*Modern Love and*
*Poems of the English Roadside, with*
*Poems and Ballads*

Jacques Reich

# MODERN LOVE

## AND

## POEMS OF THE

## ENGLISH ROADSIDE,

### WITH

## POEMS AND BALLADS

*George Meredith*

EDITED BY Rebecca N. Mitchell and Criscillia Benford

### Yale

#### UNIVERSITY PRESS

NEW HAVEN & LONDON

IN ASSOCIATION WITH

THE BEINECKE RARE BOOK AND MANUSCRIPT LIBRARY

*Frontispiece*: Portrait of George Meredith by Jacques Reich, pencil on paper, before 1910. Image courtesy of Beinecke Rare Book and Manuscript Library, Yale University, New Haven, CT. MS Vault Shelves Meredith Notebooks 1–10, 10A.

Published with assistance from the foundation established in memory of Calvin Chapin of the Class of 1788, Yale College.

Yale University Press books may be purchased in quantity for educational, business, or promotional use. For information, please e-mail sales.press@yale.edu (U.S. office) or sales@yaleup.co.uk (U.K. office).

Set in Fournier MT type by Newgen North America.
Printed in the United States of America.

Library of Congress Cataloging-in-Publication Data

Meredith, George, 1828–1909.
Modern love and Poems of the English roadside, with poems and ballads / George Meredith ; edited by Rebecca N. Mitchell and Criscillia Benford.
p.   cm.
Includes bibliographical references and index.
ISBN 978-0-300-17317-8 (cloth : alk. paper)

I. Mitchell, Rebecca N. (Rebecca Nicole), 1976–.   II. Benford, Criscillia.
III. Meredith, George, 1828–1909. Poems of the English roadside.   IV. Title.
PR5008.M6 2013
821'.8—dc23
2012012358

A catalogue record for this book is available from the British Library.

This paper meets the requirements of ANSI/NISO Z39.48-1992 (Permanence of Paper).

10 9 8 7 6 5 4 3 2 1

# Contents

## Contexts

# *Plates*

# Note on the Text

In honor of the 150th anniversary of its first publication, *Modern Love and Poems of the English Roadside, with Poems and Ballads* has been newly edited and annotated. Our goal has been twofold: 1) to return Meredith's poetic masterpiece "Modern Love" to its original textual context, allowing *Modern Love* to be received, once again, as a meaningful whole; and 2) to provide readers with a readable and reliable reprint of Meredith's second volume of poetry, one that is suitable for classroom use, scholarly work, and pleasure reading.

Our copy-text is Chapman and Hall's 1862 edition of *Modern Love*. To facilitate discussion of the kinds of revisions Meredith made to his poetry, we have collated the poems in this text with manuscript versions held by Yale's Beinecke Rare Book and Manuscript Library and by the New York Public Library's Henry W. and Albert A. Berg Collection of English and American Literature, as well as the versions of the poems that appear in Constable's *The Works of George Meredith*, the last edition of these poems that Meredith saw through the press. Commonly referred to as the Edition de Luxe, Constable's *The Works of George Meredith* was edited by Meredith's son William Maxse Meredith and appeared in thirty-six volumes from 1896 to 1911. Meredith oversaw his son's work through volume 32. Meredith's poetry appears in volumes 29–31 (1898) and 33 (1910); these volumes are also titled *Poems, Volumes 1–4*. Poems that were first published in the journal *Once a Week* have been collated with the version published in that periodical. Readers will find the results of our collation work in our "Textual Variants" appendix.

Because, as Meredith's letters document, he and his son were imperfect proofreaders, we have also emended the text to reflect the hand corrections that Meredith made to presentation copies of the 1862 edition, where appropriate. We have refrained from making silent corrections, instead opting to note changes based upon these sources in our "Variants" appendix. In poems more than one page long, we include an ornament ✦ to indicate when the page break in the current volume corresponds to a stanza break in the original.

We are indebted, as is any scholar of Meredith's work, to Phyllis Bartlett's *The Poems of George Meredith* (Yale University Press, 1978). Her edition, with its extensive notes and detailed variants, was a foundational resource for our work. Further, she narrates the composition and publication history of each poem; we have not reproduced those narratives here. We encourage anyone interested in further exploring these issues to consult Bartlett.

This edition includes a "Contexts" section designed to situate *Modern Love* within contemporary debates about poetics, sensory perception, and marriage. These supplementary readings have been reprinted faithfully, with few exceptions: when Meredith's verse is quoted, we have standardized the quotations to reflect the 1862 copy text. We reprint quotations of two lines or fewer; for longer quotations, we direct readers to the appropriate lines in the full poems. We have standardized notation of the title "Modern Love," using quotation marks when the sonnet sequence is cited and italics when the volume title is intended. We have also standardized punctuation order and removed quotation marks around block quotations. We have used [*sic*] sparingly, only in cases when an author's mistakes might otherwise lead to readerly confusion. All other instances of variation in capitalization and spelling, as well as Victorian syntactic idiosyncrasies and penchant for misquoting, are rendered as in the originals. For corrected clarifications and versions of content-related misquotations, see footnotes.

In helping readers create a rich context for *Modern Love*, we hope that this edition will allow a fuller appreciation of its "modernity," emotional complexity, and playful weirdness. We have annotated most obscure or confusing words, allusions, and some matters of historical context. Still, Meredith's poetry is infamously difficult; no amount of annotation can obviate the need for careful reading.

# Acknowledgments

The editors would like to thank the staff of Beinecke Rare Book and Manuscript Library, especially Eva Guggemos, Anne Marie Menta, Ellen Doon, and Timothy Young. A special thanks is due to the late Frank Turner, who championed this project from the start. The staff of the Henry W. and Albert A. Berg Collection of English and American Literature at the New York Public Library was also helpful in facilitating our access to Meredith's manuscripts, especially Dr. Isaac Gerwirtz and Anne Garner.

Thanks to John E. Donatich, Dan Heaton, and Niamh Cunningham at Yale University Press. We'd also like to thank our assiduous copy editor, Kate Davis. Thanks also to Kathy Psomiades, for her valuable input on the proposal, and to Alison MacKeen, without whom this project would not have come to fruition.

Mrs. P. M. Sedgwick, great-granddaughter of George Meredith, generously granted permission from Meredith's estate to reprint pages from the holograph "Modern Love" manuscript held in the Beinecke Library. We sincerely thank her for this graciousness.

For permission to reprint Sir John Squire's translation of Baudelaire's "Causerie" from *Poems and Baudelaire Flowers*, we are indebted to his estate, and especially to his grandson, Roger Squire.

The letter from Gerard Manley Hopkins to Robert Bridges appears by permission of Oxford University Press on behalf of the British Province of the Society of Jesus. The images from *Once a Week* and the edition of *Modern Love* inscribed to Robert Browning are held in Yale University's Beinecke Library, which granted permission for their reproduction here.

We also thank Marty Gould for his inimitable wit and moral support. Criscillia Benford would like to thank Duke and Stanford Universities for their financial and practical support, as well as William Softky for his impressive power to amuse and his patience with having George Meredith as his rival for so very long. To the "old friends of her halts"—Danika Brown, Ljiljana Coklin, Susan Derwin, Anna Maria Jones, Marci McMahon, Ivan Montiel, Anna Tillett, and Kay Young—Rebecca Mitchell sends the "kind thanks" she owes them.

# Abbreviations

| | |
|---|---|
| 1862 | Meredith, George. *Modern Love and Poems of the English Roadside, with Poems and Ballads*. London: Chapman and Hall, 1862. |
| Beinecke | The Beinecke Rare Book and Manuscript Library, Yale University. |
| Berg | Interleaved "Copy 7" of Meredith's *Poems* in the Henry W. and Albert A. Berg Collection of English and American Literature of the New York Public Library. |
| EdL | Meredith, George. *The Works of George Meredith*. Ed. William Maxse Meredith. London: Constable, 1898–1911. Known as the Edition de Luxe. The poems are contained in volumes 29–31 (also numbered 1–3), published in 1898 under GM's supervision, and volume 33 (also numbered 4), published posthumously in 1910. |
| errata | "Errata in the Poems." Bibliography and Various Readings. Volume 36 of *The Works of George Meredith*. |
| GM | George Meredith. |
| Johnson | Johnson, Diane. *The True History of the First Mrs. Meredith and Other Lesser Lives*. New York: Knopf, 1972. |
| Letters | Cline, C. L. *The Letters of George Meredith*. London: Oxford University Press, 1970. |
| ms | manuscript. |

| | |
|---|---|
| NB A | Early notebook belonging to George Meredith held by the Beinecke Library, beginning after endpaper with bookplate. |
| NB B | Opposite end of NB A. |
| OaW | *Once a Week.* |
| PB | Meredith, George. *The Poems of George Meredith.* Ed. Phyllis B. Bartlett. New Haven: Yale University Press, 1978. Based upon Edition de Luxe versions, the poems from *Modern Love and Poems of the English Roadside, with Poems and Ballads* are contained in volume 1. |
| Poems | Meredith, George. *Poems.* London: John W. Parker and Son, 1851. |
| Stevenson | Stevenson, Lionel. *The Ordeal of George Meredith: A Biography.* New York: Charles Scribner's Sons, 1953. |
| BEIN MSS 7 | BEIN GEN MSS 7: George Meredith's copy of 1862 edition with his ms corrections. Bookplate of Paul Lemperly, hand-corrected by Meredith. |
| BEIN 862.1 | BEIN Meredith 862, Copy 1: 1862 edition presentation copy inscribed to "Robert Browning from the author" in Meredith's hand. Hand-corrected errata. |
| BEIN 862.2 | BEIN Meredith 862, Copy 2: 1862 edition corrected by GM. Cross-referencing these changes with those in the EdL and PB, these changes seem to be his revisions for the EdL. They are extensive and do not appear in any other presentation copy. Revisions are, alas, undated. |
| BEIN 862.5 | BEIN Meredith 862, Copy 5: 1862 edition presentation copy inscribed to "Mrs. Thomas Carlyle, from the author" in Meredith's hand. Hand-corrected errata. |
| BEIN 862.6 | BEIN Meredith 862, Copy 6: 1862 edition autograph copy, corrected in Meredith's hand. |

BEIN Purdy      BEIN Purdy 433: 1862 edition presentation copy inscribed
to William Virtue by GM with notation "Full of errata, too
numerous to indicate," though some are indeed indicated.
On frontispiece: "Meredith's 2nd book of poems. This is
the original binding, and rare." (Copies are sometimes
found in a much more modern-looking blue cloth bind-
ing, which was used in later years for the copies sold after
GM's poetry had become appreciated.)

# George Meredith:
## A Brief Chronology

1828    Born in Portsmouth on 12 February.

1842–44 Studies at a school run by the Moravian Brothers in
        Neuwied, Germany.

1845    Is articled to Richard Charnock (a London solicitor).

1849    First published poem, "Chillianwallah," appears in
        *Chambers's Edinburgh Journal* on 7 July.

        Number 11 (the first of five numbers) of the "Monthly
        Observer," a handwritten journal started by Meredith
        and his friends, appears in January; subsequent numbers
        appear in March, April, June, and July.

        Marries Mary Ellen Peacock Nicolls on 9 August.

1851    Publishes *Poems* with John W. Parker and Son at his own
        expense in May.

1853    Arthur Gryffydh Meredith born on 13 June.

1856    Publishes *The Shaving of Shagpat: An Arabian Entertain-
        ment* with Chapman and Hall.

1855    Sits for Henry Wallis's *Chatterton*, a painting exhibited to
        much acclaim at the Royal Academy in 1856.

1856    Mary Ellen and Wallis begin their affair sometime between
        July and August; by this time she is no longer living with
        George Meredith.

1857    Publishes *Farina: A Legend of Cologne* with Chapman
        and Hall.

Takes over "Belle Lettres" section from George Eliot in *Westminster Review* in April.

1858    Stops writing "Belle Lettres" for *Westminster Review* in January.

Harold Meredith (nicknamed Felix), son of Mary Ellen and Wallis, born on 18 April.

Mary Ellen elopes with Wallis to Capri that autumn.

Begins life-long friendship with Captain Frederick Augustus Maxse.

1859    Publishes *The Ordeal of Richard Feverel* in three volumes with Chapman and Hall.

Mary Ellen returns to England without Wallis.

1860    *Evan Harrington* appears in *Once a Week* from 11 February to 13 October.

Publishes three-volume American edition of *Evan Harrington*.

Begins working for Chapman and Hall as a reader.

1861    Publishes three-volume English edition of *Evan Harrington* with Bradbury and Evans.

Mary Ellen dies (probably from Bright's Disease) in October.

1862    Publishes *Modern Love and Poems of the English Roadside, with Poems and Ballads* with Chapman and Hall on 28 April.

Shares Queen's House in Chelsea with D. G. Rossetti, W. M. Rossetti, and Swinburne.

1864    Marries Marie Vulliamy on 20 September.

*Emilia in England* appears in *Revue des deux Mondes* from 15 November to 15 December.

Publishes an expanded, three-volume version of *Emilia in England* (renamed *Sandra Belloni*) with Chapman and Hall.

1865    Publishes *Rhoda Fleming* in three volumes with Tinsley Brothers.

William Maxse Meredith born to George and Marie on 26 July.

1866    *Vittoria* appears in *Fortnightly Review* from 15 January to 1 December.

1867    Publishes three-volume version of *Vittoria* with Chapman and Hall.

Moves to Box Hill, Surrey, his home for the rest of his life.

1870    *The Adventures of Harry Richmond* appears in *Cornhill*, illustrated by George Du Maurier, from September 1870 to November 1871.

1871    Marie Eveleen Meredith born to George and Marie on 10 June.

Publishes three-volume version of *Harry Richmond* with Smith and Elder.

1874    *Beauchamp's Career* appears in *Fortnightly Review* from August 1874 to December 1875.

1876    Publishes three-volume version of *Beauchamp's Career* with Chapman and Hall.

1877    Delivers "On the Idea of Comedy, and the Uses of the Comic Spirit" on 2 February; the lecture is published in *New Quarterly Magazine* that April.

1879    *Sir Willoughby Patterne the Egoist* appears in *Glasgow Weekly Herald* from 21 June 1879 to 10 January 1880.

Publishes three-volume version of *Sir Willoughby Patterne the Egoist* as *The Egoist* with Kegan Paul.

1880    *The Tragic Comedians* appears in *Fortnightly Review* from October 1880 to February 1881.

Publishes two-volume version of *The Tragic Comedians* with Chapman and Hall.

1883    Publishes, at his own expense, *Poems and Lyrics of the Joy of the Earth* (his first book of poetry since *Modern Love*) with Macmillan on 20 July.

1884    *Diana of the Crossways*, Meredith's first popular novel, appears in *Fortnightly Review* from June to December.

1885    Publishes three-volume version of *Diana of the Crossways* with Chapman and Hall.

Marie Meredith dies of cancer on 17 September.

1887    Publishes *Ballads and Poems of Tragic Life* with Macmillan.

1888    Publishes *A Reading of Earth* with Macmillan.

1890    Arthur Gryffydh Meredith dies on 3 September.

Publishes *One of Our Conquerors* in three volumes with Chapman and Hall.

1892    Publishes *Modern Love, A Reprint, to which is added The Sage Enamoured and the Honest Lady* with Macmillan on 26 January.

Publishes *Poems: The Empty Purse, with Odes to the Comic Spirit, To Youth in Memory, and Verses* with Macmillan in October.

Is elected President of the Society of Authors.

1893    *Lord Ormont and His Aminta* appears in *Pall Mall Magazine* from December 1893 to July 1894.

1894    Publishes three-volume version of *Lord Ormont and His Aminta* with Chapman and Hall.

1895    *The Amazing Marriage* appears in *Scribner's Magazine* from January to December.

Publishes two-volume version of *The Amazing Marriage* with Constable.

1896    First volumes of Constable's Edition de Luxe issued.

1897    Publishes *Selected Poems* with Constable.

1898    Publishes *Odes in Contribution to the Song of French History* with Constable on 21 October.

1901    Publishes *A Reading of Life* with Constable in May.

1905    Becomes the twelfth member of the Order of Merit.

1909    Dies on 18 May.

Constable publishes *Poems Written in Early Youth* and *Last Poems*.

First volumes of Constable's *Memorial Edition* are issued.

1910    *Celt and Saxon* appear in *Fortnightly Review* from January to August, and in *The Forum* (New York) from January to June.

Constable publishes *Celt and Saxon* in volume form.

1911    Last volumes of Constable's Edition de Luxe are issued.

# Introduction

"They," said George Meredith to his friend Edward Clodd, "say this or that is Meredithian; I have become an adjective."[1] "They" were the literary critics of Meredith's day who had, toward the end of his life, turned from writing censorious reviews of his poetry and prose to writing countless articles and even a few books praising the work of "the sage of Box Hill."[2] No longer deemed a menace to Victorian morality, George Meredith was by the end of the nineteenth century a venerated elder statesman of English letters. He succeeded Alfred, Lord Tennyson as president of the Society of Authors in 1892. Collected editions of his work began to appear in England and America in 1896. Numerous younger writers, including J. M. Barrie, Arthur Conan Doyle, Alice Meynell, and Robert Louis Stevenson, made pilgrimages to his home in Box Hill, Surrey, during the final decade of his life. And in 1905, King Edward VII made Meredith the twelfth member of the Order of Merit in recognition of his intellectual and artistic achievements. If "Meredithian" had once been an insult, it was no longer so.

Perhaps the rehabilitation of Meredith's literary reputation should not have surprised him, since such a process had already occurred on a smaller scale with regard to his most enduring poem, the sonnet sequence "Modern Love" (1862). Consider, for instance, the about-face performed by the *Saturday Review*. In 1862, an unsigned reviewer dismissed "Modern Love" as a "sickly little peccadillo," insisting that Meredith's decision to write a vivid sonnet sequence that thematized infidelity and sexual desire was "a mistake so grave as utterly to disqualify [him] from achieving any great and worthy

---

1. Edward Clodd, *Memories* (New York: G. P. Putnam's Sons, 1916), 146.
2. Alice Gordon, "The First Meeting between George Meredith and Robert Louis Stevenson," *Bookman* (January 1895): 111.

result in art."[3] Yet by 1901 another critic for the *Saturday Review* would take the greatness and worthiness of "Modern Love" as givens. "Modern Love," this critic wrote, is "Mr. Meredith's masterpiece in poetry, and it will always remain, besides certain things of Donne and Browning, an astonishing feat in the vivisection of the heart in verse."[4] Perhaps it should be no surprise, then, that on the occasion of Meredith's eightieth birthday in 1908 the *Saturday Review* would offer the following breezy account of the shift in critical regard for the man and his work: "Everyone knows, and now everyone says, that Mr. Meredith is a genius, and supreme artist. There was a time when not everyone did know it, and when hardly anyone said it."[5]

Such a revolution in critical regard is hardly unique in the annals of literary history, but the extreme reactions to "Modern Love" tell us something about the heterogeneity that animates the poem itself, not just about a fickle readership. "Modern Love," and the volume in which it first appeared, derives much of its power from its juxtaposition of nostalgia and prescience, its allegiance to traditional forms and playful disregard of those forms. The sonnet sequence delineates a thoroughly ambivalent set of emotions, documenting a husband's simultaneous desire for and repulsion from his estranged wife; the couple enacts a traditional Victorian marriage—sometimes literally acting out the parts, as in Sonnet XVII—all the while demonstrating the limitations of the institution. Similar contrasts are writ large upon the *Modern Love* volume as a whole: while "Modern Love" foregrounds modernity in its very title, the poems that surround it evoke forms and subjects from the past, from a rusticated, rural England to Ancient Greece. Meredith deftly exploits the power of these and other contrasts, developing a unique voice that acknowledges the poetic discourse of his day and anticipates the sensibilities that defined literature for decades to come. One can trace the links between his verse and that of the Romantics, particularly John Keats, but also between his work and Charles Baudelaire's as well as the Symbolists and Modernists who followed. Meredith's verse does not fit comfortably under any single label, as it manipulates the defining traits of all of these movements, leading to an amalgam that resists easy definition or, some would argue, easy com-

---

3. "Mr. George Meredith's Poems," *Saturday Review* (24 October 1863): 562. See "Contemporary Reactions" in "Contexts" section for full review.

4. "George Meredith as Poet," *Saturday Review* (13 July 1901): 49.

5. "Notes of the Week," *Saturday Review* (15 February 1908): 192.

prehension. No wonder he has been characterized as a Pre-Raphaelite poet, a Spasmodic poet, a Victorian poet, and a proto-Modernist poet.

Such plasticity is perhaps the characteristic of Meredith's verse oeuvre that ensures its enduring relevance. Unfortunately, much of that oeuvre is unavailable to today's readers. Though "Modern Love"—or more often excerpts from "Modern Love"—is frequently anthologized, the majority of the other poems in the *Modern Love* volume are available only in Phyllis Bartlett's 1978 *The Poems of George Meredith*, which is itself out of print. Returning *Modern Love and Poems of the English Roadside, with Poems and Ballads* to print, on the sesquicentennial of its original publication, allows a new generation of readers to appreciate Meredith's early verse. Moreover, restoring the titular sonnet sequence to its original textual context allows for a richer interpretative experience. That "Modern Love" is not the first poem in the volume is just one of several indicators of the need to broaden the interpretive horizon that we have previously associated with it. As Isobel Armstrong warned in 1993, the other poems in the *Modern Love* volume have been "obscured" by the "dominance of the title poem in Meredith's reputation," a situation that "has paradoxically obscured the way in which 'Modern Love' itself might be read."[6] Attention to what Neil Fraistat calls the "structural framing and symmetries, as well as the development of thematic progressions and verbal echoes among the poems" in a volume such as *Modern Love* allows readers to view it as a "poetic aggregate" or "contexture."[7] Such an approach makes plain that "Modern Love" is both title and topic. Mixing age-old poetic tropes and structures with playful and innovative forms and images, Meredith meditates upon the relationship between idealized conceptions of romantic love and the physical sensation of sexual desire. Using similar strategies, Meredith also dissects the love of abstractions such as Country, Family, and Nature. Juxtaposing multiple versions of "modern love," the volume thus explores a range of contemporary sociocultural issues, including English cosmopolitanism, the so-called Woman Question, and the diffusion of democratic ideas about social equality.

---

6. Isobel Armstrong, *Victorian Poetry: Poetry, Poetics, and Politics*. (London: Routledge, 1996), 441.

7. Neil Fraistat, "Introduction," in *Poems in their Place: The Intertextuality and Order of Poetic Collections* (Chapel Hill, NC: University of North Carolina Press, 1986), 5–6. See also Jerome McGann's, *The Textual Condition* (Princeton, NJ: Princeton University Press, 1991), for a consonant discussion of the importance of apprehending poems within their original textual context.

## A Meredithian Life

The germs of these themes likely came from Meredith's own background, though the details of his early life are as obscure as his most idiosyncratic metaphors. Meredith was a private man who drew from his own life for his creative work yet remained averse to providing biographers with accurate information about his childhood and adolescence. No doubt some of this reticence was due to embarrassment. Social status and class were troublesome forces in Meredith's life from the beginning, and this is perhaps why the figures of the social climber and social outsider appear throughout his oeuvre. He was born in Portsmouth on 12 February 1828 to Augustus Meredith, a reluctant tailor, and Jane Eliza Meredith (née Macnamara), the daughter of an innkeeper. Despite their lower-middle-class status, the Merediths were a proud family who traced their lineage back to Welsh princes. Meredith himself was not immune to the stories his father liked to tell of their royal ancestry. The sons of the other Portsmouth tradesmen gave him the nickname "Gentleman Georgy" in consequence of his well-made clothes and affable yet aloof demeanor.[8] Financial hardship loomed on the horizon, however. Augustus had inherited a popular shop that specialized in naval uniforms from his own flamboyant father, Melchizedek Meredith. Melchizedek—the model for *Evan Harrington*'s "The Great Mel"—was handsome and dashing, though an indifferent businessman. Along with Melchizedek's shop, good looks, and deep pride, Augustus had also inherited his father's spending habits. Making matters worse, the business that Melchizedek bequeathed to his son was not nearly as prosperous as it had seemed. When George was nine, Augustus declared bankruptcy, losing the family business and home. Thanks to a small inheritance left to him by his mother (who died when he was five) and her sister, young George was still able to attend the Moravian Brothers school in Neuwied, Germany, from 1842 to 1844, an experience that not only erased his Hampshire accent, but also provided him with a cosmopolitan outlook, profoundly shaped his progressive views on the education of women as well as his more retrograde ones about male courage, and planted seeds for his philosophical interest in nature.

These interests would later sound as keynotes in his creative work, and the writerly phase of his life began around the same time that he met the

8. Stevenson, 8.

woman who inspired "Modern Love." When Meredith returned to England he was articled to Richard Stephen Charnock, a London solicitor with literary ambitions. Soon the two men were involved with a manuscript journal called the "Monthly Observer," to which they and a small group of friends were the sole contributors. The only woman belonging to this group was a young widow and mother named Mary Ellen Peacock Nicolls. She was witty, intelligent, and beautiful, like so many of the heroines Meredith would later create. George and Mary Ellen married on 9 August 1849, the same year that George published his first poem, "Chillianwallah" in *Chambers's Edinburgh Journal*. After a brief honeymoon in Germany and a short residence in London, the young couple settled in to The Limes in Weybridge, Surrey. They were inspired by their new surroundings and the creative energy derived from the community of writers, artists, and musicians living there. Mary Ellen wrote her own poetry, published articles and reviews, and collaborated on a cookbook with her father, the English satirist Thomas Love Peacock. George read widely—including the works of Tennyson, Keats, and Shelley—and "applied himself to a course of self-training in poetic forms," particularly the English and Scottish folk ballad.[9] Under the guidance of the poet Edmund Hornby, Meredith began to bring more "modern ingredients" to bear on his poetry.[10] Soon he published his first collection, *Poems* (1851). Although the volume was published at his own expense, it was relatively well received.

Despite these successes, and despite George and Mary Ellen's much-noted physical attraction to each other, their marriage was a volatile one haunted by poverty and filled with sorrow and resentment. The money that the couple earned from their writing was not enough to support them comfortably. No doubt Meredith's refusal to allow Peacock to obtain for him an appointment in the East India House exacerbated household tensions. Moreover, Mary Ellen was continuously pregnant, giving birth to several stillborn children between 1850 and 1852; their son, Arthur Gryffydh Meredith, was not born until 13 June 1853. Living in a small home with frustrated ambitions and decreasing sympathy for each other, George and Mary Ellen, according to Mary Ellen's daughter from her first marriage, "sharpened their wits on each other"[11] and began to isolate themselves socially. By the end of 1856

---

9. Ibid., 32.
10. *Letters*, I.8.
11. Stevenson, 47.

the couple spent more time apart than they did together. Yet when a pregnant Mary Ellen left him for the Pre-Raphaelite painter Henry Wallis in 1858, Meredith was devastated. Although he never forgave her, prevented her from seeing their son, and would in later years imply that she suffered from hereditary madness,[12] Meredith never sought to divorce her. As the excerpt from John Paget's essay on English divorce law makes clear (see "Contexts"), to have attempted to do so would have likely amplified the scandal and may not have even resulted in a legal separation.

The trials of their marriage served as inspiration for the emotional currents in much of his later prose and verse and the seductive, lively, progressive, and intelligent Mary Ellen seems to have been the model for Meredith's most notable female characters, including the wife in "Modern Love." Written in the wake of Mary Ellen's premature death in 1861, "Modern Love" unquestionably recalls Meredith's experiences with her. To this day, many scholarly assessments of the poem are built upon the assumption that it is autobiographical, with some critics ascribing the power of the poem—and its continued popularity—to the emotional precision that could only be drawn from experience. Yet while the Victorians understood the sonnet form as "a site of privileged autobiographical utterance,"[13] to understand "Modern Love" *only* as thinly veiled autobiography risks undervaluing its ironic distance, its narratorial ambiguity, and its position within the volume.

Unillustrated and containing a total of twenty-three heterogeneous yet thematically linked poems, *Modern Love and Poems of the English Roadside, with Poems and Ballads* was published on 28 April 1862 by Chapman and Hall in a small print run. It was Meredith's second volume of poetry. He dedicated it to Frederick Maxse, a naval officer and reformer he had met toward the end of 1858, who would become his lifelong friend and advocate. By this time, Meredith was regularly publishing poems in Samuel Lucas's journal *Once a Week*, many of which were illustrated by artists connected with the Pre-Raphaelite Brotherhood (see figs. 3, 5–8, and 10). Nine of these poems—"The Meeting," "Juggling Jerry," "The Old Chartist," "The Beggar's Soliloquy," "The Patriot Engineer," "The Head of Bran," "Autumn Even-Song," "Phantasy," and "By the Rosanna"—were collected in *Modern*

---

12. See for example his 3 June 1864 letter to William Hardman in *Letters*, I.262.
13. Joseph Phelan, *The Nineteenth-Century Sonnet* (London: Palgrave Macmillan, 2005), 43.

*Love*. The titular sonnet sequence, first referred to as "The Love-Match" in 1861, was the result of relatively quick work. By January 1862, Meredith sent Maxse proofs of thirty-six of the final fifty sonnets, by then called "A Tragedy of Modern Love." Three months later, upon its publication, the title was truncated to "Modern Love."

Since its initial release in 1862, "Modern Love" has stood apart from the other poems in the volume, receiving the lion's share of scorn and— later—of praise. That said, the poem's situation within the collection is as important as the poem itself; Meredith was particular about how he ordered his poems, giving his publishers careful instructions. As its full title suggests, *Modern Love* is divided into several parts. Preceding the sonnet sequence are "Grandfather Bridgeman" and "The Meeting." Following "Modern Love" is the "Roadside Philosophers" section, comprising "Juggling Jerry," "The Old Chartist," "The Beggar's Soliloquy," and the "Patriot Engineer." The remaining poems in the volume fall under the heading "Poems and Ballads," an organizational strategy that suggests that "Grandfather Bridgeman" and "The Meeting," along with those poems spoken by Meredith's Roadside Philosophers, are to be understood collectively as "Poems of the English Roadside." As a group, these poems balance the abstractions of the later poems in the collection as well as the structural and thematic difficulty of "Modern Love." That said, one must not dismiss the Roadside poems because of their accessibility; the feelings of regret, anticipation, religious faith, and unsanctioned love that define these poems also define "Modern Love" as well. Although contemporary reviewers described the Roadside poems as "wholesome," Meredith himself called them "flints perhaps, and not flowers."[14] Indeed, despite the seemingly stark differences in tone, form, and content between "Modern Love" and the Roadside poems, Meredith saw them as united by frank depiction seated in observation and experience: "Thus my Jugglers, Beggars, etc., I have met on the road, and have idealized but slightly. I desire to strike the poetic spark out of absolute human clay."[15] The Roadside poems are not caricatures or fanciful idylls; they depict characters attempting to reconcile their traditional lifestyles and ideologies with a changing world.

14. *Letters*, I.110.
15. Ibid.

## The Critics Respond

The Roadside poems were favorites among the Victorian critical establishment. J. W. Marston, writing in the *Athenaeum*, called them "wholesome" and claimed to have turned to them with a "sense of relief," and the critic for the *Saturday Review* suggested the Roadside poems showcased the "racy and vigorous style of composition" which was Meredith's "real forte."[16] To the extent that early reviews praised the Roadside poems ("Juggling Jerry" and "The Old Chartist" were especially admired), they protested against the others. "Modern Love" received the most attention and the most sharply derisive reviews. Critics did not merely dislike the sequence; they reviled it, finding it an affront to prevailing moral and aesthetic sensibilities. More than a few contemporary critics resorted to the rhetoric of disease to justify their negative response to the sonnet sequence's subject matter. Answering Meredith's claim in Sonnet XXV that "these things are life: And life, they say, is worthy of the Muse," the *Saturday Review*'s critic objected, "A more flimsy sophism could hardly be devised. The Muse is undoubtedly concerned with all forms of life, but these things are decay, and deformity, and death." It would be just as reasonable, the critic concludes, "to compose a sonnet to the gout or an ode on the small-pox."[17] The *Athenaeum* was slightly more measured. Good poetry often reveals "the diseases of our nature," its critic admitted, yet in so doing, such poetry shows "the virtue of the antidote"; the problem with "Modern Love" is that it shows us "disease, and nothing else."[18]

In addition to Meredith's choice of content, reviewers responded negatively to the poem's stylistic obscurity, a trait that they associated with the so-called Spasmodic school of poetry. Made popular by poets Alexander Smith, Sidney Dobell, and Philip James Bailey, Spasmodic poetry sought to evoke visceral responses in readers by advancing the Romantic cultivation of heightened sensory perception and subjective points of view. It was initially welcomed by writers such as George Henry Lewes, Arthur Hugh Clough, and George Gilfillan, who praised its edifying vividness. Others regarded Spasmodic poetry with suspicion and even derision, characteriz-

---

16. J. W. Marston, "*Modern Love and Poems of the English Roadside, with Poems and Ballads,*" *Athenaeum* (31 May 1862): 719; "Mr. George Meredith's Poems," *Saturday Review* (24 October 1863): 562. For full versions of these reviews, see "Contemporary Reactions."

17. "Mr. George Meredith's Poems," 563.

18. Marston, 720.

ing it as egoistic, overwrought, and dangerously focused on the body. The Spasmodic display of embodied emotions was viewed by some critics as science masquerading as art. Coventry Patmore, for instance, claimed that poets had no business writing about "the facts of science" unless they related those facts to "universal truth and permanent humanity."[19] "Mere physical interests are best discoursed in prose," Patmore insisted.[20] More common objections were leveled at Spasmodic obscurity, not its physical specificity: according to this line of reasoning, poetry that appeals to a reader's sensory experience or organic reactions, as opposed to a reader's intellect, often does so at the expense of clarity. Charges of Spasmodic obscurity thus became synonymous with charges of self-indulgence or writerly laziness. J. W. Marston contrasted the "real force and imagination" that he found in some parts of "Modern Love" with the "spasmodic indistinctness" that he felt characterized most of it.[21] R. H. Hutton, writing for the *Spectator*, complained that the energy of Meredith's verse was not produced by "intellectual courage" or "buoyancy of spirit," but rather by "a spasmodic ostentation of fast writing."[22]

Although Hutton's comment implies that Spasmodism was anti-intellectual and unsophisticated, recent critical reappraisals suggest otherwise. Jason Rudy writes that Spasmodic poetry "operated very much within the mainstream of mid-Victorian philosophy and social science,"[23] a claim supported by the selections from the work of Bain, Johnson, and Wilson included in the "Contexts" section of this volume. And, as Herbert Tucker has demonstrated, the Spasmodists' interest in "embodied intuition" and their efforts to lyricize narrative were taken up by a number of now-canonical Victorian poets[24]—including George Meredith, particularly in "Modern Love." Putting Victorian critiques of the movement into sociopolitical perspective, Tucker reminds us that "the premium that spasmodist poetry placed in theory on subjective power, and exemplified in the rolling fluency of its creative practice,

19. Coventry Patmore, "Art II. Festus: A Poem," *Edinburgh Review* 104 (October 1865): 338.

20. Ibid.

21. Marston, 719.

22. R. H. Hutton, "Mr. George Meredith's 'Modern Love,'" *Spectator* (24 May 1862): 580–81. See "Contemporary Reactions" for full review.

23. Jason Rudy, "Rhythmic Intimacy, Spasmodic Epistemology," *Victorian Poetry* 42, no. 4 (Winter 2004): 453.

24. Herbert Tucker, "Glandular Omnism and Beyond: The Victorian Spasmodic Epic," *Victorian Poetry* 42, no. 4 (Winter 2004): 430, 444.

bespoke cultural values" that many Victorian conservatives associated with Chartism as well as "sexual and other kinds of emancipation."[25]

Freighted with intertwining aesthetic and political meanings, the label "Spasmodic" nevertheless functioned as shorthand for poorly written poetry. This seems to be the way poet Algernon Swinburne understood Hutton's use of the term. Rebuking Hutton's old-fashioned and thoughtless response to *Modern Love*, Swinburne described "Modern Love" as a serious and "progressive poem" displaying "the finest and most studied workmanship." He exhorted readers to value poets such as Meredith for writing verse that looked beyond the "nursery walls."[26] Swinburne's praise of the sonnet sequence did not come at the expense of the Roadside poems, however. He found "The Beggar's Soliloquy" and "The Old Chartist" to be particularly "valuable," commending them for their "completeness of effect," "exquisite justice of style," and "thorough dramatic insight."[27]

Swinburne's assessment of "Modern Love" was, as it turns out, prophetic. And while this critical resuscitation has been welcomed by those who admire the sonnet sequence, the remaining poems in the volume—which were almost universally regarded as superior to "Modern Love" in early reviews—have fallen into obscurity. To this day, scholarly considerations of Meredith's verse oeuvre reflect and perpetuate this lopsided approach.

## The Roadside Poems

The structure of the volume itself—with the sharp contrast between the homespun warmth and formal familiarity of the "Poems of the English Roadside," the experimental and progressive feel of "Modern Love," and the richly textured abstraction of many of the other poems—may well have led critics to evaluate the work comparatively. If critics regarded "Modern Love" as needlessly obscure and focused on a needlessly prurient topic, the Roadside poems served as a counterpoint, offering easily accessible verse detailing rustic, wholesome characters; it is no surprise that many contemporary critics regarded the Roadside poems as the best in the volume. Contributing to this sense of accessibility is a general lack of the formal innovation

---

25. Ibid., 441–42.
26. Algernon C. Swinburne, "Letter to the Editor," *Spectator* (7 June 1862): 632–33. See "Contemporary Reactions" for full review.
27. Ibid., 632.

that often appears in Meredith's more-complex poems. Most of the Roadside poems eschew literary allusions and imagistic or sensual description in favor of contemporary or recent events—such as the Crimean War or Chartist uprisings—that would have been widely if not intimately known by readers, and most adopt comfortable and familiar patterns of meter and rhyme. These poems attempt to absorb the diction and rhythm of working-class speech, creating metrical irregularities that some thought unwitting.[28] "The Road" is a rich trope, associated with cross-class encounters, chance, and adventure; thus, the Roadside poems as a group seem to comprise a kind of poetic exploration of the world beyond the libraries, bedrooms, and dining rooms of "Modern Love." If there is a sensibility uniting these poems, it seems that of a unique Englishness conferred through their speakers, social outliers though they may be. Notions of direct patriotism, expressed often by speakers who have left England, permeate the poems: "Grandfather Bridgeman" offers a glimpse of the experience of a soldier injured in the Crimean War, as related through the expectations and longing of those at home; the title character of "The Old Chartist," having returned to England after a life of exile in Australia following a conviction for inciting a Chartist riot, muses that after all, England is still his "dam"; and in "The Patriot Engineer," an expat waxes nostalgic on the greatness of the oaklike English character to bemused British passengers in his boat.

The nature of the national character gives way to its singular incarnations in "The Meeting," "Juggling Jerry," and "The Beggar's Soliloquy." "The Meeting," a brief encounter between erstwhile lovers, is a scene perfectly at home in a Thomas Hardy novel. "Juggling Jerry," a favorite among early readers, details the final thoughts of an old carnival performer. His metaphysical theory figures a god in terms he knows best: as a great juggler who must keep a number of spheres moving continuously. Thus imagining himself as part of a cosmic continuum, the juggler elevates himself to an equality with all other individuals. In "The Beggar's Soliloquy," the beggar stands outside of a church, pondering the seeming disconnect between Christian charity and the unwillingness of those he entreats to give him money. In each instance, the context is always expressly English: the juggler revels in

---

28. "I claim rather to be something of a metricist," wrote Meredith, "as you would see, if you came across a boyish volume of poems of mine. . . . I wish to [see the proofs], especially as I want to turn a phrase of or two in 'Juggling Jerry,' which piece, remember, must not be too rigidly criticised in its rhythm, being the supposed speech of a vagabond freethinker." *Letters*, I.38.

the English countryside of willows, sheep, and "thatch'd ale-houses," and even the beggar at the church imagines his plight in the binary terms of the Conservative and the Radical, and takes pride in his passing connection with the "Lord Mayor o' London," whose title he invokes for effect.

The Roadside poems represent Meredith's deployment of the dramatic monologue, a peculiarly Victorian form that multiplies voices and perspectives while purporting to be the utterance of a single speaker. The form developed at the same time as theories of the mind and consciousness were exploding, "driven," as Linda Hughes writes, "by intensified interest in introspection as both a philosophical and scientific method."[29] Meredith's use of the form, then, subtly unites the Roadside poems to the introspective, sense-based explorations of other poems in the volume. Moreover, like the form of "Modern Love," the formal qualities of the Roadside poems are also an expression of Meredith's ambivalent embrace of Modernity. On the one hand the quotidian narrative situations of these poems establish their contemporary-ness, yet on the other, they suggest a class- and location-based nostalgia, one that regards rural people from the lower classes as a source of national strength because they live perpetually in a more innocent time.

## On "Modern Love"

The relative innocence of the rural lifestyle depicted in the Roadside poems is emphasized through the subject and title of the sonnet sequence "Modern Love." Simply put, the sonnets tell the story of a marriage in crisis, precipitated by the husband's realization of his wife's infidelity. The sonnets detail the husband's ambivalent feelings about his wife, working through his alternating sense of physical attraction and emotional repulsion. In between moments of introspection and reflection, touchstones of plot arise: the wife—called "Madam" throughout the poem—focuses her attention on household matters to assuage her guilt (V); the husband finds a letter his wife has written to her lover (XV); the husband and wife host a dinner party, convincingly playing happily married host and hostess (XVII); the husband takes a mistress—whom he calls "Lady"—of his own (XXXII); the wife and the mistress meet (XXXVI); the husband and wife attempt to resume sexual

---

29. Linda K. Hughes, *The Cambridge Introduction to Victorian Poetry* (Cambridge, UK: Cambridge University Press, 2010), 16.

relations (XLII); finally, the wife commits suicide (XLIX). Complicating an easy understanding of the plot is the frequently shifting narratorial perspective: some sonnets present the husband's point of view, others employ a third-person narrative stance, and in some cases multiple perspectives are used in the same sonnet.

Meredith's adaptations of the sonnet form demonstrate the way he leverages formal choice to further his thematic interests. Perspectival shifts are only one of his deviations from the traditional sonnet form, a form so heavy with history that understanding its provenance is essential to recognizing Meredith's interventions. One of the oldest poetic forms in English verse, the sonnet was brought from Italy to England in the sixteenth century by Sir Thomas Wyatt (1503–1542), who translated sonnets written by the poet and humanist Francesco Petrarch (1304–1374) and circulated them among his aristocratic friends in manuscript form. The credit for inventing what we now call the "Shakespearean" sonnet pattern, named after the man most believe to be the greatest practitioner of the form in English, goes to Henry Howard, Earl of Surrey (ca. 1517–1547), another sixteenth-century English translator of Petrarch's sonnets. The English sonnet is traditionally regarded as a fixed or closed form that follows a normative rhyme scheme and consists of fourteen lines in iambic pentameter. Nevertheless, sonneteers have tinkered with it from the beginning—a situation that led some English poets/critics, among them Leigh Hunt, to refer to the Petrarchan pattern as "the Sonnet Proper" or "the Legitimate Sonnet."[30] There are now numerous acknowledged variants of the sonnet form, including the Spenserian, the caudate sonnet, the curtal sonnet, the enclosed sonnet, and the reversed sonnet, among others.[31]

To obtain a better grasp of what's at stake in Meredith's idiosyncratic variant of the sonnet form, it is useful to think more carefully about the two most popular sonnet patterns: the Italian/Petrachan and the English/Shakespearean. As with any closed form, the Italian and English sonnet patterns establish a tight relationship between formal structure and content—usually a single idea, articulated in several stages. Normative rhyme schemes draw

---

30. Leigh Hunt and S. Adams Lee, *The Book of the Sonnet* (Boston: Robert's Brothers, 1867), 9.

31. Mid-nineteenth-century poets frequently modified these structures: for example, Gerard Manley Hopkins wrote several curtal sonnets—e.g., "Pied Beauty," which has only eleven lines—and Charles Baudelaire used the enclosed sonnet, which sandwiches tercets between the quatrains, and the reversed sonnet (also called the sonettessa) in which the sestet precedes the octave.

attention to a sonnet's functional parts, enhancing the reader's ability to chart the development of its argument. In the Italian pattern, for instance, a sonnet's fourteen-line stanza divides into two semantic units: an eight-line octave and a six-line sestet that begins with a "volta" (turn) in thought. The octave is further subdivided into two four-line quatrains, and the sestet is subdivided into two three-line tercets. A poet may use syntax and grammar to draw attention to or detract from these subdivisions. As a whole, the octave states a dilemma or proposition and follows a brace rhyme scheme of *abbaabba*. The sestet, the first line of which enacts the volta, offers a solution to the dilemma or confirmation of the proposition and follows a *cdecde* or *cdcdcd* rhyme scheme. In contrast, the Shakespearean pattern—*abab cdcd efef gg*—invites the poet to articulate her sonnet's controlling idea in four stages. Each of three quatrains describes the sonnet's dilemma or central proposition in different ways, highlighting variations in content by introducing new rhyme schemes. A rhyming couplet concludes a Shakespearean sonnet.

The "Modern Love" sonnets are sixteen lines long and feature four rhyme schemes (*abba cddc effe ghhg*), each of which signals a new shift in thought. At least one contemporary assumed that Meredith was using a version of the caudate form, a form of the sonnet that we now associate with Gerard Manley Hopkins. Taking its name from the Latin *cauda* (tail), the caudate sonnet adds a "tail" (or tails) of a half line plus a couplet to the traditional fourteen-line sonnet. Hopkins, a contemporary of Meredith, used this form to create strikingly weird poems that defy nearly every aspect of the conventional sonnet. His poem "Harry Ploughman" and his letter to Robert Bridges describing his intentions in writing "Harry Ploughman" can be found in the "Contexts" section of this volume. Meredith denied using this form for his "Modern Love" sonnets.[32] Indeed, the "Modern Love" sonnets are better understood as combining aspects of both the Italian and the Shakespearean sonnet. Their extended length allows them to appropriate the Shakespearean organizational pattern while avoiding the glibness sometimes associated with concluding couplets. And, as a formal structure, the sequence as a whole draws heavily from the formal conventions of the Petrarchan pattern, though multiple readings are likely necessary to grasp how "Modern

---

32. See William Sharp's *Sonnets of This Century* in "Contemporary Reactions" section and, for a contrasting view, Kenneth Crowell's "*Modern Love* and the *Sonetto Caudato*: Comic Intervention through the Satiric Sonnet Form" in *Victorian Poetry* 48, no. 4 (Winter 2010): 539–57.

Love" recycles Petrarchan conceits and conventions to dissect Victorian "sentimental passion."[33]

The Victorian reader would have had no difficulty identifying these conceits and conventions, although they may be obscure to most twenty-first-century readers. To understand not only why Meredith would have regarded the sonnet form as an effective dissection tool, but also the kinds of ideals against which the husband in "Modern Love" struggles, one must familiarize oneself with these conventions. Petrarchan sonnets purport to be confessional and are conventionally associated with an ennobling love. The speaker in such sonnets is usually a man; his sonnets address a cold, beautiful, and unattainable woman who is, of course, not his wife.[34] The poet-lover may idealize his beloved, reproach her for her indifference, plead with her, reflect upon his own poetic activity, and/or reflect upon his feelings and thoughts about his unrequited love. The poet-lover often spiritualizes his desire, making his love object an inspiration for faithfulness and adherence to the moralized codes of behavior associated with courtly love. He is inspired by her beauty and purity and bewitched by her eyes, bosom, lips, and hair. He will, over the course of many lines, draw elaborate parallels (for example, the poet-lover is a ship in a storm, the lady is a sun), paradoxes, and oxymora. By the end of the sequence, the poet-lover may, thanks to his lady's angelic purity, become a better man and earn his place in heaven.

Meredith's poet-lover meditates upon the real-life actions that correspond to these Petrarchan conventions. For instance, in Sonnet XXIX: "Am I failing? for no longer can I cast," the speaker reworks the beloved-as-sun convention, troping the despondency that he feels about his relationship with his blond mistress as an inability to "cast / A glory round about this head of gold" (lines 1–2). Moreover, as Cynthia Tucker explains, by repeatedly

---

33. Meredith claimed that "Modern Love" was "a dissection of the sentimental passion of these days" and insisted that it "could only be apprehended by the few who would read it many times." *Letters*, I.160. For an alternate take on the relationship between "Modern Love" and the Petrarchan sonnet, see Alison Chapman, "Sonnets and Sonnet Sequences," in *A Companion to Victorian Poetry* (London: Blackwell, 2002), 111: "The extra two lines attempt to delay the sonnet's traditional volta and closure, just as the tortured speaker attempts to postpone the final dissolution of his marriage. . . . 'Modern Love' is a sustained and tortured parody of Petrarchism (see in particular sonnet 30), which mourns figuratively and literally the fruitless, barren marriage."

34. For detailed information on mid-century challenges by female poets to this particular convention, see Marianne Van Remoortel's "Elizabeth Barrett Browning's *Sonnets from the Portuguese* and Women's Sonnets of the 1800s–1840s," in *Lives of the Sonnet, 1787–1895* (Farnham, UK: Ashgate, 2011), 89–114.

citing Petrarchan conventions, Meredith is able to highlight the gap between "the ideals which sonnets normally celebrated" and the reality of unrequited love, allowing Petrarchan "standard expressions of woe" to "become unmetaphored and moved into a bleak and untraditional reality."[35]

Exploiting the tension between narrative progression and lyric stasis, Meredith's expansion of the sonnet form becomes a necessary part of his effort to reinvest Petrarchan conceits with modern emotions. Dividing his sonnets into four semantic units, each of which corresponds to a quatrain, gives them a dynamic quality. Consider the four quatrains that make up Sonnet IX: "He felt the wild beast in him betweenwhiles." In the first, the omniscient speaker informs readers that the "wild beast" within the husband is "masterfully rude," posing a threat to the wife's safety. The second quatrain subjects this portrait to comic deflation by incorporating dialogue and converting the fact of the husband's violent desire (articulated without equivocation in the first quatrain) into an enigma: "Had he not teeth to rend, and hunger too?" The husband would surely answer yes! He regards himself as a model of masculine strength and control, as is clear when he asks his wife, "Have you no fear?"; her laughing response—"No, surely; am I not with you?"—simultaneously invokes an image of masculinity consonant with the husband's self-conception (the husband/protector) and dissonant with it (the emasculated husband).[36] The third quatrain, also in the voice of the omniscient speaker, fills in the latter portrait by describing the husband in thrall to his wife's posture, tone, and facial expressions. The final quatrain enacts the semantic "turn," and is also the site of transition from the unconventional "omniscient" speaker to the Petrarchan "I," the distressed poet-lover. Here the husband insists upon his self-mastery and the supremacy of his physical strength.

Like so many nineteenth-century narratives, the end of this sonnet appears to be the mirror image of the beginning, one that represents a restoration of order. The two quatrains calling attention to the wife's subtle, femi-

---

35. Cynthia Tucker, "Meredith's Broken Laurel: 'Modern Love' and the Renaissance Sonnet Tradition," *Victorian Poetry* 10, no. 4 (Winter 1972): 354. See also Stephen Regan, "The Victorian Sonnet, from George Meredith to Gerard Manley Hopkins," *Yearbook of English Studies* 36, no. 2 (2006): 17–34; and Dorothy Mermin, "Poetry as Fiction: Meredith's Modern Love," *ELH* 43 (1976): 100–19. On the numerous efforts to narrativize "Modern Love," see Van Remoortel's "The Inconstancy of Genre: Meredith's *Modern Love*," in *Lives of the Sonnet*, 115–39.

36. Cf. Sonnet V.4–5: "She treated him as something that is tame, / And but at other provocation bites."

nized powers are sandwiched between two quatrains about the husband's sense of his own masculinized strength. And yet, the formal dynamics of this sonnet work to destabilize such a reading at the same time that they prompt it. The structure of the sonnet allows readers to regard the husband from his own perspective and from an externalized perspective, one that hints at his delusions of power. Eschewing enjambment between quatrains emphasizes their distinctness, inviting the reader to linger over each shift in thought and perspective. The grammatical complexity of the second and fourth quatrains not only calls attention to the husband's mental confusion, but also the plurisignificance of key words and phrases. What does the wife mean by her answer? What does Meredith mean by ending this sonnet with the word *supreme*? Although the husband insists in the final quatrain that by mastering his inner beast he keeps his wife safe, these claims cannot overwrite the third quatrain's depiction of his wife's powerful wit and beauty. Much more than the mere depiction of a psychologically significant event in a story about a troubled marriage, this sonnet meditates on the difference between mastering one's impulses and being mastered by an external force. Here and elsewhere, Meredith uses poetic form to render adulterated, "modern" emotions.

"Modern Love" also explores marriage/gender roles while mixing avantgarde and traditional poetic techniques to express the emotional conflict and intersubjectivity at its center. It is indeed more than simply a story about a troubled marriage, but the union at the center of its plot links the sonnets not only to a poetic tradition centuries old, but also to the very real, very pressing issues of the day. Women's idealized love was a common subject of Victorian writing. Perhaps the best known poetic example is Coventry Patmore's *The Angel in the House*, excerpts of which appear in the "Contexts" section. This poem's title became shorthand for the stereotypical adoring, self-abnegating Victorian wife. John Ruskin echoes Patmore's portrait in his lecture "On Queens' Gardens" from *Sesame and Lilies*, a lecture that describes a woman's role as being the passive complement to her husband's active will. A woman's infidelity, on the other hand, was unconventional fodder for poetry, but an ideal platform for exploring social anxiety and/or progress. Laws and social expectations alike accorded disproportionate attention to women's adultery. Though a woman could not seek a divorce based solely on her husband's infidelity, a man could divorce his wife if she was unfaithful, and as the complex legal system allowed an accused wife little recourse, it was relatively easy for a man to manipulate the bureaucracy. Paget's explanation of the divorce process offers insight into the complexity and overwhelming gender disparity of the Victorian divorce process. Conduct manuals for both men and women warned against a wife's infidelity in the strongest possible terms: William Cobbett's manual for husbands (also in the "Contexts" section) argues that a wife's adultery is far more pernicious than a man's, not only because of the affective transgression, but because it opened the family to the social and economic degradation of bastard children. Meredith's engagement with female adultery bears the mark of these conventional attitudes: after all, the husband has been unfaithful before (as evidenced by the lock of hair he finds in Sonnet XX, a remembrance from a former dalliance) and is having an affair in the course of events depicted in the sonnets, but he seems to be untroubled by the effect of *his* infidelity on his wife, focusing solely on how her infidelity affects him. Nevertheless, the sonnets present a remarkably nuanced understanding of the conflicting emotions arising from the marriage's dissolution, especially when compared to works like Patmore's or Ruskin's. The husband details his conflicting feelings toward a wife he still finds desirable and alluring, even as he is pained by her actions. Yet, questions of blame arise frequently in the sonnets (Sonnets X, XIX, and XLIII), and the husband concludes that neither individual is solely responsible.

Probing the complexity of mutual affection and disaffection is the most identifiable trait of the sonnets' engagement with modernity; Meredith challenges the simple binary formulation of male/female gender and marital roles, even as he demonstrates the power and appeal of those binaries. The sonnets evince an uneasy relationship to modernity in other ways. Nature, to whom the Romantics would look for a mirroring of their own situation, no longer mirrors the husband's anxieties, and instead of providing respite, seems to mock him. Past notions of love—recalled from courtly romances, fairy tales, and classical myths—no longer remain relevant, even if they provide tropes the poet can deploy. Nostalgia permeates the poem, both for the shared past of the husband and his wife and for a time and place where the intrusions of the present, with its uncertainty and pain, are absent. Consider Sonnet XVIII, where the speaker regards the rural revelers at a country fair as happy in their simple ignorance. Even that nostalgic drive, though, is short-lived; in the opening line of the following sonnet the speaker insists that "No state is enviable." Indeed, to value the happiness of Jack, Tom, Moll, and Meg is to assume that their exterior pleasure belies no interior pain, a belief challenged throughout the sequence, as when the husband and wife are regarded as an ideal couple by their dinner guests (Sonnet XVII). This attempt to depict the insurmountable psychological differences between the agents, mirrored in the shifting narratorial perspective and polyvocality, situates the sequence as a precursor to the psychological probing of works written much later. Norman Friedman, in his seminal reading of "Modern Love," compares the investigation of the protagonist's consciousness to "the manner of Henry James."[37]

"Modern Love" renders this exploration of interiority in terms of the physical manifestations of psychical experience; Meredith draws from current Victorian sensory theory to invigorate his depiction of emotions. From the very opening of the sequence, intellectual or emotional cognition is couched firmly in the body. In Sonnet I, for example, the psychical devastation felt by the wife is evidenced by the sobs shaking her body even as she sleeps. Her husband witnesses that physical manifestation of tortured emotion, and the impact of those sobs on him is rendered through a striking visual image— "gaping snakes"—that has little to do with the literal action in the scene, but communicates the poisonous impact of the wife's actions as well the impact of her *own* emotional pain on the husband. The couple remain "moveless," asleep, yet "looking thro' their dead black years" and *seeing* their regret "scrawl'd over the black wall." If the couple imagines their unhappiness visually, as a sign, so too can the reader. The sonnet ends with a picture of the pair: "Like sculptured effigies they might be seen / Upon their marriage-tomb, the sword between." The sense of sight is called upon to render the emotional landscape of the couple's interiority; the senses, the intellect, and the emotions present ways of knowing, and Meredith is careful not to privilege one epistemological mode over another. Recalling Alexander Johnson's division of man as tripartite, and depending variously on the emotions, intellect, and senses for distinct though interrelated information, Meredith shows that these modes of knowing are mutually constitutive.

It makes sense, then, that many of the interpretive mistakes that the husband makes arise through his reliance on sight to the exclusion of his other faculties. He is an astute reader, to be sure, and often an insightful one, recognizing mutual pleasure in the couple's performance at a dinner party (see Sonnet XVII), recognizing her handwriting on a letter to her lover (Sonnet

---

37. Norman Friedman, "The Jangled Harp—Symbolic Structure in *Modern Love*," *Modern Language Quarterly* 18, no. 1 (1957): 12.

XV), and even recognizing that though his moods might change, his interiority is not reflected in nature: "What's this, when Nature swears there is no change / To challenge eyesight?" (Sonnet XI). Nevertheless, he is often blind to similarly obvious facts: though he keenly feels the impact of her affair, as when prompted by the errant love letter, he does not imagine the impact of his affair on her, even when he comes across a reminder in his own desk (Sonnet XX). He imagines that he "can interpret where the mouth is dumb" (Sonnet XXVI), yet is caught off guard by her suicide. Despite constant evidence to the contrary, he insists on believing that physical affection—touch—will provide the comfort he seeks (Sonnet XXXII).

These limitations, though, are perhaps not a failing on the husband's part, but rather an indication of the ultimate impossibility of the senses to facilitate intersubjectivity, a theme that is emphasized through form as well as through narrative. In Sonnet V, for example, the husband's old desire is ignited, and he is caught off guard by his wife's inability to recognize it. The sonnet features four semantic shifts, but they do not correspond to the quatrains. The first point ("She treated him as something that is tame") is made in lines 1–4; the shift in line 5 ("but at other provocation bites") is followed by the fact that her body inspires tender feelings in him, a sentiment that bleeds over into the third quatrain by one line; the first line of the fourth quatrain completes grammatically the thought that ends the last line of the third quatrain: "Love's inmost sacredness, / Call'd to him, 'Come!'" Allowing the semantic content of the quatrains to bleed over in this way throws the first line of each quatrain into stark relief, highlighting the husband's desire, a desire that he believes his wife understands as dangerous ("but at other provocation bites") and that he feels to be both sinful ("tempting") and sanctified ("Love's inmost sacredness"). Only after this virtuosic presentation of ambivalence, does the volta begin, in which the wife cannot see his momentary desire to repair their relationship:

> —In that restraining start,
> Eyes nurtured to be look'd at, scarce could see
> A wave of the great waves of Destiny
> Convulsed at a check'd impulse of the heart.

As is clear in these lines, the depiction of the limits of the senses is made possible through Meredith's use of shifting narratorial perspectives, for though the wife's insight is necessarily thwarted by the limitations of her subjectivity, the poetic voice is able to render what she cannot see. The ease of movement between first- and third-person narrators, and between distanced reflection and direct reporting of ideas spoken or thought, signifies a development in poetics that was not Meredith's alone. Such shifts in point of view are, for example, one link between emerging theories of the mind and emerging theories of poetry, links that other poets exploited. In his verse, Baudelaire similarly combined introspection and reported dialogue or conversation; other elements of Baudelaire's style—a strict and relatively conservative poetic structure with synesthesia-driven images, a predilection for shifts in temporal order, and a penchant for drawing his subjects from the lower classes—resonate with Meredith's work as well as ongoing discussions about the proper content for poetry (See Arnold, Hallam, and Massey's excerpts in the "Contexts" section).

## Poems and Ballads

If Meredith links the Roadside Philosophers—the Juggler, the Chartist, the Beggar, and the Engineer—through their use of the dramatic monologue and cannily manipulates the sonnet structure in "Modern Love," in the volume's other poems, collected under the heading "Poems and Ballads," he demonstrates his command of an impressive variety of poetic forms. Meredith's ballads are, like the Philosophers' monologues, more folksy than urban, more nostalgic than experimental; and while they bear self-conscious traces of oral transmission, their diction is more elevated than that of the Roadside poems. Like so many Victorian ballads, Meredith's are essentially narrative poems, sometimes spoken by an impersonal voice—the public voice made univocal as in a Greek chorus. They focus on a single episode and usually thematize the relationship between violence and love. They feature repetition, avoid exploring the psychological motives of their dramatis personae, and lead toward an emotional climax. These aspects are obvious in a poem like "Cassandra" but evident in "Margaret's Bridal-Eve" and "Grandfather Bridgeman" as well. The ballad is a form that had become extremely popular in the Romantic period, thanks to Bishop Percy's anthology of British balladry. As W. E. Aytoun quipped in an 1847 review on a series of books published on the ballad, "ballad poetry in all its forms and ramifications has become inconceivably rampant."[38] More important than the fashion, however, were the poets who influenced Meredith, adepts at the form: Goethe, Wordsworth, and Keats. Meredith's own ballads earned praise from his contemporaries: Swinburne thought that "Margaret's Bridal-Eve" was "pathetic and splendid," one of the best examples of the form in English.[39] The *Athenaeum* found "Cassandra" to be "free from the blemishes of caprice and obscurity" that ruined so many of the volume's poems.[40]

With the ode, Meredith introduces "high" poetry to the volume. The ode is a term used to describe a complexly organized lyric poem, serious and meditative in tone. While at first glance "Ode to the Spirit of Earth in Autumn" may seem to resonate more with the nature poetry Meredith wrote in later years, in fact its inclusion in the *Modern Love* volume casts into sharper relief the role of nature in poems throughout the collection: for Meredith, nature functions not as something to be conquered, but rather as a retreat from the vicissitudes of a society defined by institutions and progress, a retreat that is only sometimes effective. In light of the odes, the philosophies forwarded throughout the volume can be understood as more than simple folksiness: they also function as social commentary. In "Margaret's Bridal-Eve," for example, the garden becomes a site of constricting cultivation, where flowers— and young women—are grown only to be plucked, a state of affairs that leads to the death of both.

The promise of nature also figures in "By the Rosanna," a poem often criticized for being too cryptic. It was originally written as a "rallying" cry to raise the spirits of Meredith's friend Maxse, though in subsequent editions it was cut down dramatically to eliminate the more opaque content.[41] The version of "By the Rosanna" found in *Modern Love* can be read as a meditation upon the compensatory power of nature, and offers an example of a recurring idea in Meredith's poetry: an emphatic insistence on the disparity between

---

38. W. E. Aytoun, "Ancient and Modern Ballad Poetry," *Blackwood's Edinburgh Magazine* 379 (May 1847): 623.

39. Algernon Swinburne, "The Poems of Dante Gabriel Rossetti," in *Essays and Studies* (London: Chatto and Windus, 1875), 87.

40. Marston, 720.

41. In a letter to Augustus Jessopp, 13 November 1861, Meredith writes: "Apropos of the 'Rosanna,' it was written from the Tyrol, to a friend, and was simply a piece of friendly play. Which should not have been published, you add? Perhaps not, but it pleased my friend, and the short passage of description was a literal transcript of the scene. Moreover, though the style is open to blame, there is an idea running through the verses, which, while I was rallying my friend, I conceived to have some point for a larger audience." *Letters*, I.109.

"human values and the facts of Nature."[42] Those facts of nature arise, in part, through descriptions rife with a Keatsian sensuousness that annoyed many contemporary readers. He invokes the rushing movement of both London traffic and the unbridled waters of the Rosanna, in order to frame a choice: "Life, or London."[43] That contrast persists through the poem: turning from social life toward the solitude of the river, the speaker imagines the Rosanna becomes a "nymph" capable of giving much more fulfillment, if less stability, than the "Season-Beauty."

The attention accorded Meredith's powerful natural philosophy, both here and in his later works, must not overwhelm our recognition of his use of similar poetic strategies in poems that treat other subjects. Those that deal with legends and ancient texts are, for example, woefully ignored in critical treatments of Meredith's verse. "Cassandra" is replete with arresting imagery that is enhanced by the refusal of chronological narrative. "The Head of Bran" similarly marshals the resources of rhythm to convey a sense of Bran's legendary power. In "Shemselnihar," the speaker highlights the bodily effects of her anguished longing for her lover and her freedom by metaphorizing her body as various forms of desiccated plant life and refusing to describe in visual terms her luxurious surroundings. We find a similarly effective use of selective sensory description in "Phantasy," a poem that seeks to translate two fantastical worlds—that of the Wilis described in Heinrich Heine's *De l'Allemagne* and *Giselle*, the ballet based on the story—into a dream vision.[44]

If the senses can provide an avenue for the individual to commune with nature and to explore the exotic, they also provide a basis for poetic explorations of introspection and alienation: in a series of three lyric poems, each originally untitled, Meredith leverages a single sense over others to communicate the unbreachable alterity of the other. In "When I would image her features," the speaker fails to banish feelings of alienation by conjuring a vision of his beloved's face. In "A roar thro' the tall twin elm-trees," the speaker imagines that the sound of wind outside his home voices the estrangement it feels from him, an estrangement that is ironically similar to what he feels from his beloved. And, finally, "I chafe at darkness" uses the sense of

42. Arthur Simpson, "Meredith's Alien Vision: 'In the Woods,'" *Victorian Poetry* 20, no. 2 (Summer 1982): 113.

43. "By the Rosanna," line 30.

44. For more on this connection, see Carl Ketcham, "Meredith and the Wilis," *Victorian Poetry* 1, no. 4 (November 1963): 241–48.

touch to articulate the emotional feeling of disconnection. "The Doe" can be understood as offering a response to these failures. In this narrative poem, we find nature (as represented by a doe named Nancy) in Wordsworthian sympathy with a small group of country folk.

## Modern Love in Context

Readers familiar only with the sonnet sequence "Modern Love" might be surprised to learn that the last poem in the *Modern Love* volume recounts a rustic family's encounter with a deer. The volume's variety is, however surprising, an indicator of the complexity and idiosyncrasy of Meredith's poetry. The supplementary prose and verse selections in the "Contexts" section of this edition are intended to complement the *Modern Love* poems by providing insight into the social, cultural, and aesthetic landscape of Meredith's time. In addition to social commentary and texts on poetic and sensory theory, the "Contexts" section includes contemporary reviews of *Modern Love*, along with a number of poems by contemporary writers. Baudelaire's sonnet "Causerie," as mentioned previously, offers one touchstone; others include two sonnets by Keats, Gerard Manley Hopkins's innovative "Harry Ploughman," as well as selections from Tennyson's *Maud*, Barrett Browning's *Sonnets from the Portuguese*, and Christina Rossetti's "Monna Innominata." These poems exemplify several key themes in nineteenth-century poetry. Compare, for example, the sublimity of nature in Keats's "On the Sea" to its more intimate depiction in Meredith's "Autumn Even-Song," the unhinged speaker in Tennyson's *Maud* to the hysterical Margaret who collapses on her wedding night in "Margaret's Bridal-Eve," or the faithful Honoria of Patmore's "The Angel of the House" to the inconstant "Madam" of "Modern Love." In each instance, Meredith recuperates an image while transforming it, lovingly ironizing the tropes, stretching standard forms and thematic expectations to accommodate the demands of a modern life defined by evolving pressures and endless changes—the "On-on-on" described in "By the Rosanna." Modernity in *Modern Love* is not merely shocking, overtly sexual, or intentionally amoral. The poems are equally nostalgic, idyllic, and sometimes even a little cheesy. While other poets may adopt a single affective register more consistently, one of the great achievements of the *Modern Love* volume is its sustained ambivalence toward contemporary life and literature, an ambivalence that is at once sincerely Victorian and vividly fresh.

This introduction has enumerated only some of the connections between Meredith's poems and these supplementary texts, but scholars, students, and interested readers alike are sure to draw additional parallels. Much of the complexity and richness of Meredith's poetry arises from his ability to synthesize the many, varied sources that influenced his writing, so that their traces are evident even as his poetry is unmistakably his. Meredith had indeed, by the end of the nineteenth century, "become an adjective," but it is a testament to the quality of his writing that the connotations of that adjective—"Meredithian"—are myriad. To be "Meredithian" is to be penetrating, ironic, obscure, witty, acerbic, intellectual, imaginative, eccentric, sensitive, or playful. Today's reader will doubtless find these traits and more in this complete edition of *Modern Love and Poems of the English Roadside, with Poems and Ballads.*

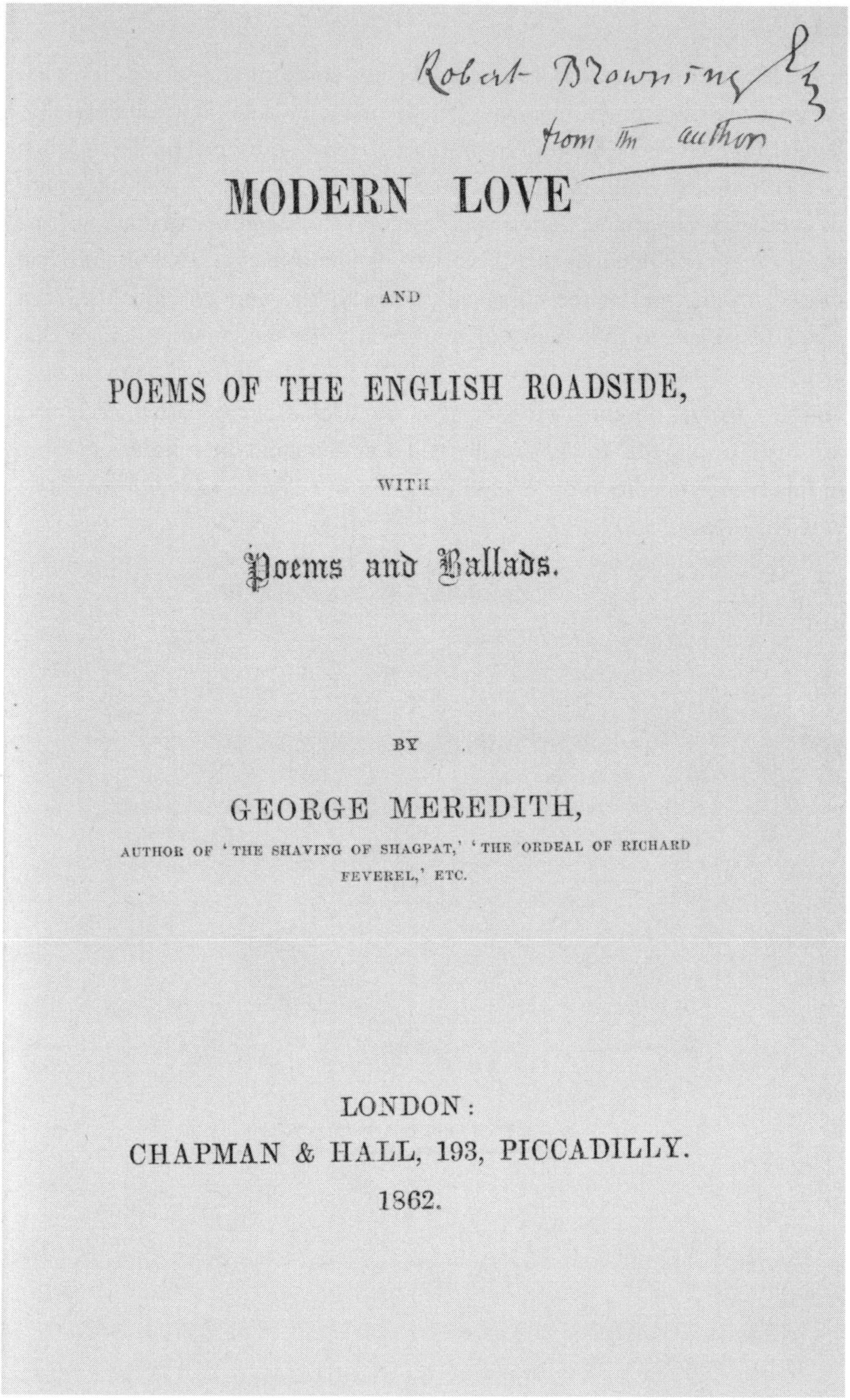

*Robert Browning*
*from the author*

# MODERN LOVE

AND

## POEMS OF THE ENGLISH ROADSIDE,

WITH

### Poems and Ballads.

BY

## GEORGE MEREDITH,

AUTHOR OF 'THE SHAVING OF SHAGPAT,' 'THE ORDEAL OF RICHARD
FEVEREL,' ETC.

LONDON:
CHAPMAN & HALL, 193, PICCADILLY.
1862.

FIGURE 2: Title page of *Modern Love and Poems of the English Roadside, with Poems and Ballads*, inscribed in the author's hand to Robert Browning. Image courtesy of Beinecke Rare Book and Manuscript Library, Yale University, New Haven, CT. BEIN Meredith 862 Copy 1.

# MODERN LOVE

### AND

## POEMS OF THE

## ENGLISH ROADSIDE,

### WITH

## POEMS AND BALLADS

Affectionately Inscribed
to
Captain Maxse, R.N.[1]

1. Frederick Augustus Maxse (1833–1900), lifelong friend of Meredith. Though eventually a Rear Admiral in the Royal Navy, Maxse turned to Radical politics after becoming disillusioned during his service in the Crimean War. He would be the model of the hero of Meredith's *Beauchamp's Career* (1875). Meredith's son William takes his middle name from Maxse.

# Grandfather Bridgeman

## I.

"Heigh, boys!" cried Grandfather Bridgeman, "it's time before
    dinner to-day."
He lifted the crumpled letter, and thump'd a surprising "Hurrah!"
Up jump'd all the echoing young ones, but John, with the starch in
    his throat,
Said, "Father, before we make noises, let's see the contents of the
    note."
The old man glared at him harshly, and, twinkling made answer:
    "Too bad!
"John Bridgeman, I'm always the whisky, and you are the water,
    my lad!"

## II.

But soon it was known thro' the house, and the house ran over
    for joy,
That news, good news, great marvels, had come from the
    solider boy;
Young Tom, the luckless scapegrace,[1] the offshoot of Methodist
    John;
His grandfather's evening tale, whom the old man hail'd as his son.
And the old man's shout of pride was a shout of his victory, too;
For he call'd his affection a method: the neighbours' opinions he
    knew.

## III.

Meantime, from the morning table, removing the stout breakfast
    cheer,
The drink of the three generations, the milk, the tea, and the beer,
(Alone in its generous reading of pints stood the Grandfather's jug)
The women for sight of the missive came pressing to coax and
    to hug.
He scatter'd them quick, with a buss[2] and a smack; thereupon he
    began
Diversions with John's little Sarah: on Sunday, the naughty
    old man!

---

1. *scapegrace*: reckless person
2. *buss*: kiss

## IV.

Then messengers sped to the maltster,[3] the auctioneer, miller,
and all
The seven sons of the farmer who housed in the range of his call.
Likewise the married daughters, three plentiful ladies, prime cooks,
Who bow'd to him while they condemned, in meek hope to stand
high in his books.
"John's wife is a fool at a pudding," they said, and the light carts
up hill
Went merrily, flouting the Sabbath: for puddings well made mend
a will.

## V.

The day was a van-bird of summer:[4] the robin still piped, but the
blue,
A warm and dreamy palace with voices of larks ringing thro,'
Look'd down as if wistfully eyeing the blossoms that fell from
its lap:
A day to sweeten the juices: a day to quicken the sap!
All round the shadowy orchard sloped meadows in gold, and the
dear
Shy violets breathed their hearts out: the maiden breath of the year!

---

3. *maltster*: a person who makes malt from grain
4. *van-bird of summer*: harbinger of summer, first bird indicating summer is on its way

# VI.

Full time there was before dinner to bring fifteen of his blood,
To sit at the old man's table: they found that the dinner was good.
But who was she by the lilacs and pouring laburnums[5] conceal'd,
When under the blossoming apple the chair of the Grandfather
    wheel'd?
She heard one little child crying, "Dear, brave Cousin Tom!" as it
    leapt:
Then murmur'd she: "Let me spare them!" and pass'd round the
    walnuts, and wept.

# VII.

Yet not from sight had she slipped ere sharp feminine eyes could
    detect
The figure of Mary Charlworth. "It's just what we all might
    expect,"
Was utter'd: and: "Didn't I tell you?" Of Mary the rumour
    resounds,
That she is now her own mistress, and mistress of five thousand
    pounds.
'Twas she, they say, who cruelly sent young Tom to the war.
Miss Mary, we thank you now! If you knew what we're thanking
    you for!

---

5. *laburnums*: flowering trees or bushes with bright yellow flowers

## VIII.

But, "Have her in: let her hear it," call'd Grandfather Bridgeman,
    elate,
While Mary's black-gloved fingers hung trembling with flight on
    the gate.
Despite the women's remonstrance, two little ones, lighter than
    deer,
Were loosed, and Mary imprison'd, her whole face white as a tear,
Came forward with culprit footsteps. Her punishment was to
    commence:
The pity in her pale visage they read in a different sense.

## IX.

"You perhaps may remember a fellow, Miss Charlworth, a sort of
    black sheep,"
The old man tuned his tongue to ironical utterance deep:
"He came of a Methodist dad, so it wasn't his fault if he kick'd.
"He earn'd a sad reputation, but Methodists *are* mortal strict.
"His name was Tom, and, dash me! but Bridgeman I think you
    might add:
"Whatever he was, bear in mind that he came of a Methodist dad."

## X.

This prelude dismally lengthen'd, till Mary, starting, exclaim'd,
"A letter, Sir, from your grandson?" "Tom Bridgeman that rascal is
    named,"
The old man answer'd, and further, the words that sent Tom to the
    ranks,
Repeated as words of a person to whom they all owed mighty
    thanks.
But Mary never blush'd: with her eyes on the letter, she sate,
And twice interrupting him falter'd, "The date, may I ask, Sir, the
    date?"

## XI.

"Why, that's what I never look at in a letter," the farmer replied:
"Facts first! and now I'll be parson." The Bridgeman women
    descried
A quiver on Mary's eyebrows. One turn'd, and while shifting her
    comb,
Said low to a sister: "I'm certain she knows more than we
    about Tom.
"She wants him now he's a hero!"[6] The same, resuming her place,
Begg'd Mary to check them the moment she found it a tedious case.

## XII.

Then as a mastiff swallows the snarling noises of cats,
The voice of the farmer open'd. "'Three cheers, and off with your
    hats!'
"—That's Tom! 'We've beaten them, daddy, and tough work it
    was, to be sure!
"'A regular stand-up combat: eight hours smelling powder and
    gore.
"'I enter'd it Serjeant-Major,'—and now he commands a salute,
"And carries the flag of old England! Heigh! see him lift his foes on
    his foot!

---

6. Mary, it seems, rejected Tom as a suitor before he went off to war.

## XIII.

"—An officer! ay, Miss Charlworth, he is, or he is so to be;
"You'll own war isn't such humbug: and Glory means something,
you see.
"'But don't say a word,' he continues, 'against the brave French
any more.'
"—That stopt me: we'll now march together. I couldn't read fur-
ther before.
"That 'brave French' I couldn't stomach. He can't see their cun-
ning to get
"Us Britons to fight their battles, while best half the winnings
they net!"

## XIV.

The old man sneer'd, and read forward. It was of that desperate
fight;—
The Muscovite[7] stole thro' the mist-wreaths that wrapp'd the chill
Inkermann[8] height,
Where stood our silent outposts: old England was in them that day!
O sharp work'd his ruddy wrinkles, as if to the breath of the fray
They moved! He sat bare-headed: his long hair over him slow,
Swung white as the silky bog-flowers in purple heath-hollows that
grow.

---

7. *Muscovite*: man from Moscow
8. *Inkermann*: the Ukrainian site of a major battle and turning point in the Crimean War, fought
5 November 1854. The allied British and French forces fought against the Russians.

## XV.

And louder at Tom's first person: acute and in thunder the 'I'
Invaded the ear with a whinny of triumph, that seem'd to defy
The hosts of the world. All heated, what wonder he little could
    brook
To catch the sight of Mary's demure puritanical look?
And still as he led the onslaught, his treacherous side-shots he sent
At her who was fighting a battle as fierce, and who sat there unbent.

## XVI.

"'We stood in line, and like hedgehogs the Russians, roll'd under us
    thick.
"'They frighten'd me there.'—He's no coward; for when, Miss,
    they came at the quick,
"The sight he swears, was a breakfast. 'My stomach felt tight: in a
    glimpse
"'I saw you snoring at home with the dear cuddled-up little imps.
"'And then like the winter brickfields at midnight, hot fire
    lengthen'd out.
"'Our fellows were just leash'd bloodhounds: no heart of the lot
    faced about.

## XVII.

"'And only that grumbler, Bob Harris, remarked that we stood one
    to ten:
"'Ye fool, says Mick Grady, just tell 'em they know how to compli-
    ment men!
"'And I sang out your old words: 'If the opposite side isn't God's,
"'Heigh! after you've counted a dozen, the pluckiest lads have the
    odds.'
"'Ping-ping flew the enemies' pepper: the Colonel roar'd, For-
    ward, and we
"'Went at them. 'Twas first like a blanket: and then a long plunge in
    the sea.

## XVIII.

"'Well, now about me and the Frenchman: it happen'd I can't tell
　　you how:
"'And, Grandfather, hear, if you love me, and put aside
　　prejudice now:'
"He never says 'Grandfather'—Tom don't—unless it's a serious
　　thing.
"'Well, there were some pits for the rifles, just dug on our French-
　　leaning wing:
"'And backwards, and forwards, and backwards we went, and at
　　last I was vex'd,
"'And swore I would never surrender a foot when the Russians
　　charged next.

## XIX.

"'I know that life's worth keeping.'—Ay, so it is, lad; so it is!
"'But my life belongs to a woman.'—Does that mean Her Majesty,
　　Miss?[9]
"'These Russians came lumping and grinning: they're fierce at it,
　　though they are blocks.
"'Our fellows were pretty well pump'd, and look'd sharp for the
　　little French cocks.
"'Lord, didn't we pray for their crowing! when over us, on the
　　hill-top,
"'Behold the first line of them skipping, like kangaroos seen on
　　the hop!

9. Grandfather teases Mary, who stands listening to the letter.

# XX.

"'That sent me into a passion, to think of them spying our flight!'
"Heigh, Tom! you've Bridgeman blood, boy! And, 'face them!' I
    shouted: 'all right;
"'Sure, Serjeant, we'll take their shot d*a*cent,[10] like gentlemen,'
    Grady replied.
"'A ball in his mouth, and the noble old Irishman dropp'd by my
    side.
"'Then there was just an instant to save myself, when a short
    wheeze
"'Of bloody lungs under the smoke, and a red-coat[11] crawl'd up on
    his knees.

# XXI.

"''Twas Ensign Baynes[12] of our parish.' Ah, ah, Miss Charlworth,
    the one
"Our Tom fought for a young lady? Come, now we've got into the
    fun!
"'I shoulder'd him: he primed his pistol, and I trailed my musket,
    prepared.'
"Why, that's a fine pick-a-back[13] for ye, to make twenty Russians
    look scared!
"'They came—never mind how many: we couldn't have run very
    well,
"'We fought back to back:' 'face to face, our last time!' he said,
    smiling, and fell.

---

10. *dacent*: Irish, decent
11. *red-coat*: a soldier in the British army
12. *Baynes*: Tom Bridgeman's rival for Mary Charlworth's affection
13. *pick-a-back*: piggyback; Tom is carrying Ensign Baynes over his shoulder.

## XXII.

"'Then I strove wild for his body: the beggars saw glittering rings,
"'Which I vow'd to send to his mother. I got some hard knocks and
sharp stings,
"'But felt them no more than an angel, or devil, except in the wind.
"'I know that I swore at a Russian for showing his teeth, and he
grinn'd
"'The harder: quick, as from heaven, a man on a horse rode
between,
"'And fired, and swung his bright sabre: I can't write you more of
the scene.

## XXIII.

"'But half in his arms, and half at his stirrup, he bore me right
forth,
"'And pitch'd me among my old comrades: before I could tell south
from north,
"'He caught my hand up, and kiss'd it! Don't ever let any man
speak
"'A word against Frenchmen, I near him! I can't find his name, tho'
I seek.
"'But French, and a General, surely he was, and, God bless him!
thro' him
"'I've learnt to love a whole nation.' The ancient man paused,
winking dim.

## XXIV.

A curious look, half woeful, was seen on his face as he turn'd
His eyes upon each of his children, like one who but faintly
    discern'd
His old self in an old mirror. Then gathering sense in his fist,
He sounded it hard on his knee-cap. "Your hand, Tom, the French
    fellow kiss'd!
"He kiss'd my boy's old pounder! I say he's a gentleman!" Straight
The letter he toss'd to one daughter; bade her the remainder relate.

## XXV.

Tom properly stated his praises in facts, but the lady preferr'd,
To deck the narration with brackets, and drop her additional word.
What nobler Christian natures these women could boast, who 'twas
    known,
Once spat at the name of their nephew, and now made his praises
    their own!
The letter at last was finish'd, the hearers breath'd freely, and sign
Was given, 'Tom's health!'—Quoth the farmer: "Eh, Miss? are you
    weak in the spine?"

## XXVI.

For Mary had sunk, and her body was shaking, as if in a fit,
Tom's letter she held, and her thumb-nail the month when the let-
    ter was writ
Fast-dinted, while she hung sobbing: "O, see, Sir, the letter is old!
"O, do not be too happy!"—"If I understand you, I'm bowl'd!"
Said Grandfather Bridgeman, "and down go my wickets!14—not
    happy! when here,
"Here's Tom like to marry his General's daughter—or widow—
    I'll swear!

---

14. *wickets*: In a game of cricket, the wicket consists of three vertical posts set into the ground; if a bowler knocks the wicket down, the batter is out.

## XXVII.

"I wager he knows how to strut, too! It's all on the cards that the
    Queen
"Will ask him to Buckingham Palace, to say what he's done and
    he's seen.
"Victoria's fond of her soldiers: and she's got a nose for a fight.
"If Tom tells a cleverish story—there is such a thing as a knight!
"And don't he look roguish and handsome!—To see a girl snivel-
    ling there—
"By George, Miss, it's clear that you're jealous!"—"I love him!"
    she answered his stare.

## XXVIII.

"Yes! *now*!" breathed the voice of a woman.—"Ah! now!" quiver'd
    low the reply.
"And 'now' 's just a bit too late, so it's no use your piping[15] your eye,"
The farmer added bluffly. "Old lawyer Charlworth was rich;
"You follow'd his instructions in kicking Tom into the ditch.
"If you're such a dutiful daughter, that doesn't prove Tom is a fool.
"Forgive and forget's my motto! and here's my grog[16] growing
    cool!"

## XXIX.

"But, Sir," Mary faintly repeated: "for four long weeks I have fail'd
"To come and cast on you my burden; such grief for you always
    prevail'd!"
"My heart has so bled for you!" The old man burst on her speech:
"You've chosen a likely time, Miss! a pretty occasion to preach!"
And was it not outrageous, that now, of all times, one should come
With incomprehensible pity! Far better had Mary been dumb.

---

15. *piping*: to produce a shrill sound; colloquially, to weep
16. *grog*: a drink made of equal parts spirits (usually rum) and water

## XXX.

But when again she stammer'd in this bewildering way,
The farmer no longer could bear it, and begg'd her to go, or to stay,
But not to be whimpering nonsense at such a time. Prick'd by a
  goad,
"'Twas you who sent him to glory:—you've come here to reap
  what you sow'd.
"Is that it?" he ask'd; and the silence the elders preserved, plainly
  said,
On Mary's heaving bosom this begging petition was read.

## XXXI.

And that it was scarcely a bargain that she who had driven him
  wild,
Should share, now, the fruits of his valour, the women express'd, as
  they smiled.
The family pride of the Bridgemans was comforted; still, with
  contempt,
They look'd on a monied damsel of modesty quite so exempt.
"O give me force to tell them!" cried Mary, and even as she spoke,
A shout and a hush of the children: a vision on all of them broke.

## XXXII.

Wheel'd, pale, in a chair, and shatter'd, the wreck of their hero was
  seen;
The ghost of Tom drawn slow o'er the orchard's shadowy green.
Could this be the martial darling they joy'd in a moment ago?
"He knows it?" to Mary Tom murmur'd, and closed his weak lids
  at her, "No."
"Beloved!" she said, falling by him, "I have been a coward: I
  thought
"You lay in the foreign country, and some strange good might be
  wrought.

## XXXIII.

"Each day I have come to tell him, and failed, with my hand on
    the gate.
"I bore the dreadful knowledge, and crush'd my heart with its
    weight.
"The letter brought by your comrade—he has but just read it
    aloud!
"It only reach'd him this morning!" Her head on his shoulder she
    bow'd.
Then Tom with Pity's tenderest lordliness patted her arm,
And eyed the old white-head fondly, with something of doubt and
    alarm.

## XXXIV.

O, take to your fancy a sculptor whose fresh marble offspring
    appears
Before him, shiningly perfect, the laurel-crown'd issue of years:
Is Heaven offended? for lightning behold from its bosom escape,
And those are mocking fragments that made the harmonious shape!
He cannot love the ruins, till feeling that ruins alone
Are left, he loves them threefold. So pass'd the old grandfather's
    moan!

## XXXV.

John's text for a sermon on Slaughter, he heard, and he did not
    protest.
All rigid as April snow-drifts, he stood, hard and feeble; his chest
Just showing the swell of the fire as it melted him. Smiting a rib,
"Heigh! what have we been about, Tom! Was this all a terrible fib?"
He cried, and the letter forth-trembled. Tom told what the cannon
    had done.
Few present but ached to see falling those aged tears on his
    heart's son!

## XXXVI.

Up lanes of the quiet village, and where the mill-waters rush red

Thro' browning summer meadows to catch the sun's crimsoning
head,

You meet an old man and a maiden who has the soft ways of a wife

With one whom they wheel, alternate; whose delicate flush of new
life

Is prized like the early primrose. Then shake his right hand, in the
chair—

The old man fails never to tell you: "You've got the French Gen-
eral's there!"

# The Meeting[1]

The old coach-road thro' a common[2] of furze,[3]
  With knolls of pines, ran white:
Berries of autumn, with thistles, and burrs,
  And spider-threads, droop'd in the light.

The light in a thin blue veil peer'd sick;
  The sheep grazed close and still;
The smoke of a farm by a yellow rick[4]
  Curl'd lazily under a hill.

No fly shook the round of the silver net;
  No insect the swift bird chased;                    10
Only two travellers moved and met
  Across that hazy waste.

One was a girl with a babe that throve,
  Her ruin and her bliss;
One was a youth with a lawless love,
  Who claspt it the more for this.

---

1. Originally published in *Once a Week* on 1 September 1860, illustrated by J. E. Millais (see fig. 3).
2. *common*: unenclosed and uncultivated land belonging to the community, hence "waste" land
3. *furƺe*: evergreen shrub
4. *rick*: haystack

The girl for her babe humm'd prayerful speech;
    The youth for his love did pray;
Each cast a wistful look on each,
    And either went their way.         20

*Modern Love*

This is not meat
For little people or for fools.

—BOOK OF THE SAGES[1]

---

1. Meredith did not include this epigraph in later editions. It appears to be his invention.

# I.

By this he knew she wept with waking eyes:
That, at his hand's light quiver by her head,
The strange low sobs that shook their common bed
Were called into her with a sharp surprise,                                    4
And strangled mute, like little gaping snakes,
Dreadfully venomous to him. She lay
Stone-still, and the long darkness flow'd away
With muffled pulses. Then, as midnight makes                                    8
Her giant heart of Memory and Tears
Drink the pale drug of silence, and so beat
Sleep's heavy measure, they from head to feet
Were moveless, looking thro' their dead black years,                          12
By vain regret scrawl'd over the blank wall.
Like sculptured effigies they might be seen
Upon their marriage-tomb, the sword between;[2]
Each wishing for the sword that severs all.                                    16

---

2. *Like sculptured . . . between*: Medieval tombs of married couples often featured images of both, lying side by side as if in bed. The sword between, however, suggests emotional or, as in Medieval courtly narratives, physical separation.

## II.

It ended, and the morrow brought the task:
Her eyes were guilty gates that let him in
By shutting all too zealous for their sin:
Each suck'd a secret, and each wore a mask.                    4
But, oh the bitter taste her beauty had!
He sicken'd as at breath of poison-flowers:[3]
A languid humour stole among the hours,
And if their smiles encounter'd, he went mad,                  8
And raged, deep inward, till the light was brown
Before his vision, and the world forgot,
Look'd wicked as some old dull murder spot.
A star with lurid beams, she seem'd to crown                   12
The pit of infamy: and then again
He fainted on his vengefulness, and strove
To ape the magnanimity[4] of love,
And smote himself, a shuddering heap of pain.                  16

---

3. *poison-flowers*: cf. Baudelaire's 1857 volume of poetry, Les *Fleurs du Mal* (1857) (*The Flowers of Evil*), a collection of poems that thematized sexuality, carnality, and the allure of the beautiful female body
4. *magnanimity*: generosity of spirit

## III.

This was the woman; what now of the man?[5]
But pass him! If he comes beneath our heel[6]
He shall be crush'd until he cannot feel,
Or, being callous, haply[7] till he can.                    4
But he is nothing:—nothing? Only mark
The rich light striking from her unto him:
Ha! what a sense it is when her eyes swim
Across the man she singles, leaving dark                    8
All else! Lord God, who mad'st the thing so fair,
See that I am drawn to her even now!
It cannot be such harm on her cool brow
To put a kiss? Yet if I meet him there!                    12
But she is mine! Ah, no! I know too well
I claim a star whose light is overcast:
I claim a phantom-woman in the Past.
The hour has struck, though I heard not the bell!          16

---

5. *the man?*: the wife's lover
6. *beneath our heel*: cf. Genesis 3:15. God says to the serpent that tempted Eve: "I will put enmity between thee and the woman, and between thy seed and her seed; it shall bruise thy head, and thou shalt bruise his heel."
7. *haply*: maybe

## IV.

All other joys of life he strove to warm,
And magnify, and catch them to his lip:
But they had suffered shipwreck with the ship,[8]
And gazed upon him sallow from the storm.                    4
Or if Delusion came, 'twas but to show
The coming minute mock the one that went.
Cold as a mountain in its star-pitch'd tent
Stood high Philosophy, less friend than foe:                 8
Whom self-caged Passion, from its prison-bars,
Is always watching with a wondering hate.[9]
Not till the fire is dying in the grate,
Look we for any kinship with the stars.[10]                  12
Oh, wisdom never comes when it is gold,
And the great price we pay for it full worth.
We have it only when we are half earth.
Little avails that coinage to the old![11]                   16

---

8. *shipwreck . . . ship*: Meredith develops this image, which resonates with Sir Thomas Wyatt's sonnet "My galley, charged with forgetfulness" and is also a version of a common Victorian trope for personal destiny, as the sequence unfolds. In Victorian literature, the ship often represents an individual soul on the sea of destiny; here it represents the couple's marriage.

9. *Cold as a mountain . . . wondering hate*: one of several images that represent the battle between rational thought (Philosophy) and feeling (Passion)

10. *Not till . . . kinship with the stars*: We only look to Nature for consolation when all simple satisfactions (e.g., warmth) are exhausted.

11. *Oh, wisdom . . . to the old*: Wisdom is wasted on the old.

## V.

A message from her set his brain aflame.
A world of household matters fill'd her mind,
Wherein he saw hypocrisy design'd:
She treated him as something that is tame,     4
And but at other provocation bites.
Familiar was her shoulder in the glass
Through that dark rain: yet it may come to pass
That a changed eye finds such familiar sights,     8
More keenly tempting than new loveliness.
The 'What has been' a moment seem'd his own:
The splendours, mysteries, dearer because known,
Nor less divine: Love's inmost sacredness,     12
Call'd to him, "Come!"—In that restraining start,
Eyes nurtured to be look'd at, scarce could see
A wave of the great waves of Destiny
Convulsed at a check'd impulse of the heart.     16

## VI.

It chanced his lips did meet her forehead cool.
She had no blush, but slanted down her eye.
Shamed nature, then, confesses love can die:
And most she punishes the tender fool                    4
Who will believe what honours her the most!
Dead! is it dead? She has a pulse, and flow
Of tears, the price of blood-drops, as I know
For whom the midnight sobs around Love's ghost,          8
Since then I heard her, and so will sob on.
The love is here; it has but changed its aim.
O bitter barren woman! what's the name?
The name, the name, the new name thou hast won?          12
Behold me striking the world's coward stroke!¹²
That will I not do, though the sting is dire.
—Beneath the surface this, while by the fire
They sat, she laughing at a quiet joke.                  16

---

12. *coward's stroke*: to strike someone down when he or she is not looking

## VII.

She issues radiant from her dressing room,
Like one prepared to scale an upper sphere:
—By stirring up a lower, much I fear!
How deftly that oil'd barber lays his bloom!                    4
That long-shank'd dapper Cupid with frisk'd curls,
Can make known women torturingly fair;[13]
The gold-eyed serpent dwelling in rich hair,
Awakes beneath his magic whisks and twirls.                    8
His art can take the eyes from out my head,
Until I see with eyes of other men;
While deeper knowledge crouches in its den,
And sends a spark up:—is it true we're wed?                    12
Yea! filthiness of body is most vile,
But faithlessness of heart I do hold worse.
The former, it were not so great a curse
To read on the steel-mirror of her smile.                      16

13. *How deftly . . . torturingly fair*: The wife's hairstyle accentuates her beauty; that a "known woman" is made "torturingly fair" suggests that the husband sees her beauty as a painful cover for her certain guilt. Cf. Sarah Stickney Ellis's discussion of the power of a woman's "personal attractions" in "Advice Manuals and Social Commentary" in the "Contexts" section.

## VIII.

Yet it was plain she struggled, and that salt
Of righteous feeling made her pitiful.
O abject worm, so queenly beautiful!
Where came the cleft between us? whose the fault?[14]          4
My tears are on thee, that have rarely dropp'd
As balm for any bitter wound of mine:
My breast will open for thee at a sign!
But, no: we are two reed-pipes, coarsely stopp'd:          8
The God[15] once fill'd them with his mellow breath;
And they were music till he flung them down,
Used! used! Hear now the discord-loving clown
Puff his gross spirit in them, worse than death!          12
I do not know myself without thee more:
In this unholy battle I grow base:
If the same soul be under the same face,
Speak, and a taste of that old time restore![16]          16

---

14. *whose the fault?*: a constant refrain throughout the sequence
15. *The God*: Pan, the reed-pipe-playing Greek god connected with nature, spring, fertility, and lust. Elizabeth Barrett Browning's "A Musical Instrument," first published in 1860, describes Pan's construction of his reed pipes.
16. *If the same soul . . . old time restore!*: These lines are addressed to his wife.

# IX.

He felt the wild beast in him betweenwhiles[17]
So masterfully rude, that he would grieve
To see the helpless delicate thing receive
His guardianship through certain dark defiles.[18]                4
Had he not teeth to rend, and hunger too?
But still he spared her. Once: "Have you no fear?"
He said: 'twas dusk; she in his grasp; none near.
She laughed: "No, surely; am I not with you?"                    8
And uttering that soft starry 'you,' she lean'd
Her gentle body near him, looking up;
And from her eyes, as from a poison-cup,
He drank until the flittering eyelids screen'd.                 12
Devilish malignant witch! And oh, young beam
Of Heaven's circle-glory![19] Here thy shape
To squeeze like an intoxicating grape—
I might, and yet thou goest safe, supreme.                      16

---

17. *betweenwhiles*: at intervals
18. *defiles*: literally, narrow passes or gorges. As a verb, *defile* can also mean to maul or to take someone's virginity.
19. *Heaven's circle-glory*: the sun

## X.[20]

But where began the change; and what's my crime?
The wretch condemn'd, who has not been arraign'd,[21]
Chafes at his sentence. Shall I, unsustain'd,
Drag on Love's nerveless body thro' all time?                    4
I must have slept, since now I wake. Prepare,
You lovers, to know Love a thing of moods:
Not like hard life, of laws. In Love's deep woods
I dreamt of loyal Life:—the offence is there!                    8
Love's jealous woods about the sun are curl'd;
At least, the sun far brighter there did beam.—
My crime is that, the puppet of a dream,
I plotted to be worthy of the world.                            12
Oh, had I with my darling help'd to mince[22]
The facts of life, you still had seen me go
With hindward feather and with forward toe,
Her much-adored delightful Fairy Prince!                        16

---

20. This sonnet is not in the manuscript version. See "Textual Variants" for original "Sonnet X."
21. *arraign'd*: brought before a court of law to answer charges
22. *mince*: literally, to chop up into tiny pieces; also, to make light of or to disparage

# XI.

Out in the yellow meadows where the bee
Hums by us with the honey of the Spring,
And showers of sweet notes from the larks[23] on wing,
Are dropping like a noon-dew, wander we.                    4
Or is it now? or was it then? for now,
As then, the larks from running rings send showers:
The golden foot of May is on the flowers,
And friendly shadows dance upon her brow.                   8
What's this, when Nature swears there is no change
To challenge eyesight?[24] Now, as then, the grace
Of Heaven seems holding Earth in its embrace.
Nor eyes, nor heart, has she to feel it strange?[25]        12
Look, woman, in the west. There wilt thou see
An amber cradle near the sun's decline:
Within it, featured even in death divine,
Is lying a dead infant, slain by thee![26]                  16

---

23. *showers . . . from the larks*: In Shelley's 1820 "To a Skylark," the lark "showers a rain of melody" (line 35) upon the speaker. Larks often connote happiness.

24. *What's this . . . eyesight?*: The husband notices that Nature is indifferent to his moods; the world looks just as beautiful now that he is tormented by the knowledge of his wife's infidelity as it did when he believed himself to be happily in love.

25. *Nor eyes . . . strange*: The husband wonders if his wife feels the disconnect between their turbulent emotions and the beauty of the external world.

26. *Within it . . . thee!*: The husband projects their anguish onto the external world, imagining he can read the death of their relationship in the sunset. While there is room to interpret the "dead infant" literally, as the child the couple will never have, the first line of the following sonnet suggests that the "dead infant" represents the future.

## XII.

Not solely that the Future she destroys,
And the fair life which in the distance lies
For all men, beckoning out from dim rich skies:
Nor that the passing hour's supporting joys                    4
Have lost the keen-edged flavour, which begat
Distinction in old time, and still should breed
Sweet Memory, and Hope,—Earth's modest seed,
And Heaven's high-prompting: not that the world is flat        8
Since that soft-luring creature I embraced,
Among the children of Illusion went:
Methinks with all this loss I were content,
If the mad Past, on which my foot is based,                   12
Were firm, or might be blotted: but the whole
Of life is mixed: the mocking Past must stay:
And if I drink oblivion of a day,
So shorten I the stature of my soul.                          16

# XIII.

"I play for Seasons; not Eternities!"
Says Nature, laughing on her way. "So must
All those whose stake is nothing more than dust!"
And lo, she wins, and of her harmonies                             4
She is full sure! Upon her dying rose
She drops a look of fondness, and goes by,
Scarce any retrospection in her eye;
For she the laws of growth most deeply knows,                      8
Whose hands bear, here, a seed-bag; there, an urn.
Pledged she herself to aught, 'twould mark her end!
This lesson of our only visible friend,[27]
Can we not teach our foolish hearts to learn?                      12
Yes! yes!—but oh, our human rose is fair
Surpassingly! Lose calmly Love's great bliss,
When the renew'd forever of a kiss
Sounds thro' the listless hurricane of hair![28]                  16

---

27. *our only visible friend*: Nature

28. Lines 15 and 16 received particular scorn in Hutton's review for the *Spectator*. See "Contemporary Reactions." Meredith rewrote 16 for subsequent editions: "Whirls life within the shower of loosened hair!"

# XIV.

What soul would bargain for a cure that brings
Contempt the nobler agony to kill?
Rather let me bear on the bitter ill,
And strike this rusty bosom with new stings!                     4
It seems there is another veering fit,
Since on a gold-hair'd lady's[29] eyeballs pure,
I look'd with little prospect of a cure,
The while her mouth's red bow loosed shafts of wit.               8
Just Heaven! can it be true that jealousy
Has deck'd the woman thus? and does her head
Whirl giddily for what she forfeited?
Madam![30] you teach me many things that be.                    12
I open an old book, and there I find
That 'Women still may love whom they deceive.'[31]
Such love I prize not, Madam: by your leave,
The game you play at is not to my mind.                          16

---

29. *gold-hair'd lady*: the husband's mistress. He will refer to her as "My Lady" in subsequent
sonnets.

30. *Madam*: the husband's wife. He will continue to refer to her as "Madam" in subsequent
sonnets.

31. *'Women still . . . deceive'*: likely Meredith's invention; no source has ever been identified

## XV.

I think she sleeps: it must be sleep, when low
Hangs that abandon'd arm towards the floor:
The head turn'd with it. Now make fast the door.
Sleep on: it is your husband, not your foe!                    4
The Poet's black stage-lion of wrong'd love,[32]
Frights not our modern dames:—well, if he did!
Now will I pour new light upon that lid,
Full-sloping like the breasts beneath. "Sweet dove,            8
"Your sleep is pure. Nay, pardon: I disturb.
"I do not? well!" Her waking infant stare
Grows woman to the burden my hands bear:
Her own handwriting to me when no curb                        12
Was left on Passion's tongue.[33] She trembles thro';
A woman's tremble—the whole instrument:—
I show another letter lately sent.
The words are very like: the name is new.[34]                 16

---

32. *The Poet's black stage-lion*: Shakespeare's Othello

33. *Her own . . . tongue*: The husband holds a love letter that his wife wrote to him early in their relationship.

34. *The words . . . new*: He compares the letter to him with a second letter that she has recently written to her lover.

## XVI.

In our old shipwreck'd days there was an hour,
When in the firelight steadily aglow,
Join'd slackly, we beheld the chasm grow
Among the clicking coals. Our library-bower          4
That eve was left to us: and hush'd we sat
As lovers to whom Time is whispering.
From sudden-open'd doors we heard them sing:
The nodding elders mix'd good wine with chat.         8
Well knew we that Life's greatest treasure lay
With us, and of it was our talk. "Ah, yes!
"Love dies!" I said: I never thought it less.
She yearn'd to me that sentence to unsay.            12
Then when the fire domed blackening, I found
Her cheek was salt against my kiss, and swift
Up the sharp scale of sobs her breast did lift:—
Now am I haunted by that taste! that sound!          16

# XVII.

At dinner she is hostess, I am host.
Went the feast ever cheerfuller? She keeps
The Topic over intellectual deeps
In buoyancy afloat. They see no ghost.                    4
With sparkling surface-eyes we ply the ball:
It is in truth a most contagious game;
HIDING THE SKELETON shall be its name.
Such play as this the devils might appal!                 8
But here's the greater wonder; in that we,
Enamour'd of our acting and our wits,
Admire each other like true hypocrites.
Warm-lighted glances, Love's Ephemeræ,[35]                12
Shoot gaily o'er the dishes and the wine.
We waken envy of our happy lot.
Fast, sweet, and golden, shows our marriage-knot.
Dear guests, you now have seen Love's corpse-light shine![36]   16

---

35. *Ephemeræ*: flies or other insects with extremely short life spans
36. *corpse-light*: according to superstition, a ball of light portending death often seen over church-
yards and ships

# XVIII.

Here Jack and Tom are pair'd with Moll and Meg.[37]
Curved open to the river-reach is seen
A country merry-making on the green.[38]
Fair space for signal shakings of the leg.[39]                    4
That little screwy fiddler from his booth,
Whence flows one nut-brown stream,[40] commands the joints
Of all who caper here at various points.
I have known rustic revels in my youth:                           8
The May-fly[41] pleasures of a mind at ease.
An early goddess was a country lass:
A charm'd Amphion-oak[42] she tripped the grass.
What life was that I lived? The life of these?                    12
God keep them happy! Nature they are near.
They must, I think, be wiser than I am:
They have the secret of the bull and lamb.[43]
'Tis true that when we trace its source, 'tis beer.               16

---

37. *Jack . . . Meg*: names of random, ordinary villagers

38. *country . . . green*: a country fair

39. *signal shakings . . . leg*: dancing

40. *nut-brown stream*: ale

41. *May-fly*: insect that lives only one day, so short-lived pleasures

42. *Amphion-oak*: Amphion, a figure from Greek mythology, whose music made the trees and stones do his bidding. In Tennyson's "Amphion" (1842) the oak trees dance to the music of Amphion's hornpipes. *Amphion* is also a genus of moths, an image that resonates in this sonnet.

43. *bull and lamb*: The bull is a symbol of fertilizing strength; the lamb is not only a symbol for Christ, but also (and more generally) a symbol of humility, innocence, and patience.

# XIX.

No state is enviable. To the luck alone
Of some few favour'd men I would put claim.
I bleed, but her who wounds I will not blame.
Have I not felt her heart as 'twere my own,                4
Beat thro' me? could I hurt her? Heaven and Hell!
But I could hurt her cruelly! Can I let
My Love's old time-piece to another set,
Swear it can't stop, and must for ever swell?              8
Sure, that's one way Love drifts into the mart
Where goat-legg'd[44] buyers throng. I see not plain:—
My meaning is, it must not be again.
Great God! the maddest gambler throws his heart.           12
If any state be enviable on earth,
'Tis yon born idiot's, who, as days go by,
Still rubs his hands before him like a fly,
In a queer sort of meditative mirth.                       16

---

44. *goat-legg'd*: a reference to Pan (see note 15)

# XX.

I am not of those miserable males
Who sniff at vice, and, daring not to snap,
Do therefore hope for Heaven. I take the hap[45]
Of all my deeds. The wind that fills my sails,                    4
Propels; but I am helmsman.[46] Am I wreck'd,
I know the devil has sufficient weight
To bear: I lay it not on him, or fate.
Besides, he's damn'd. That man I do suspect                        8
A coward, who would burden the poor deuce[47]
With what ensues from his own slipperiness.
I have just found a wanton-scented tress[48]
In an old desk, dusty for lack of use.                            12
Of days and nights it is demonstrative,
That like a blasted star gleam luridly.
If for that time I must ask charity,
Have I not any charity to give?                                   16

---

45. *hap*: chance, happenstance
46. *helmsman*: navigator; person who steers a ship; cf. Sonnet IV
47. *deuce*: devil
48. *wanton-scented tress*: lock of hair from one of his old lovers. He has thus also been unfaithful.

## XXI.

We three are on the cedar-shadow'd lawn;
My friend being third. He who at love once laugh'd,
Is in the weak rib by a fatal shaft
Struck through[49] and tells his passion's bashful dawn,                    4
And radiant culmination, glorious crown,
When 'this' she said: went 'thus': most wondrous she!
Our eyes grow white, encountering; that we are three,
Forgetful; then together we look down.                                      8
But he demands our blessing; is convinced
That words of wedded lovers must bring good.
We question: if we dare! or if we should!
And pat him, with light laugh. We have not winced.                          12
Next, she has fallen. Fainting points the sign
To happy things in wedlock.[50] When she wakes
She looks the star that thro' the cedar shakes:
Her lost moist hand clings mortally to mine.                                16

---

49. *Struck through*: by cupid's arrow
50. *Fainting points . . . wedlock*: Fainting is considered a sign of pregnancy.

# XXII.

What may this woman labour to confess?[51]
There is about her mouth a nervous twitch.
'Tis something to be told, or hidden:—which?
I get a glimpse of Hell in this mild guess.                          4
She has desires of touch, as if to feel
That all the household things are things she knew.
She stops before the glass.[52] What does she view?
A face that seems the latest to reveal!                             8
For she turns from it hastily, and toss'd
Irresolute, steals shadow-like to where
I stand; and wavering pale before me there,
Her tears fall still as oak-leaves after frost.                     12
She will not speak. I will not ask. We are
League-sunder'd[53] by the silent gulf between.
You burly lovers on the village green,
Yours is a lower, but a happier star!                               16

---

51. *labour to confess?*: The husband's grotesque pun underscores his conviction that his relationship with his wife shall never again give birth to anything good.
52. *glass*: mirror
53. *League-sunder'd*: miles separated

## XXIII.

'Tis Christmas weather, and a country house
Receives us: rooms are full: we can but get
An attic-crib.[54] Such lovers will not fret
At that, it is half-said. The great carouse[55]                    4
Knocks hard upon the midnight's hollow door.
But when I knock at hers, I see the pit.
Why did I come here in that dullard[56] fit?
I enter, and lie couch'd upon the floor.                           8
Passing, I caught the coverlid's quick beat:—
Come, Shame, burn to my soul! and Pride, and Pain—
Foul demons that have tortured me, sustain![57]
Out in the freezing darkness the lambs bleat.                      12
The small bird stiffens in the low starlight.
I know not how, but, shuddering as I slept,
I dream'd a banish'd Angel to me crept:
My feet were nourish'd on her breasts all night.                   16

54. *attic-crib*: room on the topmost floor
55. *carouse*: a bout of drinking
56. *dullard*: stupid, inert, dull
57. *sustain!*: support

## XXIV.[58]

The misery is greater, as I live!
To know her flesh so pure,[59] so keen her sense,
That she does penance now for no offence,
Save against Love. The less can I forgive!                  4
The less can I forgive, though I adore
That cruel lovely pallor which surrounds
Her footsteps; and the low vibrating sounds
That come on me, as from a magic shore.                     8
Low are they, but most subtle to find out
The shrinking soul. Madam, 'tis understood
When women play upon their womanhood.
It means, a Season gone. And yet I doubt                    12
But I am duped. That nun-like look waylays
My fancy. Oh! I do but wait a sign!
Pluck out the eyes of Pride! thy mouth to mine!
Never! though I die thirsting. Go thy ways!                 16

---

58. For an image of the manuscript version of this sonnet, see fig. 12.

59. *The misery . . . pure*: This suggests that it makes the husband more miserable to suppose that his wife's relationship with her lover is not physical.

# XXV.

You like not that French novel?[60] Tell me why.
You think it most unnatural. Let us see.
The actors are, it seems, the usual three:
Husband, and wife, and lover. She—but fie!                    4
In England we'll not hear of it. Edmond,
The lover, her devout chagrin[61] doth share;
Blanc-mange[62] and absinthe[63] are his penitent fare,
Till his pale aspect makes her overfond:                      8
So, to preclude fresh sin, he tries rosbif.[64]
Meantime the husband is no more abused:[65]
Auguste forgives her ere[66] the tear is used.
Then hangeth all on one tremendous If:—                       12
IF she will choose between them! She does choose;
And takes her husband like a proper wife.
Unnatural? My dear, these things are life:
And life, they say, is worthy of the Muse.                    16

---

60. *French novel?*: Victorians tended to associate French novels, like Flaubert's *Madame Bovary* (1857), with sexual immorality and infidelity.

61. *chagrin*: distress or worry

62. *Blanc-mange*: French, a sweet custard

63. *absinthe*: French liquor distilled from wormwood, thought to lead to insanity and popular among nineteenth-century bohemians

64. *rosbif*: French, "roast beef"

65. *abused*: deceived and/or wronged

66. *ere*: before

## XXVI.

Love ere he bleeds, an eagle in high skies,
Has earth beneath his wings: from redden'd eve
He views the rosy dawn. In vain they weave
The fatal web below while far he flies.                         4
But when the arrow strikes him, there's a change.
He moves but in the track of his spent pain,
Whose red drops are the links of a harsh chain,
Binding him to the ground with narrow range.                   8
A subtle serpent then has Love become.
I had the eagle in my bosom erst.[67]
Henceforward with the serpent I am curs'd.[68]
I can interpret where the mouth is dumb.[69]                   12
Speak, and I see the side-lie of a truth.
Perchance my heart may pardon you this deed:
But be no coward:—you that made Love bleed,
You must bear all the venom of his tooth!                      16

---

67. *erst*: first
68. *with . . . cursed*: This sonnet's imagery alludes to Satan's fall from Heaven, his transformation into a serpent before tempting Eve, and God's subsequent curse upon the serpent. See note 6.
69. *dumb*: silent

## XXVII.

Distraction is the panacea,[70] Sir!
I hear my Oracle of Medicine say.
Doctor! that same specific yesterday
I tried, and the result will not deter                    4
A second trial. Is the devil's line
Of golden hair, or raven black, composed?[71]
And does a cheek, like any sea-shell rosed,
Or fair as widow'd Heaven, seem most divine?              8
No matter, so I taste forgetfulness.
And if the devil snare me, body and mind,
Here gratefully I score:—he seeméd kind,
When not a soul would comfort my distress!               12
O sweet new world in which I rise new made!
O Lady, once I gave love: now I take!
Lady, I must be flatter'd. Shouldst thou wake
The passion of a demon, be not afraid.                   16

---

70. *panacea*: cure-all
71. *Is the devil's . . . composed?*: The husband wonders whether his mistress (who is blond) or his wife (who is brunette) poses the most damning temptation.

## XXVIII.

I must be flatter'd. The imperious
Desire speaks out. Lady, I am content
To play with you the game of Sentiment,
And with you enter on paths perilous:                              4
But if across your beauty I throw light,
To make it threefold, it must be all mine.
First secret; then avow'd. For I must shine
Envied,—I, lessen'd in my proper sight!                            8
Be watchful of your beauty, Lady dear!
How much hangs on that lamp you cannot tell.
Most earnestly I pray you, tend it well:
And men shall see me like the burning sphere:                     12
And men shall mark you eyeing me, and groan
To be the God of such a grand sunflower!
I feel the promptings of Satanic power,
While you do homage unto me alone.                                16

# XXIX.

Am I failing? for no longer can I cast
A glory round about this head of gold.
Glory she wears, but springing from the mould:
Not like the consecration of the Past!                          4
Is my soul beggar'd? Something more than earth
I cry for still: I cannot be at peace
In having Love upon a mortal lease.
I cannot take the woman at her worth!                           8
Where is the ancient wealth wherewith I clothed
Our human nakedness,[72] and could endow
With spiritual splendour a white brow
That else had grinn'd at me the fact I loath'd?                 12
A kiss is but a kiss now! and no wave
Of a great flood that whirls me to the sea.
But, as you will! we'll sit contentedly,
And eat our pot of honey on the grave.                          16

---

72. *human nakedness*: cf. Adam and Eve in the garden before the fall

# XXX.

What are we first? First, animals; and next,
Intelligences at a leap; on whom
Pale lies the distant shadow of the tomb,
And all that draweth on the tomb for text.[73]                    4
Into this state comes Love, the crowning sun:
Beneath whose light the shadow loses form.
We are the lords of life, and life is warm.
Intelligence and instinct now are one.                           8
But Nature says: 'My children most they seem
When they least know me: therefore I decree
That they shall suffer.' Swift doth young Love flee:
And we stand waken'd, shivering from our dream.                 12
Then if we study Nature we are wise.
Thus do the few who live but with the day.
The scientific animals are they.—
Lady, this is my Sonnet to your eyes.[74]                       16

---

73. *Pale lies . . . for text*: Death seems far away to most humans. However, death inspires most of
our (religious) writings.

74. *Lady . . . eyes*: both a categorical label for these poems and a metacritical comment upon son-
net conventions; cf. Shakespeare's Sonnet 130 and Philip Sidney's *Astrophel and Stella*, no. 7

## XXXI.

This golden head has wit in it. I live
Again, and a far higher life, near her.
Some women like a young philosopher;
Perchance because he is diminutive.                        4
For woman's manly god must not exceed
Proportions of the natural nursing size.
Great poets and great sages draw no prize
With women: but the little lap-dog breed,                  8
Who can be hugg'd, or on a mantel-piece
Perch'd up for adoration, these obtain
Her homage. And of this we men are vain?
Of this! 'Tis order'd for the world's increase!           12
Small flattery! Yet she has that rare gift
To beauty, Common Sense. I am approved.
It is not half so nice as being loved,
And yet I do prefer it. What's my drift?                   16

# XXXII.

Full faith I have she holds that rarest gift
To beauty, Common Sense. To see her lie
With her fair visage[75] an inverted sky
Bloom-cover'd, while the underlids uplift,[76]                    4
Would almost wreck the faith; but when her mouth
(Can it kiss sweetly? sweetly!) would address
The inner me that thirsts for her no less,
And has so long been languishing in drouth,[77]                  8
I feel that I am match'd: that I am man!
One restless corner of my heart, or head,
That holds a dying something never dead,
Still frets, though Nature giveth all she can.                   12
It means, that woman is not, I opine,
Her sex's antidote. Who seeks the asp[78]
For serpents' bites? 'Twould calm me could I clasp
Shrieking Bacchantes[79] with their souls of wine!              16

---

75. *visage*: face
76. In the manuscript, the line reads "Beneath me, while the underlids uplift," suggesting more overtly that the husband has consummated his affair. See "Textual Variants."
77. *drouth*: drought
78. *asp*: poisonous snake
79. *Bacchantes*: female followers of Bacchus, god of wine and intoxication, who are often portrayed in states of violent, erotic frenzy

# XXXIII.

'In Paris, at the Louvre,[80] there have I seen
The sumptuously-feather'd angel pierce
Prone Lucifer, descending.[81] Look'd he fierce,
Showing the fight a fair one? Too serene!                     4
The young Pharsalians[82] did not disarray
Less willingly their locks of floating silk:
That suckling mouth of his, upon the milk
Of stars might still be feasting through the fray.            8
Oh, Raphael! when men the Fiend do fight,
They conquer not upon such easy terms.[83]
Half serpent in the struggle grow these worms.
And does he grow half human, all is right.'                   12
This to my Lady in a distant spot,
Upon the theme: *'While mind is mastering clay,*
*Gross clay invades it.'* If the spy you play,
My wife, read this! Strange love-talk, is it not?             16

---

80. *Louvre*: Musée du Louvre, one of the world's largest museums

81. *The sumptuously . . . descending*: Raphael's painting *St. Michael striking down the Demon* (1518), held at the Louvre. The image is a common one and refers to a passage in Revelation (12:7–9): "And there was war in heaven: Michael and his angels fought against the dragon. . . . And the great dragon was cast out, that old serpent, called the Devil, and Satan, which deceiveth the whole world: he was cast out into the earth, and his angels were cast out with him" (see fig. 4).

82. *Pharsalians*: those from the Pharsalus region of ancient Greece. In the painting, St. Michael (and his hair) appears perfectly composed.

83. *Oh, Raphael . . . terms*: Meredith was associated with the Pre-Raphaelites, a mid-nineteenth-century "brotherhood" of English artists who repudiated Raphael's imitators and claimed to take their inspiration from nature rather than artistic convention.

## XXXIV.

Madam would speak with me. So, now it comes:
The Deluge,[84] or else Fire! She's well; she thanks
My husbandship. Our chain through silence clanks.
Time leers between us, twiddling his thumbs.                    4
Am I quite well? Most excellent in health!
The journals, too, I diligently peruse.
Vesuvius[85] is expected to give news:
Niagara[86] is no noisier. By stealth                          8
Our eyes dart scrutinizing snakes. She's glad
I'm happy, says her quivering under-lip.
"And are not you?" "How can I be?" "Take ship!
"For happiness is somewhere to be had."                        12
"Nowhere for me!" Her voice is barely heard.
I am not melted, and make no pretence.
With truisms I freeze her, tongue and sense.
Niagara, or Vesuvius, is deferr'd.                             16

---

84. *The Deluge*: Genesis (6–9) describes the great flood that destroyed nearly all of mankind as punishment for their disobedience. The term *deluge* also connotes the self-absorption of France's King Louis XV. Caring little about the results of his extravagance and lack of foresight, he famously said, "*Après moi, le déluge*" ("After me, the flood."). The French Revolution began some fifteen years after his death.
85. *Vesuvius*: volcano in Naples that erupted in 1861
86. *Niagara*: waterfall in Ontario, Canada

## XXXV.

It is no vulgar nature I have wived.
Secretive, sensitive, she takes a wound
Deep to her soul, as if the sense had swoon'd,
And not a thought of vengeance had survived.                    4
No confidences has she: but relief
Must come to one whose suffering is acute.
O have a care of natures that are mute!
They punish you in acts: their steps are brief.                 8
What is she doing? What does she demand
From Providence,[87] or me? She is not one
Long to endure this torpidly,[88] and shun
The drugs that crowd about a woman's hand.                      12
At Forfeits[89] during snow we play'd, and I
Must kiss her. "Well perform'd!" I said: then she:
"'Tis hardly worth the money, you agree?"
Save her? What for? To act this wedded lie!                     16

---

87. *Providence*: God; God's power
88. *torpidly*: listlessly, numbly
89. *Forfeits*: a game in which players give up a personal item as a penalty and redeem themselves
by performing a task

# XXXVI.

My Lady unto Madam makes her bow.
The charm of women is, that even while
You're probed by them for tears, you yet may smile,
Nay, laugh outright, as I have done just now.                    4
The interview was gracious: they anoint
(To me aside) each other with fine praise:
Discriminating compliments they raise,
That hit with wondrous aim on the weak point.                    8
My Lady's nose of nature might complain.
It is not fashion'd aptly to express
Her character of large-brow'd[90] stedfastness.
But Madam says: Thereof she may be vain!                        12
Now, Madam's faulty feature is a glazed
And inaccessible eye, that has soft fires,
Wide gates, at love-time only. This admires
My Lady. At the two I stand amazed.                             16

90. *large-brow'd*: phrenology, the study of the shape of the head, accorded intelligence and be-
nevolence to those with large foreheads (brows)

# XXXVII.

Along the garden terrace, under which
A purple valley (lighted at its edge
By smoky torch-flame on the long cloud-ledge
Whereunder dropp'd the chariot),[91] glimmers rich,          4
A quiet company we pace, and wait
The dinner-bell in pre-digestive calm.
So sweet up violet banks the Southern balm
Breathes round, we care not if the bell be late:          8
Tho' here and there gray seniors question Time
In irritable coughings. With slow foot
The low, rosed moon, the face of Music mute,
Begins among her silent bars to climb.          12
As in and out, in silvery dusk, we thread,
I hear the laugh of Madam, and discern
My Lady's heel before me at each turn.
Our Tragedy, is it alive or dead?          16

---

91. *the chariot*: the sun; Greek god Helios (also identified with Apollo) drives the chariot of the
sun across the sky each day.

# XXXVIII.

Give to imagination some pure light
In human form to fix[92] it, or you shame
The devils with that hideous human game:—
Imagination urging appetite!                                    4
Thus fallen have earth's greatest Gogmagogs,[93]
Who dazzle us, whom we cannot revere.
Imagination is the charioteer
That, in default of better, drives the hogs.                    8
So, therefore, my dear Lady, let me love!
My soul is arrow'd[94] to the light in you.
You know me that I never can renew
The bond that woman broke: what would you have?                 12
'Tis Love, or Vileness! not a choice between,
Save petrification![95] What does Pity here?
She kill'd a thing, and now it's dead, 'tis dear.
O, when you counsel me, think what you mean!                    16

---

92. *fix*: to make permanent, as in photography
93. *Gogmagogs*: The word derives from the biblical "Gog" and "Magog," but here refers to gi-
ants of British folklore.
94. *arrow'd*: attracted, pulled like an arrow
95. *petrification*: turning into stone, as when facing the Medusa

## XXXIX.

She yields: my Lady in her noblest mood
Has yielded: she, my golden-crownëd rose!
The bride of every sense! more sweet than those
Who breathe the violet breath of maidenhood.                    4
O visage of still music in the sky!
Soft moon! I feel thy song, my fairest friend!
True harmony within can apprehend
Dumb harmony without. And hark! 'tis nigh!                      8
Belief has struck the note of sound: a gleam
Of living silver shows me where she shook
Her long white fingers down the shadowy brook,
That sings her song, half waking, half in dream.               12
What two come here to mar this heavenly tune?
A man is one: the woman bears my name,[96]
And honour. Their hands touch! Am I still tame?
God, what a dancing spectre seems the moon!                    16

---

96. *the woman . . . name*: the wife

## XL.

I bade my Lady think what she might mean.
Know I my meaning, *I?* Can I love one,
And yet be jealous of another? None
Commit such folly. Terrible Love, I ween,[97]                    4
Has might, even dead, half sighing to upheave
The lightless seas of selfishness amain:[98]
Seas that in a man's heart have no rain
To fall and still them. Peace can I achieve                      8
By turning to this fountain-source of woe,
This woman, who's to Love as fire to wood?
She breath'd the violet breath of maidenhood
Against my kisses once! but I say, No!                           12
The thing is mock'd at! Helplessly afloat,
I know not what I do, whereto I strive.
The dread that my old love may be alive,
Has seiz'd my nursling new love by the throat.                   16

---

97. *ween*: think, suspect
98. *amain*: quickly and/or violently, with full force

# XLI.

How many a thing which we cast to the ground,
When others pick it up becomes a gem!
We grasp at all the wealth it is to them;
And by reflected light its worth is found.                    4
Yet for us still 'tis nothing! and that zeal
Of false appreciation quickly fades.
This truth is little known to human shades,[99]
How rare from their own instinct 'tis to feel!               8
They waste the soul with spurious desire,
That is not the ripe flame upon the bough:
We two have taken up a lifeless vow
To rob a living passion: dust for fire!                      12
Madam is grave, and eyes the clock that tells
Approaching midnight. We have struck despair
Into two hearts. O, look we like a pair
Who for fresh nuptials[100] joyfully yield all else?         16

---

99. *shades*: ghosts or souls
100. *nuptials*: weddings; in zoology, mating season

## XLII.

I am to follow her. There is much grace
In women when thus bent on martyrdom.
They think that dignity of soul may come,
Perchance, with dignity of body. Base!     4
But I was taken by that air of cold
And statuesque sedateness, when she said,
"I'm going"; lit the taper, bow'd her head,
And went, as with the stride of Pallas[101] bold.     8
Fleshly indifference horrible! The hands
Of Time now signal: O, she's safe from me!
Within those secret walls what do I see?
Where first she set the taper down she stands:     12
Not Pallas: Hebe shamed![102] Thoughts black as death,
Like a stirr'd pool in sunshine break. Her wrists
I catch: she faltering, as she half resists,
"You love . . . ? love . . . ? love . . . ?" all in an indrawn breath.     16

---

101. *Pallas*: Athena, the Greek goddess of war, wisdom, and strength; a virgin goddess, she fights on behalf of just causes.

102. *Hebe shamed!*: Daughter of Zeus and Hera and cupbearer to the gods, Hebe is said to have dropped the wine she carried to them and, ashamed, never appeared again. Thomas Moore's "The Fall of Hebe: A Dithyrambic Ode" (1806) describes the scene.

## XLIII.

Mark where the pressing wind shoots javelin-like,
Its skeleton shadow on the broad-back'd wave!
Here is a fitting spot to dig Love's grave;
Here where the ponderous breakers[103] plunge and strike,                4
And dart their hissing tongues high up the sand:
In hearing of the ocean, and in sight
Of those ribb'd wind-streaks running into white.
If I the death of Love had deeply plann'd,                8
I never could have made it half so sure,
As by the unbless'd kisses which upbraid
The full-waked sense; or, failing that, degrade!
'Tis morning: but no morning can restore                12
What we have forfeited. I see no sin:
The wrong is mix'd. In tragic life, God wot,[104]
No villain need be![105] Passions spin the plot:
We are betray'd by what is false within.                16

---

103. *breakers*: dangerous ocean waves that break violently against a rocky coast or as they pass over reefs or shallows

104. *wot*: knows

105. *No villain need be!*: a resolution to the question of blame: "the wrong is mixed" and "no villain need be"

# XLIV.

They say that Pity in Love's service dwells,
A porter at the rosy temple's gate.
I miss'd him going: but it is my fate
To come upon him now beside his wells;                    4
Whereby I know that I Love's temple leave,
And that the purple doors have closed behind.
Poor soul! if in those early days unkind,
Thy power to sting had been but power to grieve,          8
We now might with an equal spirit meet,
And not be match'd like innocence and vice.
She for the Temple's worship has paid price,
And takes the coin of Pity as a cheat.                   12
She sees thro' simulation to the bone:
What's best in her impels her to the worst.
Never, she cries, shall Pity soothe Love's thirst,
Or foul hypocrisy for truth atone!                       16

# XLV.

It is the season of the sweet wild rose,
My Lady's emblem in the heart of me!
So golden-crownëd shines she gloriously,
And with that softest dream of blood she glows:      4
Mild as an evening Heaven round Hesper[106] bright!
I pluck the flower, and smell it, and revive
The time when in her eyes I stood alive.
I seem to look upon it out of Night.      8
Here's Madam, stepping hastily. Her whims
Bid her demand the flower, which I let drop.
As I proceed, I feel her sharply stop,
And crush it under heel with trembling limbs.      12
She joins me in a cat-like way, and talks
Of company, and even condescends
To utter laughing scandal of old friends.
These are the summer days, and these our walks.      16

---

106. *Hesper*: the evening star (Venus when visible after sunset)

## XLVI.

At last we parley:[107] we so strangely dumb
In such a close communion! It befell
About the sounding of the Matin-bell,[108]
And lo! her place was vacant, and the hum          4
Of loneliness was round me. Then I rose,
And my disorder'd brain did guide my foot
To that old wood where our first love-salute[109]
Was interchanged: the source of many throes!        8
There did I see her, not alone. I moved
Towards her, and made proffer of my arm.
She took it simply, with no rude alarm;
And that disturbing shadow pass'd reproved.         12
I felt the pain'd speech coming, and declared
My firm belief in her, ere she could speak.
A ghastly morning[110] came into her cheek,
While with a widening soul on me she stared.        16

107. *parley*: talk
108. *Matin-bell*: bell for morning prayer service
109. *love-salute*: kiss
110. *morning*: sudden realization, horrifying new thought

# XLVII.

We saw the swallows gathering in the sky,
And in the osier-isle[111] we heard their noise.
We had not to look back on summer joys,
Or forward to a summer of bright dye.[112]                      4
But in the largeness of the evening earth
Our spirits grew as we went side by side.
The hour became her husband, and my bride.
Love that had robb'd us so, thus bless'd our dearth!           8
The pilgrims of the year wax'd very loud
In multitudinous chatterings, as the flood
Full brown came from the west, and like pale blood
Expanded to the upper crimson cloud.                          12
Love that had robb'd us of immortal things,
This little moment mercifully gave,
And still I see across the twilight wave,
The swan sail with her young beneath her wings.               16

111. *osier*: willow tree
112. *dye*: color

# XLVIII.

Their sense is with their senses all mix'd in.
Destroy'd by subtleties these women are!
More brain, O Lord, more brain! or we shall mar
Utterly this fair garden we might win.[113]                    4
Behold! I looked for peace, and thought it near.
Our inmost hearts had open'd, each to each.
We drank the pure daylight of honest speech.
Alas! that was the fatal draught, I fear.                      8
For when of my lost Lady came the word,
This woman, O this agony of flesh!
Jealous devotion bade her break the mesh,
That I might seek that other like a bird.                     12
I do adore the nobleness! despise
The act! She has gone forth, I know not where.
Will the hard world my sentience[114] of her share?
I feel the truth; so let the world surmise.                   16

.

---

113. *or we shall . . . win*: reference to Eve, who gives in to temptation and thus gives up the Garden of Eden

114. *sentience*: consciousness, susceptibility to sensation

## XLIX.

He found her by the ocean's moaning verge,
Nor any wicked change in her discern'd;
And she believed his old love had return'd,
Which was her exultation, and her scourge.                    4
She took his hand, and walked with him, and seem'd
The wife he sought, tho' shadowlike and dry.
She had one terror, lest her heart should sigh,
And tell her loudly she no longer dream'd.                    8
She dared not say, "This is my breast: look in."
But there's a strength to help the desperate weak.
That night he learnt how silence best can speak
The awful things when Pity pleads for Sin.                    12
About the middle of the night her call
Was heard, and he came wondering to the bed.
"Now kiss me, dear! it may be, now!" she said.
Lethe[115] had pass'd those lips, and he knew all.            16

---

115. *Lethe*: In Greek mythology, a river of Hades; those who drink from it forget all. The wife
has taken poison.

## L.

Thus piteously Love closed what he begat:
The union of this ever-diverse pair!
These two were rapid falcons in a snare,
Condemn'd to do the flitting of the bat.                    4
Lovers beneath the singing sky of May,
They wander'd once; clear as the dew on flowers:
But they fed not on the advancing hours:
Their hearts held cravings for the buried day.              8
Then each applied to each that fatal knife,
Deep questioning, which probes to endless dole.[116]
Ah, what a dusty answer gets the soul
When hot for certainties in this our life!—                12
In tragic hints here see what evermore
Moves dark as yonder midnight ocean's force,
Thundering like ramping hosts of warrior horse,
To throw that faint thin line upon the shore!             16

---

116. *dole*: dolor; grief, sorrow, or division

*Roadside Philosophers*

# Juggling Jerry[1]

## I.

Pitch here the tent, while the old horse grazes:
    By the old hedge-side we'll halt a stage.
It's nigh my last above the daisies:[2]
    My next leaf'll be man's blank page.
Yes, my old girl! and it's no use crying:
    Juggler, constable, king, must bow.
One that outjuggles all's[3] been spying
    Long to have me, and he has me now.

1. Originally published in *Once a Week* on 3 September 1859 under the title "The Last Words of Juggling Jerry," and illustrated by H. K. Browne (see fig. 5).

2. *It's nigh . . . daisies*: last night alive; he thinks he'll die the next day.

3. *One that outjuggles all*: God

## II.

We've travelled times to this old common:[4]
    Often we've hung our pots in the gorse.[5]
We've had a stirring life, old woman!
    You, and I, and the old grey horse.
Races, and fairs, and royal occasions,
    Found us coming to their call:
Now they'll miss us at our stations:
    There's a Juggler outjuggles all!

## III.

Up goes the lark, as if all were jolly!
    Over the duck-pond the willow shakes.
Easy to think that grieving's folly,
    When the hand's firm as driven stakes!
Ay! when we're strong, and braced, and manful,
    Life's a sweet fiddle: but we're a batch
Born to become the Great Juggler's han'ful:
    Balls he shies up, and is safe to catch.

## IV.

Here's where the lads of the village cricket:
    I was a lad not wide from here:
Couldn't I whip off the bale from the wicket?[6]
    Like an old world those days appear!
Donkey, sheep, geese, and thatch'd ale-house—I know them!
    They are old friends of my halts,[7] and seem,
Somehow, as if kind thanks I owe them:
    Juggling don't hinder the heart's esteem.

---

4. *common*: unenclosed and uncultivated land belonging to the community

5. *gorse*: evergreen shrub

6. *Couldn't I . . . wicket?*: In a game of cricket, the wicket consists of three vertical posts set into the ground with two crossbars on top, called bales.

7. *halts*: stops

## V.

Juggling's no sin, for we must have victual:[8]
    Nature allows us to bait for the fool.
Holding one's own makes us juggle no little;
    But, to increase it, hard juggling's the rule.
You that are sneering at my profession,
    Haven't you juggled a vast amount?
There's the Prime Minister, in one Session,
    Juggles more games than my sins'll count.

## VI.

I've murder'd insects with mock thunder:
    Conscience, for that, in men don't quail.[9]
I've made bread from the bump of wonder:[10]
    That's my business, and there's my tale.
Fashion and rank all praised the professor:
    Ay! and I've had my smile from the Queen:
Bravo, Jerry! she meant: God bless her!
    Ain't this a sermon on that scene?

## VII.

I've studied men from my topsy-turvy
    Close, and, I reckon, rather true.
Some are fine fellows: some, right scurvy:[11]
    Most, a dash between the two.
But it's a woman, old girl, that makes me
    Think more kindly of the race:
And it's a woman, old girl, that shakes me
    When the Great Juggler I must face.

---

8. *victual*: food

9. *quail*: recoil, flinch

10. *bump of wonder*: In phrenology, the study of the personality based on the shape of one's head; various "bumps" on the skull correspond to certain faculties. Those with pronounced "bumps of wonder" would likely be curious about the juggler's abilities and would pay to see him.

11. *scurvy*: low, base, or miserable

## VIII.

We two were married, due and legal:
    Honest we've lived since we've been one.
Lord! I could then jump like an eagle:
    You danced bright as a bit o' the sun.
Birds in a May-bush we were! right merry!
    All night we kiss'd—we juggled all day.
Joy was the heart of Juggling Jerry!
    Now from his old girl he's juggled away.

## IX.

It's past parsons to console us:
    No, nor no doctor fetch for me:
I can die without my bolus;[12]
    Two of a trade, lass, never agree!
Parson and Doctor!—don't they love rarely,
    Fighting the devil in other men's fields!
Stand up yourself and match him fairly:
    Then see how the rascal yields!

## X.

I, lass, have lived no gipsy, flaunting
    Finery while his poor helpmate grubs:
Coin I've stored, and you won't be wanting:
    You shan't beg from the troughs and tubs.
Nobly you've stuck to me, though in his kitchen
    Many a Marquis would hail you Cook!
Palaces you could have ruled and grown rich in,
    But your old Jerry you never forsook.

---

12. *bolus*: medication or drug

## XI.

Hand up the chirper![13] ripe ale winks in it;
  Let's have comfort and be at peace.
Once a stout draught made me light as a linnet.[14]
  Cheer up! the Lord must have his lease.
May be—for none see in that black hollow—
  It's just a place where we're held in pawn,
And, when the Great Juggler makes as to swallow,
  It's just the sword-trick—I ain't quite gone!

## XII.

Yonder came smells of the gorse, so nutty,
  Gold-like and warm: it's the prime of May.
Better than mortar, brick, and putty,
  Is God's house on a blowing day.
Lean me more up the mound; now I feel it:
  All the old heath-smells! Ain't it strange?
There's the world laughing, as if to conceal it,
  But He's by us, juggling the change.

## XIII.

I mind it well, by the sea-beach lying,
  Once—it's long gone—when two gulls we beheld,
Which, as the moon got up, were flying
  Down a big wave that spark'd and swell'd.
Crack! went a gun: one fell: the second
  Wheel'd round him twice, and was off for new luck:
There in the dark her white wing beckon'd:—
  Drop me a kiss—I'm the bird dead-struck!

13. *chirper*: cup to toast with
14. *linnet*: small finch

# The Old Chartist[1]

## I.

Whate'er I be, old England is my dam![2]
  So there's my answer to the judges, clear.
I'm nothing of a fox, nor of a lamb;
  I don't know how to bleat nor how to leer:
    I'm for the nation!
  That's why you see me by the wayside here,
  Returning home from transportation.[3]

---

1. Chartism was a social and political reform movement peaking in England between 1838 and 1848. Chartists sought the expansion of the vote to the working classes. A series of coordinated labor strikes and uprisings led to violent interactions with the state, and ultimately, many Chartist leaders were, as was the speaker of the poem, arrested and transported to Australia. The poem was originally published in *Once a Week* on 8 February 1862, illustrated by Frederick Sandys (see fig. 6).

2. *dam!*: mother (female parent); also, a barrier

3. *Returning . . . transportation*: The speaker had been sent to Australia after arrest for participation in Chartist activities and has now returned to England.

## II.

It's Summer in her bath this morn, I think.
    I'm fresh as dew, and chirpy as the birds:
And just for joy to see old England wink
    Thro' leaves again, I could harangue[4] the herds:
        Isn't it something
    To speak out like a man when you've got words,
        And prove you're not a stupid dumb thing?

## III.

They shipp'd me off for it: I'm here again.
    Old England is my dam, whate'er I be!
Says I, I'll tramp it home, and see the grain:
    If you see well, you're king of what you see:
        Eyesight is having,
    If you're not given, I said, to gluttony.
        Such talk to ignorance sounds as raving.

## IV.

You dear old brook, that from his Grace's park
    Come bounding! on you run near my old town:
My lord can't lock the water; nor the lark,
    Unless he kills him, can my lord keep down.
        Up, is the song-note!
    I've tried it, too:—for comfort and renown,
        I rather pitch'd upon the wrong note.

---

4. *harangue*: rant; to deliver a forceful address

# V.

I'm not ashamed: Not beaten's still my boast:
    Again I'll rouse the people up to strike.[5]
But home's where different politics jar most.
    Respectability the women like.
        This form, or that form—
    The Government may be hungry pike,[6]
        But don't you mount a Chartist platform!

# VI.

Well, well! Not beaten—spite of them, I shout;
    And my estate is suffering for the Cause.—
Now, what is yon brown water-rat about,
    Who washes his old poll[7] with busy paws?
        What does he mean by't?
    It's like defying all our natural laws,
    For him to hope that he'll get clean by't.

# VII.

His seat is on a mud-bank, and his trade
    Is dirt:—he's quite contemptible; and yet
The fellow's all as anxious as a maid
    To show a decent dress, and dry the wet.
        Now it's his whisker,
    And now his nose, and ear: he seems to get
    Each moment at the motion brisker!

---

5. *Again I'll . . . strike*: The Chartist was likely transported for inciting a strike among workers.
6. *pike*: fish
7. *poll*: head

## VIII.

To see him squat like little chaps at school,
  I can't help laughing out with all my might.
He peers, hangs both his fore-paws:—bless that fool,
  He's bobbing at his frill[8] now!—what a sight!
    Licking the dish up,
  As if he thought to pass from black to white,
    Like parson into lawny[9] bishop.


## IX.

The elms and yellow reed-flags in the sun,
  Look on quite grave:—the sunlight flecks his side;
And links of bindweed-flowers[10] round him run,
  And shine up doubled with him in the tide.
    *I*'m nearly splitting,
  But nature seems like seconding his pride,
    And thinks that his behaviour's fitting.


## X.

That isle o' mud looks baking dry with gold.
  His needle-muzzle still works out and in.
It really is a wonder to behold,
  And makes me feel the bristles of my chin.
    Judged by appearance,
  I fancy of the two I'm nearer Sin,
    And might as well commence a clearance.

---

8. *frill*: neck
9. *lawny*: Lawn is a kind of crisp white cloth commonly used in liturgical vestments; the parson would normally wear black, but the bishop would wear white lawn.
10. *bindweed-flowers*: bell-shaped flowers on a climbing vine

## XI.

And that's what my fine daughter said:—she meant:
    Pray, hold your tongue, and wear a Sunday face.
Her husband, the young linendraper, spent
    Much argument thereon:—I'm their disgrace.
        Bother the couple!
I feel superior to a chap whose place
    Commands him to be neat and supple.

## XII.

But if I go and say to my old hen:[11]
    I'll mend the gentry's boots, and keep discreet,
Until they grow *too* violent,—why, then,
    A warmer welcome I might chance to meet:
        Warmer and better.
And if she fancies her old cock is beat,
    And drops upon her knees—so let her!

## XIII.

She suffered for me:—women, you'll observe,
    Don't suffer for a Cause, but for a man.
When I was in the dock she show'd her nerve:
    I saw beneath her shawl my old tea-can[12]
        Trembling . . . . she brought it
To screw[13] me for my work: she loath'd my plan,
    And therefore doubly kind I thought it.

---

11. *old hen*: his wife
12. *tea-can*: Laborers would bring their tea to work in a can, which they set in the sun to warm.
13. *screw*: to encourage, to steady

## XIV.

I've never lost the taste of that same tea:
    That liquor on my logic floats like oil,
When I state facts, and fellows disagree.
    For human creatures all are in a coil;
        All may want pardon.
I see a day when every pot will boil
    Harmonious in one great Tea-garden!


## XV.

We wait the setting of the Dandy's day,
    Before that time!—He's furbishing his dress—
He *will* be ready for it!—and I say,
    That yon old dandy rat amid the cress,—[14]
        Thanks to hard labour!—
If cleanliness is next to godliness,
    The old fat fellow's Heaven's neighbour!


## XVI.

You teach me a fine lesson, my old boy!
    I've looked on my superiors far too long,
And small has been my profit as my joy.
    You've *done* the right while I've denounced the wrong.
        Prosper me later!
Like you I will despise the sniggering throng,
    And please myself and my Creator.

---

14. *cress*: low lying green plant

## XVII.

I'll bring the linendraper and his wife
  Some day to see you; taking off my hat.
Should they ask why, I'll answer: in my life
  I never found so true a democrat.
      Base occupation
  Can't rob you of your own esteem, old rat!
    I'll preach you to the British nation.

# The Beggar's Soliloquy[1]

## I.

Now, this, to my notion, is pleasant cheer,
    To lie all alone on a ragged heath,
Where your nose isn't sniffing for bones or beer,
    But a peat-fire[2] smells like a garden beneath.
The cottagers bustle about the door,
    And the girl at the window ties her strings.
She's a dish for a man who's a mind to be poor;
    Lord! women are such expensive things.

---

1. Originally published in *Once a Week* on 30 March 1861, illustrated by Charles Keene (see fig. 7).

2. *peat-fire*: Peat is dried, decomposed plant matter, often used by the poor as fuel in place of wood or coal.

## II.

We don't marry beggars, says she: why, no:
    It seems that to make 'em is what you do;
And as I can cook, and scour, and sew,
    I needn't pay half my victuals for you.
A man for himself should be able to scratch,
    But tickling's a luxury:—love, indeed!
Love burns as long as the lucifer match,[3]
    Wedlock's the candle! Now, that's my creed.

## III.

The church-bells sound water-like over the wheat;
    And up the long path troop pair after pair.
The man's well-brushed, and the woman looks neat:
    It's man and woman everywhere!
Unless, like me, you lie here flat,
    With a donkey for friend, you must have a wife:
She pulls out your hair, but she brushes your hat.
    Appearances make the best half of life.

## IV.

You nice little madam! you know you're nice.
    I remember hearing a parson say
You're a plateful of vanity pepper'd with vice;
    Yon chap at the gate thinks t'other way.
On his waistcoat you read both his head and his heart:
    There's a whole week's wages there figured in gold!
Yes! when you turn round you may well give a start:
    It's fun to a fellow who's getting old.

---

3. *lucifer match*: strikable, quick-burning match

## V.

Now, that's a good craft, weaving waistcoats and flowers,
    And selling of ribbons, and scenting of lard:[4]
It gives you a house to get in from the showers,
    And food when your appetite jockeys you hard.
You live a respectable man; but I ask
    If it's worth the trouble? You use your tools,
And spend your time, and what's your task?
    Why, to make a slide for a couple of fools.

## VI.

You can't match the colour o' these heath[5] mounds,
    Nor better that peat-fire's agreeable smell.
I'm cloth'd-like with natural sights and sounds;
    To myself I'm in tune: I hope you're as well.
You jolly old cot! though you don't own coal:
    It's a generous pot that's boil'd with peat.
Let the Lord Mayor o' London roast oxen whole:
    His smoke, at least, don't smell so sweet.

## VII.

I'm not a low Radical, hating the laws,
    Who'd the aristocracy rebuke.
I talk o' the Lord Mayor o' London because
    I once was on intimate terms with his cook.
I served him a turn, and got pensioned on scraps,
    And, Lord, Sir! didn't I envy his place,
Till Death knock'd him down with the softest of taps,
    And I knew what was meant by a tallowy[6] face!

---

4. *scenting of lard*: an early process of making perfume
5. *heath*: evergreen shrub with pink or purple flowers
6. *tallowy*: having the properties of tallow, a pale-yellow fat-based substance used to make candles and soap

# VIII.

On the contrary, I'm Conservative quite;
 There's beggars in Scripture 'mongst Gentiles and Jews:
It's nonsense, trying to set things right,
 For if people will give, why, who'll refuse?
That stopping cold custom wakes my spleen:
 The poor and the rich both in giving agree:
Your tight-fisted shopman's the Radical mean:
 There's nothing in common 'twixt him and me.

# IX.

He says I'm no use! but I won't reply.
 You're lucky not being of use to him!
On week-days he's playing at Spider and Fly,[7]
 And on Sundays he sings about Cherubim![8]
Nailing shillings to counters is his chief work:
 He nods now and then at the name on his door:
But judge of us two at a bow and a smirk,
 I think I'm his match: and I'm honest—that's more.

# X.

No use! well, I mayn't be. You ring a pig's snout,
 And then call the animal glutton! Now, he,
Mr. Shopman, he's nought but a pipe and a spout
 Who won't let the goods o' this world pass free.
This blazing blue weather all round the brown crop,
 He can't enjoy! all but cash he hates.
He's only a snail that crawls under his shop;
 Though he has got the ear o' the magistrates.

---

7. *Spider and Fly*: preying on his customers like a spider would a fly
8. *Cherubim!*: angels

## XI.

Now, giving and taking's a proper exchange,
  Like question and answer: you're both content.
But buying and selling seems always strange;
  You're hostile, and that's the thing that's meant.
It's man against man—you're almost brutes;
  There's here no thanks, and there's there no pride.
If Charity's Christian, don't blame my pursuits,
  I carry a touchstone by which you're tried.

## XII.

—"Take it," says she, "it's all I've got":
  I remember a girl in London streets:
She stood by a coffee-stall, nice and hot,
  My belly was like a lamb that bleats.
Says I to myself, as her shilling I seized,
  You haven't a character[9] here, my dear!
But for making a rascal like me so pleased,
  I'll give you one, in a better sphere![10]

## XIII.

And that's where it is—she made me feel
  I *was* a rascal: but people who scorn,
And tell a poor patch-breech[11] he isn't genteel,
  Why, they make him kick up—and he treads on a corn.
It isn't liking, it's curst ill-luck,
  Drives half of us into the begging-trade:
If for taking to water you praise a duck,
  For taking to beer why a man upbraid?

---

9. *character*: a letter of reference
10. *a better sphere!*: in heaven, likely
11. *patch-breech*: literally, one whose pants are patched; also a clown in Shakespeare's *Pericles*, but doubtful the speaker would know that

## XIV.

The sermon's over: they're out of the porch,
   And it's time for me to move a leg;
But in general people who come from church,
   And have called themselves sinners, hate chaps to beg.
I'll wager they'll all of 'em dine to-day!
   I was easy half a minute ago.
If that isn't pig that's baking away,
   May I perish!—we're never contented—heigho!

# The Patriot Engineer[1]

"Sirs! *may* I shake your hands?
　My countrymen, I see!
I've lived in foreign lands
　Till England's Heaven to me.
A hearty shake will do me good,
And freshen up my sluggish blood."

Into his hard right hand we struck,
Gave the shake, and wish'd him luck.

"—From Austria I come,
　An English wife to win,　　　　　　　10
　And find an English home,
　And live and die therein.
Great Lord! how many a year I've pined
To drink old ale and speak my mind!"

✦

---

1. Originally published in *Once a Week* on 14 December 1861, illustrated by Charles Keene (see fig. 8).

Loud rang our laughter, and the shout
Hills round the Meuse-boat[2] echoed about.

"—Ay, no offense: laugh on,
　　Young gentlemen: I'll join.
　Had you to exile gone,
　　Where free speech is base coin,     20
You'd sigh to see the jolly nose
Where Freedom's native liquor flows!"

He this time the laughter led,
Dabbing his oily bullet head.

"—Give me, to suit my moods,
　　An ale-house on a heath,
　I'll hand the crags and woods
　　To B'elzebub[3] beneath.
A fig for scenery! what scene
Can beat a Jackass on a green?"     30

Gravely he seem'd, with gaze intense,
Putting the question to common sense.

"—Why, there's the ale-house bench:
　　The furze-flower[4] shining round:
　And there's my waiting-wench,
　　As lissome[5] as a hound.
With 'hail Britannia!' ere I drink,
I'll kiss her with an artful wink."

---

2. *Meuse*: a river that flows through France, Belgium, and the Netherlands before emptying into the North Sea
3. *B'elzebub*: the devil
4. *furze-flower*: yellow flowers of the evergreen furze shrub
5. *lissome*: limber

Fair flash'd the foreign landscape while
Breath'd we thus our native Isle.                                    40

"—The geese may swim hard-by;
      They gabble, and you talk:
    You're sure there's not a spy
      To mark your name with chalk.
My heart's an oak, and it won't grow
In flower-pots, foreigners must know."

Pensive he stood: then shook his head
Sadly; held out his fist, and said:

"—You've heard that Hungary's floor'd?
      They've got her on the ground.                                 50
    A traitor broke her sword:[6]
      Two despots[7] hold her bound.
I've seen her gasping her last hope:
I've seen her sons strung up b' the rope.

"Nine gallant gentlemen
      In Arad they strung up![8]
    I work'd in peace till then:—
      That poison'd all my cup.
A smell of corpses haunted me:
My nostril sniff'd like life for sea.                                60

"Take money for my hire
      From butchers?—not the man!
    I've got some natural fire,
      And don't flash in the pan;—

---

6. *You've heard . . . sword*: The engineer refers to the Magyar revolt of 1849, when the Magyars, an ethnic group native to Hungary, took on both Austrian and Russian forces as part of an ongoing revolution and bid for independence; the traitor was Arthur Gyorgy, a Magyar general who commanded the Magyars' surrender to the Russians.

7. *Two despots*: Austria and Russia

8. *Nine . . . strung up!*: Army leaders of the revolution were executed by the Austrians in Arad.

A few ideas I reaveal'd:—
'Twas well old England stood my shield!

"Said I, 'The Lord of Hosts
    Have mercy on your land!
  I see those dangling ghosts,—
    And you may keep command,        70
And hang, and shoot, and have your day:
They hold your bill, and you must pay.

"'You've sent them where they're strong,
    You carrion Double-Head!
  I hear them sound a gong
    In Heaven above!'—I said.
My God, what feathers won' you moult
For this! says I: and then I bolt.[9]

"The Bird's a beastly Bird,
    And what is more, a fool.        80
  I shake hands with the herd
    That flock beneath his rule.
They're kindly; and their land is fine.
I thought it rarer once than mine.

"And rare would be its lot,
    But that he baulks its powers:
  It's just an earthen pot
    For hearts of oak like ours.
Think! think!—four days from those frontiers,
And I'm a-head full fifty years.        90

"It tingles to your scalps,
    To think of it, my boys!

---

9. *I bolt*: The engineer leaves the mercenary forces.

Confusion on their Alps,
    And all their baby toys!
The mountains Britain boasts are men:
And scale you them, my brethren!"

Cluck, went his tongue; his fingers, snap.
Britons were proved all heights to cap.

    And we who worshipp'd crags,
       Where purple splendours burn'd,        100
    Our idol saw in rags,
       And right about were turn'd.
Horizons rich with trembling spires
On violet twilights, lost their fires.

    And heights where morning wakes
       With one cheek over snow;—
    And iron-wallëd lakes
       Where sits the white moon low;—
For us on youthful travel bent,
The robing picturesque was rent.        110

    Wherever Beauty show'd
       The wonders of her face,
    This man his Jackass rode,
       Despotic in the place.
Fair dreams of our enchanted life,
Fled fast from his shrill island fife.

    And yet we liked him well;
       We laugh'd with honest hearts:—
    He shock'd some inner spell,
       And rous'd discordant parts.       120
We echoed what we half abjured;
And hating, smilingly endured.

Moreover, could we be
　　To our dear land disloyal?
And were not also we
　　Of History's blood-Royal?
We glow'd to think how donkeys graze
In England, thrilling at their brays.

For there a man may view
　　An aspect more sublime                    130
Than Alps against the blue:—
　　The morning eyes of Time!
The very Ass participates
The glory Freedom radiates!

*Poems and Ballads*

# Cassandra[1]

## I.

Captive on a foreign shore,
Far from Ilion's[2] hoary wave,
Agamemnon's bridal slave
Speaks futurity no more:
Death is busy with her grave.

## II.

Thick as water, bursts remote
Round her ears the alien din,
While her little sullen chin
Fills the hollows of her throat:
Silent lie her slaughter'd kin.

---

1. In Greek mythology, Cassandra of Troy is cursed by Apollo to predict the future but have no one believe her prophesies. Daughter to King Priam and Queen Hecuba, Cassandra is taken to Argos by King Agamemnon as his concubine after Troy is captured by the Greeks and set on fire. Dante Gabriel Rossetti composed a drawing (see fig. 9), which, though difficult to date exactly, was likely inspired by Meredith's poem.

2. *Ilion's*: Troy's

## III.

Once, to many a pealing shriek,
Lo, from Ilion's topmost tower,
Ilion's fierce prophetic flower[3]
Cried the coming of the Greek!
Black in Hades[4] sits the hour.

## IV.

Eyeing phantoms of the Past,
Folded like a prophet's scroll,
In the deep's long shoreward roll
Here she sees the anchor cast:
Backward moves her sunless soul.[5]

## V.

Chieftains, brethren of her joy,
Shades, the white light in their eyes
Slanting to her lips, arise,
Crowding quick the plains of Troy:
Now they tell her not she lies.

## VI.

O the bliss upon the plains
Where the joining heroes clash'd
Shield and spear, and, unabashed,
Challeng'd with hot chariot-reins
Gods!—they glimmer ocean-wash'd.

---

3. *Ilion's . . . flower*: clearly a reference to Cassandra's powers of prophesy, but perhaps also a gesture toward Aeschylus's *Agamemnon* (the first play of the *Oresteia*), in which Agamemnon describes Cassandra as "the finest flower of all our loot" (line 955)

4. *Hades*: the kingdom of the underworld that bears its ruler's name

5. *Backward . . . soul*: Apollo, the Greek god of light, music, poetry, and prophecy, is often identified with Helios, the charioteer of the sun. Deprived of Apollo's protection, Cassandra's soul moves "backward" and is "sunless."

## VII.

Alien voices round the ships,
Thick as water, shouting Home,
Argives,[6] pale as midnight foam,
Wax before her awful lips:
White as stars that front the gloom.

## VIII.

Like a torch-flame that by day
Up the daylight twists, and, pale,
Catches air in leaps that fail,
Crush'd by the inveterate ray,
Through her shines the Ten-Years' Tale![7]

## IX.

Once, to many a pealing shriek,
Lo, from Ilion's topmost tower,
Ilion's fierce prophetic flower
Cried the coming of the Greek!
Black in Hades sits the hour.

## X.

Still upon her sunless soul,
Gleams the narrow hidden space
Forward, where her fiery race
Falters on its ashen goal:
Still the Future strikes her face.

6. *Argives*: the inhabitants of Argos
7. *Ten-Years' Tale!*: According to legend, the Trojan War lasted ten years.

## XI.

See, towards the conqueror's car
Step the purple Queen[8] whose hate
Wraps red-armed her royal mate
With his Asian tempest-star:
Now Cassandra views her Fate.

## XII.

King of men! the blinded host
Shout:—she lifts her brooding chin:
Glad along the joyous din
Smiles the grand majestic ghost:[9]
Clytemnestra leads him in.

## XIII.

Lo, their smoky limbs aloof,
Shadowing Heaven and the seas,
Fates and Furies, tangling Threes,
Tear and mix above the roof:
Fates and fierce Eumenides.[10]

## XIV.

Is the prophetess with rods
Beaten, that she writhes in air?
With the gods who never spare,
Wrestling with the unsparing gods,
Lone, her body struggles there.

---

8. *towards the . . . Queen*: In Aeschylus's *Agamemnon*, Clytemnestra goads her husband into dis-
respecting the gods by walking with dirty feet upon expensive purple fabric as he enters the palace.

9. *grand majestic ghost*: Agamemnon, who is fated to be murdered by Clytemnestra for sacrificing
their daughter to Artemis

10. *Eumenides*: the Furies, Greek gods of vengeance. In Aeschylus's *Eumenides*—the third and
final play of the *Oresteia*—the Eumenides punish Orestes for killing Clytemnestra, his mother.

## XV.

Like the snaky torch-flame white,
Levell'd as aloft it twists,—
She, with soaring arms, and wrists
Drooping, struggles with the light,
Helios, bright above all mists!

## XVI.

In his orb she sees the tower,
Dusk against its flaming rims,
Where of old her wretched limbs
Twisted with the stolen power:
Ilion all the lustre dims!

## XVII.

O the bliss upon the plains,
Where the joining heroes clash'd
Shield and spear, and, unabash'd,
Challenged with hot chariot-reins
Gods!—they glimmer ocean-wash'd.

## XVIII.

Thrice the sun-god's name she calls;
Shrieks the deed that shames the sky;[11]
Like a fountain leaping high,
Falling as a fountain falls:
Lo, the blazing wheels go by!

---

11. *Thrice . . . sky*: Cassandra accurately predicts that both she and Agamemnon will be murdered by Clytemnestra; of course, she is not believed.

## XIX.

Captive on a foreign shore,
Far from Ilion's hoary wave,
Agamemnon's bridal slave
Speaks Futurity no more:
Death is busy with her grave.

# The Young Usurper

On my darling's bosom
Has dropp'd a living rosy-bud,
   Fair as brilliant Hesper[1]
   Against the brimming flood.
       She handles him,
       She dandles[2] him,
   She fondles him and eyes him:
And if upon a tear he wakes,
   With many a kiss she dries him:
She covets every move he makes,
   And never enough can prize him.
       Ah, the young Usurper!
       I yield my golden throne:
   Such angel bands attend his hands
   To claim it for his own.

10

---

1. *Hesper*: the evening star (Venus when visible after sunset)
2. *dandles*: bounces gently on the knee

# Margaret's Bridal-Eve

## I.

The old grey mother she thrumm'd on her knee:
  *There is a rose that's ready;*
And which of the handsome young men shall it be?
  *There's a rose that's ready for clipping.*[1]

My daughter, come hither, come hither to me:
  *There is a rose that's ready;*
Come, point me your finger on him that you see:
  *There's a rose that's ready for clipping.*

O mother, my mother, it never can be:
  *There is a rose that's ready;*                                    10
For I shall bring shame on the man marries me:
  *There's a rose that's ready for clipping.*

Now let your tongue be deep as the sea;
  *There is rose that's ready;*

---

1. *There's a . . . clipping*: Gardeners are encouraged to clip spent roses off the shrub ("deadhead")
in order to encourage it to produce more blooms. Alternatively, a gardener may wish to clip a plump
bud that is just about to open in order to display it in the house. Pre-Raphaelite poet Dante Gabriel
Rossetti's "Sister Helen" (1854) is a precedent for ballad refrains like those used here.

And the man'll jump for you, right briskly will he:
> *There's a rose that's ready for clipping.*

Tall Margaret wept bitterly;
> *There is a rose that's ready;*

And as her parent bade did she;
> *There's a rose that's ready for clipping.*                    20

O the handsome young man dropp'd down on his knee;
> *There is a rose that's ready;*

Pale Margaret gave him her hand, woe's me!
> *There's a rose that's ready for clipping.*

## II.

O mother, my mother, this thing I must say,
> *There is a rose in the garden;*

Ere he lies on the breast where that other lay:
> *And the bird sings over the roses.*

Now, folly, my daughter, for men are men:
> *There is a rose in the garden;*

You marry them blindfold, I tell you again:
> *And the bird sings over the roses.*

O mother, but when he kisses me!
> *There is a rose in the garden;*                               10

My child, 'tis which shall sweetest be!
> *And the bird sings over the roses.*

O mother, but when I awake in the morn!
> *There is a rose in the garden;*

My child, you are his, and the ring is worn;
> *And the bird sings over the roses.*

Tall Margaret sigh'd and loosen'd a tress;
> *There is a rose in the garden;*

Poor comfort she had of her comeliness;
*And the bird sings over the roses.*                    20

My mother will sink if this thing be said:
*There is a rose in the garden;*
That my first betrothed came thrice to my bed;
*And the bird sings over the roses.*

He died on my shoulder the third cold night;
*There is a rose in the garden;*
I dragged his body all through the moonlight;
*And the bird sings over the roses.*

But when I came by my father's door;
*There is a rose in the garden;*                        30
I fell in a lump on the stiff dead floor;
*And the bird sings over the roses.*

O neither to heaven, nor yet to hell;
*There is a rose in the garden;*
Could I follow the lover I loved so well!
*And the bird sings over the roses.*

## III.

The bridesmaids slept in their chambers apart;
*There is a rose that's ready;*
Tall Margaret walk'd with her thumping heart;
*There's a rose that's ready for clipping.*

The frill of her nightgown below the left breast,
*There is a rose that's ready;*
Had fall'n like a cloud of the moonlighted west;
*There's a rose that's ready for clipping.*

But where the west-cloud breaks to a star;
  *There is rose that's ready;*       10
Pale Margaret's breast show'd a winding scar;
  *There's a rose that's ready for clipping.*

O few are the brides with such a sign!
  *There is a rose that's ready;*
Tho' I went mad the fault was mine;
  *There's a rose that's ready for clipping.*

I must speak to him under this roof to-night;
  *There is a rose that's ready;*
I shall burn to death if I speak in the light;
  *There's a rose that's ready for clipping.*   20

O my breast! I must strike you a bloodier wound;
  *There is a rose that's ready;*
Than when I scored you red and swoon'd,
  *There's a rose that's ready for clipping.*

I will stab my honour under his eye;
  *There is a rose that's ready;*
Tho' I bleed to the death, I shall let out the lie;
  *There's a rose that's ready for clipping.*

O happy my bridesmaids! white sleep is with you!
  *There is a rose that's ready;*      30
Had he chosen among you he might sleep too!
  *There's a rose that's ready for clipping.*

O happy my bridesmaids! your breasts are clean;
  *There is a rose that's ready;*
You carry no mark of what has been!
  *There's a rose that's ready for clipping.*

# IV.

An hour before the chilly beam,
  *Red rose and white in the garden;*[2]
The bridegroom started out of a dream,
  *And the bird sings over the roses.*

He went to the door, and there espied
  *Red rose and white in the garden;*
The figure of his silent bride,
  *And the bird sings over the roses.*

He went to the door, and let her in;
  *Red rose and white in the garden;*                    10
Whiter look'd she than a child of sin;
  *And the bird sings over the roses.*

She look'd so white, she look'd so sweet;
  *Red rose and white in the garden;*
She look'd so pure he fell at her feet;
  *And the bird sings over the roses.*

He fell at her feet with love and awe;
  *Red rose and white in the garden;*
A stainless body of light he saw;
  *And the bird sings over the roses.*                    20

O Margaret, say you are not of the dead!
  *Red rose and white in the garden;*
My bride! by the angels at night are you led?
  *And the bird sings over the roses.*

---

2. *Red rose . . . garden*: Red roses are often symbols of passion, love, and/or desire; white roses often symbolize purity and/or innocence.

I am not led by the angels about;
  *Red rose and white in the garden;*
But I have a devil within to let out;
  *And the bird sings over the roses.*

O Margaret! my bride and saint!
  *Red rose and white in the garden;*          30
There is on you no earthly taint:
  *And the bird sings over the roses.*

I am no saint, and no bride can I be,
  *Red rose and white in the garden;*
Until I have open'd my bosom to thee;
  *And the bird sings over the roses.*

To catch at her heart she laid one hand;
  *Red rose and white in the garden;*
She told the tale where she did stand;
  *And the bird sings over the roses.*          40

She stood before him pale and tall;
  *Red rose and white in the garden;*
Her eyes between his, she told him all;
  *And the bird sings over the roses.*

She saw how her body grew freckled and foul;
  *Red rose and white in the garden;*
She heard from the woods the hooting owl;
  *And the bird sings over the roses.*

With never a quiver her mouth did speak;
  *Red rose and white in the garden;*          50
O when she had done she stood so meek!
  *And the bird sings over the roses.*

The bridegroom stamp'd and call'd her vile;
  *Red rose and white in the garden;*
He did but waken a little smile;
  *And the bird sings over the roses.*

The bridegroom raged and call'd her foul;
  *Red rose and white in the garden;*
She heard from the woods the hooting owl;
  *And the bird sings over the roses.*                    60

He mutter'd a name full bitter and sore:
  *Red rose and white in the garden;*
She fell in a lump on the stiff dead floor;
  *And the bird sings over the roses.*

O great was the wonder, and loud was the wail,
  *Red rose and white in the garden;*
When through the household flew the tale;
  *And the bird sings over the roses.*

The old grey mother she dress'd the bier;[3]
  *Red rose and white in the garden;*                     70
With a shivering chin and never a tear;
  *And the bird sings over the roses.*

O had you but done as I bade you, my child!
  *Red rose and white in the garden;*
You would not have died and been reviled;
  *And the bird sings over the roses.*

The bridegroom he hung at midnight by the bier;
  *Red rose and white in the garden;*

---

3. *bier*: the movable stand on which a corpse, whether in a coffin or not, is placed before burial and on which it is carried to the grave

He eyed the white girl thro' a dazzling tear;
    *And the bird sings over the roses.*           80

O had you been false as the women who stray;
    *Red rose and white in the garden;*
You would not be now with the Angels of Day!
    *And the bird sings over the roses.*

# Marian[1]

## I.

She can be as wise as we,
   And wiser when she wishes;
She can knit with cunning wit,
   And dress the homely dishes.
She can flourish staff or pen,
   And deal a wound that lingers;
She can talk the talk of men,
   And touch with thrilling fingers.

---

1. Many readers regard this poem as a sketch of Mary Peacock Nicolls, Thomas Love Peacock's daughter and Meredith's first wife.

## II.

Match her ye across the sea,
  Natures fond and fiery;
Ye who zest the turtle's nest[2]
  With the eagle's eyrie.[3]
Soft and loving is her soul,
  Swift and lofty soaring;
Mixing with its dove-like dole
  Passionate adoring.

## III.

Such a she who'll match with me?
  In flying or pursuing,
Subtle wiles are in her smiles
  To set the world a-wooing.
She is steadfast as a star,
  And yet the maddest maiden:
She can wage a gallant war,
  And give the peace of Eden.

---

2. *turtle's nest*: Female turtles create nest cavities by digging in the beach with their hind flippers; after depositing numerous eggs, the mother will use her hind flippers to hide the nest with sand.

3. *eyrie*: a nest of any large bird, especially one that nests high on cliffs or tall trees

# The Head of Bran[1]

## I.

When the Head of Bran
    Was firm on British shoulders,
God made a man!
    Cried all beholders.

Steel could not resist
    The weight his arm would rattle;
He, with naked fist,
    Has brain'd[2] a knight in battle.

He march'd on the foe,
    And never counted numbers;          10

---

1. "The Head of Bran" initially appeared in *Once a Week* (4 February 1860) with an illustration by John Everett Millais (see fig. 10) and a foreword by Meredith glossing the poem's subject. Bran was a British king said to be the first Christian convert. Mortally injured in battle, he is said to have instructed seven princes to chop off his head and bury it facing France, at the site where the Tower of London now stands. The head is said to have protected Britain from invasion until King Arthur dug it up, refusing (in Meredith's words) "in his pride, to trust to the charm." This act was followed, Meredith continues, "by invasion and general disaster."

2. *brain'd*: hit on the head

Foreign widows know
   The hosts he sent to slumbers.

As a street you scan,
   That's tower'd by the steeple,
So the Head of Bran
   Rose o'er his people.

## II.

"Death's my neighbour,"
   Quoth Bran the Blest;
"Christian labour
   Brings Christian rest.
From the trunk sever
   The Head of Bran,
That which never
   Has bent to man!

"That which never
   To men has bow'd,          10
Shall live ever
   To shame the shroud:
Shall live ever
   To face the foe;
Sever it, sever,
   And with one blow.

"Be it written,
   That all I wrought
Was for Britain,
   In deed and thought:        20
Be it written,
   That, while I die,

Glory to Britain!
   Is my last cry.
"'Glory to Britain!'
   Death echoes me round.
Glory to Britain!
   The world shall resound.
Glory to Britain!
   In ruin and fall,           30
Glory to Britain!
   Is heard over all."

## III.

Burn, Sun, down the sea!
Bran lies low with thee.

Burst, Morn, from the main!
Bran so shall rise again.

Blow, Wind, from the field!
Bran's Head is the Briton's shield.

Beam, Star, in the west!
Bright burns the Head of Bran the Blest.

## IV.

Crimson-footed, like the stork,
   From great ruts of slaughter,
Warriors of the Golden Torque,[3]
   Cross the lifting water.
Princes seven, enchaining hands,
   Bear the live head homeward.[4]

---

3. *Torque*: a collar, bracelet, or similar ornament consisting of a twisted narrow band or strip, usually of precious metal, worn especially by the ancient Gauls and Britons
4. Millais's illustration (fig. 10) depicts the action in this stanza.

Lo! it speaks, and still commands;
   Gazing far out foamward.

Fiery words of lightning sense,
   Down the hollows thunder;         10
Forest hostels know not whence
   Comes the speech, and wonder.
City-castles, on the steep,
   Where the faithful Seven
House at midnight, hear, in sleep,
   Laughter under heaven.

Lilies, swimming on the mere,[5]
   In the castle shadow,
Under draw their heads, and Fear
   Walks the misty meadow.         20
Tremble not! it is not Death
   Pledging dark espousal:
'Tis the Head of endless breath,
   Challenging carousal!

Brim the horn! a health is drunk,
   Now, that shall keep going:
Life is but the pebble sunk;
   Deeds, the circle growing!
Fill, and pledge the Head of Bran!
   While his lead they follow,         30
Long shall heads in Britain plan
   Speech Death cannot swallow!

---

5. *mere*: a lake, a pond, or a pool

# By Morning Twilight

## I.

Night like a dying mother,
   Eyes her young offspring, Day.
The birds are dreamily piping.
And O, my love, my darling!
   The night is life ebb'd away:
   Away beyond our reach!
A sea that has cast us pale on the beach;
   Weeds with the weeds and the pebbles
That hear the lone tamarisk[1] rooted in sand,
     Sway
With the song of the sea to the land.

10

---

1. *tamarisk*: evergreen shrub or small tree, with slender feathery branches and minute scalelike leaves

## II.

Night has eyes of Heaven:
　　Eyes of Earth has Day.
How darkly over the pillow
　　The locks from your forehead stray!
How like yon tangled darkness
　　From the arch of pearly gray!
And now the blush steals on it, like the stream
Of rose across the crocus-bed[2]
　　In the pearly eastern arch.
I'm half in love with morning,　　　　　　　10
　　Morning fresh on her march,
To see you: but O for the shadowy gleam
Of our dark-jewell'd mistress,
　　Bearing the baby-dream
On the infinite vales of her bosom!
　　My love! I must up and away.

---

2. *crocus*: a small plant with brilliant flowers, which are usually deep yellow or purple

# Autumn Even-Song[1]

The long cloud edged with streaming gray,
    Soars from the west;
The red leaf mounts with it away,
    Showing the nest
A blot among the branches bare:
There is a cry of outcasts in the air.

Swift little breezes, darting chill,
    Pant down the lake;
A crow flies from the yellow hill,
    And in its wake          10
A baffled line of labouring rooks:[2]
Steel-surfaced to the light the river looks.

---

1. "Autumn Even-Song" first appeared in *Once a Week* (3 December 1859).
2. *rooks*: loud Eurasian crows which nest in colonies in the tops of trees

Pale on the panes of the old hall
   Gleams the lone space
Between the sunset and the squall;[3]
   And on its face
Mournfully glimmers to the last:
Great oaks grow mighty minstrels[4] in the blast.

Pale the rain-rutted roadways shine
   In the green light          20
Behind the cedar and the pine:
   Come, thundering night!
Blacken broad earth with hoards of storm:
For me yon valley-cottage beckons warm.

---

3. *squall*: a loud, harsh cry or a sudden and violent gust of wind

4. *minstrels*: singers or musicians of the medieval period, especially those who sing heroic or lyric poetry

# Unknown Fair Faces[1]

Though I am faithful to my loves lived through,
And place them among Memory's great stars,
Where burns a face like Hesper:[2] one like Mars:
Of visages I get a moment's view,
Sweet eyes that in the Heaven of me, too,
Ascend, tho' virgin to my life they pass'd.
Lo, these within my destiny seem glass'd[3]
At times so bright, I wish that Hope were new.
A gracious freckled lady, tall and grave,
Went in a shawl voluminous and white,                        10
Last sunset by; and going sow'd a glance.
Earth is too poor to hold a second chance;
I will not ask for more than Fortune gave:
My heart she goes from—never from my sight!

---

1. PB suggests that this sonnet may have been inspired by Keats's "To a Lady Seen for a Few Moments at Vauxhall."

2. *Hesper*: the evening star (Venus when visible after sunset)

3. *glass'd*: either to set (an object, oneself) before a mirror or other reflecting surface, so as to cause an image to be reflected, or, more simply, to reflect

# Phantasy[1]

## I.

Within a Temple of the Toes,
    Where twirl'd the passionate Wili,[2]
I saw full many a market rose,
    And sigh'd for my village lily.

## II.

With cynical Adrian[3] then I took flight
    To that old dead city[4] whose carol
Bursts out like a reveller's loud in the night,
    As he sits astride his barrel.

---

1. Originally published in *Once a Week* (23 November 1861).
2. According to Slavic folklore, the Wili (or Wilis) are mischievous female spirits who can use their powers to help humans or to lure them into danger. Meredith may have become familiar with them through the ballet *Giselle, ou Les Wilis* (first performed in Paris in 1841 and in London in 1842) or through Heinrich Heine, a German poet and essayist who was extremely popular among mid-Victorian authors—including Meredith.
3. *cynical Adrian*: likely a reference to Meredith's friend, Maurice Fitzgerald, the model for Adrian (the "wise youth") in Meredith's novel *The Ordeal of Richard Feverel*
4. *old dead city*: Bruges

## III.

We two were bound the Alps to scale,
    Up the rock-reflecting river;[5]
Old times blew thro' me like a gale,
    And kept my thoughts in a quiver.

## IV.

Hawking ruin, wood-slope, and vine,
    Reel'd silver-laced under my vision,
and into me pass'd, with the green-eyed wine[6]
    Knocking hard at my head for admission.

## V.

I held the village lily cheap,
    And the dream around her idle:
Lo, quietly as I lay to sleep,
    The bells led me off to a bridal.

## VI.

My bride wore the hood of a Beguine,[7]
    And mine was the foot to falter;
Three cowl'd monks, rat-eyed, were seen;
    The Cross was of bones o'er the altar.

---

5. *rock-reflecting river*: Carl Ketcham identifies this as the Rhine, and suggests that the description of the speaker's journey here may have been based on Meredith's journey with his son Arthur to the Swiss Alps. Carl H. Ketcham, "Meredith and the Wilis," *Victorian Poetry* 1, no. 4 (November 1963): 241–48.

6. *green-eyed wine*: perhaps wine in a Bocksbeutel, a squat green bottle used in Franconia

7. *Beguine*: a name for members of certain lay sisterhoods that began in the Low Countries in the twelfth century; they devoted themselves to a religious life but did not bind themselves by strict vows and were able to leave their societies for marriage.

## VII.

The Cross was of bones; the priest that read,
    A spectacled necromancer:[8]
But at the fourth word, the bride I led,
    Changed to an Opera dancer.

## VIII.

A young ballet beauty who perk'd in her place,
    A darling of pink and spangles;
One fair foot level with her face,
    And the hearts of men at her ankles.

## IX.

She whirl'd, she twirl'd; the mock-priest grinn'd,
    And quickly his mask unriddled;
'Twas Adrian! loud his old laughter dinn'd;
    Then he seized a fiddle, and fiddled.

## X.

He fiddled, he glow'd with the bottomless fire,
    Like Sathanas[9] in feature:
All thro' me he fiddled a wolfish desire
    To dance with that bright creature.

## XI.

And gathering courage I said to my soul,
    Throttle the thing that hinders!
When the three cowl'd monks, from black as coal,
    Wax'd hot as furnace-cinders.

---

8. *necromancer*: sorcerer
9. *Sathanas*: Satan

## XII.

They caught her up, twirling; they leapt between-whiles:
  The fiddler flicker'd with laughter:
Profanely they flew down the awful aisles,
  Where I went sliding after.

## XIII.

Down the awful aisles, by the fretted walls,
  Beneath the Gothic arches:—
King Skull in the black confessionals
  Sat rub-a-dub-dubbing his marches.

## XIV.

Then the silent cold stone warriors frown'd,
  The pictured saints strode forward:
A whirlwind swept them from holy ground;
  A tempest puff'd them nor'ward.

## XV.

They shot through the great cathedral door;
  Like mallards they traversed ocean:
And gazing below, on its boiling floor,
  I mark'd a horrid commotion.

## XVI.

Down a forest's long alleys they spun like tops:
  It seem'd that for ages and ages,
Thro' the Book of Life bereft of stops,
  They waltz'd continuous pages.

## XVII.

And ages after, scarce awake,
    And my blood with the fever fretting,
I stood alone by a forest-lake,[10]
    Whose shadows the moon were netting.

## XVIII.

Lilies, golden and white, by the curls
    Of their broad flat leaves hung swaying.
A wreath of languid twining girls
    Stream'd upward, long locks disarraying.

## XIX.

Their cheeks had the satin frost-glow of the moon;
    Their eyes the fire of Sirius.[11]
They circled, and droned a monotonous tune,
    Abandon'd to love delirious.

## XX.

Like lengths of convolvulus[12] torn from the hedge,
    And trailing the highway over,
The dreamy-eyed mistresses circled the sedge,[13]
    And call'd for a lover, a lover!

---

10. *I stood . . . forest-lake*: The second act of *Giselle* takes place on the shores of a lake.

11. *Sirius*: the chief star of the constellation Canis Major or Great Dog, and the brightest in the heavens; the Dog Star

12. *convolvulus*: a plant with slender twining stems and trumpet-shaped flowers

13. *sedge*: a name for various coarse grassy plants growing in wet places

## XXI.

I sank, I rose through seas of eyes,
  In odorous swathes delicious:
They fann'd me with impetuous sighs,
  They bit me with kisses vicious.

## XXII.

My ears were spell'd, my neck was coil'd,
  And I with their fury was glowing,
When the marbly waters bubbled and boil'd
  At a watery noise of crowing.

## XXIII.

They dragg'd me low and low to the lake:
  Their kisses more stormily shower'd;
On the emerald brink, in the white moon's wake,
  An earthly damsel cower'd.

## XXIV.

Fresh heart-sobs shook her knitted hands
  Beneath a tiny suckling,
As one by one of the doleful bands
  Dived like a fairy duckling.

## XXV.

And now my turn had come—O me!
  What wisdom was mine that second!
I dropp'd on the adorer's knee;
  To that sweet figure I beckon'd.

## XXVI.

Save me! save me! for now I know
   The powers that nature gave me,
And the value of honest love I know:—
   My village lily! save me!

## XXVII.

Come 'twixt me and the sisterhood,
   While the passion-born phantoms are fleeing!
Oh, he that is true to flesh and blood
   Is true to his own being!

## XXVIII.

And he that is false to flesh and blood,
   Is false to the star within him:
And the mad and hungry sisterhood
   All under the tides shall win him!

## XXIX.

My village lily! save me! save!
   For strength is with the holy:—
Already I shudder'd to feel the wave,
   As I kept sinking slowly:—

## XXX.

I felt the cold wave and the under-tug
   Of the Brides, when—starting and shrinking—
Lo, Adrian tilts the water-jug!
   And Bruges with morn is blinking.

# XXXI.

Merrily sparkles sunny prime
   On gabled peak and arbour:
Merrily rattles belfry-chime
   The song of Sevilla's Barber.

# Shemselnihar[1]

## I.

O my lover: the night like a broad smooth wave
    Bears us onward, and morn, a black rock, shines wet.
How I shudder'd!—I knew not that I was a slave,
    Till I look'd on thy face:—then I writhed in the net.
Then I felt like a thing caught by fire, that her star
Glow'd dark on the bosom of Shemselnihar.

## II.

And he came, whose I am: O my lover! he came:
    And his slave, still so envied of women, was I:
And I turned as a hissing leaf spits from the flame,
    Yes, I shrivell'd to dust from him, haggard and dry.
O forgive her:—she was but as dead lilies are:
The life of her heart fled from Shemselnihar.

---

1. Shemselnihar, a character from one of Meredith's favorite books, the *Arabian Nights*, is a concubine belonging to the Prince of the Faithful, the Caliph. Her lover is Ali the son of Becar. Upon meeting, the two fall violently in love. When the Caliph hears that Shemselnihar loves another, he refuses to believe it and, in fact, begins to love her all the more. In the story, Shemselnihar and Ali are essentially killed by their susceptibility to poetry and the force of their passion for each other.

## III.

Yet with thee like a full throbbing rose how I bloom!
    Like a rose by the fountain whose showering we hear,
As we lie, O my lover! in this rich gloom,
    Smelling faint the cool breath of the lemon-groves near.
As we lie gazing out on that glowing great star—
Ah! dark on the bosom of Shemselnihar.

## IV.

Yet with thee am I not as an arm of the vine,
    Firm to bind thee, to cherish thee, feed thee sweet?
Swear an oath on my lip to let none disentwine
    The fair life that here fawns to give warmth to thy feet.
I on thine, thus! no more shall that jewelled Head jar
The music thou breathest on Shemselnihar.

## V.

Far away, far away, where the wandering scents
    Of all flowers are sweetest, white mountains among,
There my kindred abide in their green and blue tents:
    Bear me to them, my lover! they lost me so young.
Let us slip down the stream and leap steed till afar
None question thy claim upon Shemselnihar.

## VI.

O that long note the bulbul[2] gave out—meaning love!
  O my lover, hark to him and think it my voice:
The blue night like a great bell-flower from above
  Drooping low and gold-eyed: O, but hear him rejoice!
Can it be? 'twas a flash! that accurst scimitàr[3]
In thought even cuts thee from Shemselnihar.


## VII.

Yes, I would that, less generous, he would oppress,
  He would chain me, upbraid me, burn deep brands for hate,
Than with this mask of freedom, and gorgeousness,
  Spangle over my slavery, mock my strange fate.
Would, would, would, O my lover, he knew—dared debar
Thy coming, and earn curse of Shemselnihar!

---

2. *bulbul*: a species of bird belonging to the thrush family, much admired in the East for its song; sometimes called the "nightingale" of the East
  3. *scimitàr*: a short, curved, single-edged sword, used especially by Turks and Persians

# [A roar thro' the tall twin elm-trees]

A roar thro' the tall twin elm-trees
    The mustering storm betray'd:
The south-wind seiz'd the willow
    That over the water sway'd.

Then fell the steady deluge
    In which I strove to doze,
Hearing all night at my window
    The knock of the winter rose.

The rainy rose of winter!
    An outcast it must pine.
And from thy bosom outcast
    Am I, dear lady mine.

# [When I would image her features][1]

When I would image her features,
    Comes up a shrouded head:
I touch the outlines, shrinking;
    She seems of the wandering dead.

But when love asks for nothing,
    And lies on his bed of snow,
The face slips under my eyelids,
    All in its living glow.

Like a dark cathedral city
    Whose spires, and domes, and towers,      10
Quiver in violet lightnings,
    My soul basks on for hours.

---

1. Section LXX of Tennyson's *In Memoriam* ("I cannot see the features right") offers a compelling antecedent to this poem.

# [I chafe at darkness in the night]

I chafe at darkness in the night;
    But when 'tis light,
  Hope shuts her eyes: the clouds are pale;
The fields stretch cold into a distance hard:
  I wish again to draw the veil
    Thousand-starr'd.

Am I of them whose blooms are shed,
    Whose fruits are spent,
  Who from dead eyes see Life half dead;—
Because desire is feeble discontent?
  Ah, no! desire and hope should die,
    Thus were I.

But in me something clipp'd of wing,
    Within its ring
  Frets; for I have lost what made
The dawn-breeze magic, and the twilight beam
  A hand with tidings o'er the glade
    Waving, seem.

10

# By the Rosanna[1]

TO F. M.[2]

*Stanzer Thal, Tyrol*[3]

The old grey Alp[4] has caught the cloud,
And the torrent river sings aloud;
The glacier-green Rosanna sings
An organ song of its upper springs.
Foaming under the tiers of pine,
I see it dash down the dark ravine,
And it tumbles the rocks in boisterous play,
With an earnest will to find its way.
Sharp it throws out an emerald shoulder,
    And, thundering ever of the mountain,        10
Slaps in sport some giant boulder,
    And tops it in a silver fountain.
A chain of foam from end to end,
And a solitude so deep, my friend,
You may forget that man abides
Beyond the great mute mountain-sides.

---

1. "By the Rosanna" first appeared in *Once a Week* (19 October 1861). Lines 21–179 were cut from the version that appeared in the Edition de Luxe.

2. *F. M.*: Meredith's long-time friend, Frederick A. Maxse. On 26 July 1861, Meredith wrote to Maxse: "The Rosanna, by the way, put me in mind of you—nay, sang of you with a mountain voice. . . . Perhaps because it is both hearty and gallant, subtle and sea-green." *Letters*, I.106.

3. *Stanzer Thal, Tyrol*: Meredith, his son Arthur, and Bonaparte Wyse vacationed in the low Alpine valley of Stanzer Thal in Austria, Tyrol, in the summer of 1861.

4. *old grey Alp*: Mount Hoher Riffler

Yet to me, in this high-walled solitude
Of river and rock and forest rude,
The roaring voice through the long white chain,
Is the voice of the world of bubble and brain.                    20

I find it where I sought it least;
I sought the mountain and the beast,
The young thin air that knits the nerves,
The chamois ledge, the snowy curves;
Earth in her whiteness looking bold
To Heaven for ever as of old.

And lo, if I translate the sound
Now thundering in my ears around,
'Tis London rushing down a hill:
Life, or London; which you will!                                  30

And men with brain who follow the bubble,
    And hosts without, who hurry and eddy,
And still press on: joy, passion, and trouble!
    Necessity's instinct; true, though unsteady.

Yea, letting alone the roar and the strife,
This On-on-on is so like life!
Here's devil take the hindmost, too;
And an amorous wave has a beauty in view;
And lips of others are kissing the rocks:
Here's chasing of bubbles, and wooing of blocks.                  40
And through the resonant monotone
    I catch wild laughter mix'd with shrieks;
And a wretched creature's stifled moan,
    Whom Time, the terrible usurer, tweaks.

Is it enough to profane your mood,
    Arcadian[5] dreamer, who think it sad

---

5. *Arcadian*: ideally rural or rustic

If a breath of the world on your haunts intrude,
    Though in London you're hunting the bubble like mad?

For you are one who raise the Nymph
    Wherever Nature sits alone;                50
Who pitch your delight in a region of lymph,[6]
    Rejoiced that its arms evade your own.

I see you lying here, and wistfully
    Watching the dim shape, tender and fresh:
Your Season-Beauty[7] faithless, or kiss'd fully,
    You're just a little tired of flesh.

She[8] dances, and gleams, now under the wave,
    Now on a fern-branch, or fox-glove[9] bell;
Thro' a wreath of the bramble she eyes me grave;
    She has a secret she will not tell.          60

But if I follow her more and more,
    If I hold her sacred to each lone spot,
She'll tell me—what I knew before;
    For the secret is, that she can't be caught!

She lives, I swear! We join hands there.
But what's her use? Can you declare?
If she serves no purpose, she must take wing:
Art stamps her for an ugly thing.

Will she fly with the old gods, or join with the new?
    Is she made of the stuff for a thorough alliance?    70

---

6. *lymph*: literally, a clear bodily fluid; figuratively, as here, pure water
7. *Season-Beauty*: In Victorian society, the London social season, roughly during the months of May, June, and July, was when socially and politically connected families attended exclusive balls, dinner parties, and charity events. It was also the time when debutants (or, as Meredith calls them here, Season-Beauties) were presented to the queen—a social ritual known as "coming out."
8. *She*: the Nymph
9. *fox-glove*: a common ornamental flowering plant

Or, standing alone, does she dare to go thro'
    The ordeal of a scrutiny of Science?

What say you, if, in this retreat,
    While she poises tiptoe on yon granite slab, man,
I introduce her, shy and sweet,
    To a short-neck'd, many-caped, London cabman?

You gasp!—she totters! And is it too much?
Mayn't he take off his hat to her? hope for a touch?
Get one kind curtsey of aërial grace
For his most liberal grimace?                                    80

It would do him a world of good, poor devil!
And Science makes equal on this level:
Remember that!—and his friend, the popular
Mr. Professor, the learned and jocular,
Were he to inspect her and call her a foam-bow,
I very much fear it would prove a home-blow.
We couldn't save her!—she'd vanish, fly;
    Tho' she's more than that, as we know right well;
But who shall expound to a hard cold eye,
    The infinite impalpable?                                     90

A Queen on sufferance must not act
    My Lady Scornful:—thus presuming,
If Sentiment won't wed with Fact,
    Poor Sentiment soon needs perfuming.
Let her curtsey with becoming tact
    To cabman caped and poet blooming!—

No, I wouldn't mix Porter with Montepulciano![10]
    I ask you merely, without demanding,

---

10. *Porter with Montepulciano!*: Porter is a dark-brown, bitter beer; Montepulciano is an Italian red wine. Francesco Redi called Montepulciano "the king of all wine" in his "Bacco in Toscana," a popular Italian poem translated into English by Leigh Hunt after a wine-soaked trip to Italy in the 1820s.

To give a poor beggar his *buon' mano:*——[11]
    Make my meaning large with your understanding!      100

The cicada sits spinning his wheel on the tree;
    The little green lizard slips over the stone
    Like water: the waters flash, and the cone
Drops at my feet. Say, how shall it be?
    Your Nymph is on trial. Will she own
Her parentage Humanity?
Of her essence these things but form a part;
Her heart comes out of the human heart.

Tremendous thought, which I scarce dare blab, man!
    The soul she yet lacks—the illumination      110
    Immortal!—it strikes me like inspiration,
She must get her that soul by wedding the cabman!

Don't ask me why:—when instinct speaks,
    Old Mother Reason is not at home.
But how gladly would dance the days and the weeks!
    And the sky, what a mirth-embracing dome!
If round sweet Poesy's waist were curl'd
The arm of him who drives the World!

Could she claim a higher conquest, she?
And a different presence his would be!      120
I see him lifting his double chin
    On his threefold comforter, sniffing and smirking,
And showing us all that the man within
    Has had his ideas of her secretly lurking.

Confess that the sight were as fine—ay, as fair!
As if from a fire-ball in mid-air

---

11. *buon' mano*: Italian; literally, "good hand"; normally means a tip, but in this context, a handout

She glow'd before you woman, spreading
With hands the hair her foot was treading!

'Twere an effort for Nature both ways, and which
    The mightier I can't aver:                               130
If we screw ourselves up to a certain pitch,
    She meets us—that I know of her.

She is ready to meet the grim cabman half-way!
    Now! and where better than here, where, with thunder
Of waters, she might bathe his clay,
    And enter him by the gate of wonder?

It takes him doubtless long to peel,
    Who wears at least a dozen capes:
Yet if but once she makes him feel,
    The man comes of his multiform shapes.                   140

To make him feel, friend, is not easy.
    *I* once did nourish that ambition:
But there he goes, purple, and greasy, and wheezy,
    And waits a greater and truer magician!

Hark to the wild Rosanna cheering!
    Never droops she, while changing clime
At every leap, the levels nearing:
    Faith in ourselves is faith in Time!

And faith in Nature keeps the force
    We have in us for daily wear.                            150
Come from thy keen Alp down, and, hoarse,
    Tell the valleys the tale I hear,
O River!

        Now, my friend, adieu!
In contrast, and in likeness, you
Have risen before me from the tide,

Whose channel is narrow, whose noise is wide;
Whose rage is that of your native seas;
Buzzing of battle like myriad bees,
Which you have heard on the Euxine shore[12]                    160
    Sounding in earnest. Here have I placed
The delicate spirit with which you adore
    Dame Nature in lone haunts embraced.
Have I affrighted it, frail thing, aghast?
I have shown it the way to live and last!

    How often will those long links of foam
    Cry to me in my English home,
    To nerve me, whenever I hear them bellow,
    Like the smack of the hand of a gallant fellow!

    I give them my meaning here, and they             170
    Will give me theirs when far away.
    And the snowy points, and the ash-pale peaks,
    Will bring a trembling to my cheeks,
    The leap of the white-fleck'd, clear light, green
    Sudden the length of its course be seen,
    As, swift it launches an emerald shoulder,
        And, thundering ever of the mountain,
    Slaps in sport some giant boulder,
        And tops it in a silver fountain.

12. *Euxine shore*: the shore of the Black Sea, where Maxse fought in the Crimean War

# Ode to the Spirit of Earth in Autumn

Fair mother Earth lay on her back last night,
To gaze her fill on Autumn's sunset skies,
When at a waving of the fallen light,
Sprang realms of rosy fruitage o'er her eyes.
A lustrous heavenly orchard hung the West,
Wherein the blood of Eden bloom'd again.
Red were the myriad cherub mouths that press'd
Among the clusters, rich with song, full fain,
But dumb,[1] because that overmastering spell
Of rapture held them dumb, then, here and there,    10
A golden harp lost strings; a crimson shell
Burnt grey; and sheaves of lustre fell to air.
The illimitable eagerness of hue
Bronzed, and the beamy winged bloom that flew
'Mid those bunch'd fruits and thronging figures, fail'd.
A green-edged lake of saffron[2] touch'd the blue,
With isles of fireless purple lying thro':
And Fancy on that lake to seek lost treasures sail'd.

✦

---

1. *dumb*: silent
2. *saffron*: dried crocus stamens, bright orange-yellow in color, used as a spice

Not long the silence follow'd:
The voice that issues from the breast,                                    20
    O, glorious South-West,
Along the gloom-horizon holloa'd;
Warning the valleys with a mellow roar
Thro' flapping wings; then, sharp the woodland bore
    A shudder, and a noise of hands:
    A thousand horns from some far vale
    In ambush sounding on the gale.
    Forth from the cloven sky came bands
Of revel-gathering spirits; trooping down,
Some rode the tree-tops; some, on torn cloud-strips,              30
    Burst screaming thro' the lighted town:
And scudding seaward, some fell on big ships:
    Or mounting the sea-horses blew
    Bright foam-flakes on the black review
    Of heaving hulls and burying beaks.

Still on the farthest line, with outpuff'd cheeks,
'Twixt dark and utter dark, the great wind drew
From heaven that disenchanted harmony
To join earth's laughter in the midnight blind:³
Booming a distant chorus to the shrieks                               40
            Preluding him: then he,
His mantle streaming thunderingly behind,
Across the yellow realm of stiffen'd Day,
Shot thro' the woodland alleys signals three;
    And with the pressure of a sea,
Plunged broad upon the vale that under lay.

Night on the rolling foliage fell:
But I, who love old hymning night,
And know the Dryad⁴ voices well,
Discerned them as their leaves took flight,                          50

---

3. *blind*: here, a drunken bout or orgy
4. *Dryad*: wood nymph

Like souls to wander after death:
Great armies in imperial dyes,
And mad to tread the air, and rise,
The savage freedom of the skies
To taste before they rot. And here,
Like frail white-bodied girls in fear,
The birches swung from shrieks to sighs;
The aspens, laughers at a breath,
In showering spray-falls mixed their cries,
Or raked a savage ocean-strand                            60
With one incessant drowning screech.
Here, stood a solitary beech,
That gave its gold with open hand,
And all its branches, toning chill,
Did seem to shut their teeth right fast,
To shriek more mercilessly shrill,
And match the fierceness of the blast.

But heard I a low swell that noised
Of far-off ocean, I was 'ware
Of pines upon their old roots poised,                     70
Whom never madness in the air
Can draw to more than loftier stress
Of mournfulness not mournfulness,
Not mournfulness, but Joy's excess
That singing, on the lap of sorrow faints:
And Peace, as in the hearts of saints
Who chant unto the Lord their God,
Deep Peace below upon the muffled sod,
The stillness of the sea's unswaying floor.
Could I be sole there not to see                          80
The life within the life awake;
The spirit bursting from the tree,
And rising from the troubled lake?
Pour, let the wines of Heaven pour!
The Golden Harp is struck once more,
And all its music is for me!

Pour, let the wines of Heaven pour!
And, ho, for a night of Pagan glee!

    There is a curtain o'er us.
For once, good souls, we'll not pretend        90
To be aught better than her who bore us,[5]
And is our only visible friend.[6]
Hark to her laughter! who laughs like this,
Can she be dead, or rooted in pain?
She has been slain by the narrow brain,
But for us who love her she lives again.
    Can she die? O, take her kiss!

The crimson-footed nymph is panting up the glade,
With the wine-jar at her arm-pit, and the drunken ivy-braid
Round her forehead, breast, and thighs: starts a Satyr, and they
    speed:        100
Hear the crushing of the leaves: hear the cracking of the
    bough!
And the whistling of the bramble, the piping of the weed![7]

    But the bull-voiced oak is battling now!
    The storm has seized him half asleep,
    And round him the wild woodland throngs
    To hear the fury of his songs,
    The uproar of an outraged deep.
    He wakes to find a wrestling giant
    Trunk to trunk and limb to limb,
    And on his rooted force reliant,        110
    He laughs and grasps the broaden'd giant,
    And twist and roll the Anakim;[8]

---

5. *her who bore us*: Nature

6. *visible friend*: Nature; Meredith uses the same epithet in Sonnet XIII of "Modern Love."

7. *piping of the weed!*: playing the panpipes

8. *Anakim*: biblical giants whom Joshua sent from Israel into Gaza, Gath, and Ashdod (see Numbers, Deuteronomy, and Joshua)

And multitudes acclaiming to the cloud,
　Cry which is breaking, which is bowed.


　Away, for the cymbals clash aloft
　In the circle of pines, on the moss-floor soft.
　The nymphs of the woodland are gathering there.
　They huddle the leaves, and trample, and toss;
　They swing in the branches, they roll in the moss,
　　They blow the seed on the air.　　　　　　　　120
　Back to back they stand and blow
　The winged seed[9] on the cradling air,
　A fountain of leaves over bosom and back!
　The pipe of the Faun[10] comes on their track,
　And the weltering alleys overflow
　With musical shrieks and wind-wedded hair.
　The riotous companies melt to a pair.
　　Bless them, mother of kindness!


　A star has nodded thro'
　The depths of the flying blue.　　　　　　　　130
　Time only to plant the light
　Of a memory in the blindness.
　But time to show me the sight
　Of my life thro' the curtain of night.
　Shining a moment, and mix'd
　With the onward-hurrying stream,
　Whose pressure is darkness to me,
　Behind the curtain, fix'd,
　Beams with endless beam,
　That star on the changing sea!　　　　　　　　140


Oh, mother Nature! teach me, like thee,
To kiss the season, and shun regrets.

---

9. *winged seed*: cf. Shelley's "Ode to the West Wind," l.1–14
10. *the Faun*: Pan, the reed-pipe-playing Greek god connected with nature, spring, fertility, and lust

And am I more than the mother who bore,
Mock me not with thy harmony!
   Teach me to blot regrets,
   Great mother! me inspire
   With faith that forward sets
   But feeds the living fire.
   Faith that never frets
   For vagueness in the form.                          150
   In life, O keep me warm!
   For, what is human grief?
   And what do men desire?
Teach me to feel myself the tree,
   And not the wither'd leaf.
Fix'd am I and await the dark to-be!


   And O, green bounteous earth!
Bacchante[11] Mother! stern to those
Who live not in thy heart of mirth;
Death shall I shrink from, loving thee?            160
Into the breast that gives the rose,
   Shall I with shuddering fall?


   Earth, the mother of all,
   Moves on her steadfast way,
   Gathering, flinging, sowing.
   Mortals, we live in her day,
   She in her children is growing.


She can lead us, only she,
Unto God's footstool, whither she reaches:
Loved, enjoy'd, her gifts must be;             170
Reverenced the truths she teaches,
Ere a man may hope that he

---

11. *Bacchante*: female followers of Bacchus, god of wine and intoxication, who are often portrayed in states of violent, erotic frenzy

Ever can attain the glee
Of things without a destiny!

Hark to her laughter! And would you wonder
To hear amazing laughter thunder
From one who contemplateth man?—
    Knowing the plan!

The great procession of the Comedy,
Passes before her. Let the curtain down!                    180
For she must laugh to shake her starry crown,
To mark the strange perversions that are we;
Who hoist our shoulders confident of wings,
When we have named her Ashes, dug her ditch;
Who do regard her as a damnëd witch,
Fair to the eye, but full of foulest things.
We, pious humpback mountebanks[12] meanwhile,
Break off our antics to stand forth, white-eyed,
And fondly hope for our Creator's smile,
By telling him that his prime work is vile,                  190
Whom, through our noses, we've renounced, denied.

Good friends of mine, who love her,
And would not see her bleeding:
The light that is above her,
From eyesight is receding,
As ever we grow older,
And blood is waxing colder.
But grasp in spirit tightly,
That she is no pretender,
While still the eye sees brightly,—                          200
Then darkness knows her splendour,
And coldness feels her glory.
As in yon cloud-scud hoary,[13]

12. *mountebanks*: sellers of quack medicines
13. *cloud-scud hoary*: a wispy, fast-moving cloud

From gloom to gloom swift winging,
The sunset beams have found me:
I hear the sunset singing
In this blank roar around me!

Friends! we are yet in the warmth of our blood,
And swift as the tides upon which we are borne.
There's a long blue rift in the speeding scud,                    210
That shows like a boat on a sea forlorn,
With stars to man it! That boat is ours,
And we are the mariners on the great flood
Of the shifting slopes and the drifting flowers,
That oar unresting towards the morn!
And are we the children of Heaven and earth,
We'll be true to the mother with whom we are,
So to be worthy of Him who afar,
Beckons us on to a brighter birth.

  She knows not loss:                                   220
  She feels but her need,
  Who the winged seed
  With the leaf doth toss.

And may not men to this attain?
That the joy of motion, the rapture of being,
 Shall throw strong light when their season is fleeing,
 Nor quicken aged blood in vain,
At the gates of the vault, on the verge of the plain?
Life thoroughly lived is a fact in the brain,
 While eyes are left for seeing.                              230

Behold, in yon stripp'd Autumn, shivering gray,
 Earth knows no desolation.
 She smells regeneration
 In the moist breath of decay.

Prophetic of the coming joy and strife,
   Like the wild western war-chief sinking
   Calm to the end he eyes unblinking,
Her voice is jubilant in ebbing life.

   He for his happy hunting-fields
   Forgets the droning chant, and yields        240
   His number'd breaths to exultation
   In the proud anticipation:
   Shouting the glories of his nation,
   Shouting the grandeur of his race,
   Shouting his own great deeds of daring!
   And when at last death grasps his face,
   And stiffen'd on the ground in peace
He lies with all his painted terrors glaring;
Hush'd are the tribe to hear a threading cry:
   Not from the dead man;        250
   Not from the standers-by:
   The spirit of the red man
Is welcomed by his fathers up on high.

# The Doe:

## A Fragment

### (*From* "Wandering Willie")

And—"Yonder look! yoho! yoho!
"Nancy is off!" the farmer[1] cried,
Advancing by the river side,
Red-kerchieft and brown-coated;—"So,
"My girl, who else could leap like that?
"So neatly! like a lady! Zounds!
"Look at her how she leads the hounds!"
And waving his dusty beaver hat,
He cheer'd across the chase-fill'd water,
And clapt his arm about his daughter,                    10
And gave to Joan[2] a courteous hug,
And kiss that, like a stubborn plug
From generous vats in vastness rounded,
The inner wealth and spirit sounded:
Eagerly pointing south, where, lo!
The daintiest fleetest-footed doe
Led o'er the fields and thro' the furze[3]
Beyond; her lively delicate ears

---

1. "*Nancy . . . farmer*: Nancy is the doe, named after the farmer's dead daughter; though not mentioned in this fragment, the farmer's name is Gale. PB II.957, line 367.
2. *Joan*: Willie's wife
3. *furze*: evergreen shrub

Prickt up erect, and in her track
A dappled lengthy-striding pack.                                        20

Scarce had they cast eyes upon her,
When every heart was wager'd on her,
And half in dread, and half delight,
They watch'd her lovely bounding flight;
As now, across the flashing green,
And now, beneath the stately trees,
And now far distant in the dene,
She headed on with graceful ease:
Hanging aloft with doubled knees,
At times athwart some hedge or gate;                                    30
And slackening pace by slow degrees,
As for the foremost foe to wait.
Renewing her outstripping rate
Whene'er the hot pursuers near'd,
By garden wall and paled estate,
Where clambering gazers whoopt and cheer'd.
Here, winding under elm and oak,
And slanting up the sunny hill:
Splashing the water here, like smoke
Among the mill-holms round the mill.                                    40

And—"let her go; she shows her game,
"My Nancy girl, my pet and treasure!"
The farmer sigh'd; his eyes with pleasure
Brimming: "'tis my daughter's name,
"My second daughter lying yonder."
And Willie's eye in search did wander,
And caught at once, with moist regard,
The white gleam of a gray churchyard.

"Three weeks before my girl had gone,
"And while upon her pillows propt,                                      50
"She lay at eve; the weakling fawn—
"For still it seems a fawn just dropt

"A se'nnight,[4] to my Nancy's bed[5]
"I brought to make my girl a gift:
"The mothers of them both were dead;
"And both to bless it was my drift,
"By giving each a friend; not thinking
"How rapidly my girl was sinking.
"And I remember how, to pat
"Its neck, she stretch'd her hand so weak,          60
"And its cold nose against her cheek
"Press'd fondly; and I fetcht the mat
"To make it up a couch just by her,
"Where in the lone dark hours to lie;
"For neither dear old nurse, nor I
"Would any single wish deny her.
"And there unto the last it lay;
"And in the pastures cared to play
"Little or nothing: there its meals
"And milk I brought: and even now          70
"The creature such affection feels
"For that old room that, when and how,
"'Tis strange to mark, it slinks and steals
"To get there, and all day conceals.
"And once when nurse who, since that time,
"Keeps house for me, was very sick,
"Waking upon the midnight chime,
"And listening to the stair-clock's click,
"I heard a rustling, half uncertain,
"Close against the dark bed-curtain:          80
"And while I thrust my leg to kick,
"And feel the phantom with my feet,
"A loving tongue began to lick
"My left hand lying on the sheet;

---

4. *se'nnight*: seven nights
   5. *the weakling . . . bed*: PB writes, "The idea of a doe comforting a human being stems not only from folklore but [also] from Wordsworth's *White Doe of Rylstone* (1815)." She also notes the poem's formal resemblance to Wordworth's *The Excursion*. PB II.1141.

"And warm sweet breath upon me blew,
"And that 'twas Nancy then I knew.
"So, for her love, I had good cause
"To have the creature 'Nancy' christen'd."

He paused, and in the moment's pause,
His eyes and Willie's strangely glisten'd.                    90
Nearer came Joan, and Bessy[6] hung
With face averted, near enough
To hear, and sob unheard: the young
And careless ones had scamper'd off
Meantime, and sought the loftiest place
To beacon the approaching chase.

"Daily upon the meads to browse,
"Goes Nancy with those dairy cows
"You see behind the clematis:[7]
"And such a favourite she is,                                100
"That when fatigued, and helter skelter,
"Among them from her foes to shelter,
"She dashes when the chase is over,
"They'll close her in and give her cover,
"And bend their horns against the hounds,
"And low, and keep them out of bounds!
"From the house dogs she dreads no harm,
"And is good friends with all the farm,
"Man, and bird, and beast, howbeit
"Their natures seem so opposite.                             110
"And she is known for many a mile,
"And noted for her splendid style,
"For her clear leap and quick slight hoof;
"Welcome she is in many a roof.

---

6. *Bessy*: Nancy's older sister; in parts of the narrative not included in this fragment, she is deserted by her lover after having premarital sex.

7. *clematis*: a twining shrub with a showy flower, popularly called "Virgin's Bower," "Traveler's Joy," and "Old Man's Beard"

"And if I say, I love her, man!
"I say but little: her fine eyes full
"Of memories of my girl, at Yule
"And May-time, make her dearer than
"Dumb brute to men has been, I think.
"So dear I do not find her dumb.                                120
"I know her ways, her slightest wink,
"So well; and to my hand she'll come,
"Sideling, for food or a caress,
"Just like a loving human thing.
"Nor can I help, I do confess,
"Some touch of human sorrowing
"To think there may be such a doubt
"That from the next world she'll be shut out,
"And parted from me! And well I mind
"How, when my girl's last moments came,                         130
"Her soft eyes very soft and kind,
"She join'd her hands and pray'd the same.
"That she 'might meet her father, mother,
"Sister Bess, and each dear brother,
"And with them, if it might be, one
"Who was her last companion:'
"Meaning the fawn—the doe you mark—
"For my bay mare was then a foal,
"And time has pass'd since then:—but hark!"

For like the shrieking of a soul                                140
Stifled in a tomb, a darken'd cry
Of inward-wailing agony
Surprised them, and all eyes on each
Fixt in the mute-appealing speech
Of self-reproachful apprehension:
Knowing not what to think or do:
But Joan, recovering first, broke thro'
The instantaneous suspension,
And knelt upon the ground, and guess'd
The bitterness at a glance, and press'd                         150

Into the comfort of her breast,
The deep-throed quaking shape[8] that droop'd
In misery's willful aggravation,
Before the farmer as he stoopt'd,
Touch'd with accusing consternation:
Soothing her as she sobb'd aloud:—
"Not me! not me! Oh, no, no, no!
"Not me! God will not take me in!
"Nothing can wipe away my sin!
"I shall not see her: you will go;                                    160
"You and all that she loves so:
"Not me! not me! Oh, no, no, no!"[9]


Colourless—her long black hair,
Like seaweed in a tempest, toss'd
Tangling astray, to Joan's care
She yielded like a creature lost:
Yielded, drooping towards the ground,
As doth a shape one half-hour drown'd,
And heaved from the old sea with mast and spar,
All dark of its immortal star.                                        170
And on that tender heart, inured
To flatter basest grief, and fight
Despair upon the brink of night,
She suffered herself to sink, assured
Of refuge; and her ear inclined
To comfort; and her thoughts resigned
To counsel; and her hair let brush
From off her weeping brows; and shook
With many little sobs that took
Deeper-drawn breaths, till into sighs                                 180
Long sighs they sunk; and to the 'hush!'

---

8. *quaking shape*: Bessy, crying on the ground
9. *"Not me! . . . no, no!"*: Bessy is distraught because she believes her past actions will keep her from entering heaven.

Of Joan's gentle chide, she sought
Childlike, to check them as she ought,
Looking up at her infantwise.

And Willie, gazing on them both,
Shiver'd with bliss through blood and brain,
To see the darling of his troth
Like a maternal angel strain
The sinful and the sinless child[10]
At once on either breast, and there                    190
In peace and promise reconciled,
Unite them: nor could Nature's care
With subtler beneficence
Have fed the springs of penitence,
Still keeping true, though harshly tried,
The vital prop of human pride.

THE END

---

10. *sinless child*: Joan's infant

FIGURE 3: Illustration for "The Meeting" by John Everett Millais, from *Once a Week* (1 September 1860), p. 276. Image courtesy of Beinecke Rare Book and Manuscript Library, Yale University, New Haven, CT.

FIGURE 4: *Saint Michael striking down the Demon*, by Raphael, also called *The Large Saint Michael*, oil transferred from wood to canvas, 1518, Louvre, Paris.
© Réunion des Musées Nationaux / Art Resource, NY

FIGURE 5: Illustration for "The Last Words of Juggling Jerry" by Hablot Knight (H. K.) Browne, from *Once a Week* (3 September 1859), p. 190. Image courtesy of Beinecke Rare Book and Manuscript Library, Yale University, New Haven, CT.

FIGURE 6: Illustration for "The Old Chartist" by Frederick Sandys, from *Once a Week* (8 February 1862), p. 183. Image courtesy of Beinecke Rare Book and Manuscript Library, Yale University, New Haven, CT.

THE BEGGAR'S SOLILOQUY.

FIGURE 7: Illustration for "The Beggar's Soliloquy" by Charles Keene, from *Once a Week* (30 March 1861), p. 378. Image courtesy of Beinecke Rare Book and Manuscript Library, Yale University, New Haven, CT.

FIGURE 8: Illustration for "The Patriot Engineer" by Charles Keene, from
*Once a Week* (14 December 1861), p. 686. Image courtesy of Beinecke Rare
Book and Manuscript Library, Yale University, New Haven, CT.

FIGURE 9: Portrait of Annie Miller as Cassandra by Dante Gabriel Rossetti, pen and black ink on paper, 1861 / reworked 1867, British Museum, London. © Trustees of the British Museum.

FIGURE 10: Illustration for "The Head of Bran" by John Everett Millais, from *Once a Week* (4 February 1860), p. 132. Image courtesy of Beinecke Rare Book and Manuscript Library, Yale University, New Haven, CT.

*Contexts*

# Contemporary Reactions

The contemporary response to *Modern Love and Poems of the English Road-side, with Poems and Ballads* was largely negative, mostly due to distaste for the subject matter of the volume's titular sonnet sequence. Even Meredith's dear friend Frederick Maxse, to whom *Modern Love and Poems of the English Roadside* was dedicated, noted that some of the poems in the volume suffered from obscure passages. Champions and detractors alike, however, praised the "Poems of the English Roadside" and remarked upon the "vigour" of Meredith's verse in general. Richard Holt Hutton's review for the *Spectator* is typical of negative reactions, and it prompted poet Algernon Charles Swinburne to compose a spirited rejoinder defending Meredith's verse. The difference between these men's views is indicative not only of the divided reaction to *Modern Love*, but also of larger debates regarding Victorian poetry.

These often-vehement responses to *Modern Love* participate in ongoing Victorian discussions about intelligibility, poetic realism, sensory processing, and gender equality, as articulated in the excerpts included throughout the "Contexts" section of this edition.

# Unsigned Review, *Parthenon* (1862)[1]

Subtitled "A Weekly Journal of Literature, Science and Art," the *Parthenon* was short-lived (1862–63). This review is generally positive, admiring Meredith's descriptive powers and reverence for nature as well as his ability to portray "the subtlest workings of . . . human hearts." The author appears to be unaware that *Modern Love* is Meredith's second book of poetry.

Amid the multitude of versifiers and unfortunate persons who fancy themselves poets because their heads contain some rambling tunes, beginning with no purpose and ending with no conclusion, it is not a little gratifying to meet with the work of a conscientious artist, with distinct conceptions unflinchingly realized. Whatever difference of opinion may be excited by these poems, on one point at least we may expect agreement, viz. that they form a book not of promise, but performance; not of attempts, but results. Mr. George Meredith does not, like many, offer us a bunch of green leaves, and beg us expect that he will do wonders by-and-by—that at a future period he will give matured fruit; he has commenced with the fruit, the taste of which may be relished or disliked, but no doubt can be raised as to its full-grown ripeness.

The great variety of the contents of this volume renders it difficult to speak of it as a whole. It contains poems, such as "Grandfather Bridgeman" and the "Poems of the English Roadside," which for sunny, genial health and joyousness will compare with the most sparkling moods of Burns.[2] It contains others, which for their morbid subtlety of analysis Byron might have envied;

---

1. "Modern Love and Poems of the English Roadside, with Poems and Ballads. By George Meredith. Chapman and Hall," *Parthenon* (17 May 1862): 71–72. Maurice Buxton Forman identifies the authors of this review as J. C. Morison and N. E. S. A. Hamilton in *Meredithiana: Being a Supplement to The Bibliography of Meredith* (London: Dunedin Press, 1924), 15. We have been unable to corroborate this attribution.

2. Robert Burns (1759–1796), a Scottish poet widely regarded as a precursor of the Romantics.

and one or two which remind us of Hood.[3] Yet we fancy through all this diversity may be traced the recurrence of one under-tone, one bass-note, over which the melody is infinitely varied; and this is a deep inextinguishable love of and reliance on external nature, as the one source of joy and consolation given to man here on earth. This element is ever working in Mr. Meredith's poetry, imparting a smell of pines and gorse[4] and clover to all he touches. Doubtless a mere love of Nature as such is not very distinctive; thousands have it who are not poets, and perhaps a man cannot be a poet who has it not. But Mr. Meredith has it in a degree rare among even poets. It is at once his passion and his credo. Never is he so favoured of the Muse as when he speaks of "our only visible friend":—

[quotes "Ode to the Spirit of Earth in Autumn," lines 89–97]

There is something reverential, almost solemn, in the tone which Mr. Meredith uses with regard to Nature, which, we confess, greatly charms us. He does not, like some, condescendingly patronize and approve, implying that her merits must be very great, as he has been good enough to notice them. Neither does he affect a free and easy familiarity, which is nearly as disgusting. His feeling appears to be the yearning of love of a son to a mother to whom he owes all he is:—

[quotes "Ode to the Spirit of Earth in Autumn," lines 157–67]

Gladly would we quote the whole of the astonishing poem from which these extracts are taken. The "Ode to the Spirit of Earth in Autumn" . . . is replete with the very highest excellences of lyrical composition. It has a rush about it as of a mighty wind—the wild music of the south-west wind of which it sings—the *crescendo* roar of the rising gale, broken with lulls of flute-melody between. The volume of sound we especially notice. On this point we do not hesitate to say that Mr. Meredith need not fear comparison with even such a lyrist as Shelley, who, in his command over the most graceful, and power to paint the most evanescent, ideas, stands indeed supreme, but who never dashed from his harp such a storm of harmony as the poem before us:—

[quotes "Ode to the Spirit of Earth in Autumn," lines 98–128]

---

3. Thomas Hood (1799–1845), a British poet, illustrator, and humorist.
4. *gorse*: evergreen bush with yellow flowers

More important, and even more beautiful than Mr. Meredith's wonderful descriptive power is the spirit which prompts him to its use, the burden and meaning of his song. Mr. Meredith sings of Nature because he loves her, and wishes us to do the same, as the best thing for us. The clear tone of his voice is not falsified by any *arrière pensée*.[5] Shelley could hardly ever enjoy Nature for long without bringing in his fearful metaphysics. Wiser and better is this:—

[quotes "Ode to the Spirit of Earth in Autumn," lines 168–74, 231–38]

And so much for Mr. Meredith's treatment of outward Nature. But Mr. Meredith does not confine himself to rocks and fields, fond as he is of them. He goes without hesitation into the world of human action and suffering, and produces several pictures, some charged with the deepest and warmest colouring, others equally bright and jubilant. The tragical portion of these poems is represented by "Margaret's Bridal-Eve" and "Modern Love." As regards the first, we can only say that for delicacy of treatment and exquisite pathos it is absolutely perfect. As we cannot quote it all, we shall quote nothing, urging every reader to turn to it for himself. "Modern Love" is a poem which by no means wears its meaning conspicuous on the surface. On the contrary, it will be better understood on the second perusal than on the first, and better on the tenth than on the second. The "tragic hints" which are here given us of a great sorrow and misery will not permit us to make—even supposing that we could—a prosaic translation for the benefit of our readers. We prefer to leave the subject in the black shadows, the Rembrandt-like gloom into which the author has thrown it. This much may be said:—We perceive a man and woman—husband and wife—moving about in the darkness of shipwrecked love. With slow, deliberate analysis the artist has seized and graven the successive stages of this internal agony, decked as it is with laughing flowers to the outer world:—

[quotes "Modern Love" XVII and XXIII in their entirety]

Where every stanza is a mosaic of the closest setting, a miniature of the finest drawing, quotation is powerless or impertinent. Still, to impart some notion of this wonderful production, we give the following:—

[quotes "Modern Love" XLVI, XLVII, XLIX, and L in their entirety]

---

5. *arrière pensée*: afterthought or doubt

If the ode we first spoke of shows Mr. Meredith's poetical sympathy for and love of Nature, we think there can be no doubt that in "Modern Love" he has entered into the subtlest workings of two human hearts, and expressed the whole in the most gorgeous verse.

We have left ourselves but little space to dwell on the many other attractions of this volume. The whole series called "Poems of the English Roadside" is particularly worthy of attention. "Juggling Jerry," the first, is inimitable in its way. The worn-out old juggler coming to die on the common he had lived on as a boy, his reflections and jokes and manly resignation to his lot, are given with a broad, genial power of characterization very noteworthy. How well it begins:—

> [quotes "Juggling Jerry," lines 1–4 from stanza I,
> and stanzas II and III in their entirety]

We have spoken of these poems in terms of warm commendation, but not with one epithet more than they deserve, in our opinion. The probable addition of a new original genius to the goodly company of England's poets is not a matter on which it is easy to speak with stoical calmness. "Take special care of the beautiful," said Goethe, "for the useful can take care of itself."[6] Fully believing that Mr. Meredith is a true priest of the beautiful, ordained by Nature herself, we consider it a pleasure and a duty to give him a sincere welcome.

---

6. A common misquotation from the second volume of Goethe's *Wilhelm Meister's Apprenticeship*. Thomas Carlyle translates the sentence thusly: "The useful encourages itself; for the multitude produce it, and no one can dispense with it: the beautiful must be encouraged; for few can set it forth, and many need it" (London: Chapman and Hall, 1824), 132.

# R. H. Hutton, *Spectator* (1862)[1]

Richard Holt Hutton (1826–1897) was an English theologian, editor, and journalist. He rose to prominence thanks to his contributions to *The National Review*, a journal he coedited with Walter Bagehot from 1855 to 1862. By the time he wrote this scathing review of *Modern Love*, he had also become a coeditor and proprietor of the *Spectator*, a politically influential, liberal journal. Hutton scorned Meredith's decision to write a poem about marriage and sexual desire, denounced almost all of the volume's poems as "meretricious," and chided Meredith for failing to bring "original imaginative power or true sentiment" to the task of poetic creation. To obtain a better understanding of the kinds of ideas informing Hutton's critique, readers should refer to Massey's discussion of the Spasmodic school, Wilson's discussion of the difference between the sense of sight and the sense of hearing, and Bain's discussion of metaphor (see "On the Senses" and "Nineteenth-Century Poetics" sections).

Clever bold men with any literary capacity are always tempted to write verse, as they can say so much under its artistic cover which in common prose they could not say at all. It is a false impulse, however, for unless the form of verse is really that in which it is most natural for them to write, the effect of adopting it is to make the sharp hits which would be natural in prose, look out of place—lugged in by head and shoulders—and the audacity exceedingly repellent. This is certainly the effect upon us of this volume of verse. Mr. George Meredith is a clever man, without literary genius, taste, or judgment, and apparently aims at that sort of union of point, passion, and pictorial audacity which Byron attained in "Don Juan."[2] There is, however, no kind of harmonious concord between his ideas and

---

1. R. H. Hutton, "Mr. George Meredith's 'Modern Love,'" *Spectator* (24 May 1862): 580–81.

2. *"Don Juan"*: a playful long poem by Byron in which the legendary womanizer becomes a man who is continually seduced by women

his expressions; when he is *smart*, as he is habitually, the form of versifica-
tion makes the smartness look still more vulgar, and the jocularity jar far
more than it would in prose. On the whole the effect of the book on us is that
of clever, meretricious,[3] turbid[4] pictures, by a man of some vigour, jaunty
manners, quick observation, and some pictorial skill, who likes writing about
naked human passions, but does not bring either original imaginative power
or true sentiment to the task. The chief composition in the book, absurdly
called "Modern Love," is a series of sonnets intended to versify the leading
conception of Goethe's "elective affinities."[5] Mr. Meredith effects this with
occasional vigour, but without any vestige of original thought or purpose
which could excuse so unpleasant a subject, and intersperses it, moreover,
with sardonic grins that have all the effect of an intentional affection of cyni-
cism. This is not quite always the case, however, or we should soon throw
the book contemptuously aside; for the jocularities are intolerably feeble and
vulgar. The best, or one of the best sonnets, describes the concealed tragedy
of social life when the hero (if he is to be so called) with his wife and the lady
for whom he has since formed a passion are walking on the terrace before
dinner with a brilliant party:

[quotes "Modern Love" XXXVII in its entirety]

There is considerable vividness in this description, especially of the "grey se-
niors" who "question Time in irritable coughings," but the intended poetry
is meretricious; no one who feels truly can help feeling that to speak of "the
low, rosed moon" as "the face of Music mute," is a snatch at the glitter and
varnish of apparent, not real poetry. There is no analogy, subtle or other-
wise, between the round simplicity of the moon's face and the spirit of music,
which always involves the unity of melodious variety. A true poet has said,

> Slow, slow, fall
> With indecisive motion eddying down,
> The white-winged flakes, *calm as the sleep of sound*,
> Dim as a dream;[6]

---

3. *meretricious*: tastelessly showy

4. *turbid*: unclear, hazy

5. *"elective affinities"*: Goethe's 1809 novella *Elective Affinities* was named after the scientific
term that describes the tendency of certain chemicals or compounds to unite with others. Goethe used
the term as a metaphor for exploring the emotional chemistry between individuals, and the novella
explored the institution of marriage.

6. From David Gray's *The Luggie and Other Poems* (London: Macmillan, 1862).

and this is beautiful, for it really translates the language of hearing into the language of sight. But to speak of the moon as "[the] face of Music mute," appeals to no subtle analogy at all, and is a mere unmeaning eulogium on that admirable planet. Such a criticism is doubtless small,—but in these minute touches lies the true distinction between a poet and one

> Who hides with ornament his want of Art.[7]

Mr. George Meredith has a sense of what is graphic, but he never makes an excursion beyond that into what he intends for poetry without falling into some trick of false ornamentation. For one more example we will take the most reflective of these sonnets, in which Mr. Meredith is teaching us how to learn from Nature not to attach ourselves irretrievably to any mortal thing. The idea is forcibly expressed till it is intended to rise into a sort of tragic climax at the end, when it soars into an absurd parody of Tennysonian metaphor that is a perfect specimen of the foolish-sublime:

> [quotes "Modern Love" XIII in its entirety]

What is the "forever of a kiss"? Is Mr. Meredith trying to distinguish between "the transient" and "the permanent" in kisses, "das reine seyn" and "reine nichts" as the German sages say,[8] and to single out the permanent element, that which expresses "the infinite." If this rash suggestion be at all near the mark, we are still painfully in the dark as to the force of the word "renewed." If the "renewed forever of a kiss" in any way refers to the renewal of this infinite element, as ordinary people would suppose—why is *this* the moment when we are exhorted to "*lose* calmly love's great bliss"? If it be a leave-taking the force of the word "renewed" on this particular crisis is hid from us. And what are we to say of the last line? Surely the "sound" of a kiss is not the true poetic and permanent element therein? If there is a "forever"—an eternal element—in these expressive symbolic actions at all, we submit that it is not in the sound,—that on the contrary the sound is an accidental and rather unfortunate adjunct and accident in them. And what can Mr. Meredith mean to suggest by speaking of them as sounding through a "listless hurricane of hair"? That which is heard through a hurricane—though we will not rashly answer for a "listless" hurricane, hurricanes usually appearing to

---

7. A slight misquotation from Alexander Pope's *Essay on Criticism* (1711).

8. *"das reine seyn" and "reine nichts"*: These are Hegel's terms: "the pure being" and "the pure nothing."

us quite too much in earnest,—is usually a thunderclap and nothing less,—and if Mr. Meredith really means to be sentimental about a kiss that in any way resembles a thunderclap, we fear few will fall into his mood. Probably the "listless hurricane of hair" was meant as a gorgeous metaphor addressed to the eye and not to the ear—the hair being a non-conductor of sound, softening or smothering the loud report alluded to, and resembling a "listless hurricane," only in the tumultuous tangle of agitated locks, expressive of the *abandon* of great grief. But turn it how you will we fear this meretricious piece of fine writing turns out to mean that some very loud sound has been heard in spite of great obstacles—which sound and which obstacles are supposed to heighten the anguish of renunciation. We fear there was something of a "listless hurricane" of ideas in the author's mind when he extemporized this very noble language.

This, it will be said, is verbal criticism; but that is not so. No clever man who prizes grandiloquent ornament above modest meaning is guilty of a mere verbal negligence, for this goes to the heart of the matter. Mr. Meredith, too (though, so far as we understand the intended drift of his "Modern Love," we can accuse it of nothing worse than meddling causelessly, and somewhat pruriently, with a deep and painful subject, on which he has no convictions to express), sometimes treats serious themes with a flippant levity that is exceedingly vulgar and unpleasant, and perhaps even unjust to himself:

[quotes "Modern Love" XXV in its entirety]

This is wretched jocularity, as pointless as it is coarse, and though it is certainly the worst sonnet in the series, after reading the whole through several times, there seems to us no more purpose, poetic or moral, to be got out of the series, than out of this single sonnet,—the general drift being that there is a good deal of tragic misunderstanding, leading to desperate unfaithfulness in the marriage of proud minds who might have been very happy if they had so chosen;—a common-place which is illustrated with a freedom that mistakes itself for courage, and is simply bad and prurient taste. The thing has no kind of right to the title "Modern Love": "Modern Lust" would be certainly a more accurate though not a true title, there is something of real love, but more of the other embodied in the sonnets.

In the verses which do not hinge on this sort of subject, there is the same confusion between a "fast" taste and what Mr. Meredith mistakes for courageous realism,—poetic pre-Raphaelitism. For instance, Mr. Meredith has, in some verses on a scene in the Alps, given us a vision of the spirit of Beauty, whom he proposes in a vehement kind of half-and-half enthusiasm, one half sentiment the other half beer, to introduce to a London cabman. The poem is long and rambling, but we extract such verses as bear upon this great idea. The poet is speaking at first,—as we gather,—of the spirit of poetic beauty:

[quotes "By the Rosanna," lines 57–64, 73–80, 91–96, 109–18, and 137–44]

This is not intellectual courage, nor buoyancy of spirit, nor anything but a spasmodic ostentation of fast writing.[9] There are moods in which a man of high animal spirits is apt to think that any nonsense which amuses himself in an irrational moment is good enough to amuse the world; and because Mr. George Meredith was amused for the moment with the incongruity of fancying a greasy-coated cabman with his arm round Calliope,[10] and with his own poor pun on that person's "driving the world," he thought it, we suppose, a mark of intellectual pluck to print it. It really is only noisy vulgarity, which, in so clever a man—for he is clever and graphic in his way—is exceedingly unworthy. There is a deep vein of muddy sentiment in most men, but they should let the mud settle, and not boast of it to the world. Mr. Meredith evidently thinks mud picturesque, as, indeed, it may be, but all picturesqueness is not poetry. One gains a graphic picture of a good deal of interior mental mud without verse to help us. Mr. Meredith thinks we do not get enough, and the solution given here is sometimes a very thick one indeed. The best thing in the book is "Juggling Jerry," which is not vulgar nor tawdry, as so much of the volume is.

---

9. See excerpt from Massey's essay in the "Nineteenth-Century Poetics" section for more details regarding the Spasmodic school of poetry.

10. *Calliope*: Greek muse of heroic poetry

# J. W. Marston, *Athenaeum* (1862)[1]

John Westland Marston (1819–1890) was an English critic, poet, and playwright whose intellectual circle included Charles Dickens, Robert Browning, Philip Bailey, and D. G. Rossetti. In 1856 he co-founded *The National Maga\i{}ine*, a journal that published the work of Pre-Raphaelite and Spasmodic poets, and he wrote for the *Athenaeum* from 1850 to 1875. The *Athenaeum* was established in 1828 with the avowed aim of becoming "the resort of the distinguished philosophers, historians, and orators and poets of our day." In its early years, it took a stand against "logrolling," that is, publishing uncritically positive reviews of work by friends and business associates, and by the 1840s it had become one of England's most influential journals devoted to literature, science, and the fine arts. Criticizing the poems in *Modern Love* for their vulgarity as well as their obscurity, Marston, like those who decried the Spasmodic school and the unnamed reviewers that Hallam criticizes in his essay on Tennyson's poetry (see "Nineteenth-Century Poetics" section), insists that good poetry ought to be immediately intelligible to readers.

T he story of "Modern Love" is rather hinted at than told. There is nothing of orderly statement and little of clear and connected suggestion. These sonnets resemble scattered leaves from the diary of a stranger. The allusions, the comments, the interjections, all refer to certain particulars which are not directly related, and have to be painfully deduced. We are not sure that, after great labour, we have arrived at Mr. Meredith's drift; but we are quite sure that, if we have, we do not care for it. So far as we have groped our way, the tale seems that of a man who is jealous of his wife. It appears that she is still faithful to the bonds of wedlock, though not to

---

1. "*Modern Love and Poems of the English Roadside, with Poems and Ballads*," *Athenaeum* (31 May 1862): 719–20. In *Meredith: The Critical Heritage* (New York: Barnes & Noble, 1971), Ioan Williams attributes the review to J. W. Marston, but *Athenaeum*'s index does not corroborate this.

those of love. The phases of the husband's torture are elaborately set forth—often with spasmodic[2] indistinctness, but now and then with real force and imagination. A May-day recalls the Spring when she yet loved him. At a village festival he sardonically contrasts his refined misery with the coarse happiness of the revellers. At dinner the wedded pair play host and hostess, and mask their wretchedness with smiles. Here is a recollection of past joy, which appeals to the heart through ear and eye, like an echo from a ruin:

[quotes "Modern Love" XVI in its entirety]

Few of the sonnets, however, are so intelligible as the foregoing. The abrupt and obscure style which too often prevails may be learnt from the next example. Yet, whoever has patience to spell out its meaning, may catch a fine image in the closing lines:—

[quotes "Modern Love" V in its entirety]

It would seem—but we still write under correction—that the husband strives to console himself by the stimulant of a new passion. We infer that the expedient is a double failure. Yielding no relief to the conscientious husband, it revives, through jealousy, the all-but-dead affection of his wife. But her contrition apparently comes too late, for we think she takes poison. Still, this is a mere conjecture, from a dark hint or two, which the reader can interpret for himself:—

[quotes "Modern Love" XLIX, lines 13–16]

We have already intimated that "Modern Love" contains passages of true beauty and feeling; but they are like the casual glimpses of a fair landscape in some noxious clime, where the mists only break to gather again more densely. Besides, the best gifts of expression would be wasted on a theme so morbid as the present. It is true that poetic genius has often revealed to us the diseases of our nature; but they have been only a portion of the exhibition. The causes which produced them, and the results in which they were expiated or subdued, have also been given. The bane has shown the virtue of the antidote. In "Modern Love" we have disease, and nothing else.

With a sense of relief we turn to the more wholesome poems in the volume. "Grandfather Bridgeman" is a pathetic story, told with fair effect and

---

2. See excerpt of Massey's essay in the "Nineteenth-Century Poetics" section for more details regarding the Spasmodic school of poetry.

with some success in the delineation of character. In his portrait of the farmer, however, Mr. Meredith does not always discriminate between the homely and the coarse. The poem is disfigured, too, by abrupt transitions, and, at times, by a vagueness of style inexcusable in one who can write to the point when he pleases. "The Old Chartist," again, is well drawn upon the whole; but the lesson which he derives from a water-rat, though correct, is not sufficiently obvious. A moral of this kind should not have to be reasoned out, but, like that of the fable, should seize the reader at once. Of Mr. Meredith's character-pieces the best is "Juggling Jerry." Jerry is a conjuror struck with mortal sickness: he pitches his tent on a familiar spot, where his old horse has been used to graze, and where the gorse blooms from which he has often hung his kettle. In this scene he recalls to his wife the story of their lives, and strives to comfort her in the closing hours of their union. The pathos and humour of this conception enhance each other, while the poor juggler's love of nature is true in itself and expressed in the graphic idioms that befit the speaker. The lyric of "Cassandra" embodies a fine conception of the dying prophetess, and is free from the blemishes of caprice and obscurity. We cannot say as much for "Phantasy," which is founded on the poetical superstition of The Willis. "Phantasy" is written with spirit, and contains some striking though grotesque pictures. We grant that the subject admits of fantastic treatment; but freedom is here pushed into licence. In poetry, even humour should not be prosaic and coarse; but Mr. Meredith's is both. His dancing Phantom has nothing of the supernatural charm that belonged to her in the original legend, which, by the way, formed some years since the groundwork of a *ballet* for Taglioni.[3] The *danseuse* might have taught a lesson to the poet. She raised the invention of the *maître de ballet*[4] into poetry; Mr. Meredith takes a poetical conception and degrades it into that of a ballet-girl:—

[quotes "Phantasy" VIII, lines 2–4]

This whim of thrusting bald realities into poetry reaches its climax in the lines headed "By the Rosanna." The poem opens with a life-like description of the "torrent river," and the dash of its waters is caught happily in the verse. The grandeur of nature, however, only suggests to Mr. Meredith London by

---

3. *ballet for Taglioni*: *Giselle, ou Les Wilis*, first performed in Paris in 1841 and in London in 1842. Marie Taglioni (1804–1884) was a leading ballerina of the Romantic era, but *Giselle* was created for ballerina Carlotta Grisi, not Taglioni.

4. *maître de ballet*: ballet master

gaslight; and, for the Naiad[5] who should haunt the solitude, he invokes the "Season-Beauty," who, in this case, seems to be an inveterate jilt. After other profound questions touching the lady, he demands,—

[quotes "By the Rosanna," lines 73–76]

Of course there is a philosophy running through this doggerel, and we subscribe to the writer's doctrine when he says,—

If Sentiment won't wed with Fact,
    Poor Sentiment soon needs perfuming. ["By the Rosanna," lines 93–94]

—Still, the "fact," however plain, must have a poetic life in it. Of course there may be such life in a cabman; but to find it we must see the man's nature, not merely the "short neck" and "many capes" which represent him here. Mr. Meredith's forced transitions from the ideal to the prosaic are merely an outrage upon taste. The versatility at which he aims is admirable when shown within the limits of Art, but worthless as easy when it transgresses them.

The absurdities of this volume are the more to be lamented because, in spite of them, it displays some fine qualities. There is an Autumnal Ode, for instance, which, though not free from the author's besetting vagueness, has noble passages. The wild evening finds its faithful mirror and the wind its own turbulent chant in the lines that follow:—

[quotes "Ode to the Spirit of the Earth in Autumn," lines 28–46]

Few readers, we think, will deny the poetic feeling and the truth of observation which our extract reveals. But if these gifts are to produce a lasting result, Mr. Meredith must add to them a healthier purpose, a purer taste and a clearer style.

---

5. *Naiad*: water nymph

# A. C. Swinburne, *Spectator* (1862)[1]

Algernon Charles Swinburne (1837–1909) was a cosmopolitan poet, playwright, and literary critic who wrote for the *Fortnightly Review*, the *Athenaeum*, and the *Spectator*—among other periodicals. His poetry, starting with his *Poems and Ballads* (1866), is associated with the Decadent and Art for Art's Sake movements. A friend of D. G. Rossetti's since their Oxford days, Swinburne shared a house in London with him, William Michael Rossetti, and Meredith from 1862 to 1863. A direct response to Hutton's *Spectator* review (provided earlier), Swinburne's passionate defense of *Modern Love* asks readers to judge the quality of Meredith's verse for themselves and censures Hutton's review for (what Swinburne regards as) its insolence and old-fashioned demand that poetry take conventionally moral positions thereby limiting its "scope of sight" to "the nursery walls." We include here Hutton's printed editorial response to this letter.

Sir,—I cannot resist asking the favour of admission for my protest against the article on Mr. Meredith's last volume of poems in the *Spectator* of May 24th. That I personally have for the writings, whether verse or prose, of Mr. Meredith a most sincere and deep admiration is no doubt a matter of infinitely small moment. I wish only, in default of a better, to appeal seriously on general grounds against this sort of criticism as applied to one of the leaders of English literature. To any fair attack Mr. Meredith's books of course lie as much open as another man's; indeed, standing where he does, the very eminence of his post makes him perhaps more liable than a man of less well-earned fame to the periodical slings and arrows of publicity. Against such criticism no one would have a right to appeal, whether for his own work or for another's. But the writer of the article in question blinks at starting [*sic*] the fact that he is dealing with no unfledged pretender. Any

1. Algernon C. Swinburne, "Letter to the Editor," *Spectator* (7 June 1862): 632–33.

work of a man who has won his spurs, and fought his way to a foremost place among the men of his time, must claim at least a grave consideration and respect. It would hardly be less absurd, in remarking on a poem by Mr. Meredith, to omit all reference to his previous work, and treat the present book as if its author had never tried his hand at such writing before, than to criticize the *Légende des Siècles*,[2] or (coming to a nearer instance) the *Idylls of the King*, without taking into account the relative position of the great English or the greater French poet. On such a tone of criticism as this any one who may chance to see or hear of it has a right to comment.

But even if the case were different, and the author were now at his starting-point, such a review of such a book is surely out of date. Praise or blame should be thoughtful, serious, careful, when applied to a work of such subtle strength, such depth of delicate power, such passionate and various beauty, as the leading poem of Mr. Meredith's volume: in some points, as it seems to me (and in this opinion I know that I have weightier judgments than my own to back me) a poem above the aim and beyond the reach of any but its author. Mr. Meredith is one of the three or four poets now alive whose work, perfect or imperfect, is always as noble in design as it is often faultless in result. The present critic falls foul of him for dealing with "a deep and painful subject on which he has no conviction to express." There are pulpits enough for all preachers in prose; the business of verse-writing is hardly to express convictions; and if some poetry, not without merit of its kind, has at times dealt in dogmatic morality, it is all the worse and all the weaker for that. As to subject, it is too much to expect that all schools of poetry are to be for ever subordinate to the one just now so much in request with us, whose scope of sight is bounded by the nursery walls; that all Muses are to bow down before her who babbles, with lips yet warm from their pristine pap, after the dangling delights of a child's coral;[3] and jingles with flaccid fingers one knows not whether a jester's or a baby's bells. We have not too many writers capable of duly handling a subject worth the serious interest of men. As to execution, take almost any sonnet at random out of the series, and let any man qualified to judge for himself of metre, choice of expression, and splendid language, decide on its claims. And, after all, the test will be unfair, except as regards metrical or pictorial merit; every section of this great progressive poem being

---

2. *La Légende des Siècles*: a poem by French author Victor Hugo
3. *child's coral*: teether

connected with the other by links of the finest and most studied workman-ship. Take, for example, that noble sonnet, beginning

We saw the swallows gathering in the skies, ["Modern Love" XLVII]

a more perfect piece of writing no man alive has ever turned out; witness these three lines, the grandest perhaps of the book:

[quotes "Modern Love" XLVII, lines 5–7]

but in transcription it must lose the colour and effect given it by its place in the series; the grave and tender beauty, which makes it at once a bridge and a resting-place between the admirable poems of passion it falls among. As specimens of pure power, and depth of imagination at once intricate and vig-orous, take the two sonnets on a false passing reunion of wife and husband; the sonnet on the rose; that other beginning:

[quotes "Modern Love" XX, lines 1–3]

And, again, that earlier one:

All other joys of life he strove to warm, ["Modern Love" IV, line 1]

Of the shorter poems which give character to the book I have not space to speak here; and as the critic has omitted noticing the most valuable and important (such as the "Beggar's Soliloquy," and "The Old Chartist," equal to Béranger[4] for completeness of effect and exquisite justice of style, but no-ticeable for a thorough dramatic insight, which Béranger missed through his personal passions and partialities), there is no present need to go into the matter. I ask you to admit this protest simply out of justice to the book in hand, believing as I do that it expresses the deliberate unbiassed opinion of a sufficient number of readers to warrant the insertion of it, and leaving to your consideration rather their claims to a fair hearing than those of the book's author to a revised judgment. A poet of Mr. Meredith's rank can no more be profited by the advocacy of his admirers than injured by the rash or partial attack of his critics.

—A. C. Swinburne

---

4. Pierre-Jean de Béranger (1780–1857), French poet, songwriter, political satirist; Chapman and Hall published a translation of his songs in 1847.

[We insert this gladly, from personal respect to our correspondent, whose opinion on any poetical question should be worth more than most men's, but must reiterate that it was not after a hasty, but the most careful study of Mr. Meredith's book that we passed our judgment upon it, a judgment which would not have been so severe had not Mr. Meredith earned a right to be judged as a man of some mark. We do not know to what school Mr. Swinburne may allude as writing the childish-moral poetry. No eminent poets of the kind are known to us. —Ed. *Spectator*.]

# Frederick Maxse, *Morning Post* (1862)[1]

Although he dedicated *Modern Love* to his friend Frederick Maxse, Meredith nevertheless asked the young captain to review the volume for the *Morning Post*. Maxse's review was based upon a partial manuscript of the volume, and despite minor criticisms, is little more than a puff piece. "You should have whipped me on the score of the absurdities, obscurities, and what not. I feel you have been sparing me, and though I don't love the rod, I don't cry for mercy," Meredith wrote to Maxse after reading it.[2]

All lovers of literature have long been aware that among the large group of authors now distinguishing the country, there is no more rising man than Mr. George Meredith; neither is it necessary with them, as it may be with the ordinary reader, to warn against the confusion of his name with that of Mr. Owen Meredith.[3] George Meredith has been slow in acquiring his audience; but the audience once gained remember his last words and wait patiently for the next, their number steadily increasing, and desertion not known among them. Excepting a small but remarkable volume of verse which appeared 10 years ago, his claim on the public has been purely as a prose writer, first in the *Shaving of Shagpat*, where, in the license of Oriental romance, he gave legitimate proof of a brilliancy of imagination which he has since, however tempting the circumstances, sternly subdued to the requirements of art; secondly, in the *Ordeal of Richard Feverel*, perhaps somewhat too blunt in its truth, too indifferent in a better stuff to the mere velvet of morality, and injudiciously interrupted by the contents of a certain "Scrip of Proverbs," which, though original and striking by themselves, serve to trip

1. Frederick Maxse, "Poems of George Meredith," *Morning Post* (London), 20 June 1862: 6.
2. *Letters*, I.75.
3. Owen Meredith was the pseudonym of the first Earl of Lytton, Edward Robert Bulwer-Lytton, a poet, novelist, and public servant.

the heels of most readers without obtaining the attention which is their due; yet, notwithstanding these drawbacks, a book wherein a real master seizes the mind with Carlyle-like fascination from the first page to the last, and niches one character, that of Adrian, the stomach-philosopher, a permanent figure in memory; and, lastly, in *Evan Harrington*, in which, the rapidity of work for weekly issue allowing no time for that vigorous condensation Mr. George Meredith has the rare strength to apply, the public received a better opportunity of learning the prolific conception and vast store of humour, pathos, and fancy he has so abundantly and unrestrictedly at command, and impressing both reader and critic with the richness yet reserved.

In the present instance it is a volume of poetry with which Mr. George Meredith favours us, dedicated to Captain Maxse, R. N. Hitherto it has been the poet writing prose; but if an author possesses the power of being concrete with any sense of music, there can be no doubt but what his proper field is that of verse, no there can be none that it is the higher form of expression and the surer mode of influence. This, notwithstanding Mr. Disraeli's dissertation on the matter,[4] and his dictum that it is time to have done with the "barbaric clash of rhyme"—a sentiment implying a preference for the diffuseness of little to the concentration of much, and of fatal encouragement to several voluminous writers, who would be so much improved were they occasionally to exercise themselves with the trammels of verse. It is a good sign when a writer returns to poetry after a due performance in prose; it shows an increase of power and a genuine vitality in the muse, in contradistinction to the mere lyrical exuberance of youth which puts out at 19 the one thin volume of verse, and henceforth finds an easy exhaustion in prose. It is the later desire for the concentration of "thick coming fancies" away from prose that marks the true poet, and which with high satisfaction we find in George Meredith. Also, because poetry is so much worthier of the twofold nature perceivable in this author's writings, the "androgynal"[5] nature which Coleridge has remarked as appertaining to great, but which more properly belongs to "poetical," minds, and which feminine intuition is indispensable to the poet, the two married natures combining largeness of sympathy with keenness of instinct. The volume now published is characterised by this qualification, and

---

4. Before serving as conservative prime minister of England in 1868 and again from 1874 to 1880, Benjamin Disraeli (1804–1881) was a man of letters; the quote is from his 1832 novel *Contarini Fleming*.

5. "*androgynal*": having qualities of both sexes; Coleridge's line was "The truth is, a great mind must be androgynous," as recorded in *Specimens of the Table Talk of Samuel Taylor Coleridge* (1835).

it is the more striking on account of the rugged force there is in the verse. There is a strength reactionary from the tenderness, a tenderness approved by the strength, and a creation arising from the two which, if taken up in any way but superficially, must permanently establish its author's reputation. But, alas! there is so much smooth and glib verse current that it is doubtful whether there is any very large public left with a sense of what is fine and subtle. The slightest obscurity or difficulty in a passage, though the passage contain a true diamond, will intimidate those who have become accustomed to seize paste with avidity; and, therefore, while George Meredith's poetry is appreciated by the few preserving their purity, it is doubtful whether it will become popular until these leaders have made it standard.

Still, while certain of the eventual acknowledgement of this writer's claim to repute, we may in common with other well-wishers desire that he would cast less often mantles of obscurity over some of his very finest passages. It may be desirable perhaps that all readers should equally enjoy cerebral exercise with poetic sympathy; but the combination of taste is not that of any large public, as Mr. Tennyson and Mr. Robert Browning both discovered, though but the former to profit by. It is not want of simplicity with which Mr. George Meredith can be charged as a rule, for it exists in the most frequent and homely manner; but apparently only spontaneously. There seems some obstinacy to adopt that high essential when the idea has once fallen in its first crude and vigorous obscurity.

The present publication opens with a ballad entitled "Grandfather Bridgeman"—stirring and bright as only an English brook can be, and equally strong and healthy under its passing cloud; after which comes the most important piece in the volume, a poem in 50 sonnets, entitled "Modern Love." The tale told is the hidden and inner tragedy of a false love which is flowing blackly beneath the semblance of a happy married life:—

[quotes "Modern Love" I, lines 3–6, 8–13; and II, lines 1–4, 12–16]

As the husband's Palace of Love lies in mere shards at his feet, the fearfulness of passionate despair is divulged partly in its own cries, partly in the revealing stroke of the poet:—

[quotes "Modern Love" X, lines 1–3, 11–16]

He invokes nature to solve the hideous paradox. There she is, leaning over human misery with the smile adamant, still

[quotes "Modern Love" XI, lines 6–10]

And thus she answers:—

[quotes "Modern Love" XIII, lines 1–2, 5–10]

From which, though he breaks off impetuously:—

[quotes "Modern Love" XIII, lines 13–16]

and comes an exquisite sonnet of bereavement and loss:—

[quotes "Modern Love" XVI in its entirety]

The poet here bares all the delicate agony of the large heart whose faith and stake were in the one love—whose fealty had been ever to the divine exaltation of the passion in contrast to its commoner abasement to animalism, but to which now, transformed, subjugated to the flinty skepticism of the world:—

[quotes "Modern Love" XXIX, lines 13–16]

Shrouded in cynicism, his stupefied nature observes a trenchant irony to the wife, while at the same time indulging in a contemptuous appetite towards a certain "golden-headed" lady who is near. There is a skin of poetry even over his passage with her; he could notice how:—

[quotes "Modern Love" XXXVII, lines 10–12]

The course and conclusion of the two guilts, the deliberate and the desperate, are shadowed forth in "tragic hints," which, in conformity with the wreck of the two lives, permits of no consecutive sketch. There comes no angel to mediate, albeit each hour held salvation, especially one, in which, however, but freezing conjugal formalities pass, or:—

Our chain through silence clanks. ["Modern Love" XXXIV, line 3]

For after all it seems the wife, pure, was reclaimable; but he relentlessly held to distraction in the "golden-headed" one, though at times alarmed, lest the old love still breathed,

[quotes "Modern Love" XL, lines 4–6 and 15–16]

As a strange climax to the terrible drama, the wife sacrifices her home rather to the desire of peace for her husband, who might then "seek that other," than to any search of a drug for herself, or infatuation for the original "disturbing shadow." After which there is an abrupt conclusion in her death, and a laconic epitaph on the part of the author.

Turning from the spell of this powerful production, here is a sweet lyric, called "The Young Usurper":—

[quotes "The Young Usurper" in its entirety]

To classical taste the following poem of "Cassandra" may be submitted; there is a roll through it, and so true a ring of inspiration that (with previous commendation of the choral cast of each final line) we can only present it to the reader entire:—

[quotes "Cassandra" in its entirety]

Entirely Mr. George Meredith's own are his "Roadside Philosophers," a set of ballads in the form of monologues, and placed in the mouth of men lowest in the social scale, such as a juggler, an old Chartist returned from transportation, a beggar, and a working engineer. The writer evidently enjoys the study of this class of character, and the interpretation of their souls, in much the same manner as the great artist of *Adam Bede* and *Silas Marner.*[6] Poor old "Juggling Jerry" is dying out on the common, and expatiates to his faithful "old girl" upon the

[quotes "Juggling Jerry" XII, lines 1–4]

And informs her at such a moment

[quotes "Juggling Jerry" IX, lines 1–8]

The old Chartist draws his moral, as he sits by a ditch, from an old brown rat, who sits on a mudbank trying to clean himself, though "his trade is dirt," bent notwithstanding this upon his own self-esteem: and the "Beggar's Soliloquy" is full of rough and humourous perception, as one Sunday he lies on the heath watching the people go to church:—

[quotes "The Beggar's Soliloquy" III, lines 1–8]

Thus curtly the vagabond disposes of the grand sentiment:—

---

6. *Adam Bede* (1859) and *Silas Marner* (1861): two novels by George Eliot (née Mary Ann Evans, 1819–1880), considered masterworks of Realism and valued for frank depictions of rural life

> Love burns as long as the lucifer match,
>      Wedlock's the candle! Now, that's my creed. [II, lines 7–8]

The "Meeting" may be remembered as published in *Once a Week*, with a felicitous illustration by Mr. Millais:—

[quotes "The Meeting" in its entirety]

"Margaret's Bridal Eve" is another passionate woe tale, wherein is the same mastery of stroke in stamping and linking together what traits are most powerful in portraying drama. A beautiful lost but noble creature, Margaret is, after the lover's death, in spite of her own protests, about to be palmed off in marriage by an old quean[7] of a mother upon a new lover, but the girl, though she "bleeds to death," is determined to "let out the lie" to him; so, on the bridal eve

[quotes "Margaret's Bridal-Eve" IV, lines 41–44]

The burden of the rose which runs through the ballad is seemingly designed to relieve the tragic incident in the mind of the reader. There is a whole volume in the "eyes between his." In a piece called "Phantasy" occurs this voluptuous picture of Naiads:—[8]

[quotes "Phantasy" XVIII, lines 1–4]

But the temptation to extract is leading to excess of space, and probably enough has been given to make all genuine lovers of poetry prefer the satisfaction of referring to the volume for themselves.

---

7. *quean*: hussy
8. *Naiads*: water nymphs

# From Unsigned Review, *Westminster Review* (1862)[1]

The *Westminster Review* was a radical quarterly journal edited by a variety of luminaries, such as Jeremy Bentham, George Eliot, John Stuart Mill, and Mark Pattison. From the latter half of 1857 through January 1858, Meredith himself wrote the "Belles Lettres" column, taking it over from Eliot. This review begins with a discussion about meter in modern translations of ancient poetry before comparing *Modern Love* with the recent work of several other English poets. The author praises Meredith's poetic technique but laments his evident interest in "guilt and sin."

In Mr. George Meredith's poems, there is a freshness and vigour not often met with at the present day. Moreover, there are no traces in them of imitation of any of our popular poets. Their faults are frequent roughness and occasional obscurity. Some of Mr. Meredith's lines are very terse and effective. Several passages in his poems prove him to be a sharp observer and skillful analyst of human motives. Let the following serve as an example:—

[quotes "Modern Love" XLI, lines 1–6]

There is much truth in this remark by "The Old Chartist":—

> She suffered for me:—women, you'll observe,
> Don't suffer for a Cause, but for a man. [XIII, lines 1–2]

There is both truth and force in the lines employed by a beggar to characterize a lady:—

[quotes "The Beggar's Soliloquy" IV, lines 1–3]

---

1. "Belles Lettres," *Westminster Review* (July 1862): 284–86. The Wellesley Index offers no authorial attribution for this review.

How much is condensed in the following short lines:—

> Life is but the pebble sunk;
>> Deeds, the circle growing! ["The Head of Bran," lines 27–28]

It is unfortunate that the subjects of many of these poems are tales of guilt and sin, of women's temptation and fall. The manner in which Mr. Meredith treats his subjects convinces us that he has real poetical talents, and is capable, too, of producing still more effective poems than those contained in this volume.

# Unsigned Review, *Saturday Review* (1863)[1]

Founded in 1855 just after the repeal of the Newspaper Stamp Act, which by reducing per-page taxes on newspapers lowered the costs of production and subscriptions, the politically conservative *Saturday Review of Politics, Literature, Science and Art* soon gained a large readership. Known for its misogyny and elitist, caustic tone, it was nicknamed the "Saturday Reviler." This review opens by praising the "obvious and simple design" of "The Old Chartist," yet ultimately finds the more "ambitious" poems in the volume—particularly "Modern Love" and the usually admired "Ode to the Spirit of Earth in Autumn"—to be pretentious and in bad taste.

We are in the present day overrun by clever writers of fiction, and of that species of verse which is spun from the same kind of intellectual web that produces fiction. But the names of English novelists and versifiers now living who may be said to unite real originality of thought and aim with conspicuous cleverness in workmanship are almost few enough to be counted on the fingers. Among these few Mr. George Meredith unquestionably holds a place. His novel of *Evan Harrington*, which appeared three or four years ago, contained some of the most purely original conceptions that have been attempted by any writer of novels of character for a long time past. The same may be said of the volume of poems which he has, like Professor Kingsley, Miss Muloch, Mr. Farrar,[2] and half a score more, as in duty bound, composed and published. He is in the habit of genuinely

---

1. "Mr. George Meredith's Poems," *Saturday Review* (24 October 1863): 562–63. The Wellesley Index offers no authorial attribution for this review.

2. Charles Kingsley (1819–1875), a professor of history, is perhaps best known for his fiction, including *Westward, Ho!* (1855) and *The Water Babies* (1863); Dinah Maria Mulock (1826–1887), later Mrs. Craik, is a novelist most famous for writing *John Halifax, Gentleman* (1857); Frederick William Farrar (1831–1903), a novelist and theologian, was author of *Eric, or Little by Little* (1858). All three also composed poetry.

drawing from his own resources of observation and reflection, and his strong thought and quaint expression remind us, here and there—though at a considerable interval—of Robert Browning. In skill of phrase and rhyme he is quite as happy as his greater contemporary, and often less obscure. The poem of "The Old Chartist" is, for instance, a capital piece of writing, with an obvious and simple design. An ancient shoemaker, who in early life has had the misfortune to cross the water on account of misbehaviour on a Chartist platform, returns to his native town at the expiration of his time, and is converted to common sense by seeing a water-rat scrubbing his face contentedly by a brookside. The fresh-hearted old vagabond is made to soliloquize thus:—

[quotes "The Old Chartist" I–II]

He presently espies the water-rat going through his morning's washing, and the train of natural thought and feeling set in motion by that sight is exceedingly well described. The first wonder is the apparent incongruity of cleanliness with the antecedents and present position of a rat:—

[quotes "The Old Chartist" VII, lines 1–4]

In the eye of nature, however, there seems to be nothing incongruous:—

[quotes "The Old Chartist" IX]

This simple spectacle introduces into the breast of the old grumbler the thin end of the wedge of self-knowledge. He has been picking holes in his superiors' coats and denouncing the wrong, while he ought to have been *doing* the right. He will henceforward be wiser, and live the life of the rat, "pleasing himself and his Creator." He will go quietly home, mend the gentry's boots, comfort his old wife—who, while detesting his ways and his views, had faithfully stood by him with the consoling tea-can in the dock—and on some future Sunday he will bring his fine daughter, with her smug draper-husband, to see the model democrat of the mud-bank. The "Old Chartist" is certainly a good piece of writing of its kind, and "Juggling Jerry," the "Beggar's Soliloquy," and "Grandfather Bridgeman," are nearly, if not quite, up to the same standard.

It is in the direction of this racy and vigorous style of composition that Mr. George Meredith's real *forte* lies, though he would hardly be inclined to subscribe to that opinion. Few people who have aimed at fine writing find it easy or pleasant to believe that their strength lies, after all, in something which, from the fine writer's point of view, seems to be very far below. However, a perusal of Mr. George Meredith's more ambitious productions, and especially of "Modern Love"—the composition which he has thought worthy of giving a name to his collection—leads one reluctantly to the conclusion that he has entirely mistaken his powers, and has utterly marred what might have been a rare and successful volume. It was bad enough to quit the "English Roadside" for a ranting rhapsody like the "Ode to the Spirit of Earth in Autumn," which we should conjecture to have been written at a very early age, when Shelley was less perfectly understood than ardently and blindly adored. The lines which follow, and which are supposed to indicate the rising of a violent south-wester, are among the milder and less uproarious passages of the ode:—

[quotes "Ode to the Spirit of Earth in Autumn," lines 36–46]

The first line reminds one of the old illustration to the fable, where the traveller, wrapped in a cloak, is plodding along beneath the influence of two round faces, one representing the north wind and the other the sun. The single voice issuing from the "outpuff'd cheeks" is made to boom "a chorus" to the preluding shrieks, the nature of which last we should conceive that it must be equally difficult to imagine and to describe. The "yellow realm of stiffen'd Day" no doubt sounds as if something like it might have occurred in *In Memoriam*; but we venture to assert that no parallel passage to the line is to be found in that poem, any more than to the "thunderingly streaming" [*sic*] appearance which was remarked in the south-west wind's mantle. There is a passage in the otherwise excellent poem called "Grandfather Bridgeman" which is congenial to these extracts, and seems too good of its sort to be omitted. It is not often that metaphor is confused with more completeness than in this description of a summer morning:—

[quotes "Grandfather Bridgeman" V, lines 1–3]

It is, as we have said, bad enough that a writer of real ability and skill should allow himself to associate this kind of fustian[3] with poems of worth and merit. But Mr. George Meredith's descent from his "roadside" style of

---

3. *fustian*: bombastic, pretentious speech or writing

thought and composition to his lyrical mood is, we regret to say, only trifling compared with the change which he undergoes when he indulges in an elaborate analysis of a loathsome series of phenomena which he is pleased to call "modern love." The poem called "Modern Love" is of considerable length, and has clearly had a large share of labour bestowed on its preparation. The mere composition is sometimes very graceful, and always exceedingly ingenious. The few short passages quoted below appear to us to contain real beauty:—

[quotes "Modern Love" XXXVII, lines 10–12; XLI, lines 1–6; XI, lines 7–8, and XXII, lines 11–12]

But no word-painting or clever analysis can atone for a choice of subject which we cannot help regarding as involving a grave moral mistake—a mistake so grave as utterly to disqualify the chooser from achieving any great and worthy result in art. The whole of this poem is occupied in portraying the miseries of married life as it exists in our modern society. The writer's apology for his choice would probably be the same that he has put into the mouth of one of his characters:—

These things are life;
And life, they say, is worthy of the Muse. ["Modern Love" XXV, lines 15–16]

A more flimsy sophism could hardly be devised. The Muse is undoubtedly concerned with all forms of life, but these things are decay, and deformity, and death. So far from a condition of doubt and uncertainty on the general tone of matrimonial morality being in any sense an interesting or attractive thing, it is one of the most disastrous calamities that can befall a nation. To write of the rotten places of our social system as if they were fitting subjects for the Muse is just as reasonable as it would be to compose a sonnet to the gout or an ode on the small-pox. Besides, the subject is old and outworn, exhausted by far abler hands then those of Mr. George Meredith. With the great literary error of *Don Juan* before his eyes, it was scarcely worth his while to commit the sickly little peccadillo of "Modern Love." It was no doubt his conviction, derived from French authorities, that there is a species of nineteenth-century infidelity, more recondite, more interesting, more intellectual forsooth, than those which have gone before, and that this novelty was not undeserving of a bard. If he should be at any time desirous of taking the measure of his work, it would not be an uninstructive process to read over the poem of "Guinevere," in *Idylls of the King*,[4] and then to peruse some half-dozen of his own cantos. The contrast might disabuse him of the notion that he has succeeded in producing, under the title of "Modern Love," anything worthy of the name of art. If he could regard his clever performance as others see it, he might perhaps agree with us in thinking that his utmost achievement has been to throw the thin veil of Coan drapery[5] over a set of grinning skeletons.

---

4. Alfred, Lord Tennyson's *Idylls of the King* comprises twelve narrative poems based upon Sir Thomas Malory's *Le Morte d'Arthur* and Welsh folklore. At the time this review was written, only four of the twelve poems had been published.

5. *Coan drapery*: the look of sheer, draped fabric achieved in classical statuary, which allows all the contours of the body beneath to be visible

# William Sharp, from *Sonnets of This Century* (1886)[1]

> Scottish poet William Sharp's (1855–1905) *Sonnets of This Century* is an anthology introduced with an essay on the nature and structure of the sonnet, with particular emphasis on the English sonnet. Given that Sharp offers a list of "ten commandments" of the sonnet, a list that includes a length of fourteen lines and an octave/sestet organization, it does not surprise that he selects Meredith's "Lucifer in Starlight," from *Poems and Lyrics of the Joy of Earth*, over any of the "Modern Love" sonnets for inclusion in the main text of his volume. The excerpt that follows is drawn from a note on George Meredith in the appendix of Sharp's anthology.

M r. Meredith's fame—a steadily, and rapidly increasing fame—as the most brilliant living master of fiction, has overshadowed his claims as a poet. Out of the hundreds who have read and delighted in *The Ordeal of Richard Feverel*, in *Evan Harrington*, in *Rhoda Fleming*, etc., there are probably only two or three here and there who before the recent issue of *Poems and Lyrics of the Joy of Earth* knew that Mr. Meredith had written verse at all. Yet two very noteworthy little volumes had previously—the first a long time before—seen the light. In the second, entitled *Modern Love: and other Poems*, [*sic*] there is a very remarkable sequence of sixteen line poems comprised under the heading "Modern Love." A sad enough story is told therein, with great skill, and much poetic beauty. I had always imagined them to have been sonnets on the model of the Italian "sonnet with a tail," but Mr. Meredith tells me that they were not designed for that form. As, however, for all their structural drawbacks they are in other things essentially "caudated sonnets," I may quote the following fine examples:—

---

1. William Sharp, "George Meredith," in *Sonnets of This Century* (London: Walter Scott, 1886), 299–301.

[quotes "Modern Love" XVI, XXIX, XLIII, XLIX, and L in their entirety ]

As to the single sonnet proper by Mr. Meredith which I have given in my selection, it is quite unnecessary to point to its imaginative power—its sense of vastness. It is from his *Poems and Lyrics of the Joy of Earth*.

# Arthur Symons, from
## *Westminster Review* (1887)[1]

Arthur Symons (1865–1945), a British poet and literary critic, was a longtime admirer of Meredith's work. His own poetry was deeply influenced by the French symbolists, including Charles Baudelaire. Toward the end of the century, Symons emerged as a key figure in the Art for Art's Sake movement. His influential 1893 essay, "The Decadent Movement in Literature," is often anthologized. The excerpted review that follows was occasioned by the 1887 publication of Meredith's *Ballads and Poems of Tragic Life*. Here Symons praises the originality and intensity of Meredith's verse.

"**M**odern Love," by far the greatest of [all of Meredith's poems], . . . stands almost by itself as an analytical study of contemporary life and manners; the "Roadside" poems deal synthetically with country humours and country pathos; there is a number of romantic poems and ballads, and these have at least two remarkable divisions among themselves. "Modern Love," Mr. Meredith's longest poem—it is written in fifty sonnet-like stanzas of sixteen lines—is also, beyond a shadow of doubt (so it seems to us), by far his best work in verse. It is a most remarkable poem, and it has never received anything like due recognition at the hands of critics or public. We trace to it, perhaps wrongly, but we think not, the origin or suggestion of at least the manner of two subsequent poems of considerable importance and merit, James Thomson's "Story of Weddah and Om-el-Bonain"[2]

1. Arthur Symons, "Meredith's Poetry," *Westminster Review* (September 1887): 695–97.

2. James Thomson (1834–1882), pessimistic Scottish poet who wrote under the pseudonym Bysshe Vanolis, was best known for his 1874 poem "The City of Dreadful Night." "Weddah and Om-el-Bonain" is a tragic story of two lovers. Meredith admired his work.

and Mr. W. S. Blunt's "Love Sonnets of Proteus."[3] We have no authority but internal evidence for this supposition, though we know that James Thomson had a very great admiration for "Modern Love," and used often to speak of it. In certain qualities both "Weddah and Om-el-Bonain" and the "Love Sonnets of Proteus" are superior to Mr. Meredith's poem; but besides the extremely important fact that Mr. Meredith was first in the field, his poem as a whole is to our mind decidedly superior to either of those with which we have classed it. We have never been able to tell quite what it is that gives to these sonnet-like stanzas (with all their obscurities of allusion and their occasional faults in versification) a certain charm and power which fascinate and fasten upon mind and memory at once. Mr. Meredith has never done anything else like it; this wonderful style, acid, stinging, bittersweet, poignant, as if fashioned of the very moods of these "modern lovers," reappears in no other poem (except faintly in the "Ballad of Fair Ladies in Revolt").[4] The poem stands alone, not merely in Mr. Meredith's work, but in all antecedent literature. It is altogether a new thing; we venture to call it the most "modern" poem we have.

"Modern Love" is a poem of the drawing-rooms; it is tinged throughout with irony; it moves by "tragic hints." In the same volume we have a group of "Poems of the English Roadside," studies, as they are also termed, of "Roadside Philosophers." Here we are in a new atmosphere altogether, an atmosphere in which we can breathe more freely, under the open sky, upon the road and the heath. This little group of homely poems, to which should be added "Martin's Puzzle,"[5] a poem of the same period, seems to us, after "Modern Love," perhaps the most original and satisfying contribution made by Mr. Meredith to the poetry of his time. One poem at least is an absolute masterpiece, and of its kind it is almost without a rival. There is a sly and kindly humour in "The Beggar's Soliloquy," a quaint wit in "The Old Char-

---

3. Wilfrid Scawen Blunt (1840–1922), English writer and poet, published *Sonnets and Songs by Proteus* in 1875 and *The Love Songs of Proteus* in 1880. Symons seems to have conflated the two titles here.

4. "A Ballad of Fair Ladies in Revolt" initially appeared in the *Fortnightly Review in 1876; it was later collected in* Poems and Lyrics of the Joy of the Earth (1883).

5. "Martin's Puzzle" initially appeared in the *Fortnightly Review* in 1865; it was later collected in *Poems and Lyrics of the Joy of the Earth* (1883), before finally appearing alongside "Juggling Jerry" and "The Old Chartist" in the Edition de Luxe.

tist," a humourous wisdom tinged with pathos in "Martin's Puzzle"; each of these poems is a greater or less success in a line of work which is much more difficult than it looks; but "Juggling Jerry," notwithstanding a flaw here and there in the rhythm, quickens our blood and strikes straight from the heart to the heart as only a few poems here and there can do. We said that of its kind it is almost without a rival; we may say, indeed, quite without a rival, outside Burns.[6]

Allied to both "Modern Love" and the "Poems of the English Roadside" by the intensity of their emotion, but in tone and manner and subject removed equally from either, four or five poems, wonderfully powerful and original, form another distinct group. These are "Cassandra," in the volume of 1862, and "The Nuptials of Attila," "The Song of Theodolinda," "King Harald's Trance," and "Aneurin's Harp," in the new volume. There is something fierce, savage, convulsive almost, in the passion which informs these poems; a note sounded in our days by no other poet, not even by M. Leconte de Lisle[7] in the *Poèmes Barbares*. The words rush rattling on one another like the clashing of spears or the ring of iron on iron in a day of old-world battle. The lines are javelins, consonated lines full of savage power and fury, as if sung or played by a Northern Skald harping on a field of slain. And this is the poet of the joy of Earth!

---

6. Robert Burns (1759–1796), a Scottish poet widely regarded as a precursor of the Romantics.
7. Leconte de Lisle (1818–1894), French poet of the Parnassian school.

# From Unsigned Review,
## *Travelers Record* (1892)[1]

Debuting in 1865 with a print run of 50,000 and published by Travelers Insurance, the *Travelers Record* was one of the world's first industrial in-house magazines. It featured letters purportedly from satisfied customers, articles about the dangers of modern life, literary and fine-arts reviews, and poetry, some of which was reprinted in British periodicals. This review addresses the 1891 pirated edition of "Modern Love," published by Thomas Mosher, which included a foreword by the poet Elizabeth Cavazza. Only 400 copies of this edition were printed. Critical of Meredith's peculiar variation on the sonnet form, this review is largely negative. It is, however, unique for its attempt to imagine what motivates the wife's behavior. Readers will note that although this reviewer blames both husband and wife in "Modern Love" for their marital unhappiness, s/he—like Ellis (see "Advice Manuals and Social Commentary" in the next section)—insists that wives would do well to resign themselves to being ignored by their husbands.

Strictly speaking, it is not a poem, but a set of fifty detached scenes, exactly corresponding to the sets of panels in the comic papers which tell stories without words. The intent is a narrative; the plan is a series of photographs of various occasions during the story, mixed with reflections by the hero and the author, and independent description. Whether this is the ideal form of poetical narrative might be questioned; but an author has a right to choose his own form. It gives a Carlylean effect of seeing the action by occasional flashes of lightening, and is not favorable to obvious sequence and consequently to intelligibility of motive; it makes the action seem arbitrary and capricious beyond need. The stanzas are of sixteen lines each, rhymed in

---

1. "George Meredith's 'Modern Love,'" *Travelers Record* (February 1892): 6.

fours. Mr. Swinburne allows that they are sonnets, and in spirit and genesis they are; but in metrical and artistic effect they are certainly not, with all deference to Mr. Swinburne and Mrs. Cavazza. The four groups of lines are often not "quatrains" at all, unless any four inter-rhyming lines from any poem are a quatrain: their burden does not always begin or end with themselves, and they have no relation except to the general sense of the stanza. The question would not be of much importance except that the lack of definition of quatrains robs the strophes[2] of much potential beauty of form. But enough is left to make them exceedingly rich. By far the most luxurious in melodic beauty is No. 11, so delicious that it angers one with him. The man who can write poetry like that, and will not, deserves all the ills he has to bear. We would gladly swap all his "fire-bringing" for a hundred such poems. There are more philosophers now than the world knows what to do with; creators of beauty are always scarce, and he is a traitor to his mission in pouring out crabbed similes to be forgotten, in place of visions of loveliness to be a joy forever. The first parts of Nos. 39, 44, 45, and 47 are also very beautiful in different ways. In striking novelty and fierce strength of thought, none surpass Nos. 20 and 38, which make one wince with personal shame, like Hartley Coleridge's terrible sonnet "If I have sinned."[3] But lack of ideas is nowhere Meredith's fault.

The title assumes the story to be typical of modern love in general, the motto assumes it to concern only a few finely strung natures; and the motto is correct. Ordinary human nature even now is grosser in action and duller in feeling; both the motive and the conduct of the poem would be unintelligible to the crowd. That does not make the story not worth telling; but it prevents extracting any general formula from it (though the author deduces one which in fact has nothing at all to do with the story). Not that the situation is very rare; but the ideality of action is, though by no means unknown. (Parenthetically, we cannot but smile at the way he, like all writers who deal with strong emotions, takes care to have no children to embarrass the story, though children are inherently probable. They make havoc with heroics and hysterics, and a melodramatic story-writer nearly always makes his married couples barren, often in defiance of all probability.) The root of the trouble is a wife's unwillingness to have life progress beyond the days of courtship.

---

2. *strophe*: usually refers to a section of a choral ode in Greek drama; perhaps the author is using its more general connotation from the Latin—to turn or twist—to refer to the volta of a sonnet.

3. David Hartley Coleridge (1796–1849), the son of Samuel Taylor Coleridge, a poet and critic.

This is common enough; but here the wife goes further, and reverses a woman's usual position. She is hurt and jealous that her husband wishes to do a man's work in the world, and have a life, outside hers and unshared by her, of manly activities and worldly interest; for herself she does not wish to face the realities of life's work and duties. She wishes that both should live their whole lives in a haze of sentimentalities, possible and true for brief periods of delight, but as a continuous existence unreal and impossible. She does not tell him this, but broods over it in silent discontent; and at last he finds to his horror that she is burning incense to a new idol, not with any intent of gross infidelity, but simply to have a focus for her inner life of sentiment. The new is probably not finer than the old, but in her fancy of him his life is all her own. The husband has perfect and just confidence in his wife's virtue, even when he gets hold of love-letters she has written to his rival; but that does not content him with the loss of her love, and he values her judgment too highly even to feel superiority to the rival,—a rather overstrained modesty, seeing how wholly subjective her fancy was, and how many Titanias have loved how many Bottoms with the ass's head plainly visible.[4] Violence would be wasted, for he could not reclaim her soul with a revolver. Finally they settle down to live a whited sepulchre of a life, unchanged in surface amity but icily apart beneath; which also is not novel. This becomes so intolerable that the wife makes repeated efforts to break the barrier of silence and once more talk heart to heart; and if he really wanted back her love he would have welcomed the chance. But rankling hurt for the past, and suspicion for the present and future, are stronger than tenderness, or than his intellectual judgment that he cannot blame her when he has a certain perfumed glove in his desk; and he rebuffs all overtures. Then he takes a sentimental mate of his own to match hers, and once the two couples pass each other—a pleasant meeting. Finally she leaves him and goes into hiding, to enable him, as she believes, to possess his new love. After long search he finds her dying by the sea; and in a last kiss and a last look into each other's eyes, the truth as to both hearts and the long heart-break is revealed, too late for any further joy on earth.

The author sums up by saying that "They fed not on the advancing hours"; or in other words, would not trim their course by the sweep of life's

---

4. *Titanias . . . Bottoms*: referring to characters from Shakespeare's *A Midsummer Night's Dream*; Titania is the beautiful queen of the fairies, whose attraction to Nick Bottom, the arrogant and rude weaver whose head has been turned into that of an ass, is attributable only to a magic potion.

own channel as it momently revealed itself, but tried to make the river flow in circles where they liked best to stay. This is true of the wife, but hardly just to the husband, who fed on the advancing hours till he was wronged and endangered. His fault, it is intimated, was in not pretending unconsciousness of any change in his wife, and waiting patiently till she outgrew her folly and gave back her love; but what security had he that it would ever have come back? The end of that path is usually the divorce court or the devil; and the higher a man's nature, the less can he be satisfied with mere chastity, and let love come or go as it will. Both parties are unreal. A woman so obstinately unreasonable would not have been so high-minded and pure; a man willing to keep up the phantom of a home with his wife nestling to a neighbor, for any motive but to welcome the first hint of return, justifies her. The action will do for a poem; but it is not life.

The author draws the further deduction that the soul should not be "hot for certainties in this our life." But this is gratuitous and irrelevant, for certainties (ultimate truths) were exactly what the wife did not want, and the husband only wanted rational probabilities. It is, however, the author's grand discovery, which constitutes him a "fire-bringer"; this and that we need "more brain." That is, we take it, Accept the inevitable calmly and keep your soul at peace, for you can gain nothing and find out nothing by its tumult. Whatever comes is probably best and certainly unavoidable, so what is the good of worrying over it? Don't blink facts, don't shirk truth, but don't kick at them, nor forego possible solutions in despair of fathoming all.

Now, this in our judgment is much superior to Browning's theorem. It is eminently sensible, practical, and healthy; the soundest of advice. But novel or deep or satisfying—No! It is an insult to a struggling and aspiring soul to put that before it as a solution of its problem. It begs the very questions asked by millions of souls in this unsettled age,—by what token they may know if life is worth living, or the universe only a giant sweep of aimless forces; if effort pays in the finest sense, if duty pays, if righteousness pays, if heed to conscience pays. Once men were sure, and now they are not sure; perhaps again they will be sure. But there is no help in a seer who only tells us to be satisfied not to know, and that "the universe is all right." He is not God, and no one else can assure us of that. A great thinker and artist Mr. Meredith may be, a strong thinker and fine poet he certainly is; but we cannot accept him as a "fire-bringer" on the evidence of this poem. He brings none to us.

## Advice Manuals and Social Commentary

Many of the central emotive themes of "Modern Love"—the angst and frustration of disconnection, the jealousy precipitated by adultery or fear of adultery, the desire to assign blame in the aftermath of the breakdown of a relationship—are so universally familiar that they can be immediately appreciated. Understanding the particular social context of the middle- and upper-class Victorian couple nevertheless helps to account for the strength and intensity of those emotive themes. Sarah Stickney Ellis's conduct manual articulates some of the expectations the Victorian bride faced, and frames the wife's proper role as one of constant self-effacement in support of her husband and family. While acknowledging that the role will be difficult at times, Ellis suggests that the only real happiness available to a wife is the satisfaction of fulfilling her domestic duties. William Cobbett also frames the role of husband in terms of duty, and encourages men to tend to the emotional needs of their wives, if only to prevent possible adultery. In both manuals, the inherent inequality of the Victorian marriage is evident, as is an emphasis on dutiful obedience to social expectations. These texts, along with John Ruskin's "Of Queens' Gardens," from *Sesame and Lilies*, indicate how fraught ideas of feminine desire were in the mid-nineteenth century: Ellis's manual suggests a complete repression of a wife's desire; Ruskin, by suggesting that women are only passive beings, affirms Ellis's rejection of feminine desire; and Cobbett implicitly brings women's purported penchant for cheating to the forefront through his repeated insistence that a man must guard against his wife's infidelity. These texts help to explain why the husband in "Modern Love" is so troubled by his wife's infidelity, why he does not regard his own as similarly problematic, and why his wife might opt for suicide rather than face life after the breakdown of her marriage: the wife not only violated her marriage vows, but rejected the very definition of woman's position in the family unit and in society beyond.

Outside of the roles defined in works like Ellis's and Cobbett's, there were few practical options for the Victorian woman. Today's students might wonder why the couple did not simply seek a divorce. John Paget's description of the labyrinthine world of divorce court in mid-Victorian England helps to explain the practical difficulties in doing so; except for the very rich and those with the temperament to withstand the emotional toll of the process, divorce was not a possibility. The unhappily married couple thus found themselves with few options, and women's limited financial and legal agency meant her situation was the more precarious of the two. John Stuart Mill's call for greater equitability in marriage suggests that existing marital expectations for both women and men would more than likely lead to unhappiness. His vision of a new kind of marriage based on equality and mutual value serves as a corrective to the unaccommodating institution that lead the "Modern Love" couple to misery. It is a vision that Meredith embraced, even if he recognized (and repeatedly skewered in his verse and prose) obstacles to effecting those changes posed by the individual's ego.

"Modern Love" is not the only poem illuminated by the advice manuals and social commentary in this section. Fruitful connections can also be made to many of the *Modern Love* poems, the poetry included in "Contexts," and Meredith's broader oeuvre. For instance, Ellis advises that imagining what life would be like if your spouse died is a good way to relieve marital discontent; Mrs. Graham, a fictional character of Coventry Patmore's *The Angel in the House*, passes along similar advice to her son. Ellis's and John Ruskin's conceptions of ideal femininity are almost identical to Patmore's, and understanding the intensity of that ideal sheds light not only upon "Modern Love," but also on "The Meeting," "Juggling Jerry," "Margaret's Bridal-Eve," and "The Doe."

# Sarah Stickney Ellis, from
## *The Wives of England* (1843)[1]

Sarah Stickney Ellis (1799–1862) is widely known for her instruction
manuals, most of which are directed to young women. Here, she of-
fers a meditation on the nature of marriage, first bemoaning the fact
that many enter into marriage with little awareness about the actual
experience. She encourages women to tend to their relationships,
cultivating them like a garden, and she condemns women's desire for
public attention. Ellis's vision of the ideal Victorian wife helped es-
tablish expectations for both women and the men they would marry.
In light of these expectations, one can better understand the ambiva-
lence manifested by the couple in "Modern Love," as they tried to
reconcile their own conflicting desire with prescribed notions of be-
havior, responsibility, and duty.

I f, in the foregoing pages, I have spoken of the married state as one of
the trial of principle, rather than of the fruition of hope; and if, upon the
whole, my observations should appear to have assumed a discourag-
ing, rather than a cheering character, it has arisen in the first place, from my
not having reached, until now, that part of the subject in which the advan-
tages of this connection are fully developed; and if in the second place, I must
plead guilty to the charge of desiring to throw some hindrances in the way
of youthful aspiration, it has simply been from observing amongst young
people generally, how much greater is the tendency to make the experiment
for themselves, than to prepare themselves for the experiment. . . .

That this disproportion betwixt expectation and reality, arises from igno-
rance, rather than any other cause, I am fully prepared to believe—ignorance
of the human heart, of the actual circumstances of human life, of the operation

1. Sarah Stickney Ellis, "The Love of Married Life," in *The Wives of England: Their Relative Du-
ties, Domestic Influence, and Social Obligations* (New York: D. Appleton, 1843), 106–13, 117–23.

of cause and effect in human affairs, and of the relative duty of human beings one towards another.

The numbers who have failed in this way to realize in their experience of married life, the fair pictures which imagination painted before it was tried, it would be useless to attempt to enumerate; as well as to tell how many have thrown the blame of their disappointment upon situation or circumstances— upon husband, servants, friends, or relatives—when the whole has rested with themselves, and has arisen solely out of a want of adaptation in their views and habits to the actual requirements of the new state of existence upon which they have entered.

That this state itself is not capable of the greatest amount of happiness which is expected from it, I should be sorry to deny; and all I would attempt to prove in the way of discouragement is, that its happiness will often prove to be of a different kind from what has been anticipated. All that has been expected to be enjoyed from the indulgence of selfishness, must then of necessity be left out of our calculations, with all that ministers to the pride of superiority, all that gratifies the love of power, all that converts the woman into the heroine, as well as all that renders her an object of general interest and attraction.

It may very naturally be asked, what then remains? I answer, the love of married life; and in this answer is embodied the richest treasure which this earth affords. All other kinds of love, hold by a very slender tenure the object of supreme regard; but here the actual tie is severed only by the stroke of death, while mutual interest, instead of weakening, renders it more secure. The love of a parent for a child, natural, and pure, and holy as it is, can never bind that child beyond a certain period within its influence; while the love of a child for a parent must necessarily be interrupted in the course of nature, by the dissolution of its earthly hold. The love of a brother or a sister must ever be ready to give place to dearer claims; and that of a friend, though "very precious" while it lasts, has no real security for its continuance. And yet all these, according to the laws which regulate our being, in their own place, and measure, supply the natural craving of the human heart for something beyond itself, which it may call its own, and in the certainty of possessing which, it may implicitly repose. . . .

Nor is it only in our human sympathies that this craving is developed. . . . And strange to say, it is sometimes even thus with ambition, and with many of those aims and occupations which absorb man's life. They are followed, not for the results they bring, so much as for the promises they offer—for the vague hopes they hold out, that their entire accomplishment will satisfy the cravings of an insatiable soul.

But, perhaps, more than in any other case, is it thus with literary fame, in the pursuit of which how many are urged on by a strong, though it may seem to some a fanciful impression, that the voice of feeling which has failed to find an echo in its own immediate sphere, may, in the wide world through which it is sent forth, touch in some unknown breast a sympathetic chord, and thus awaken a responsive emotion.

But if with man, the most powerful and independent of created beings, there ever exists this want of spiritual reliance and communion, what must it be to the weaker heart of woman, to find one earthly hold after another giving way, and to look around upon the great wilderness of life, in which she stands unconnected, and consequently alone? If there be one principle in woman's nature stronger than all others, it is that which prompts her to seek sympathy and protection from some being whom she may love, and by whom she may be loved in return. The influence of fashion is, perhaps, of all others to which the female sex is exposed, the most hardening to the heart—the most chilling to its warm and genuine emotions. Yet I much question whether the successful candidate for public admiration, would not sometimes willingly retire from the splendid circle in which she is the centre of attraction, to receive in private the real homage of one unsophisticated, noble, and undivided heart. Having failed in this, woman's first and most excusable ambition, how often does she go forth into the world, to waste upon the cold and polished surface of society, those capabilities of thought and feeling which might, if more wisely directed, have made a happy home; and how often is she compelled to look, appalled and horror-struck, upon the utter emptiness of the reward which follows this expenditure, when the same outlay in a different soil, and under happier culture, might have enabled her to gather into her bosom a hundred-fold, the richer fruits of confidence and affection.

It is only in the married state that the boundless capabilities of woman's love can ever be fully known or appreciated. There may, in other situations, be occasional instances of heroic self-sacrifice, and devotion to an earthly object; but it is only here that the lapse of time, and the familiar occasions of every day, can afford opportunities of exhibiting the same spirit, operating through all those minor channels, which flow like fertilizing rills² through the bosom of every family, where the influence of woman is alike happy in its exercise, and enlightened in its character. . . .

In order to know how to avert [the death of love], it is necessary to endeavour to look calmly and dispassionately at the subject in every point of view, to dispel the visions of imagination, and to ask what is the real cause of failure, where woman has so much at stake.

Love may arise spontaneously, but it does not continue to exist without some care and culture. In a mind whose ideas are all floating at large, and whose emotions of feeling or affection are left to the prompting of impulse, unrestrained by the discipline of reason, there will naturally arise strange wandering thoughts, which will be likely at any unguarded moment to undermine so frail a fabric, as love under such circumstances must ever be.

One tendency in the mind of the married woman who has thus neglected the government of her own feelings, will be, on every occasion of momentary vexation or dissatisfaction, to compare her husband with other men to his disadvantage; than which nothing can be more dangerous, or more inconsistent with that faithfulness which ought ever to be a leading characteristic in the love of married life. Nor can any thing well be more impolitic or absurd; since there is no human being, however excellent, who may not, in some way or other, be made to suffer by comparison with others. Besides which, what right have we, as frail and erring creatures, to aspire, in this connection, to an alliance with a being entirely faultless, or even more perfect than ourselves?

If then there should occasionally arise feelings of disappointment and dissatisfaction, as the lapse of time and a nearer acquaintance develop a husband's faults, it is good to bear in mind that the same exposure of your own, from the same cause, must necessarily have taken place; and by often dwelling upon this view of the subject, a degree of charitable feeling will be excited, more calculated to humble and chasten the heart, than to imbitter it against the failings of another. . . .

Against the petulance and occasional resentment which an accumulation of [provocations] call forth, there is one great and solemn consideration, by which a woman of right feeling may, at any time, add sufficient weight to the balance in her husband's favour—she may think of his death, of the emotions

---

2. *rills*: small streams

with which she would receive his last farewell, and of what would be her situation if deprived at once of his love, his advice, and his protection. We are all perhaps too little accustomed to such thoughts as these, except where illness or accident places them immediately before us. We are too much in the habit of looking upon the thread of life with us, as far more likely to be broken first, and of thinking that the stronger frame must necessarily endure the longest. But one realizing thought that the sentence of widowed loneliness may possibly be ours—how does it sweep away, as by a single breath, the mist of little imperfections which had gathered around a beloved form, and reveal to us at one glance the manly beauties of a noble, or a generous character! . . .

. . . It must ever be borne in mind, that man's love, even in its happiest exercise, is not like woman's; for while she employs herself through every hour, in fondly weaving one beloved image into all her thoughts; he gives to her comparatively few of his, and of these perhaps neither the loftiest, nor the best. His highest hopes and brightest energies, must ever be expected to expand themselves upon the promotion of some favourite scheme, or the advancement of some public measure; and if with untiring satisfaction he turns to her after the efforts of the day have been completed; and weary, and perhaps dispirited, comes back to pour into her faithful bosom the history of those trials which the world can never know, and would not pity if it could; if she can thus supply to the extent of his utmost wishes, the sympathy, and the advice, the confidence, and the repose, of which he is in need, she will have little cause to think herself neglected.

It is a wise beginning then, for every married woman to make up her mind to be forgotten through the greater part of every day; to make up her mind to many rivals too, in her husband's attentions, though not in his love; and amongst these, I would mention one, whose claims it is folly to dispute; since no remonstrances or representations on her part, will ever be able to render less attractive the charms of this competitor. I mean the newspaper, of whose absorbing interest some wives are weak enough to evince a sort of childish jealousy, when they ought rather to congratulate themselves that their most formidable rival is one of paper.

The same observations apply perhaps in a more serious manner to those occupations which lead men into public life. If the object be to do good, either by correcting abuses, or forwarding benevolent designs, and not merely to make himself the head of a party, a judicious and right-principled woman will be too happy for her husband to be instrumental in a noble cause, to put in competition with his public efforts, any loss she may sustain in personal attention, or domestic comfort.

A system of persecution perseveringly carried on against such manly propensities as reading the newspaper, or even against the household derangements necessarily accompanying attention to public business, has the worst possible effect upon a husband's temper, and general state of feeling. So much so, that I am inclined to think a greater sum of real love has been actually teased away, than ever was destroyed by more direct, or more powerfully operating means.

The same system of teasing is sometimes most unwisely kept up, for the purpose of calling forth a succession of those little personal attentions, which, if not gratuitously rendered, are utterly destitute of value, and ought never to be required.

To all married women, it must be gratifying to receive from a husband just so much attention as indicates a consciousness of her presence; but with this acknowledgement, expressed in any manner which may be most congenial to her husband's tastes and habits, a woman of true delicacy would surely be satisfied without wishing to stipulate for more.

Still less would she annoy him with an exhibition of her own fondness, under the idea of its being necessarily returned in kind. It is a holy, and a blessed mystery, from the secrets of which, in its mastery over the human mind, almost all women who have ever been beloved, have learned the power of their own tenderness; but in proportion to the purity of its nature, and the sacredness of its exercise, is its capability of being abused and degraded. Thus, all exhibition of fondness before a third party, may justly be looked upon as indicating a total ignorance of the intensity, and the purity, of that which alone deserves the name of love; while, could one imagine the possibility of such a thing, all exercise of this fondness made use of for the purpose of obtaining advantage over a husband's judgment or inclination, could only be supposed to arise out of the meanest impulse of a low, an artful, and a degraded mind.

But we cannot for a moment imagine such things really are. We cannot believe that a woman conscious of her personal attractions, could hang about her husband's neck, or weep, or act the impassioned heroine, for the base purpose of inducing him to make some concession, which in his calmer moments he could not be prevailed upon to grant. No, the true heart of woman knows too well, that that sweet gift of heaven, granted in consideration to her weakness, was never meant to be made use of as an instrument of power to gain a selfish end; but was permitted her for the high and holy purpose of softening the harder and more obdurate nature of man, so as to render it capable of impressions upon which the seal of eternity might be set.

It requires much tact, as well as delicacy, to know how to render expressions of endearment at all times appropriate, and consequently acceptable; and as love is far too excellent a thing to be wasted, and tenderness too precious to be thrown away, a sensible woman will most scrupulously consult her husband's mood and temper in this respect, as well as remember always the consideration due to her own personal attractions; for, without some considerable portion of these advantages it will be always safest not to advance very far, unless there should be clear and direct encouragement to do so. Pitiful pictures have been drawn in works of fiction of the hopelessness of efforts of this nature; but one would willingly believe them to be confined to fiction only, for there is happily, in most enlightened female minds, an intuitive perception on these points, by which they may discover almost instantaneously from a look, a tone, a touch responsive to their own, how far it may be desirable to go, and by what shadow they ought to be warned, as well as by what ray of light they ought to be encouraged.

It may be easily imagined how an ignorant, or selfish woman, never can be able to understand all this, and how she may consequently make shipwreck of her husband's happiness, and her own peace, simply from never having known, observed, or felt, what belongs to the nature of the human heart in these its most exquisite touches of light and shade; while, on the other hand, not the highest intellectual attainments, with the noblest gifts of nature, nor all the importance and distinction which these attributes obtain for their possessor in the world, will be able to efface for a moment the delicate perceptions of a truly sensitive woman, or to render her, in the deep and fervent love of which she is capable, otherwise than humble, and easily subdued; especially when she comes with child-like simplicity, to consult the dial of her husband's love, and to read there the progress of the advancing or receding shadows, which indicate her only true position through the lapse of every hour.

It is an act of injustice towards women, and one which often brings its own punishment upon talented men, when they select as their companions for life, the ignorant or the imbecile of the other sex, believing that because they are so, they must be more capable of loving. If to be incapable of any thing else, implies this necessity, it must be granted that they are so. But of what value is that love which exists as a mere impulse of nature, compared with that, which, with an equal force of impulse, combines the highest attributes of an enlightened mind, and brings them all with their rich produce, like flowers from a delicious garden, a welcome and appropriate offering at the shrine whereon the heart is laid.

Still, I must repeat, that it is not the superiority of talent, but the early and the best use of such as we possess, which gives this power and beauty to affection, by directing it to its appropriate end. For as in other duties of woman's life, without knowledge she cannot, if she would, act properly; so in the expression and bestowment of her love, without an intimate acquaintance with the human heart, without having exercised her faculties of observation and reflection, and without having obtained by early discipline some mastery over her own feelings, she will ever be liable to rush blindly upon those fatal errors, by which the love of married life so often has been wrecked.

In connection with this subject, there is one consideration to which sufficient weight is seldom given; and that is, the importance of never trifling with affection after the nuptial knot is tied. To do this at any time, or in any way, is scarcely consistent with the feelings of a deeply sensitive and delicate mind; but leaving the display of caprice to those who think it gives zest to the familiarity of courtship, it cannot be too deeply impressed upon the female mind, that with the days of courtship it must end.

There are innumerable tests which might be applied to the love of married life, so as to ascertain the degree of its intensity, or the progress of its declension;[3] but who would wish to apply them?—or who, even if they did, would *dare* to make so critical an experiment? If there be any cause for its existence, the consciousness comes soon enough, that the wife is not all to her husband which the flattering promises of early love prepared her to expect; and if there be no cause for the slightest shadow of suspicion that her star is beginning to go down, why trouble her own repose, and that of her husband, by questioning the reality of what it would be worse than death to doubt?

All teasing, all caprice, all acting for the purpose of renewing an agreeable effect, are therefore inimical to the mutual trust, and the steady confidence in reciprocal affection, which are, or ought to be, enjoyed by individuals thus bound together by an indissoluble tie. Not that the writer would for

---

3. *declension*: decline

a moment wish to discountenance that harmless vivacity which some women know so well how to charm; or to speak of the privacy of married life as consisting of dull and sombre scenes. So far from this, it is her firm belief, that nothing tends more to animate and renew the feeling of affection in the mind of man, than the cheerfulness of his fireside companion.

# William Cobbett, from

## *Advice to Young Men, and (Incidentally) to Young Women, in the Middle and Higher Ranks of Life* (1862)[1]

William Cobbett (1763–1835), an agitator for radical parliamentary reform, was an English farmer and prolific writer who lived and worked in Britain and the United States. First published in 1829, his *Advice to Young Men* went through a number of editions and was reissued in 1862. Cobbett's advice on the subject of adultery, excerpted here, is notable for its account of shared responsibility. Although Cobbett insists that infidelity is "much worse in the wife" than in the husband, he nevertheless concedes that husbands must work to avoid being "the cause of temptation to the wife to be unfaithful" or reacting in kind. Meredith—whose "Modern Love" turns upon the fact that both husband and wife are to blame for their marital unhappiness—was a fan of Cobbett's work; he encouraged his friend William Hardman to write Cobbett's biography. The numbers preceding each section are from Cobbett's original; we retain them here for readers' convenience.

178. When we consider what a young woman gives up on her wedding-day; she makes a surrender, an absolute surrender, of her liberty, for the joint lives of the parties; she gives the husband the absolute right of causing her to live in what place, and in what manner and in what society, he pleases; she gives him the power to take from her, and to use for his own purposes, all her goods, unless reserved by

1. William Cobbett, "Letter IV, to a Husband," in *Advice to Young Men, and (Incidentally) to Young Women, in the Middle and Higher Ranks of Life: In a Series of Letters Addressed to a Youth, a Bachelor, a Husband, a Father, a Citizen or a Subject.* New Edition. (London: Griffin, Bohn, 1862), 173, 177, 181, 183–84, 189, 193–200.

some legal instrument; and, above all, she surrenders to him *her person*. Then, when we consider the pains which they endure for us, and the large share of all the anxious parental cares that fall to their lot; when we consider their devotion to us, and how unshaken their affection remains in our ailments, even though the most tedious and disgusting; when we consider the offices that they perform, and cheerfully perform, for us, when, were we left to one another, we should perish from neglect; when we consider their devotion to their children, how evidently they love them better, in numerous instances, than their own lives; when we consider these things, how can a just man think anything a trifle that effects their happiness? . . .

182. But though all the aforementioned considerations demand from us the kindest possible treatment of a wife, the husband is to expect dutiful deportment at her hands. He is not to be her slave; he is not to yield to her against the dictates of his own reason and judgment; it is her duty to obey all his lawful commands; and, if she have sense, she will perceive that it is a disgrace to herself to acknowledge as a husband a thing over which she has an absolute control. It should always be recollected that *you* are the party whose body must, if any do, lie in jail for debts, and for debts of her contracting, too, as well as of your own contracting. Over her *tongue*, too, you possess a clear right to exercise, if necessary, some control; for if she use it in an unjustifiable manner, it is against *you*, and not against her, that the law enables, and justly enables, the slandered party to proceed; which would be monstrously unjust, if the law were not founded on the *right* which the husband has to control, if necessary, the tongue of the wife, to compel her to keep it within the limits prescribed by the law. A charming, a most enchanting life, indeed, would be that of a husband, if he were bound to cohabit with and to maintain one for all the debts and all the slanders of whom he was answerable, and over whose conduct he possessed no compulsory control. . . .

186. Am I recommending *tyranny?* Am I recommending *disregard* of the wife's opinions and wishes? Am I recommending a *reserve* towards her that would seem to say that she was not trustworthy, or not a party interested in her husband's affairs? By no means: on the contrary, though I would keep anything disagreeable from her, I should not enjoy the prospect of good without making her a participator. But reason says, and God has said, that it is the duty of wives to be obedient to their husbands; and the very nature of things prescribes that there must be *a head* of every house, and an *undivided*

authority. And then it is so clearly *just* that the authority should rest with him on whose head rests the whole responsibility, that a woman, when patiently reasoned with on the subject, must be a virago[2] in her very nature not to submit with docility to the terms of her marriage vow. . . .

189. "A house divided against itself," or, rather, *in* itself, "cannot stand"; and it *is* divided against itself if there be a *divided authority*. The wife ought to be *heard*, and *patiently* heard; she ought to be reasoned with, and, if possible, convinced; but if, after all endeavours in this way, she remain opposed to the husband's opinion, his will *must* be obeyed, or he at once becomes nothing; she is, in fact, the *master*, and he is nothing but an insignificant inmate. As to matters of little comparative moment; as to what shall be for dinner; as to how the house shall be furnished; as to the management of the house and of menial servants: as to those matters, and many others, the wife may have her way without any danger; but when the questions are, what is to be the *calling* to be pursued; what is to be the *place of residence*; what is to be the *style* of living and *scale* of expense; what is to be done with *property*; what the manner and place of educating children; what is to be their *calling* or state of life; who are to be employed or entrusted by the husband; what are the principles that he is to adopt as to public matters; whom he is to have for coadjutors[3] or friends; all these must be left solely to the husband; in all these he must have his will; or there never can be any harmony in the family. . . .

195. Now I would advise a young man, especially if he have a pretty wife, not to commit her unnecessarily to the care of any other man; not to be separated from her in this studious and ceremonious manner; and not to be ashamed to prefer her company and conversation to that of any other woman. I never could discover any *good-breeding* in setting another man, almost expressly, to poke his nose up in the face of my wife, and talk nonsense to her; for, in such cases, nonsense it generally is. It is not a thing of much consequence, to be sure; but when the wife is young, especially, it is not seemly, at any rate, and it cannot possibly lead to any good, though it may not lead to any great evil. And, on the other hand, you may be quite sure that, whatever she may *seem* to think of the matter, she will not like *you* the better for your attentions of this sort to other women, especially if they be young and

---

2. *virago*: a domineering, manlike woman
3. *coadjutors*: colleagues or assistants

handsome; and as this species of fashionable nonsense can do you no good, why gratify your love of talk, or the vanity of any woman, at even the risk of exciting uneasiness in that mind of which it is your most sacred duty to preserve, if you can, the uninterrupted tranquility. . . .

199. . . . [B]ad as is conjugal infidelity in the *husband*, it is much worse in the *wife*: a proposition that it is necessary to maintain by the force of reason, because *the women*, as a sisterhood, are prone to deny the truth of it. They say that *adultery* is *adultery*, in men as well as in them; and that, therefore, the offence is *as great* in the one case as in the other. As a crime, abstractedly considered, it certainly is; but, as to the *consequences*, there is a wide difference. In both cases there is the breach of a solemn vow, but there is this great distinction, that the husband, by his breach of that vow, only brings *shame* upon his wife and family; whereas the wife, by a breach of her vow, may bring the husband a spurious offspring to maintain, and may bring that spurious offspring to rob of their fortunes, and in some cases of their bread, her legitimate children. So that here is a great and evident wrong done to numerous parties, besides the deeper disgrace inflicted in this case than in the other.

200. And why is the disgrace *deeper?* Because here is a total want of *delicacy*; here is, in fact, *prostitution*; here is grossness and filthiness of mind; here is everything that argues baseness of character. Women should be, and they are, except in a few instances, far more reserved and more delicate than men: nature bids them be such; the habits and manners of the world confirm this precept of nature; and therefore, when they commit this offence, they excite loathing, as well as call for reprobation. In the countries where a *plurality of wives* is permitted, there is no *plurality of husbands*. It is there thought not at all indelicate for a man to have several wives; but the bare thought of a woman having *two husbands* would excite horror. The *widows* of the Hindoos burn themselves in the pile that consumes their husbands;[4] but the Hindoo *widowers* do not dispose of themselves in this way. . . .

201. For these plain and forcible reasons it is that this species of offence is far more heinous in the wife than in the husband; and the people of all civilized countries act upon this settled distinction. Men who have been guilty of the offence are not cut off from society, but women who have been guilty of it

---

4. For many Victorians, the practice of suttee served as an extreme example of ideal wifely devotion.

are; for, as we all know well, no woman, married or single, of *fair reputation*, will risk that reputation by being ever seen, if she can avoid it, with a woman who has ever, at any time, committed this offence, which contains in itself, and by universal award, a sentence of social excommunication for life.

202. If, therefore, it be the duty of the husband to adhere strictly to his marriage vow: if his breach of that vow be naturally attended with the fatal consequences above described: how much more imperative is the duty on the wife to avoid even the semblance of a deviation from that vow! If the man's misconduct, in this respect, bring shame on so many innocent parties, what shame, what dishonour, what misery follow such misconduct in the wife! Her parents, those of her husband, all her relations, and all her friends, share in her dishonour. And *her children!* how is she to make atonement to them! They are commanded to honour their father and their mother; but not such a mother as this, who, on the contrary, has no claim to anything from them but hatred, abhorrence, and execration. It is she who has broken the ties of nature; she has dishonoured her own offspring; she has fixed a mark of reproach on those who once made a part of her own body: nature shuts her out of the pale of its influence, and condemns her to the just detestation of those whom it formerly bade love her as their own life.

203. But as the crime is so much more heinous, and the punishment so much more severe, in the case of the wife than it is in the case of the husband, so that caution ought to be greater in making the accusation, or entertaining the suspicion. Men ought to be very slow in entertaining such suspicions: they ought to have clear *proof* before they can *suspect*; a proneness to such suspicions is a very unfortunate turn of the mind; and, indeed, few characters are more despicable than that of a *jealous-headed husband*; rather than be tied to the whims of one of whom, an innocent woman of spirit would earn her bread over the washing-tub, or with a hay-fork, or a reap-hook. With such a man there can be no peace; and, as far as children are concerned, the false accusation is nearly equal to the reality. When a wife discovers her jealousy, she merely imputes to her husband inconstancy and breach of his marriage vow: but jealousy in him imputes to her a willingness to palm a spurious offspring upon him, and upon her legitimate children, as robbers of their birthright; and, besides this, grossness, filthiness, and prostitution. She imputes to him injustice and cruelty: but he imputes to her that which banishes her from society; that which cuts her off for life from everything connected with female purity; that which brands her with infamy to her latest breath.

204. Very slow, therefore, ought a husband to be in entertaining even the thought of this crime in his wife. He ought to be *quite sure* before he take the smallest step in the way of accusation; but if unhappily he have the proof, no consideration on earth ought to induce him to cohabit with her one moment longer. Jealous husbands are not despicable because they have *grounds*; but because they *have not grounds*; and this is generally the case. When they have grounds, their own honour commands them to cast off the object, as they would cut out a corn or a cancer. It is not the jealousy in itself which is de-spicable; but the *continuing to live in that state*. It is no dishonour to be a slave in Algiers, for instance; the dishonour begins only where you remain a slave *voluntarily*; it begins the moment you can escape from slavery, and do not. It is despicable unjustly to be jealous of your wife; but it is infamy to cohabit with her if you *know* her to be guilty.

205. I shall be told that the *law* compels you to live with her, unless you be *rich* enough to disengage yourself from her; but the law does not compel you to remain *in the same country with her*; and, if a man have no other means of ridding himself of such a curse, what are mountains or seas to traverse? And what is the risk (if such there be) of exchanging a life of bodily ease for a life of labour? What are these, and numerous other ills (if they hap-pen) superadded? Nay, what is death itself, compared with the baseness, the infamy, the never-ceasing shame and reproach of living under the same roof with a prostituted woman, and calling her your *wife?* But there are *children*, and what are to become of these? To be taken away from the prostitute, to be sure; and this is a duty which you owe to them: the sooner they forget her the better, and the farther they are from her, the sooner that will be. There is no excuse for continuing to live with an adulteress: no inconvenience, no loss, no suffering, ought to deter a man from delivering himself from such a state of filthy infamy; and to suffer his children to remain in such a state is a crime that hardly admits of adequate description; a jail is paradise compared with such a life, and he who can endure this latter, from the fear of encountering hardship, is a wretch too despicable to go by the name of man.

206. But, now, all this supposes, that the husband has *well and truly acted his part!* It supposes, not only that he has been faithful; but that he has not, in any way, been the cause of temptation to the wife to be unfaithful. If he have been cold and neglectful; if he have led a life of irregularity; if he have proved to her that *home* was not his delight; if he have made his house the place of resort for loose companions; if he have given rise to a taste for visit-

ing, junketting,[5] parties of pleasure and gaiety; if he have introduced the habit of indulging in what are called *"innocent freedoms"*; if these, or any of these, the *fault is his*, he must take the consequences, and he has *no right* to inflict punishment on the offender, the offence being, in fact, of his own creating. The laws of God, as well as the laws of man, have given him all power in this respect: it is for him to use that power for the honour of his wife as well as for that of himself: if he neglect to use it, all the consequences ought to fall on him; and, as far as my observation has gone, in nineteen out of twenty cases of infidelity in wives, the crimes have been *fairly ascribable to the husbands*. Folly or misconduct in the husband cannot, indeed, justify or even palliate[6] infidelity in the wife, whose very nature ought to make her recoil at the thought of the offence; but it may, at the same time, deprive him of the right of inflicting punishment on her: her kindred, her children, and the world, will justly hold her in abhorrence; but the husband must hold his peace.

207. *"Innocent freedoms!"* I know of none that a wife can indulge in. The words, as applied to the demeanour of a married woman, or even a single one, imply a contradiction. For *freedom*, thus used, means an exemption or departure from the *strict rules of female reserve*; and I do not see how this can be *innocent*. It may not amount to *crime*, indeed; but still it is not *innocent*; and the use of the phrase is dangerous. If it had been my fortune to be yoked to a person who liked "innocent freedoms," I should have unyoked myself in a very short time. But, to say the truth, it is all a man's own fault. If he have not sense and influence enough to prevent "innocent freedoms," even *before* marriage, he will do well to let the thing alone, and leave wives to be managed by those who have. But men will talk to your wife, and flatter her. To be sure they will, if she be young and pretty; and would you go and pull her away from them? Oh no, by no means; but you must have very little sense, or must have made very little use of it, if her manner do not soon convince them that they employ their flattery in vain.

208. So much of a man's happiness and of his *efficiency* through life depends upon his mind being quite free from all anxieties of this sort, that too much care cannot be taken to guard against them; and, I repeat, that the great preservation of all is, the young couple living as much as possible at *home*, and having as few visitors as possible. If they do not prefer the company

---

5. *junketting*: carousing
6. *palliate*: ease

of each other to that of all the world besides; if either of them be weary of the company of the other; if they do not, when separated by business or any other cause, think with pleasure of the time of meeting again, it is a bad omen. Pursue this course when young, and the very thought of jealousy will never come into your mind; and, if you do pursue it, and show by your *deeds* that you value your wife as you do your own life, you must be pretty nearly an idiot if she do not think you to be the wisest man in the world. The *best* man she will be sure to think you, and she will never forgive any one that calls your talents or your wisdom in question.

# John Paget, from
# "The English Law of Divorce" (1856)[1]

John Paget (1811–1898) was a police magistrate, barrister, and au-
thor. This selection offers insight into the logistical reasons why a
Victorian husband who suspected his wife of adultery might choose
to remain married to her, despite the fact that a wife's infidelity was
the only legal basis for divorce at the time. In this review article,
Paget purports to present his readers with a "concise and intelligible
summary" of the English court's position on divorce. The difficulty,
which the article points to with regular sarcasm, is that the laws are
so convoluted and self-contradictory, that composing a "concise and
intelligible summary" is simply impossible: the process was opaque,
expensive, and extraordinarily cumbersome. It was also open to
abuse, as a man could pay a willing agent to swear to having a re-
lationship with his wife, and she was given no recourse to defend
herself in the criminal proceeding and scant opportunity in the eccle-
siastical proceeding. Paget's argument anticipates the reforms that
the 1857 Matrimonial Causes Act attempted to effect.

O ne of the obstacles in the way of a prompt and thorough reform
of our Ecclesiastical Courts,[2] is the difficulty of obtaining accurate
information with regard to the practice and actual mode of work-
ing of those courts, divested of the technical language (which to the ears of
the uninitiated, seems an unintelligible jargon) in which their proceedings
are carried on. The phraseology of our courts of Common Law has become
grafted into our ordinary conversation, and everybody is familiar with plain-

---

1. John Paget, "The English Law of Divorce," *Westminster Review* (April 1856): 338–42, 345.
2. *Ecclesiastical Courts*: courts of the Church of England with jurisdiction over religious
matters

tiffs and defendants. It is not so with the language of Doctors' Commons;[3] and if, in a mixed company, any one were to speak of promovents, impugnants, producents and administrants,[4] he would be justly suspected of pedantry, and would probably be utterly unintelligible, unless some one of his audience had the misfortune of having at some time filled one of those characters. In such a case, the speaker would in all probability find that he had touched a very sore place, and would turn the conversation, and get out of the scrape as quickly as possible. We purpose, therefore, to place before our readers a concise and intelligible summary of the position in which the law now stands on the most important, and at the same time the most difficult matter confided to these courts, viz., that of divorce.

We shall not, in this article, enter upon the vexed questions as to what should, and what should not, be a sufficient ground for a divorce. All civilized countries which permit divorce at all, recognise the infidelity of the wife as a sufficient ground for relieving the husband from the bond of marriage. The law of England permits a legal separation, or divorce *a mensâ et thoro*,[5] on proof of such offence having been committed by either party; but in practice, and with exceptions too rare and peculiar to require notice, grants a complete divorce *a vinculo*[6] only at the suit of the husband. Continental codes grant a complete divorce to the wife, if the husband has outraged her by bringing the partner of his guilt under the roof where the wife inhabits. The law of Scotland and of the principal States of North America, visits the infidelity of the husband with the same penalty as the infidelity of the wife.

For our present purpose, we accept the law as it stands; and when the law has determined what circumstances shall entitle any party to demand a divorce, we presume it will be admitted that every delay, every expense, every difficulty, except what is necessary for satisfactorily proving the existence of those circumstances, is a wrong and an injustice. Let us see how the law of

---

3. *Doctors' Commons*: The Courts of Common Law adjudicate based upon precedent; here, the Courts of Common Law would take up criminal action as opposed to the Doctors' Commons, which would address civil actions.

4. *promovents, impugnants, producents and administrants*: terms unique to the Ecclesiastical Courts, which are not used in any other branch of the law

5. *a mensâ et thoro*: Latin, "from bed and board"; as Paget notes, a legal separation as opposed to a divorce

6. *a vinculo*: shortened form of *a vinculo matrimonii*, Latin for "from the bond of marriage"; a total and complete divorce of the marital tie

England, having determined that a husband whose wife is unfaithful shall be entitled to a complete divorce, sets about to achieve that object.

It begins hopefully, by flatly contradicting itself.

The Law says, when you have once entered into a valid marriage, no subsequent circumstance but death shall absolve you from it, and enable you to contract a second union.

The Legislature says, prove that your partner in the marriage-contract has been faithless, and we will alter the law in your individual case; but we will only do so on the condition that you shall have previously obtained every redress that law will give you for your wrongs.

The first step which a husband is thus compelled to take to obtain his freedom, is one revolting to every man of honour and high feeling. He must appraise his wife, put a money-value on the sanctity of his hearth and the purity of his bed, pocket the price of infidelity, in the form of damages in an action of crim. con.,[7] and extort by law what he would be eternally disgraced were he to accept if voluntarily offered!

He then enters the Ecclesiastical Court and sues for a divorce *a mensâ et thoro*. Hitherto, revolting as the action against his wife's seducer is to all his feelings, he has been fighting in open day. But the scene now changes. As sometimes happens in a London fog, a single step takes him from broad daylight into the thickest obscurity. He may be met with counter charges, utterly groundless but difficult to disprove, and what is the machinery which the law provides for the elimination of truth in the Ecclesiastical Courts? Here is a picture by no means overcharged of the process:—[8]

"In all courts the first material proceeding in the inquiry, and which necessarily precedes the evidence, consists in the statement of the case on each side, and these statements are technically known by the name of 'The Pleadings.'

"In a criminal case they consist of the 'Indictment' and 'Plea.'

"The 'Indictment' is a short and plain statement of the offence with which the prisoner is charged.

---

7. *crim. con.*: criminal conversation, i.e., unlawful sexual intercourse with a married person; adultery

8. The following series of quotations are from Paget's own book, *Ecclesiastical Courts. A report of the Judgment Delivered by Dr. Radcliffe, in the Case of Talbot v. Talbot, in the Consistorial Court of Dublin* (London: Thomas Blenkarn, 1854), 6–8.

"The plea of 'Not guilty' requires the prosecutor to prove the case, and entitles the prisoner to give any evidence in his power of his innocence.

"In an action at Common Law the pleadings consist of the 'Declaration,' which contains the plaintiff's statement of his ground of complaint—the 'Plea,' which contains the defendant's answer; and if anything further remains to be told, these are followed by the 'Replication' and 'Rejoinder,' and other pleadings, distinguished by various technical designations, until the story on each side is fully before the court.

"In Chancery[9] the same object is obtained by the 'Bill' of the plaintiff and the 'Answer' of the defendant.

"A suit for divorce by reason of adultery, in the Ecclesiastical Courts, partakes of the nature both of a criminal and a civil proceeding.

"The wife is on her trial for a crime, and so far as regards her the proceeding is criminal.

"The husband seeks redress for a wrong, and so far as regards him the proceeding is civil.

"The pleadings consist in the first place of the 'Libel,' which is exhibited by the husband or 'Promovent,' as he is technically called.

"This is analogous to the Indictment in a criminal or the Declaration in a civil proceeding. It contains a statement of the complaint.

"This is met by a Plea or 'Defensive Allegation,' which contains the counter-statement of the wife, who is technically designated as the 'Impugnant.'

"If further facts have to be brought forward on either side, and the nature and circumstances of the case are such as to render it necessary, each party may state those further facts and add to their original statements by pleading 'Additional Articles' until the story is complete on both sides.

"We now come to what is the pith, marrow, and essence of every judicial inquiry, however conducted—the Evidence. Each party produces his witnesses.

"Here the great and striking difference between the mode of procedure in the Ecclesiastical Courts and the Courts of Common Law commences.

"The proctor draws, or is supposed to draw, the article in support of which he produces a witness, from information furnished to him by that

---

9. *Chancery*: the court of the Lord Chancellor of England, a court of equity with jurisdiction over matters such as wills, estates, and trusts

witness. The witness tells his story to the proctor. The proctor draws the article from the information so given, and then sends the witness in to prove it.

"This is the case where proctor and witness are both honest; but there is nothing whatever, except the subsequent penalties of perjury upon the witness if he is caught out, to prevent the process from being reversed, and the proctor from drawing the article to suit what he wants to prove, and then finding a witness to prove it.

"If the witness has a tolerable memory, and is sufficiently unscrupulous, he is pretty sure to prove any article he is designed to, for he goes direct from the proctor's or attorney's office to the Examiner, who is an officer of the court; he sits with him in a private room, no eye to watch him, no ear to mark his faltering voice as he approaches the perjury he is about to commit; the article he is to prove is read over to him, and his deposition taken down, almost in the very words to which he has been drilled by the attorney or the proctor whose office he has just quitted.

"This machinery, ingeniously as it is adapted for ensuring and protecting falsehood, sometimes fails. It occasionally happens that a witness shrinks from the actual commission of the crime he has undertaken, and speaks the truth he has promised to suppress; but this, as may well be supposed, is rare, and in general it may be assumed that a witness proves in chief the article to which he is designed.

"We now come to the cross examination.

"Before a witness is produced, the proctor for the opposite party receives notice of the name of the witness and the articles he is vouched to support, and he then prepares interrogatories to be administered to the witness. These interrogatories are reduced into writing and given to the Examiner, who cross-examines the witness from them; but they are not communicated to the party who produces the witness, nor does he know what questions have been put, or what answers have been given, unless the witness divulges them, which he is cautioned not to do, a caution which, it is presumed, he does not very often obey. The proctor or counsel who prepares the interrogatories does not know what the witness has deposed in chief; and, as the examination in chief and the cross-examination are both in secret, it follows that there is no re-examination.

"The evidence remains under the seal of official secrecy until it is completed on both sides; when that is the case, each party is entitled to know what has been sworn, and, as it is technically called, 'Publication passes.' . . .

"If the ingenuity of man had been employed for the express purpose of inventing a scheme for the concealment of the truth, one more perfect could hardly have been devised.

"The evidence is given in secret. Not even the judge who has to decide upon it is present when the witness is examined. No one but the officer of the court, whose lips are sealed by his official duty, knows the manner, demeanour, or general behaviour of the witness whilst giving his evidence.

"Cross-examination, the sword of truth, is turned from steel to lead. All who have wielded that weapon know how powerless it is except in the swift thrust and parry of oral contest. It is only in the rapid movements of such a struggle that the joints of the armour of fraud open and admit its point.

"A cross-examination by written interrogatories, in secret, and where the evidence given in chief is unknown, must (except under circumstances of the most extraordinary good fortune) be a mere farce, a 'mockery, a delusion, and a snare.'"[10] . . .

[Paget next describes a similarly confounding process in the civil courts.]

Having passed this ordeal—having, notwithstanding the difficulties thus opposed, established his right to a divorce *a mensâ et thoro*, to a decree which, while it relieves him from the society of his faithless partner, sentences him to "live a man forbid,"—he is at last permitted to appear at the bar of the House of Lords, there to commence *de novo*,[11] to prove over again what he has proved twice before, and to establish, for the third time, a right to redress, so strong that it entitles him to relief by a special Act of Parliament. Thus, whilst law and justice admit that the right to relief is unanswerable, the only mode by which that relief can be obtained is when, after three tedious and expensive processes—after commencing with an action which a Lord Chancellor has denounced as "a disgrace to the country," and "a stigma on the law of England," and concluding by a process which a Chief Justice has declared to be "a scandalous practice," and a lay peer has held up to contempt, as "disgusting and demoralizing," the sword of the Legislature at last

---

10. [Paget's footnote:] Sir Anthony Hart says, speaking of the similar system which formerly prevailed in the Court of Chancery, "As cross-examinations are at present, they are mere random hits in the dark. When I was very young at the bar, I used to cross-examine, but I soon gave it up. For the last thirty years I hardly recommended it—I may say, I left it off as hopeless—I abandoned it in despair."—Per Sir Anthony Hart, Lord Chancellor of Ireland, in Booth *v.* Parks, 1 *Molloy*, 467.

11. *de novo*: Latin, "from the beginning"

cuts the knot in the individual case, and leaves the law of the land where it found it—in what law-makers themselves have designated as a "barbarous," "indecent," "oppressive," "anomalous," "preposterous," and "utterly disgraceful" condition!

Such are the means which the law provides for the vindication of an unquestioned right, in the very small number of cases in which it permits that right to be vindicated at all; for a process, the cost of which must amount, at the lowest estimate, to many hundreds of pounds, and may, and frequently does, amount to thousands, can be attainable only by a very small percentage of the persons aggrieved. But partial, costly, and inefficient as is the assertion of a right, this same law becomes the most terrible agent in the infliction of a wrong. Impotent to protect, it is powerful to oppress; weak for the weak, it is strong for the strong; powerless for good, it is omnipotent for evil.

# John Ruskin, from
## *Sesame and Lilies* (1865)[1]

John Ruskin (1819–1900) is a major figure of Victorian letters, writing widely as a critic of art, literature, and culture. In *Sesame and Lilies*, he offers a series of lectures describing education's role in man's life and—as follows—in woman's; along the way, he articulates what he considers to be the essential nature of the sexes. In this excerpt, perhaps the best known from the lectures, Ruskin depends on binary oppositions: he concludes that a "man's power is active, progressive, defensive" and that man is "the doer, the creator, the discoverer, the defender," while a woman's power and intellect is best used "not for invention or creation, but for sweet ordering, arrangement, and decision." In prose littered with literary allusions, Ruskin constructs an argument that is as conservative as Mill's is progressive; it is worth noting that Meredith challenges Ruskin's version of manhood in the *Modern Love* poems.

We cannot determine what the queenly power of women should be, until we are agreed what their ordinary power should be. We cannot consider how education may fit them for any widely extending duty, until we are agreed what is their true constant duty. And there never was a time when wilder words were spoken, or more vain imagination permitted, respecting this question—quite vital to all social happiness. The relations of the womanly to the manly nature, their different capacities of intellect or of virtue, seem never to have been yet measured with entire consent. We hear of the mission and of the rights of Woman, as if these could

---

1. John Ruskin, "Of Queens' Gardens," in *Sesame and Lilies* (London: Smith, Elder, 1865), 123–25, 146–50, 177–87.

ever be separate from the mission and the rights of Man;—as if she and her lord were creatures of independent kind and of irreconcilable claim. This, at least, is wrong. And not less wrong—perhaps even more foolishly wrong (for I will anticipate thus far what I hope to prove)—is the idea that woman is only the shadow and attendant image of her lord, owing him a thoughtless and servile obedience, and supported altogether in her weakness by the pre-eminence of his fortitude.

This, I say, is the most foolish of all errors respecting her who was made to be the helpmate of man. As if he could be helped effectively by a shadow, or worthily by a slave! . . .

We are foolish, and without excuse foolish, in speaking of the "superiority" of one sex to the other, as if they could be compared in similar things. Each has what the other has not: each completes the other, and is completed by the other: they are in nothing alike, and the happiness and perfection of both depends on each asking and receiving from the other what the other only can give.

Now their separate characters are briefly these. The man's power is active, progressive, defensive. He is eminently the doer, the creator, the discoverer, the defender. His intellect is for speculation and invention; his energy for adventure, for war, and for conquest, wherever war is just, wherever conquest necessary. But the woman's power is for rule, not for battle,—and her intellect is not for invention or creation, but for sweet ordering, arrangement, and decision. She sees the qualities of things, their claims, and their places. Her great function is Praise: she enters into no contest, but infallibly adjudges the crown of contest. By her office, and place, she is protected from all danger and temptation. The man, in his rough work in open world, must encounter all peril and trial:—to him, therefore, the failure, the offence, the inevitable error: often he must be wounded, or subdued, often misled, and *always* hardened. But he guards the woman from all this; within his house, as ruled by her, unless she herself has sought it, need enter no danger, no temptation, no cause of error or offence. This is the true nature of home—it is the place of Peace; the shelter, not only from all injury, but from all terror, doubt, and division. In so far as it is not this, it is not home; so far as the anxieties of the outer life penetrate into it, and the inconsistently-minded, unknown, unloved, or hostile society of the outer world is allowed by either husband or wife to cross the threshold, it ceases to be home; it is then only a part of that outer world which you have roofed over, and lighted fire in. But so far as it is a sacred place, a vestal temple, a temple of the hearth watched over by Household Gods, before whose faces none may come but those whom they can receive with love,—so far as it is this, and roof and fire are types only of a nobler shade and light,—shade as of the rock in a weary land, and light as of the Pharos in the stormy sea;—so far it vindicates the name, and fulfils the praise, of Home.

And wherever a true wife comes, this home is always round her. The stars only may be over her head; the glowworm in the night-cold grass may be the only fire at her foot: but home is yet wherever she is; and for a noble woman it stretches far round her, better than ceiled with cedar, or painted with vermilion,[2] shedding its quiet light far, for those who else were homeless.

This, then, I believe to be,—will you not admit it to be,—the woman's true place and power? But do not you see that, to fulfil this, she must—as far as one can use such terms of a human creature—be incapable of error? So far as she rules, all must be right, or nothing is. She must be enduringly, incorruptibly good; instinctively, infallibly wise—wise, not for self-development, but for self-renunciation: wise, not that she may set herself above her husband, but that she may never fail from his side: wise, not with the narrowness of insolent and loveless pride, but with the passionate gentleness of an infinitely variable, because infinitely applicable, modesty of service—the true changefulness of woman. In that great sense—"La donna e mobile,"[3] not "Qual piùm' al vento";[4] no, nor yet "Variable as the shade, by the light quivering aspen made";[5] but variable as the *light*, manifold in fair and serene division, that it may take the colour of all that it falls upon, and exalt it. . . .

Generally, we are under an impression that a man's duties are public, and a woman's private. But this is not altogether so. A man has a personal work or duty, relating to his own home, and a public work or duty, which is the expansion of the other, relating to the state. So a woman has a personal work or duty, relating to her own home, and a public work and duty, which is also the expansion of that.

---

2. *vermilion*: red

3. *La donna e[é] mobile*: "Woman is fickle," the opening line of a famous aria from Verdi's 1851 opera *Rigoletto*

4. *Qual piùm'[piuma] al vento*: "Like a feather on the wind," the second line of the aria

5. *Variable . . . made*: from Sir Walter Scott's *Marmion*, Canto VI, XXX.3–4

Now the man's work for his own home is, as has been said, to secure its maintenance, progress, and defence; the woman's to secure its order, comfort, and loveliness.

Expand both these functions. The man's duty, as a member of a commonwealth, is to assist in the maintenance, in the advance, in the defence of the state. The woman's duty, as a member of the commonwealth, is to assist in the ordering, in the comforting, and in the beautiful adornment of the state.

What the man is at his own gate, defending it, if need be, against insult and spoil, that also, not in a less, but in a more devoted measure, he is to be at the gate of his country, leaving his home, if need be, even to the spoiler, to do his more incumbent work there.

And, in like manner, what the woman is to be within her gates, as the centre of order, the balm of distress, and the mirror of beauty; that she is also to be without her gates, where order is more difficult, distress more imminent, loveliness more rare.

And as within the human heart there is always set an instinct for all its real duties,—an instinct which you cannot quench, but only warp and corrupt if you withdraw it from its true purpose;—as there is the intense instinct of love, which, rightly disciplined, maintains all the sanctities of life, and, misdirected, undermines them; and *must* do either the one or the other;—so there is in the human heart an inextinguishable instinct, the love of power, which, rightly directed, maintains all the majesty of law and life, and misdirected, wrecks them.

Deep rooted in the innermost life of the heart of man, and of the heart of woman, God set it there, and God keeps it there. Vainly, as falsely, you blame or rebuke the desire of power!—For Heaven's sake, and for Man's sake, desire it all you can. But *what* power? That is all the question. Power to destroy? the lion's limb, and the dragon's breath? Not so. Power to heal, to redeem, to guide, and to guard. Power of the sceptre and shield; the power of the royal hand that heals in touching,—that binds the fiend, and looses the captive; the throne that is founded on the rock of Justice, and descended from only by steps of mercy. Will you not covet such power as this, and seek such throne as this, and be no more housewives, but queens?

It is now long since the women of England arrogated, universally, a title which once belonged to nobility only; and, having once been in the habit of accepting the simple title of gentlewoman, as correspondent to that of gentle-

man, insisted on the privilege of assuming the title of "Lady,"[6] which prop-
erly corresponds only to the title of "Lord."

I do not blame them for this; but only for their narrow motive in this. I
would have them desire and claim the title of Lady, provided they claim, not
merely the title, but the office and duty signified by it. Lady means "bread-
giver" or "loaf-giver," and Lord means "maintainer of laws," and both titles
have reference, not to the law which is maintained in the house, nor to the
bread which is given to the household; but to law maintained for the mul-
titude, and to bread broken among the multitude. So that a Lord has legal
claim only to his title in so far as he is the maintainer of the justice of the
Lord of Lords; and a Lady has legal claim to her title only so far as she com-
municates that help to the poor representatives of her Master,[7] which women
once, ministering to Him of their substance, were permitted to extend to that
Master Himself; and when she is known, as He Himself once was, in breaking
of bread.

And this beneficent and legal dominion, this power of the Dominus, or
House-Lord, and of the Domina, or House-Lady, is great and venerable, not
in the number of those through whom it has lineally descended, but in the
number of those whom it grasps within its sway; it is always regarded with
reverent worship wherever its dynasty is founded on its duty, and its ambi-
tion co-relative with its beneficence. Your fancy is pleased with the thought
of being noble ladies, with a train of vassals. Be it so; you cannot be too noble,
and your train cannot be too great; but see to it that your train is of vassals
whom you serve and feed, not merely of slaves who serve and feed *you*; and
that the multitude which obeys you is of those whom you have comforted,
not oppressed,—whom you have redeemed, not led into captivity.

And this, which is true of the lower or household dominion, is equally
true of the queenly dominion;—that highest dignity is open to you, if you
will also accept that highest duty. Rex et Regina—Roi et Reine[8]—"*Right-
doers*"; they differ but from the Lady and Lord, in that their power is su-

---

6. [Ruskin's footnote:] I wish there were a true order of chivalry instituted for our English
youth of certain ranks, in which both boy and girl should receive, at a given age, their knighthood and
ladyhood by true title; attainable only by certain probation and trial both of character and accomplish-
ment; and to be forfeited, on conviction, by their peers, of any dishonourable act. Such an institution
would be entirely, and with all noble results, possible, in a nation which loved honour. That it would
not be possible among us, is not to the discredit of the scheme.

7. *Master*: Here, *Master* refers not to a wife's husband, but to the Christian God.

8. *Rex et Regina—Roi et Reine*: "King and Queen" in Latin and French, respectively

preme over the mind as over the person—that they not only feed and clothe, but direct and teach. And whether consciously or not, you must be, in many a heart, enthroned: there is no putting by that crown; queens you must always be; queens to your lovers; queens to your husbands and your sons; queens of higher mystery to the world beyond, which bows itself, and will for ever bow, before the myrtle crown, and the stainless sceptre, of womanhood. But, alas! you are too often idle and careless queens, grasping at majesty in the least things, while you abdicate it in the greatest; and leaving misrule and violence to work their will among men, in defiance of the power, which, holding straight in gift from the Prince of all Peace, the wicked among you betray, and the good forget.

"Prince of Peace." Note that name. When kings rule in that name, and nobles, and the judges of the earth, they also, in their narrow place, and mortal measure, receive the power of it. There are no other rulers than they: other rule than theirs is but *mis*rule; they who govern verily "Dei gratiâ"[9] are all princes, yes, or princesses, of peace. There is not a war in the world, no, nor an injustice, but you women are answerable for it; not in that you have provoked, but in that you have not hindered. Men, by their nature, are prone to fight; they will fight for any cause, or for none. It is for you to choose their cause for them, and to forbid them when there is no cause. There is no suffering, no injustice, no misery in the earth, but the guilt of it lies lastly with you. Men can bear the sight of it, but you should not be able to bear it. Men may tread it down without sympathy in their own struggle; but men are feeble in sympathy, and contracted in hope; it is you only who can feel the depths of pain; and conceive the way of its healing. Instead of trying to do this, you turn away from it; you shut yourselves within your park walls and garden gates; and you are content to know that there is beyond them a whole world in wilderness—a world of secrets which you dare not penetrate; and of suffering which you dare not conceive.

---

9. *Dei gratiâ*: Latin, "By the Grace of God"

# John Stuart Mill, from
## *The Subjection of Women* (1869)[1]

Social theorist and political philosopher John Stuart Mill (1806–1873) offers here an impassioned, utilitarian argument for the value of a marriage based on notions of personal and legal equality. The text made a strong impression on Meredith: John Morley writes in *Recollections* that Meredith "eagerly seized [*The Subjection of Women*], fell to devouring it in settled silence, and could not be torn from it all day."[2] In the section excerpted here, Mill outlines reasons for redressing structural imbalances regarding the rights and expectations of husbands and wives, arguing, for example, that a woman's contributions to household duties should be considered on par with a husband's income.

I readily admit (and it is the very foundation of my hopes) that numbers of married people even under the present law, (in the higher classes of England probably a great majority,) live in the spirit of a just law of equality. Laws never would be improved, if there were not numerous persons whose moral sentiments are better than the existing laws. Such persons ought to support the principles here advocated; of which the only object is to make all other married couples similar to what these are now. But persons even of considerable moral worth, unless they are also thinkers, are very ready to believe that laws or practices, the evils of which they have not personally experienced, do not produce any evils, but (if seeming to be generally approved of) probably do good, and that it is wrong to object to them. It would, however, be a great mistake in such married people to suppose, because the legal conditions of the tie which unites them do not occur to their thoughts once

1. John Stuart Mill, *The Subjection of Women* (London: Longmans, Green, Reader, and Dyer, 1870), 83–90.

2. John Morley, *Recollections* (New York: Macmillan, 1917), 47.

in a twelvemonth, and because they live and feel in all respects as if they were legally equals, that the same is the case with all other married couples, wherever the husband is not a notorious ruffian. To suppose this, would be to show equal ignorance of human nature and of fact. The less fit a man is for the possession of power—the less likely to be allowed to exercise it over any person with that person's voluntary consent—the more does he hug himself in the consciousness of the power the law gives him, exact its legal rights to the utmost point which custom (the custom of men like himself) will tolerate, and take pleasure in using the power, merely to enliven the agreeable sense of possessing it. What is more; in the most naturally brutal and morally uneducated part of the lower classes, the legal slavery of the woman, and something in the merely physical subjection to their will as an instrument, causes them to feel a sort of disrespect and contempt towards their own wife which they do not feel towards any other woman, or any other human being, with whom they come in contact; and which makes her seem to them an appropriate subject for any kind of indignity. Let an acute observer of the signs of feeling, who has the requisite opportunities, judge for himself whether this is not the case: and if he finds that it is, let him not wonder at any amount of disgust and indignation that can be felt against institutions which lead naturally to this depraved state of the human mind.

We shall be told, perhaps, that religion imposes the duty of obedience; as every established fact which is too bad to admit of any other defence, is always presented to us as an injunction of religion. The Church, it is very true, enjoins it in her formularies, but it would be difficult to derive any such injunction from Christianity. We are told that St. Paul said, "Wives, obey your husbands": but he also said, "Slaves, obey your masters." It was not St. Paul's business, nor was it consistent with his object, the propagation of Christianity, to incite anyone to rebellion against existing laws. The apostle's acceptance of all social institutions as he found them, is no more to be construed as a disapproval of attempts to improve them at the proper time, than his declaration, "The powers that be are ordained of God," gives his sanction to military despotism, and to that alone, as the Christian form of political government, or commands passive obedience to it. . . .

After what has been said respecting the obligation of obedience, it is almost superfluous to say anything concerning the more special point included in the general one—a woman's right to her own property; for I need not hope that this treatise can make any impression upon those who need anything to convince them that a woman's inheritance or gains ought to be as much her own after marriage as before. The rule is simple: whatever would be the husband's or wife's if they were not married, should be under their exclusive control during marriage; which need not interfere with the power to tie up property by settlement, in order to preserve it for children. Some people are sentimentally shocked at the idea of a separate interest in money matters, as inconsistent with the ideal fusion of two lives into one. For my own part, I am one of the strongest supporters of community of goods, when resulting from an entire unity of feeling in the owners, which makes all things common between them. But I have no relish for a community of goods resting on the doctrine, that what is mine is yours but what is yours is not mine; and I should prefer to decline entering into such a compact with anyone, though I were myself the person to profit by it.

This particular injustice and oppression to women, which is, to common apprehensions, more obvious than all the rest, admits of remedy without interfering with any other mischiefs: and there can be little doubt that it will be one of the earliest remedied. Already, in many of the new and several of the old States of the American Confederation, provisions have been inserted even in the written Constitutions, securing to women equality of rights in this respect: and thereby improving materially the position, in the marriage relation, of those women at least who have property, by leaving them one instrument of power which they have not signed away; and preventing also the scandalous abuse of the marriage institution, which is perpetrated when a man entraps a girl into marrying him without a settlement, for the sole purpose of getting possession of her money. When the support of the family depends, not on property, but on earnings, the common arrangement, by which the man earns the income and the wife superintends the domestic expenditure, seems to me in general the most suitable division of labour between the two persons. If, in addition to the physical suffering of bearing children, and the whole responsibility of their care and education in early years, the wife undertakes the careful and economical application of the husband's earnings to the general comfort of the family; she takes not only her fair share, but usually the larger share, of the bodily and mental exertion required by their joint existence. If she undertakes any additional portion, it seldom relieves her from this, but only prevents her from performing it properly. The care which she is herself disabled from taking of the children and the household, nobody else takes; those of the children who do not die, grow up as they best can, and the management of the household is likely to be so bad, as even in point of economy to be a great drawback from the value of the wife's earnings. In an otherwise just state of things, it is not, therefore, I think, a desirable custom, that the wife should contribute by her labour to the income of the family. In an unjust state of things, her doing so may be useful to her, by making her of more value in the eyes of the man who is legally her master; but, on the other hand, it enables him still farther to abuse his power, by forcing her to work, and leaving the support of the family to her exertions, while he spends most of his time in drinking and idleness. The *power* of earning is essential to the dignity of a woman, if she has not independent property. But if marriage were an equal contract, not implying the obligation of obedience; if the connexion were no longer enforced to the oppression of those to whom it is purely a mischief, but a separation, on just terms (I do not now speak of a divorce), could be obtained by any woman who was morally entitled to it; and if she would then find all honourable employments as freely open to her as to men; it would not be necessary for her protection, that during marriage she should make this particular use of her faculties. Like a man when he chooses a profession, so, when a woman marries, it may in general be understood that she makes choice of the management of a household, and the bringing up of a family, as the first call upon her exertions, during as many years of her life as may be required for the purpose; and that she renounces, not all other objects and occupations, but all which are not consistent with the requirements of this. The actual exercise, in a habitual or systematic manner, of outdoor occupations, or such as cannot be carried on at home, would by this principle be practically interdicted to the greater number of married women. But the utmost latitude ought to exist for the adaptation of general rules to individual suitabilities; and there ought to be nothing to prevent faculties exceptionally adapted to any other pursuit, from obeying their vocation notwithstanding marriage: due provision being made for supplying otherwise any falling-short which might become inevitable, in her full performance of the ordinary functions of mistress of a family. These things, if once opinion were rightly directed on the subject, might with perfect safety be left to be regulated by opinion, without any interference of law.

# On the Senses

Is poetry, as John Stuart Mill suggested, the "logical opposite" of science? While the methods and goals of each discipline may be very different, the influence of nineteenth-century science on the literary arts cannot be underestimated. It is clear from the excerpts that follow that the ways in which Victorian scientists and physiologists understood sensory experience directly influenced the ways in which poets composed verse and readers conceived of their encounters with poetry.

Victorian treatises on the material processes of sensory perception are particularly relevant with regard to Meredith's poetry. As detractors and devotees alike noted, Meredith's poetry is filled with sensuous detail. Recalling the representational strategies of Pre-Raphaelite painting, the poems of *Modern Love* render the material world as it appears to the senses—minutely, colorfully, and without conventional judgment. Meredith invites his readers to see, hear, touch, and smell worlds both ancient and modern. The excerpts included in this section reveal the ways that Meredith's use of sensory detail engages with contemporary efforts to theorize the relationship between intellectual understanding and the body.

What readers of these extracts may find most surprising is that even scientists insist that comprehending poetry is more than just an intellectual activity; it is also a physical one. Alexander Bain, for instance, explains that since the "essence of cerebral action" is "the transmission of influence along the nerve fibres from place to place," cerebral life isolated from the body does not exist; even when we reminiscence, the brain communicates with the rest of the body. The body is thus important to his understanding of a person's emotional experience of art. Bain also discusses the implications that his theory has for understanding literary tropes like metaphor, and he articulates his position on the standards by which one adjudicates art. Against those who claim that art should reflect nature and represent truth, Bain maintains that art should gratify "the senses and the aesthetic sensibilities," leaving the precise rendering of revolting facts to science. Like Bain, Alexander Bryan Johnson is particularly concerned with the difficulty of communicating sensory experience via language. He offers metaphor as a solution to this problem, arguing that our ability to create and understand metaphors is rooted in sensory experience. Johnson offers a three-part taxonomy of knowledge—"sensible" knowledge (what one can learn through sensory experience), "intellectual" knowledge (what one understands verbally or intellectually), and "emotional" knowledge (the compensatory knowledge that we gain through analogy)—which seems almost postmodern. Using highly figurative language, the excerpts from George Wilson's introduction to *The Five Senses: Or, Gateways to Knowledge* and his chapter on hearing focus on a concept central to the aforementioned discussions, most of the reviews of *Modern Love*, and the "Nineteenth-Century Poetics" selections: aesthetic pleasure. Although Wilson opens his chapter on hearing by describing how the ear works, he ends the chapter with a discussion of imagined sounds and his reasons for deeming hearing the most poetical of the five senses.

Together these selections illuminate the connections between Victorian poetic and scientific discourses, reminding readers that the boundaries between the disciplines were less rigid then than they are today.

# Alexander Bain, from
## *The Senses and the Intellect* (1855)[1]

Alexander Bain (1818–1903), one of the founders of modern psychology, was a Scottish natural philosopher, writer, and academic. A materialist and an associationist, Bain maintained that understanding how humans process sensory experiences was key to constructing a viable theory of mental life. Previously experienced sensations are revived as ideas according to "laws" of association, including the "Law of Contiguity," "Law of Similarity," and "Law of Contrast." In the excerpts that follow, Bain explains why mental life necessarily involves the body, and he describes the relationship between his model of mind and artistic creation. Against those who regard fidelity to nature as the most important standard by which to judge poetry, Bain insists that the poet's standard ought to be feeling. The numbers preceding each section are from Bain's original; we retain them here for readers' convenience.

## From "Of the Nerve Force and the Course of Power in the Brain"[2]

25. . . . The organ of mind is not the brain by itself; it is the brain, nerves, muscles, and organs of sense. When the brain is in action, there is some transmission of nerve power, and the organ that receives or that originated the power is an essential part of the mechanism. A brain bereft of the spinal cord and spinal nerves is dead though the blood continues to flow to it; and these nerves,[3] if plucked out of the limbs

---

1. Alexander Bain, *The Senses and the Intellect* (London: John W. Parker and Son, 1855).

2. Ibid., 61–62.

3. According to Bain, "*The function of a nerve is to transmit impressions, influences, or stimuli, from one part of the system to another.* The nerves originate nothing; they are exclusively a medium of communication" (*The* Senses, 38; emphasis in original).

and other parts where they terminate, would probably not suffice to sustain the currents associated with mental life.

It is, therefore, in the present state of our knowledge, an entire misconception to talk of a *sensorium* within the brain, a *sanctum sanctorum*,[4] or inner chamber, where impressions are poured in and stored up to be reproduced in a future day. There is no such chamber, no such mode of reception of outward influence. A stimulus or sensation acting on the brain exhausts itself in the production of a number of transmitted currents or influences; while the stimulus is alive, these continue, and when these have ceased the impression is exhausted. The revival of the impression is the setting on of the currents anew; such currents show themselves in actuating the bodily members,—the voice, the eyes, the features,—in productive action, or in mere expression and gesture. The currents may have all degrees of intensity, from the fury of a death struggle to the languor of a half-sleeping reverie, or the fitful flashes of a dream, but their nature is still the same.

We must thus discard for ever the notion of the *sensorium commune*, the cerebral closet, as a central seat of mind, or receptacle of sensation and imagery. We may be very far from comprehending the full and exact character of nerve force, but the knowledge we have gained is sufficient to destroy the hypothesis that has until lately prevailed as to the material processes of perception. Though we have not attained a final understanding of this obscure and complicated machinery, we can at least substitute a more exact view for a less; and such is the substitution now demanded of current action for the crude conception of a central receptacle of stored up impressions. Our present insight enables us to say with great probability, no currents, no mind. The transmission of influence along the nerve fibres from place to place, seems the very essence of cerebral action. This transmission, moreover, must not be confined within the limits of the brain: not only could no action be kept up and no sensation received by the brain alone, but it is doubtful if even thought, reminiscence, or the emotions of the past and absent, could be sustained without the more distant communications between the brain and the rest of the body—the organs of sense and of movement. It is true that between the separate convolutions of the brain, between one hemisphere and another, between the convoluted hemispheres and the corpora striata, thalami optici,

_____

4. *sanctum sanctorum*: Latin, literally, "holy of holies"; figuratively, used to mean a private retreat free from outside intrusion

corpora quadrigemina, cerebellum, medulla oblongata,[5] and spinal cord, influence might be imagined to pass and repass without flowing into the active extremities or to the five senses, and might thus constitute an isolated cerebral life; but it is in the highest degree improbable that such isolation does or can exist. Nervous influence, rising in great part in sensation, comes at last to action; short of this nothing is done, no end served. However feeble the currents may be, their natural course is towards the organs accustomed to their sway. Hence the reason for adopting language, as we have done throughout the present chapter, to imply that the brain is only a part of the machinery of mind; for although a large part of all the circles of mental action lie within the head, other parts equally indispensable extend throughout the body.

## From "Illustrative Comparisons and Literary Art"[6]

43. Of the Tropes and Figures described in Rhetoric, the largest half turn upon comparison.[7] The metaphor, the simile, the allegory—are all forms of illustration by similitude, sometimes serving for clearness, or intellectual comprehension, at other times producing animation and effect. Their invention is due to the identifying intellect, which breaks through the partition caused by difference of subject to bring together what is similar in some one striking aspect or form. The literary and poetic genius of ages has accumulated a store of such comparisons; many of them have passed into common speech to enrich the dialects of everyday life. No man has ever attained rank in literature, without possessing in some degree the power of original illustration; and the reach or interval of disparity through which new similes are brought, makes a fair measure of the intellectual force of the individual mind in one of the leading characteristics of genius. The original fetches of Homer, of Aeschylus, of Milton, and above all of Shakespeare (I do not pretend to exhaust the list even of the first-rate minds), are prodigious. How remote and yet how grand the simile describing the descent of Apollo from Olympus: "he came like night."[8] The identifying faculty, be it never so strong, would hardly suffice to bring together things so widely different, but for some

---

5. *corpora . . . oblongata*: parts of the brain

6. Bain, *The Senses*, 534–35.

7. Comparison, Bain maintains, is a process by which we extend the known into the unknown. See especially his chapter "Law of Similarity," pp. 451–543.

8. From Book I of the *Iliad*, line 54. Apollo is a Greek god associated with the sun.

previous preparation serving to approximate the nature of the two things in the first instance, as we have already had occasion to remark of some of the scientific discoveries. Night itself must have been first personified in the mind to some extent, thereby reducing the immense disparity between the closing day and the march of a living personage down the mountain slopes. But with all due allowance for the highest susceptibility of mind to the poetic aspects of things, the power of adducing comparisons from remote regions, such as we find it in the greatest literary compositions, is stupendous and sublime.

## From "Fine Art Constructions—Imagination"[9]

26. The Fine Art emotions properly so called, the emotions of harmony, beauty, sublimity, picturesqueness, pathos, humour, become associated in the artistic mind with the objects that radiate the influence on the beholder, and from the materials thus stored up and reproduced by association the artist makes his constructions. . . . The labour consists in getting up the constituent parts from the repositories of the mind, and in choosing and rejecting until the end in view is completely answered. Because the imaginations of a dreamer are easy and fluent, it does not follow that the imaginations of a musician, an architect, or a poet, shall be equally easy, although in principle the same, being governed by an emotion powerfully developed and richly associated with material. The artist has more stringent conditions to fulfill than the dreamer. He has to satisfy the reigning feeling of his piece,—the melody, harmony, pathos, humour,—of the composition; he has also to make this effect apparent to the minds of others; he has moreover to exclude many effects discordant to the taste of his audience; and if his work be the decoration of some object of common usefulness, he has to save the utilities while in search of the amenities. Every new restriction adds to the difficulty of a combining effort; and an artist may be so trammelled with conditions, that the exercise of imagination shall be rendered as laborious as any construction of the reason.[10] To call up combinations that produce powerful and rich effects upon the minds of men is not easy in any art; but the gathered abundance of the artistic intellect is the secret of the power. The more rich the granary[11] of ma-

---

9. Bain, *The Senses*, 605–9.

10. Erecting a purely functional building is one of Bain's examples of a "construction of the reason."

11. *granary*: grain warehouse

terial, the more is the artist prepared to submit to the numerous conditions involved in a really great performance.

27. I do not purpose at present to enter upon a minute illustration of the mental processes of art-construction. Not only would a large space be requisite for spreading out the examples in detail, but there would soon come to be involved a strenuous polemical discussion in consequence of the prevalence of theories of art that seem to me erroneous. Conceiving as I do that the first object of an artist is to gratify the feelings of taste, or the proper aesthetic emotions, I cannot assent to the current maxim that nature is his standard, or truth his chief end. On the contrary, I believe that these are precisely the conditions of the scientific man; he it is that should never deviate from nature, and who should care for truth before all other things. The artist's standard is *feeling*, his end is refined pleasure; he goes to nature and selects what chimes in with his feelings of artistic effect, and passes by the rest. He is not even bound to adhere to nature in her very choicest displays; his own taste being the touchstone, he alters the originals at his will. The scientific man, on the other hand, must embrace every fact with open arms; the most nauseous fungus, the most loathsome reptile, the most pestilential vapour, must be scanned and set forth in all its details.

The amount of regard that the artist owes to truth, so far as I am able to judge, is nearly as follows. In the purely effusive arts, such as music or the dance, truth and nature are totally irrelevant; the artist's feeling and the gratification of the senses of mankind generally are the sole criterion of the effect. So in the fancies of decorative art, nature has very little place; suggestions are occasionally derived from natural objects, but no one is bound to adopt more of these than good taste may allow. Nobody talks of the design of a calico as being true to nature; it is enough if it please the eye. "Art is art because it is not nature."[12] The artist provides dainties not to be found in nature. There are, however, certain departments of art that differ considerably from music and fanciful decoration, in this respect, namely, that the basis of the composition is generally something actual, or something derived from the existing realities of nature or life. Such are painting, poetry, and romance.[13] In these, nature gives the subject, and the artistic genius the adornment. Now, although in this case also the gratification of the senses and the aesthetic

---

12. From Goethe's *Wilhelm Meister's Apprenticeship* (1795–96).
13. In this context, "romance" should be understood as novel writing.

sensibilities is still the aim of the artist, he has to show a certain decent respect to our experience of reality in the management of his subject, that not being purely imaginary, like the figures of a calico, but chosen from the world of reality. Hence when a painter lays hold of the human figure in order to display his harmonies of colour and beauties of form and picturesqueness of grouping, he ought not to shock our feeling of truth and consistency by a wide departure from the usual proportions of humanity. We don't look for anatomical exactness; we know that the studies of an artist do not imply the knowledge of a professor of anatomy; but we expect that the main features of reality shall be adhered to. In like manner, a poet is not great because he exhibits human nature with literal fidelity; to do that would make the reputation of a historian or a mental philosopher. The poet is great by his metres, his cadences, his images, his picturesque groupings, his graceful narrative, his exaltation of reality into the region of ideality; and if in doing all this he avoid serious mistakes or gross exaggerations, he passes without rebuke, and earns the unqualified honours of his genius.

28. The attempt to reconcile the artistic with the true,—art with nature,—has given birth to a middle school, in whose productions a restraint is put upon the flights of pure imagination, and which claims the merit of informing the mind as to the realities of the world, while gratifying the various aesthetic emotions. Instead of the tales of Fairy-land, the Arabian nights, the Romances of chivalry, we have the modern novelist with his pictures of living men and manners. In painting we have natural scenery, buildings, men, and animals represented with scrupulous exactness. The sculptor and the painter exercise the vocation of producing portraits that shall hand down to future ages the precise lineaments of the men and women of their generation. Hence the study of nature has become an element in artistic education; and the artist often speaks as if the exhibition of truth were his prime endeavour and his highest honour. It is probably this attempt to subject imagination to the conditions of truth and reality that has caused the singular transference above mentioned, whereby the definition of science has been made the definition of art.

Now I have every desire to do justice to the merits of the truth-seeking artist. Indeed the importance of the reconciliation that he aims at is undeniable. It is no slight matter to take out the sting from pleasure, and to avoid corrupting our notions of reality while gratifying our artistic sensibilities. A sober modern romancist does not outrage the probabilities of human life, nor excite delusive and extravagant hopes, in the manner of the middle-age romances. The improvement is a most beneficial one.

Nevertheless, there is, and always will be, a distinction between the degree of truth attainable by an artist, and the degree of truth attained by a man of science or a man of business. The poet, let him desire it never so much, cannot study realities with an undivided attention. His readers in general do not desire truth simply for its own sake; nor will they accept it in the severe forms of an accurate terminology. The scientific man has not wantonly created the diagrams of Euclid, the symbols of Algebra, or the jargon of technical Anatomy; he was forced into these repulsive elements because in no other way could he seize the realities of nature with precision. It cannot be supposed that the utmost plenitude of poetic genius shall ever be able to represent the world faithfully by discarding all these devices in favour of flowery ornament and melodious metre. We ought not to look to an artist to guide us to truth; it is enough for him that he do not mis-guide us.

# A. B. Johnson, from
## *The Physiology of the Senses* (1856)[1]

Alexander Bryan Johnson (1786–1867) was an American banker, amateur scientist, and philosopher of language whose *Physiology of the Senses* was praised by the English press for its lively synthesis of contemporary thought about how sensory perception relates to understanding and language use. Words do not name the knowledge we gain through our senses, Johnson insists. Rather, words name our intellectual or emotional understanding of sensory perceptions. As Johnson puts it, "the sensible signification of language is strictly limited by the sensible knowledge of the hearer."[2] Key to Johnson's account of how language can promote or impede the communication of sensory experience from one person to another is a distinction among "sensible" knowledge (learned through sensory experience), "intellectual" knowledge (understood verbally or intellectually), and "emotional" knowledge (gained through analogy). Readers will find that Johnson's theory resonates with discussions in the "Nineteenth- Century Poetics" section (particularly the essays by Hallam and Massey). The numbers preceding each section are from Johnson's original; we retain them here for readers' convenience.

## From Part II, "Theorem II"[3]

Any feel [information received from the sense of touch, or as Johnson calls it, the sense of feeling] which feeling has not informed me of, is unknown to me. . . .

1. When I see surgical operations, my intellect learns thereby the visible effect on the sufferer, and the audible effect, so far as he expresses any sound;

1. Alexander Bryan Johnson, *The Physiology of the Senses; or, How and What We See, Hear, Taste, Feel and Smell* (New York: Derby and Jackson, 1856).

2. Ibid., 134.

3. Ibid., 139–43.

but I can learn no feel that I have not felt. The principle is general, hence language is unintelligible to me in its sensible[4] signification when it refers to feels that I have not experienced; though to the extent that I have felt analogous feels, my meaning of the words will approximate to their true meaning. The sensible experience of two men is rarely identical; but the differences are usually not sufficient to produce much ambiguity in their ordinary intercommunications. Our nomenclature of pains might alone enable us to infer that each man's personal acquaintance with pains was limited to his own experience, for we talk of headache, toothache, stomachache; designating locations rather than feelings; and of throb, ache, shoot, acute; designating classes of pains, not particularities; or of gnawing pains, piercing, lancinated,[5] stitching, burning, scalding pains; designating only effects of general processes to which the pains we would designate are deemed analogous. When, however, we speak of weight, we designate it to a grain; or of distance, we designate it to the thousandth part of an inch; practices which evince that weight and distance, with their divisions, we can manifest to each other specifically. When, therefore, a person says words cannot convey his feelings, the obstacle is in our organic inability to communicate to a man feelings he has not felt.

2. . . . . After feeling has informed me of roughness, it is known to me in the skin of a rhinoceros that I have never felt, as well as in the tongue of a cat which I have felt, while sensibly we can know such feels only as we have experienced,—the identity of every roughness being only a conception of the intellect. The inhabitants of the tropics and the inhabitants of the polar regions, speak not merely alike of cold weather generally; but of very cold, exceedingly cold, intensely cold. The poorest tenant of a log hut will discriminate some items of his food, as good, very good, excellent, delicious, rich, luscious, sumptuous; hence a sermon that should be preached in the most fashionable church of London against excessive dress, extravagant furniture, dissipation in visiting and dancing, indulgence in delicacies of eating and drinking; may be preached with equal verbal pertinancy[6] and intellectual cogency in every age and in every place. I have heard such sermons in neighbourhoods where the itinerant missionary, addressing his congregation seated on wooden benches in a district school-room, lighted with a few

---

4. *sensible*: here, and throughout the essay, sensory
5. *lancinated*: acute, piercing
6. *pertinancy*: stubbornness

tallow candles in tin candle-sticks, has made many a poor female auditor feel self-condemned at the pound of loaf sugar she recently purchased, or the new ribbon worn by her ambitious daughter.

3. In the foregoing instances, we fail to discriminate the sensible meaning of words from their intellectual meaning; so the following examples will show that we fail to discriminate intellectual intimations from sensible revelations. When I am at sea and behold a distant beacon, the sight intimates to my intellect that a tangible body is the source of what I see. The sight may indicate no such fact to an inexperienced child; but when we look at the moon, few persons discriminate its indicated tangibility from tactile perception. The intellectually conceived tangible magnitude of the stars and tangible speed of light, signify sensibly certain sensible revelations that are not tangibilities; but we rarely discriminate the intellectually conceived tangibility from a revelation of feeling. Children led by this intellectual prepossession, will, with entire unconsciousness of any delusion, deem a rainbow tangible, and chase after it if you suggest the action. Younger children evince the prepossession in their attempts to grasp a shadow on a wall, or the figures of a painting. If you fill a bladder with air, and place it in the hands of a child, he will deem the feel conclusive that the contents possess visibility; and when the wind blows against us so that we can scarcely resist its pressure, the invisibility of our seeming ghostly assailant would overwhelm us with superstitious terror, were we not familiar with this exception to the accustomed association of visibility with tangibility. So you may occasionally feel something crawling over your neck, and scarcely credit a companion who informs you that nothing is visible, his negation seeming like a contradiction of your feelings, rather than the announcement of a misconception of your intellect. . . .

## From Part II, "Theorem VI"[7]

All knowledge which none of my senses nor my intellect can inform me of, is emotional. . . .

1. . . . I have experimented with comparatively few stones, yet I pick one up anywhere with entire certainty that it will fall to the earth when I relax my hold of it. Why am I certain? You may say my intellect knows that like causes produce like effects; but this dogma cannot be authoritative till I have

7. Johnson, *The Physiology of the Senses*, 184–88, 190–92, 196, 200–5, 206.

found that the new stone is like the former ones. Here, then, is seemingly a mystery,—experience can give us only specific knowledge, yet it gives us general knowledge; but the mystery disappears when we know that knowledge is sensible, intellectual, and emotional, and that the knowledge in question is only emotional. We know sensibly the fall of a stone that is transpiring before our eyes; we know intellectually the fall that has so transpired; but we know only emotionally the fall that is future. As the fly wheel of a machine supplies a momentum during any momentary cessation of the moving power, so our emotions supply a compensating knowledge during the cessation of our sensible experience. We may never have fallen into a pit, or off a high tower, yet we have experienced analogous dangers, and a proximity to either a pit or tower excites organically emotions which obviate the danger. A man in any such position, who should seem regardless of the danger, would be stigmatized as *feeling* foolhardy—the phrase denoting the absence of a proper emotion. Phraseology testifies in the same way that our knowledge is emotional in relation to the future fall of a stone—we *feel* confident, we *feel* sure, we *feel* certain of the fall. A present fall we *see*—thus denoting our knowledge thereof to be sensible;—while a past fall we recollect—thus denoting our knowledge thereof to be intellectual. The famous puzzle of man's inability to prove the existence of an external universe, or even his own existence, is founded on the same disregard of the triplicity of knowledge. The proof applicable to the existence is emotional (our consciousness), hence the ability to prove is not contradicted, as the puzzle implies it is, by the absence of sensible and intellectual proof.

Shakespeare makes Anthony say to Cleopatra—

> Though you may know what moderation ought to be,
> You know not what it is.[8]

The knowledge thereof which she possessed was intellectual, but the knowledge she lacked was emotional; the two being generically different, and only verbally identical. Some years ago, a sect existed who believed that the world was forthwith to be destroyed. Their belief was emotional, but the public not knowing that such belief may coexist with an intellectual disbelief, supposed the believers to be either insane or hypocritical. . . .

---

8. From Shakespeare's *Antony and Cleopatra*, 3.13.122–23. The actual lines are: "Though you can guess what temperance should be, / You know not what it is."

2. Having thus endeavoured to contemplate man as tripersonal, sensible, intellectual, and emotional, we may render the division more intelligible by saying that the intellectual person remembers, thinks, reasons, reflects, speculates, guesses, calculates; the emotional person believes, doubts, disbelieves, hopes, fears, loves, contemns, envies, hates; the sensible person sees, hears, tastes, feels, and smells. The emotional person is more (feelingly) the man himself than either of the other two, our emotions being to the tripersonality what sound is to a piano; while the senses and the intellect assimilate to the keys and strings. When my intellect is uncertain as to the organism[9] to which any word refers on any given use thereof, the forms of phraseology will usually resolve the uncertainty; as, for instance, is doubt intellectual, emotional, or sensible? It is emotional, for phraseologically, we say, I *feel* in doubt, I *feel* dubious, &c. In speaking of sensible things, phraseology almost uniformly designates the sense which is the source of our information; as I *smell* fire, I *felt* an earthquake, I *saw* a volcano, I *heard* thunder, I *taste* pepper. The intellect employs verbs designative of intellections; as I think, I guess, I remember, I reason. The emotions possess verbs designative of our susceptions; as I fear, hope, love, envy, hate, &c. But we ought to note here that the intellect conceives an analogy between its own actions and the actions of the sense of seeing, hence we say indiscriminately, I *see* an argument is cogent, and I *see* a stick is straight; though one is an intellection and the other a sight. So the intellect conceives an analogy between the sense of feeling and our emotions, hence we say indiscriminately, I *feel* fear, I *feel* pain—the first being emotional and the latter physical; but the intellect of the most uneducated man discriminates accurately in all practical uses, when any word applies to vision, and when to intellection; when to physical feeling, and when to emotional. . . .

As phraseology in the foregoing examples manifests the organism to which verbs refer, so an equal tendency exists in phraseology to manifest the organism of the nominative.[10] My emotions were unpleasant; my anger was excited; my intellect is stored with examples; my taste rejected it; my sight was satisfied; my hearing is perfect: the hearing cannot refuse to hear, or the sight to see. Instead of thus making the organism act as nominative to verbs,

---

9. *organism*: For Johnson, *organism* refers to either the emotions, the intellect, or the senses.

10. *nominative*: named. Here Johnson suggests that the verb choice names the organism being used.

we more usually employ the personal pronoun; I felt unpleasant, I heard, I tasted, &c., and nothing so speculatively mystifies our knowledge as the implied oneness of such an actor, the oneness being only a contrivance of the intellect. The same may be said of the objective "me." The "me" which is afflicted by envy or jealousy is my emotional organism, the "me" which can be taught that three angles of a triangle are equal to two right angles is my intellect; while the "me" which can be tortured by fire is my sense of feeling. The several "mes" are as heterogeneous in their underlying unverbal meanings as the several organisms to which they relate. . . .

3. As phraseology can tell us the organism to which any word refers for its signification, so conversely our organisms can interpret phrases better than any other interpreter. For instance, the phrase "I thank you"; what is its meaning? Etymologists say it means, "I will think of you." We may then ask what the latter phrase means, and we can arrive at no end of such inquisition; but, by looking inwardly, we shall find an emotion which every man experiences on becoming the recipient of kind offices from other men; and that constitutes the ultimate meaning of the phrase. Adieu! God bless you! Peace go with you! refer to another emotion which is organically excited in friends when they are about to separate, hence in all languages some phrase must be employed to express the emotion, as also the former; and the phrases will be dictated by the different habits or local knowledge of the different races who use the respective phrases. Etymology may reveal to us how "I thank you," came to be applied by Englishmen to a given emotion, but when we would know the meaning of the new use we must not look to the etymology, but to the organic manifestation to which the new use refers.

. . . The intellect is continually expressing its conceptions by the use of words that originated with the senses, but to deem the new use expressive of only the original meaning is analogous to the old factious[11] cry that bank notes are only old rags and lampblack.[12] But while the conceptions angel and spirit exist probably among all peoples, a like universality is not predicable[13] of every conception, civilization influencing the intellect to conceive in some condition what in some other condition may remain unconceived; especially will different degrees of civilization influence the conceptions to which

---

11. *factious*: divisive
12. *lampblack*: black varnish or dye
13. *predicable*: able to be affirmed

names will be applied. Absent minded is an organic condition of the intellect which must be coextensive with man, but it may not be universally designated verbally; and we may say the same of ennui, which refers to a condition of our feelings. The presence or absence in any language of phrases referring to organic conditions, would yield some indication of the civilization of the people by whom the language was spoken.

Words that relate to physical objects we are accustomed to interpret by referring to the object named, but words relating to intellections and emotions we are never taught speculatively to interpret by introspection, as in the preceding examples is recommended, though the process is practised universally. The parting benediction of his parent every child thus interprets, though no word of the benediction may be to him significant otherwise. Even the cries of brute animals are understood when they proceed from wants and feelings common to the animals and to us; animals being unintelligible to each other in proportion to only the heterogeneity of their organisms. If I see hot water thrown on a dog and hear outcries from him, my intellect understands his exclamations as well as though they were English words. On the same principle my intellect will recognize the meaning of words uttered by two foreigners who shall meet suddenly in my presence after having been sometime separated. Such an interpretation of unknown words is like the trigonometrical solution by which when two angles of a given triangle are known, the third angle also becomes known. . . . I saw lately some comments on the fancied translation into French, by a Frenchman, of the exclamation "Out, brief candle!" The Frenchman is made to render it, "Get out, you short candle!" The difference in the two exclamations is ridiculous enough, but the ridiculousness depends alone on the different organisms to which the phrases refer; "out, brief candle!" expressing an emotion, and "get out, you short candle!" expressing customarily only a physical action to be performed. Irrespective of these differences in us, the two phrases are verbally much alike. So "hail, horrors hail!" were rendered into French by the same fancied Frenchman, as "how do you do, horrors, how do you do!"—two phrases which differ only in the different emotions to which they are become conventionally connected. . . .

To thus look inwardly for the subjective meaning of language, rather than outwardly for an objective meaning, will solve many mysteries. Why must time be past, present, or future, and not a continued present? Because our senses perceive by only successive sensations. Our thoughts and feelings are equally successive, and about equally transient. From these unintermitted successions, our intellect knows no continuous present, and can, therefore, conceive time as only present, past, and future, just as it can conceive ice as only hard and cold. . . .

# George Wilson, from
## *The Five Senses* (1860)[1]

George Wilson (1818–1859) was a professor at the University of Edinburgh, chemist, celebrated public speaker, museum director, and writer of popular textbooks and scientific treatises. He is perhaps best remembered for his research findings regarding color blindness, research that changed practices in railway and ship signaling. Wilson's *The Five Gateways of Knowledge* (as it was initially known) popularized scientific thought about the influence of the senses upon the mind and went through at least seven editions. Using religious rhetoric, Wilson argued against the notion that ignoring the body improves the mind and encouraged his readers to cultivate their sensory perception. Contemporary reviewers called it a "prose poem," and indeed Wilson appears to have been as fond of quoting poetry as he was of creating his own vivid images. The excerpt that follows is drawn from his introduction and his chapter on the ear. In the latter chapter, Wilson describes the structure of the ear and how it carries sound, compares the sense of hearing to the sense of sight, and concludes by explaining why he finds hearing to be the most poetical of the senses.

## From the Introduction[2]

The ivory palace of the skull, which is the central abode of the soul, although it dwells in the whole body, opens to the outer world four gateways, by which its influences may enter; and a fifth, whose alleys are innumerable, unfolds its thousand doors on the surface of every limb. These gateways, which we otherwise name the Organs of the Senses, and call

---

1. George Wilson, *The Five Senses: Or, Gateways to Knowledge* (Philadelphia: Lindsay & Blakiston, 1860).
2. Ibid., 5–8.

in our mother speech, the Eye, the Ear, the Nose, the Mouth, and the Skin— are instruments by which we see, and hear, and smell, and taste, and touch: at once loopholes through which the spirit gazes out upon the world, and the world gazes in upon the spirit; porches which the longing, unsatisfied soul would often gladly make wider, that beautiful material nature might come into it more fully and freely; and fenced doors, which the sated and dissatisfied spirit would, if it had the power, often shut and bar altogether.

I will try to picture each of those living inlets of learning, without stopping at present to inquire how much the soul knows independent of the senses, and how far it controls them. The soul and its servants were not intended to be at war with each other, and the better the wise king is served, the more kingly will he appear. We have a strange fear of our bodies, and are ever speaking as if we could right the spirit, only by wronging the flesh, and could best sharpen our intellects by blunting our senses. But our souls would be only gainers by the perfection of our bodies were they wisely dealt with; and for every human being we should aim at securing, so far as they can be attained, an eye as keen and piercing as that of the eagle; an ear as sensitive to the faintest sound as that of the hare; a nostril as far scenting as that of the wild deer; a tongue as delicate as that of the butterfly; and a touch as acute as that of the spider.

No man ever was so endowed, and no one ever will be; but all come infinitely short of what they should achieve were they to make their senses what they might be made. The old have outlived their opportunity, and the diseased never had it; but the young, who have still an undimmed eye, an undulled ear, and a soft hand; an unblunted nostril, and a tongue which tastes with relish the plainest fare, can so cultivate their senses as to make the narrow ring which for the old and infirm encircles things sensible, widen for them into an almost limitless horizon.

There are three points of view from which we are to look at the senses, viz:—

> 1st. As ministers to the merely animal wants of the Body.
> 2d. As ministers to the cultivation of the Intellect; and,
> 3d. As ministers to the gratification of the perception of Beauty and its opposite.

It is to the two last, the Intellectual and Aesthetical offices of the senses, I am mainly to refer, including that relation to our Moral Instincts which flows from the triple Corporeal, Intellectual, and Aesthetical function which is exercised by each sense.

## From "The Ear"[3]

The second of the Gateways of Wisdom is the Ear. The organ or instrument of hearing is in all its more important parts so hidden within the head, that we cannot perceive its construction by a mere external inspection. What in ordinary language we call the ear, is only the outer porch or entrance-vestibule of a curious series of intricate, winding passages, which, like the lobbies of a great building, lead from the outer air into the inner chambers. Certain of these passages are full of air; others are full of liquid; and thin membranes are stretched like parchment curtains across the corridors at different places, and can be thrown into vibration, or made to tremble, as the head of a drum or the surface of a tambourine does when struck with a stick or the fingers. Between two of those parchment-like curtains, a chain of very small bones extends, which serves to tighten or relax these membranes, and to communicate vibrations to them. In the innermost place of all, rows of fine threads, called nerves, stretch like the strings of a piano from the last points to which the tremblings or thrillings reach, and pass inwards to the brain. If these threads or nerves are destroyed, the power of hearing as infallibly departs, as the power to give out sound is lost by a piano or a violin when its strings are broken.

Without attempting to enter more minutely into a description of the ear, it may now be stated, that in order to produce sound, a solid, a liquid, or a gas, such as air, must in the first place be thrown into vibration. We have an example of a solid body giving a sound, when a bell produces a musical note on being struck; of a liquid, in the dash of a waterfall, or the breaking of the waves; and of the air, in the firing of a cannon, or the blast of a trumpet. Sounds once produced, travel along solid bodies, or through liquids, or through the air, the last being the great conveyor or conductor of sounds.

The human ear avails itself of all these modes of carrying sound; thus the walls of the skull, like the metal of a bell, convey sounds inwards to the nerves of hearing; whilst within the winding canals referred to, is inclosed a volume of liquid, which pulsates and undulates as the sea does when struck by a paddle-wheel or the blade of an oar. Lastly, two chambers divided from each

---

3. Ibid., 40–45, 50–61, 62–68.

other by a membrane, the one leading to the external ear, the other opening into the mouth, are filled with air, which can be thrown into vibration. We may thus fitly compare the organ of hearing, considered as a whole, to a musical glass, *i.e.* a thin glass tumbler containing a little water. If the glass be struck, a sound is emitted, during which, not only the solid wall of the tumbler, but the liquid in it, and the air above it, all tremble or vibrate together, and spread the sound. All this is occurring every moment in our ears; and as a final result of these complex thrillings, the nerves which I likened to the "piano strings" convey an impression inwards to the brain, and in consequence of this we hear.

We know far less, however, of the ear than of the eye. The eye is a single chamber open to the light, and we can see into it, and observe what happens there. But the ear is many-chambered, and its winding tunnels traversing the rock-like bones of the skull are narrow, and hidden from us as the dungeons of a castle are; like which, also, they are totally dark. Thus much, however, we know, that it is in the innermost recesses of these unilluminated ivory vaults, that the mind is made conscious of sound. Into these gloomy cells, as into the bright chamber of the eye, the soul is ever passing and asking for news from the world without; and ever and anon, as of old in hidden subterranean caverns where men listened in silence and darkness to the utterance of oracles, reverberations echo along the resounding walls, and responses come to the waiting spirit, whilst the world lifts up its voice and speaks to the soul. The sound is that of a hushed voice, a low but clear whisper; for as it is but a dim shadow of the outer world we see, so it is but a faint echo of the outer world we hear.

Such, then, is the Ear; and it is in some respects a more human organ than the Eye, for it is the counterpart of the human voice; and it is a sorer affliction to be cut off from listening to the tongues of our fellow-men, than it is to be blinded to the sights on which they gaze. . . .

But conceding all this, those two mighty masters [Milton and Beethoven] may be fitly regarded as furnishing characteristic examples of the relative severity of blindness and deafness, when they befall those who once saw and heard. We should every one of us, I suppose, prefer the lot of Milton to that of Beethoven, and find it more easy to console a blind painter[4] than a deaf mu-

---

4. Perhaps Wilson, following Horace's decree, "Ut pictura poesis" ("As is painting, so is poetry") considers Milton's poetry as a kind of painting.

sician. I speak thus because I presume it is a matter of universal experience, that we can more easily and vividly recall and conceive sights, than we can recall and conceive sounds. It costs us no effort to summon before us, even though destitute of the painter's gifts, endless landscapes, cities, or processions, and faces innumerable; but even rarely endowed musicians can mentally reproduce few, comparatively, of the melodies or harmonies they know, if debarred from uttering them vocally, or through some instrument. We may test this point by the experience of our dreams.

If I mistake not, though I would not speak dogmatically on this point, we never fully dream a sound. Coleridge in his "Kubla Khan" declares:—

> A damsel with a dulcimer[5]
> In a vision once I saw:
> It was an Abyssinian maid,
> And on her dulcimer she played,
> Singing of Mount Abora.

But this was the visionary vision of a poet; in dreams, I imagine, we hear no sounds, unless it be those of the world without. We carry on many conversations, and marvellous things are told us; but these, like our waking communings with ourselves, and mental hummings of tunes, are uttered by voiceless lips in a speechless tongue. Dreamland is a silent land, and all the dwellers in it are deaf and dumb.

How different is it with Sight! No objects beheld by our waking eyes impress us so vividly as the splendid and awful dissolving views which pass before us in the visions of the night. So much is this the case, that when in daylight life we encounter some reality more startling, more joyful, or terrible than most, we utter the strange paradox: "It cannot be true; it must be a dream!" I infer from this that the Blind, who must dream or imagine all the sights which they see, are, *caeteris paribus*,[6] more fortunate than the Deaf, who must dream the sounds which they hear. In the *Life of Niebuhr*[7] there is a striking description of the long and happy hours which his blind old father spent in recalling the striking scenes which in early life he had witnessed in

---

5. *dulcimer*: a trapezoid-shaped stringed instrument played with light wooden hammers

6. *caeteris paribus*: Latin, "all other things being equal"

7. Barthold George Niebuhr (1776–1831) was a Danish-German historian of ancient Rome; Wilson refers to a book about him by the Chevalier Bunsen and Professors Brandis and Loeball.

the Holy Land and other Eastern countries; and every child who looks into its pillow to see wonders there, could record a parallel experience: but I know of no corresponding fact in the history of the deaf. At all events, an active and joyous memory of sounds is rare among them. The ear is accordingly an organ which we can worse afford to lose than the eye; and one, therefore, which should be all the more cared for. It is still more susceptible of education than the eye, and can be educated more quickly.

Thus a love of music is much more frequent than a love of painting or sculpture; and you will reach the hearts and touch the feelings of the majority of mankind more quickly by singing them a song, than by showing them a picture. In truth, the sensitiveness of the ear to melody and to harmony is so great, that we not only seek to gratify it when bent upon recreation, but even in the midst of the hardest labor we gratify it if we can. Two carpenters planing the same piece of wood will move their planes alternately; so that, when the one is pushing his forward, the other is drawing his back, thereby securing a recurrence of sounds, which, from their inequality, would be harsh if they were heard simultaneously. In the same way two paviors,[8] driving in stones, bring down their mallets time about; and so do working engineers when they are forging a bar; and the smith, when he has dealt a succession of monotonous blows, relieves his ear by letting his hammer ring musically on the anvil; and I need not tell you how sailors, heaving the anchor or hoisting the sails, sing together in chorus; nor remind you that the most serious of all hard work, fighting, is helped on by the drum and the trumpet.

This natural inclination of man towards music shows itself from the first. The infant's eye, we have seen, is aimless for a season; but its ear is alert from the beginning. It enters upon life with a cry; and its first sorrow, expressed in a sound, is soothed by the first sound of its mother's voice. One half of the nurse's time, I suppose, is spent in singing; and baby, when not sleeping or drinking, is either making or hearing music.

Now is it not a thing to be deeply lamented, that the sensitive ears with which almost every one of us has been gifted by God, are so little educated, that they might as well be stuffed with tow,[9] or plugged with lead, for any good use we make of them? To be sure we keep them sufficiently open to hear

---

8. *paviors*: pavers
9. *tow*: short fibers of flax or hemp

all gossip about us, and can most of us tell when the cannons are firing; but as for training them to that exquisite sense of melody or harmony of which they are susceptible, how few do it!

Our national music is famous all the world over; our song-tunes and our psalm-tunes are listened to with delight in every clime. Yet how few can sing the ever-welcome songs of Burns:[10] in how few churches will you hear psalm-singing that, as music, is other than a grief to an educated ear! This must be mended! Let every one so train, and educate, and fully develop the faculty of hearing that is in those ears of his, that he may listen with full delight and appreciation to the songs of birds, and the roar of the sea, the wailing of the winds, and the roll of the thunder; and may be able to cheer his soul and calm his heart by hearkening to the music of his fellow-men, and in turn rejoice their hearts by making music for them. . . .

. . . . It is not necessary to enlarge upon the aesthetics of hearing. All great poets have been passionate lovers of music, and it has received due honor at their hands. Most of the great painters and sculptors have been lovers of music also, in this respect being more catholic than their brethren the great musicians, who have often been totally indifferent to the arts which appeal to the eye; and double honor has thus been paid to the ear.

. . . . Of all the senses [hearing] is the one which most readily and most largely lends itself to impassioned, emotional, or, as we otherwise name it, poetical or aesthetical feeling. The retiringness of the ear is one great cause of this. The mechanism of hearing does not obtrude itself. The conditions of sound are known only to a small fraction of mankind; and the great majority of us die without even faintly realizing that the chief vehicle of sound, the atmosphere, has any existence. Music thus comes to us we cannot tell whence or how; and the less we are reminded of the mechanical or formal appliances by which an art appeals to our emotions, the more surely and profoundly are they stirred by it. The nostril is the only organ of sense that can compare with the ear in this respect, but its range is far more limited. The eye is much less fortunately circumstanced. The threads of the canvas, the shape and carving of the picture-frame, the string that suspends it, the nail on which it hangs, and the wall behind it, all disturb our delight at a picture, as the stains on a piece of marble, and the tarnish on bronze, do our delight at sculpture. The

---

10. Robert Burns (1759–1796), a Scottish poet widely regarded as a precursor of the Romantics.

substantial material in which the painter and sculptor must work, continually, and often harshly, force themselves upon the fleshly sense, and conflict with the purely emotional appreciation of their works. But music is never more delightful than when listened to in utter darkness, without obtrusion of the music-paper, or instrument, or performer; and whilst we forget that we have ears, and are content to be living souls floating in a sea of melodious sound. To be awaked from sleep by splendid music is to me the highest conceivable sensuous pleasure. A certain ethereality thus belongs pre-eminently to music, as it does in a lesser degree to fragrance. The most prosaic, formal, and utilitarian of mankind, for whom no other fine art has any charms, acknowledge the attractions of music. Alone of all the arts, it has suffered nothing from the intensely scientific and strongly utilitarian temper of modern times; and, even in the most faithless of recent epochs, music has thriven when every other aesthetic development was reduced to zero.

Whatever accordingly we envy the ancients, we need not envy them their music; they paid no such honor to the ear as we do; and it is remarkable that, at the deadest period of the last century, from the sleep of which nothing short of the French Revolution was sufficient to awake us, when only physical science was progressing, Handel and Haydn gave to us works which will be forgotten only when music of more amazing genius shall startle the world; and, in unbroken succession from their day, Mozart, Beethoven, Weber, Rossini, Mendelssohn, Meyerbeer, and many more, have placed us, in the matter of music, in advance of all the earlier ages.

. . . The peculiar ethereality of music is doubtless one of the reasons why we so willingly believe that creatures of a higher order than ourselves are especially given to song; and accept, as most credible, the declaration that immortal beings find the only sufficient expression of their emotions in praise. It was a splendid theory of the ancient Pagan sages, that the whole visible heavens were melodious with a music, which gifted ears were privileged to hear, when star sang to star, and constellations rejoiced together. And it is a still grander belief of modern Christian men, that within the invisible heavens angels that excel in strength, and undying human spirits, never cease their immortal song. But apart from the sympathy which the imagination has with such a belief, it commends itself to our reason by an argument which none can disown, and which supplies the justification of that pre-eminent importance which, from the days of King David the Psalmist, to our own, has been attached to the musical part of public religious worship.

Music forms the universal language which, when all other languages were confounded, the confusion of Babel left unconfounded. The white man and the black man, the red man and the yellow man, can sing together, however difficult they may find it to be to talk to each other. And both sexes and all ages may thus express their emotions simultaneously; for, in virtue of the power of the ear to distinguish, side by side, those differing but concordant notes which make up harmony, there is not only room but demand for all the qualities of voice which childhood, adolescence, maturity, and old age supply. . . .

# Nineteenth-Century Poetics

This section is not intended to offer a comprehensive overview of the numerous (and often elaborate) theories of Victorian prosody. Instead, it provides a series of texts that articulate some of the abiding aesthetic concerns of the period, chosen both for their representative nature and their relevance to Meredith's verse and its contemporary reception.

Each of these excerpts raises questions that shaped Meredith's poetry: What is poetry's purview? Are the ancients relevant to modern poets and readers? What role, if any, should the present play in contemporary poetry? How should poetry handle subjective and emotive experience? Is highly sensual poetry morally dangerous? Should poetry reflect things as they are or as they ought to be? The expansive and generous quality of Meredith's literary tastes becomes clear when we realize that he offered no single answer to any of these questions. Instead, he experimented from poem to poem, and sometimes within poems, using poetic form, literary allusion, and contemporary subjects to develop a singularly provocative style. Meredith's poetry thus seems bound to upset some, if not most, Victorian critics, who frequently linked moral value to compositional choices.

We begin with an excerpt from Arthur Henry Hallam's review of Alfred, Lord Tennyson's first volume of poetry. One of the "high points of early Victorian criticism," as Isobel Armstrong has noted, its analyses of the poetry of Tennyson, John Keats, Percy Bysshe Shelley, and William Wordsworth "resonate throughout the century."[1] The excerpt that follows

---

1. Isobel Armstrong, *Victorian Poetry: Poetry, Poetics and Politics* (London: Routledge, 1996), 60.

focuses on Keats and Shelley, two second-generation Romantics whose lega-
cies loom large over Victorian poetry. Many of the men and women who were
labeled Spasmodists by the Victorian critical establishment were inspired by
Keats and Shelley's poetry of "sensation" (as Hallam calls it). While moral
prejudices may prevent a reader from grasping the import of this kind of
poetry, understanding it "is never *physically* impossible," Hallam insists "be-
cause nature has placed in every man the simple elements, of which art is the
sublimation."

In his preface to his 1853 *Poems*, Matthew Arnold discusses what readers
have in common with one another and with poets, though the essay's central
focus is the question of whether or not poets should draw their "subjects
from matters of present import." Arnold answers with a resounding "no."
Meredith's answer to the question is more complicated. As is suggested by
this volume's title, the *Modern Love* poems contrast contemporary depictions
of love with "ancient" and old-fashioned versions to explore the nature of
modernity itself.

Arnold's insistence that modern life is too bewildering to serve as a fit
subject for poetry resonates with Massey's critique of Spasmodism. The con-
troversy surrounding Spasmodism helps explain the critical reaction to Mer-
edith's poetry. Peaking in the 1840s and 1850s, Spasmodic poetry was marked
by a neo-Romantic sensibility, favoring emotion and rich imagery, often with
a working-class bent.[2] Early endorsers of the Spasmodic school included
George Henry Lewes, who argued in 1853 that "one of the poet's functions
is that of beautifying and ennobling" feelings of passion or sensuousness. A
poet, Lewes insisted, "only merits reprobation, when, by cynicism, irrever-
ence, and insinuation, or conscious lubricity, he disgraces his office."[3] Ger-
ald Massey's 1858 essay on Spasmodism harkens back to the key concerns
in Hallam's essay and initially seems consonant with Lewes's, defining the
work of poetry as the translation of feeling into thought—a process that en-
ables readers "to realise in thought what [they] may have once experienced
in feeling." Unlike Lewes, however, Massey faults the Spasmodists for being
too self-absorbed. In his estimation, they fail to give their particular, subjec-
tive feelings and experiences an objective, timeless quality. Rather than seek-

---

2. For an overview of Spasmodic poetry, see Charles LaPorte and Jason Rudy's "Spasmodic
Poetry and Poetics," *Victorian Poetry* 42, no. 4 (Winter 2004): 421–27.

3. George Henry Lewes, "Poems of Alexander Smith," *Westminster Review* (April 1853): 271.

ing inspiration in "primal truths," the Spasmodists, Massey claims, not only evidence a "willful delight in remote and involved thinking" and "abrupt and jerking mental movements," but also prefer creating extravagant (but not necessarily intelligible) imagery and speculating "on bones and membranes, cells and blood-vessels." By the time *Modern Love* was published, Massey's view had taken hold: the charges of Spasmodism leveled at Meredith's poetry were intended as insults, not compliments.

Henry James's essay on Baudelaire, like Arnold's "Preface" and Massey's essay on the Spasmodists, addresses the question of poetic content, demonstrating that this issue remained a contested one through the latter half of the century. James's essay ties the question of sensory detail to the concepts of truth and sincerity in fresh ways, criticizing Baudelaire's *Les Fleurs du Mal* for addressing our senses rather than our "consciousness": "evil for [Baudelaire] begins outside and not inside, and consists primarily of a great deal of lurid landscape and unclean furniture."

And, finally, the excerpts by Gerard Manley Hopkins explicitly address the issue of obscurity and the question of how poetry communicates with readers. In his "Author's Preface," Hopkins discusses poetic rhythm as a means of making difficult poems more intelligible and looks to English medieval verse as well as Latin and Greek lyric for inspiration. These issues hover in the background of his letter to Robert Bridges regarding the clarity and force of the sonnet "Harry Ploughman."

# Arthur Henry Hallam, from "On Some of the Characteristics of Modern Poetry" (1831)[1]

Arthur Henry Hallam (1811–1833) is now, perhaps, best known as the man whose death occasioned one of the Victorian period's most powerful elegies: Tennyson's *In Memoriam*. Before he died, however, Hallam was a promising poet and critic who planned to make a living at law. A love of poetry drew Tennyson and Hallam together while students at Cambridge. Tennyson's first published volume of poems initially found few sympathetic readers among the critical establishment. No surprise, then, that Hallam's review of the same volume begins by telling its readers to judge the book (and indeed all poetry) for themselves. In the excerpt that follows, Hallam articulates a set of criteria by which to adjudicate poetry—criteria that take as foundational the claim that poetic creation and understanding can be intellectual, moral, and physical.

... [K eats and Shelley] are both poets of sensation rather than reflection. Susceptible of the slightest impulse from external nature, their fine organs trembled into emotion at colours, and sounds, and movements, unperceived or unregarded by duller temperaments. Rich and clear were their perceptions of visible forms; full and deep their feelings of music. So vivid was the delight attending the simple exertions of eye and ear, that it became mingled more and more with their trains of active thought, and tended to absorb their whole being into the energy of sense. Other poets *seek* for images to illustrate their conceptions; these men had no need to

---

1. Arthur Henry Hallam, "On Some of the Characteristics of Modern Poetry, And on the Lyrical Poems of Alfred Tennyson," *Englishman's Magazine* (August 1831): 617–20. Paragraph breaks have been added to Hallam's text to increase readability.

seek; they lived in a world of images; for the most important and extensive portion of their life consisted in those emotions, which are immediately conversant with sensation. Like the hero of Goethe's novel, they would hardly have been affected by what are called the pathetic parts of a book; but the *merely beautiful* passages, "those from which the spirit of the author looks clearly and mildly forth,"[2] would have melted them to tears. Hence they are not descriptive; they are picturesque. They are not smooth and *negatively* harmonious; they are full of deep and varied melodies.

This powerful tendency of imagination to a life of immediate sympathy with the external universe, is not nearly so liable to false views of art as the opposite disposition of purely intellectual contemplation. For where beauty is constantly passing before "that inward eye, which is the bliss of solitude";[3] where the soul seeks it as a perpetual and necessary refreshment to the sources of activity and intuition; where all the other sacred ideas of our nature, the idea of good, the idea of perfection, the idea of truth, are habitually contemplated through the medium of this predominant mood, so that they assume its colour, and are subject to its peculiar laws—there is little danger that the ruling passion of the whole mind will cease to direct its creative operations, or the energetic principle of love for the beautiful sink, even for a brief period, to the level of a mere notion in the understanding. We do not deny that it is, on other accounts, dangerous for frail humanity to linger with fond attachment in the vicinity of sense. Minds of this description are especially liable to moral temptations, and upon them, more than any, it is incumbent to remember that their mission as men, which they share with all their fellow-beings, is of infinitely higher interest than their mission as artists, which they possess by rare and exclusive privilege. But it is obvious that, critically speaking, such temptations are of slight moment. Not the gross and evident passions of our nature, but the elevated and less separable desires are the dangerous enemies which misguide the poetic spirit in its attempts at self-cultivation.

That delicate sense of fitness, which grows with the growth of artist feelings, and strengthens with their strength, until it acquires a celerity[4] and weight of decision hardly inferior to the correspondent judgments of con-

---

2. *Wilhelm Meister's Apprenticeship* (1795–96). Hallam's quotation comes from book 5, chapter 6.
3. Wordsworth's "I Wandered Lonely as a Cloud," lines 21–22.
4. *celerity*: swiftness

science, is weakened by every indulgence of heterogeneous aspirations, however pure they may be, however lofty, however suitable to human nature. We are therefore decidedly of opinion that the heights and depths of art are most within the reach of those who have received from Nature the "fearful and wonderful"[5] constitution we have described, whose poetry is a sort of magic, producing a number of impressions too multiplied, too minute, and too diversified to allow of our tracing them to their causes, because just such was the effect, even so boundless, and so bewildering, produced on their imaginations by the real appearance of Nature. These things being so, our friends of the new school[6] had evidently much reason to recur to the maxim laid down by Mr. Wordsworth, and to appeal from the immediate judgments of lettered or unlettered contemporaries to the decision of a more equitable posterity. How should they be popular, whose senses told them a richer and ampler tale than most men could understand, and who constantly expressed, because they constantly felt, sentiments of exquisite pleasure or pain, which most men were not permitted to experience? The public very naturally derided them as visionaries, and gibbeted[7] *in terrorem*[8] those inaccuracies of diction, occasioned sometimes by the speed of their conceptions, sometimes by the inadequacy of language to their peculiar conditions of thought. But, it may be asked, does not this line of argument prove too much? Does it not prove that there is a barrier between these poets and all other persons, so strong and immovable, that, as has been said of the Supreme Essence, we must be themselves before we can understand them in the least? Not only are they not liable to sudden and vulgar estimation, but the lapse of ages, it seems, will not consolidate their fame, nor the suffrages of the wise few produce any impression, however remote or slowly matured, on the judgments of the incapacitated many. We answer, this is not the import of our argument.

Undoubtedly the true poet addresses himself, in all his conceptions, to the common nature of us all. Art is a lofty tree, and may shoot up far beyond our grasp, but its roots are in daily life and experience. Every bosom contains the elements of those complex emotions which the artist feels, and every head

---

5. Psalm 139:14.

6. *new school*: The "Cockney School," as it was derisively known. Leigh Hunt, a poet and political radical, was regarded by the mainstream press as the school's leader; he introduced Keats and Shelley to the public via his journal *The Examiner*.

7. *gibbet*: a post from which the corpses of executed criminals were displayed

8. *in terrorem*: Latin legal term, literally "in order to frighten," a warning

can, to a certain extent, go over in itself the process of their combination, so as to understand his expressions and sympathize with his state. But this requires exertion; more or less, indeed, according to the difference of occasion, but always some degree of exertion. For since the emotions of the poet, during composition, follow a regular law of association, it follows that to accompany their progress up to the harmonious prospect of the whole, and to perceive the proper dependence of every step on that which preceded, it is absolutely necessary *to start from the same point*, i.e., clearly to apprehend that leading sentiment in the poet's mind, by their conformity to which the host of suggestions are arranged. Now this requisite exertion is not willingly made by the large majority of readers. It is so easy to judge capriciously, and according to indolent impulse! For very many, therefore, it has become *morally* impossible to attain the author's point of vision, on account of their habits, or their prejudices, or their circumstances; but it is never *physically* impossible, because nature has placed in every man the simple elements, of which art is the sublimation.[9]

Since then this demand on the reader for activity, when he wants to peruse his author in a luxurious passiveness, is the very thing that moves his bile, it is obvious that those writers will be always most popular, who require the least degree of exertion. Hence, whatever is mixed up with art, and appears under its semblance, is always more favourably regarded than art free and unalloyed. Hence, half the fashionable poems in the world are mere rhetoric, and half the remainder are perhaps not liked by the generality for their substantial merits. Hence, likewise, of the really pure compositions those are most universally agreeable, which take for their primary subject the *usual* passions of the heart, and deal with them in a simple state, without applying the transforming powers of high imagination. Love, friendship, ambition, religion, &c., are matters of daily experience, even amongst imaginative tempers. The forces of association, therefore, are ready to work in these directions, and little effort of will is necessary to follow the artist. For the same reason such subjects often excite a partial power of composition, which is no sign of a truly poetic organization. We are very far from wishing to depreciate this class of poems, whose influence is so extensive, and communicates so refined a pleasure.

---

9. *sublimation*: literally, both the chemical process by which heat converts a solid substance into a vapor that upon cooling resolidifies, and the solid substance itself that results from this cooling; figuratively, a distillation

We contend only that the facility with which its impressions are communicated, is no proof of its elevation as a form of art, but rather the contrary. . . .

With the close of the last century came an era of reaction, an era of painful struggle, to bring our overcivilised condition of thought into union with the fresh productive spirit that brightened the morning of our literature. But repentance is unlike innocence: the laborious endeavour to restore has more complicated methods of action, than the freedom of untainted nature. Those different powers of poetic disposition, the energies of Sensitive,[10] of Reflective, of Passionate Emotion, which in former times were intermingled, and derived from mutual support an extensive empire over the feelings of men, were now restrained within separate spheres of agency. The whole system no longer worked harmoniously, and by intrinsic harmony acquired external freedom; but there arose a violent and unusual action in the several component functions, each for itself, all striving to reproduce the regular power which the whole had once enjoyed. Hence the melancholy, which so evidently characterises the spirit of modern poetry; hence that return of the mind upon itself, and the habit of seeking relief in idiosyncrasies rather than community of interest.

---

10. [Hallam's footnote:] We are aware that this is not the right word, being appropriated by common use to a different signification. Those who think the caution given by Caesar should not stand in the way of urgent occasion, may substitute "sensuous," a word in use amongst our elder divines, and revived by a few bold writers in our own time.

# Matthew Arnold, from
## "Preface" to *Poems* (1853)[1]

Although Matthew Arnold (1822–1888) earned his living as a school
inspector, he was also a prominent poet, essayist, and social critic.
This is Arnold's first published essay; it is important not only as an
influential account of readers' aesthetic responses to poetry, but also
as a statement of Arnold's own classicist aesthetic. Fundamentally,
this is an essay about language and style. In the excerpt that follows,
Arnold praises the ancients for subordinating style to subject matter
and overall design—a strategy which (according to Arnold) enabled
their work to produce a clear and profound moral impression in au-
diences. He advises would-be poets and critics who seek to remain
relevant to posterity to liberate themselves from the particular and
"bewildering" concerns of the present and to seek inspiration and
training from the ancients.

"The Poet," it is said, and by an apparently intelligent critic, "the Poet
who would really fix the public attention must leave the exhausted
past, and draw his subjects from matters of present import, and
*therefore* both of interest and novelty."[2]

Now this view I believe to be completely false. It is worth examining,
inasmuch as it is a fair sample of a class of critical dicta everywhere current at
the present day, having a philosophical form and air, but no real basis in fact;
and which are calculated to vitiate the judgment of readers of poetry, while
they exert, so far as they are adopted, a misleading influence on the practice
of those who write it.

---

1. Matthew Arnold, "Preface" in *Poems* (London: Longman, Brown, Green and Longmans,
1853), ix–xix, xxi–xxxi.

2. [Arnold's footnote:] In *The Spectator*, of April 2nd, 1853. The words quoted were not used
with reference to poems of mine.

What are the eternal objects of Poetry, among all nations, and at all times? They are actions; human actions; possessing an inherent interest in themselves, and which are to be communicated in an interesting manner by the art of the Poet. Vainly will the latter imagine that he has everything in his own power; that he can make an intrinsically inferior action equally delightful with a more excellent one by his treatment of it: he may indeed compel us to admire his skill, but his work will possess, within itself, an incurable defect.

The Poet, then, has in the first place to select an excellent action; and what actions are the most excellent? Those, certainly, which most powerfully appeal to the great primary human affections: to those elementary feelings which subsist permanently in the race, and which are independent of time. These feelings are permanent and the same; that which interests them is permanent and the same also. The modernness or antiquity of an action, therefore, has nothing to do with its fitness for poetical representation; this depends upon its inherent qualities. To the elementary part of our nature, to our passions, that which is great and passionate is eternally interesting; and interesting solely in proportion to its greatness and to its passion. A great human action of a thousand years ago is more interesting to it than a smaller human action of to-day, even though upon the representation of this last the most consummate skill may have been expended, and though it has the advantage of appealing by its modern language, familiar manners, and contemporary allusions, to all our transient feelings and interests. These, however, have no right to demand of a poetical work that it shall satisfy them; their claims are to be directed elsewhere. Poetical works belong to the domain of our permanent passions: let them interest these, and the voice of all subordinate claims upon them is at once silenced.

Achilles, Prometheus, Clytemnestra, Dido[3]—what modern poem presents personages as interesting, even to us moderns, as these personages of an "exhausted past"? We have the domestic epic dealing with the details of modern life which pass daily under our eyes; we have poems representing modern personages in contact with the problems of modern life, moral, intellectual, and social; these works have been produced by poets the most distinguished of their nation and time; yet I fearlessly assert that "Hermann and

---

3. *Achilles . . . Dido*: primary characters of Homer's *Iliad*, Aeschylus's *Prometheus Bound* and *Oresteia*, and Virgil's *Aeneid*

Dorothea," *Childe Harold*, "Jocelyn," "The Excursion,"[4] leave the reader cold in comparison with the effect produced upon him by the latter books of the *Iliad*, by the *Oresteia*, or by the episode of Dido. And why is this? Simply because in the three latter cases the action is greater, the personages nobler, the situations more intense: and this is the true basis of the interest in a poetical work, and this alone.

It may be urged, however, that past actions may be interesting in themselves, but that they are not to be adopted by the modern Poet, because it is impossible for him to have them clearly present to his own mind, and he cannot therefore feel them deeply, nor represent them forcibly. But this is not necessarily the case. The externals of a past action, indeed, he cannot know with the precision of a contemporary; but his business is with its essentials. The outward man of Oedipus or of Macbeth, the houses in which they lived, the ceremonies of their courts, he cannot accurately figure to himself; but neither do they essentially concern him. His business is with their inward man; with their feelings and behaviour in certain tragic situations, which engage their passions as men; these have in them nothing local and casual; they are as accessible to the modern Poet as to a contemporary.

The date of an action, then, signifies nothing: the action itself, its selection and construction, this is what is all-important. This the Greeks understood far more clearly than we do. The radical difference between their poetical theory and ours consists, as it appears to me, in this: that, with them, the poetical character of the action in itself, and the conduct of it, was the first consideration; with us, attention is fixed mainly on the value of the separate thoughts and images which occur in the treatment of an action. They regarded the whole; we regard the parts. With them, the action predominated over the expression of it; with us, the expression predominates over the action. Not that they failed in expression, or were inattentive to it; on the contrary, they are the highest models of expression, the unapproached masters of the *grand style*:[5] but their expression is so excellent because it is so admirably kept in its right degree of prominence; because it is so simple and so well subordinated; because it draws its force directly from the pregnancy of the matter which it conveys. For what reason was the Greek tragic poet confined to so limited a range of subjects? Because there are so few actions

---

4. *"Hermann . . . Excursion"*: names of poems by Goethe, Byron, Lamartine, and Wordsworth
5. For more on Arnold's conception of "grand style," see his *On Translating Homer*.

which unite in themselves, in the highest degree, the conditions of excellence: and it was not thought that on any but an excellent subject could an excellent Poem be constructed. A few actions, therefore, eminently adapted for tragedy, maintained almost exclusive possession of the Greek tragic stage; their significance appeared inexhaustible; they were as permanent problems, perpetually offered to the genius of every fresh poet. This too is the reason of what appears to us moderns a certain baldness of expression in Greek tragedy; of the triviality with which we often reproach the remarks of the chorus, where it takes part in the dialogue: that the action itself, the situation of Orestes, or Merope, or Alcmaeon,[6] was to stand the central point of interest, unforgotten, absorbing, principal; that no accessories were for a moment to distract the spectator's attention from this; that the tone of the parts was to be perpetually kept down, in order not to impair the grandiose effect of the whole. The terrible old mythic story on which the drama was founded stood, before he entered the theatre, traced in its bare outlines upon the spectator's mind; it stood in his memory, as a group of statuary, faintly seen, at the end of a long and dark vista: then came the Poet, embodying outlines, developing situations, not a word wasted, not a sentiment capriciously thrown in: stroke upon stroke, the drama proceeded: the light deepened upon the group; more and more it revealed itself to the riveted gaze of the spectator: until at last, when the final words were spoken, it stood before him in broad sunlight, a model of immortal beauty.

This was what a Greek critic demanded; this was what a Greek poet endeavoured to effect. It signified nothing to what time an action belonged; we do not find that the *Persae*[7] occupied a particularly high rank among the dramas of Aeschylus, because it represented a matter of contemporary interest: this was not what a cultivated Athenian required; he required that the permanent elements of his nature should be moved; and dramas of which the action, though taken from a long-distant mythic time, yet was calculated to accomplish this in a higher degree than that of the *Persae*, stood higher in his estimation accordingly. The Greeks felt, no doubt, with their exquisite sagacity of taste, that an action of present times was too near them, too much mixed up with what was accidental and passing, to form a sufficiently grand, detached, and self-subsistent object for a tragic poem: such objects belonged

---

6. Each of these characters avenged the murder of a family member.

7. *Persae*: *The Persians*, a historical drama by Aeschylus

to the domain of the comic poet, and of the lighter kinds of poetry. For the more serious kinds, for *pragmatic* poetry, to use an excellent expression of Polybius,[8] they were more difficult and severe in the range of subjects which they permitted. But for all kinds of poetry alike there was one point on which they were rigidly exacting; the adaptability of the subject to the kind of poetry selected, and the careful construction of the poem. Their theory and practice alike, the admirable treatise of Aristotle, and the unrivalled works of their poets, exclaim with a thousand tongues—"All depends upon the subject; choose a fitting action, penetrate yourself with the feeling of its situations; this done, everything else will follow."

How different a way of thinking from this is ours! We can hardly at the present day understand what Menander[9] meant, when he told a man who enquired as to the progress of his comedy that he had finished it, not having yet written a single line, because he had constructed the action of it in his mind. A modern critic would have assured him that the merit of his piece depended on the brilliant things which arose under his pen as he went along. We have poems which seem to exist merely for the sake of single lines and passages; not for the sake of producing any total-impression. We have critics who seem to direct their attention merely to detached expressions, to the language about the action, not to the action itself. I verily think that the majority of them do not in their hearts believe that there is such a thing as a total-impression to be derived from a poem at all, or to be demanded from a poet; they think the term a commonplace of metaphysical criticism. They will permit the Poet to select any action he pleases, and to suffer that action to go as it will, provided he gratifies them with occasional bursts of fine writing, and with a shower of isolated thoughts and images. That is, they permit him to leave their poetical sense ungratified, provided that he gratifies their rhetorical sense and their curiosity. Of his neglecting to gratify these, there is little danger; he needs rather to be warned against the danger of attempting to gratify these alone; he needs rather to be perpetually reminded to prefer his action to everything else; so to treat this, as to permit its inherent excellences to develope themselves, without interruption from the intrusion of his personal peculiarities: most fortunate, when he most entirely succeeds in effacing himself, and in enabling a noble action to subsist as it did in nature.

---

8. *Polybius*: Greek historian (ca. 200–118 B.C.)

9. *Menander*: Greek dramatist associated with the "New Comedy" (ca. 342–292 B.C.)

But the modern critic not only permits a false practice; he absolutely prescribes false aims. —"A true allegory of the state of one's own mind in a representative history," the Poet is told, "is perhaps the highest thing that one can attempt in the way of poetry."[10]— And accordingly he attempts it. An allegory of the state of one's own mind, the highest problem of an art which imitates actions! No assuredly, it is not, it never can be so: no great poetical work has ever been produced with such an aim. *Faust*[11] itself, in which something of the kind is attempted, wonderful passages as it contains, and in spite of the unsurpassed beauty of the scenes which relate to Margaret, *Faust* itself, judged as a whole, and judged strictly as a poetical work, is defective: its illustrious author, the greatest poet of modern times, the greatest critic of all times, would have been the first to acknowledge it; he only defended his work, indeed, by asserting it to be "something incommensurable."

The confusion of the present times is great, the multitude of voices counselling different things bewildering, the number of existing works capable of attracting a young writer's attention and of becoming his models, immense: what he wants is a hand to guide him through the confusion, a voice to prescribe to him the aim which he should keep in view, and to explain to him that the value of the literary works which offer themselves to his attention is relative to their power of helping him forward on his road towards this aim. Such a guide the English writer at the present day will nowhere find. Failing this, all that can be looked for, all indeed that can be desired, is, that his attention should be fixed on excellent models; that he may reproduce, at any rate, something of their excellence, by penetrating himself with their works and by catching their spirit, if he cannot be taught to produce what is excellent independently. . . .

[In the excised paragraph, Arnold extols the virtues of Shakespeare's poetry, but laments the fact that his so-called followers rarely produce comparable work.]

Let me give an instance of what I mean. I will take it from the works of the very chief among those who seem to have been formed in the school of Shakespeare: of one whose exquisite genius and pathetic death render him for ever interesting. I will take the poem of "Isabella, or the Pot of Basil," by Keats. I choose this rather than the *Endymion*, because the latter work,

---

10. David Masson, "Theories of Poetry and a New Poet" *North British Review* 19 (1853): 338.
11. *Faust*: verse drama by Goethe

(which a modern critic has classed with the *Fairy Queen!*) although undoubt-
edly there blows through it the breath of genius, is yet as a whole so utterly
incoherent, as not strictly to merit the name of a poem at all. The poem of
"Isabella," then, is a perfect treasure-house of graceful and felicitous words
and images: almost in every stanza there occurs one of those vivid and pictur-
esque turns of expression, by which the object is made to flash upon the eye
of the mind, and which thrill the reader with a sudden delight. This one short
poem contains, perhaps, a greater number of happy single expressions which
one could quote than all the extant tragedies of Sophocles. But the action, the
story? The action in itself is an excellent one; but so feebly is it conceived by
the Poet, so loosely constructed, that the effect produced by it, in and for it-
self, is absolutely null. Let the reader, after he has finished the poem of Keats,
turn to the same story in the *Decameron*:[12] he will then feel how pregnant and
interesting the same action has become in the hands of a great artist, who
above all things delineates his object; who subordinates expression to that
which it is designed to express.

I have said that the imitators of Shakespeare, fixing their attention on his
wonderful gift of expression, have directed their imitation to this, neglect-
ing his other excellences. These excellences, the fundamental excellences of
poetical art, Shakespeare no doubt possessed them—possessed many of them
in a splendid degree; but it may perhaps be doubted whether even he himself
did not sometimes give scope to his faculty of expression to the prejudice
of a higher poetical duty. For we must never forget that Shakespeare is the
great poet he is from his skill in discerning and firmly conceiving an excellent
action, from his power of intensely feeling a situation, of intimately associat-
ing himself with a character; not from his gift of expression, which rather
even leads him astray, degenerating sometimes into a fondness for curiosity
of expression, into an irritability of fancy, which seems to make it impossible
for him to say a thing plainly, even when the press of the action demands the
very directest language, or its level character the very simplest. Mr. Hallam,[13]
than whom it is impossible to find a saner and more judicious critic, has had
the courage (for at the present day it needs courage) to remark, how ex-
tremely and faultily difficult Shakespeare's language often is. It is so: you
may find main scenes in some of his greatest tragedies, *King Lear* for instance,

---

12. *Decameron*: a bawdy collection of tales by the fourteenth-century Italian, Giovanni Boccaccio
13. *Mr. Hallam*: Henry Hallam (1777–1859), historian and father to Arthur Henry Hallam

where the language is so artificial, so curiously tortured, and so difficult, that every speech has to be read two or three times before its meaning can be comprehended. This over-curiousness of expression is indeed but the excessive employment of a wonderful gift—of the power of saying a thing in a happier way than any other man; nevertheless, it is carried so far that one understands what M. Guizot[14] meant, when he said that Shakespeare appears in his language to have tried all styles except that of simplicity. He has not the severe and scrupulous self-restraint of the ancients, partly no doubt, because he had a far less cultivated and exacting audience: he has indeed a far wider range than they had, a far richer fertility of thought; in this respect he rises above them: in his strong conception of his subject, in the genuine way in which he is penetrated with it, he resembles them, and is unlike the moderns: but in the accurate limitation of it, the conscientious rejection of superfluities, the simple and rigorous development of it from the first line of his work to the last, he falls below them, and comes nearer to the moderns. In his chief works, besides what he has of his own, he has the elementary soundness of the ancients; he has their important action and their large and broad manner: but he has not their purity of method. He is therefore a less safe model; for what he has of his own is personal, and inseparable from his own rich nature; it may be imitated and exaggerated, it cannot be learned or applied as an art; he is above all suggestive; more valuable, therefore, to young writers as men than as artists. But clearness of arrangement, rigour of development, simplicity of style—these may to a certain extent be learned: and these may, I am convinced, be learned best from the ancients, who although infinitely less suggestive than Shakespeare, are thus, to the artist, more instructive.

What then, it will be asked, are the ancients to be our sole models? the ancients with their comparatively narrow range of experience, and their widely different circumstances? Not, certainly, that which is narrow in the ancients, nor that in which we can no longer sympathize. An action like the action of the *Antigone* of Sophocles, which turns upon the conflict between the heroine's duty to her brother's corpse and that to the laws of her country, is no longer one in which it is possible that we should feel a deep interest. I am speaking too, it will be remembered, not of the best sources of intellectual stimulus for the general reader, but of the best models of instruction for the individual writer. This last may certainly learn of the ancients, bet-

14. François Pierre Guillaume Guizot, an eighteenth-century French politician and orator

ter than anywhere else, three things which it is vitally important for him to know:—the all-importance of the choice of a subject; the necessity of accurate construction; and the subordinate character of expression. He will learn from them how unspeakably superior is the effect of the one moral impression left by a great action treated as a whole, to the effect produced by the most striking single thought or by the happiest image. As he penetrates into the spirit of the great classical works, as he becomes gradually aware of their intense significance, their noble simplicity, and their calm pathos, he will be convinced that it is this effect, unity and profoundness of moral impression, at which the ancient Poets aimed; that it is this which constitutes the grandeur of their works, and which makes them immortal. He will desire to direct his own efforts towards producing the same effect. Above all, he will deliver himself from the jargon of modern criticism, and escape the danger of producing poetical works conceived in the spirit of the passing time, and which partake of its transitoriness.

The present age makes great claims upon us: we owe it service, it will not be satisfied without our admiration. I know not how it is, but their commerce with the ancients appears to me to produce, in those who constantly practise it, a steadying and composing effect upon their judgment, not of literary works only, but of men and events in general. They are like persons who have had a very weighty and impressive experience: they are more truly than others under the empire of facts, and more independent of the language current among those with whom they live. They wish neither to applaud nor to revile their age: they wish to know what it is, what it can give them, and whether this is what they want. What they want, they know very well; they want to educe and cultivate what is best and noblest in themselves: they know, too, that this is no easy task . . . and they ask themselves sincerely whether their age and its literature can assist them in the attempt. If they are endeavouring to practise any art, they remember the plain and simple proceedings of the old artists, who attained their grand results by penetrating themselves with some noble and significant action, not by inflating themselves with a belief in the preeminent importance and greatness of their own times. They do not talk of their mission, nor of interpreting their age, nor of the coming Poet; all this, they know, is the mere delirium of vanity; their business is not to praise their age, but to afford to the men who live in it the highest pleasure which they are capable of feeling. If asked to afford this by means of subjects drawn from the age itself, they ask what special fitness the present age has for supplying them: they are told that it is an era of progress, an age commissioned to carry out the great ideas of industrial development and social amelioration. They reply that with all this they can do nothing; that the elements they need for the exercise of their art are great actions, calculated powerfully and delightfully to affect what is permanent in the human soul; that so far as the present age can supply such actions, they will gladly make use of them; but that an age wanting in moral grandeur can with difficulty supply such, and an age of spiritual discomfort with difficulty be powerfully and delightfully affected by them.

A host of voices will indignantly rejoin that the present age is inferior to the past neither in moral grandeur nor in spiritual health. He who possesses the discipline I speak of will content himself with remembering the judgments passed upon the present age, in this respect, by the men of strongest head and widest culture whom it has produced; by Goethe and by Niebuhr.[15] It will be sufficient for him that he knows the opinions held by these two great men respecting the present age and its literature; and that he feels assured in his own mind that their aims and demands upon life were such as he would wish, at any rate, his own to be; and their judgment as to what is impeding and disabling such as he may safely follow. He will not, however, maintain a hostile attitude towards the false pretensions of his age; he will content himself with not being overwhelmed by them. He will esteem himself fortunate if he can succeed in banishing from his mind all feelings of contradiction, and irritation, and impatience; in order to delight himself with the contemplation of some noble action of a heroic time, and to enable others, through his representation of it, to delight in it also.

I am far indeed from making any claim, for myself, that I possess this discipline; or for the following Poems, that they breathe its spirit. But I say, that in the sincere endeavour to learn and practise, amid the bewildering confusion of our times, what is sound and true in poetical art, I seemed to myself to find the only sure guidance, the only solid footing, among the ancients. They, at any rate, knew what they wanted in Art, and we do not. It is this uncertainty which is disheartening, and not hostile criticism. How often have I felt this when reading words of disparagement or of cavil:[16] that it is the uncertainty as to what is really to be aimed at which makes our difficulty, not the

---

15. *Niebuhr*: See note 7 in excerpt from Wilson's *The Five Senses* in "On the Senses."
16. *cavil*: trivial objection

dissatisfaction of the critic, who himself suffers from the same uncertainty. *Non me tua turbida terrent Dicta: Dii me terrent, et Jupiter hostis.*[17]

Two kinds of *dilettanti*, says Goethe, there are in poetry: he who neglects the indispensable mechanical part, and thinks he has done enough if he shows spirituality and feeling; and he who seeks to arrive at poetry merely by mechanism, in which he can acquire an artisan's readiness, and is without soul and matter. And he adds, that the first does most harm to Art, and the last to himself. If we must be *dilettanti*: if it is impossible for us, under the circumstances amidst which we live, to think clearly, to feel nobly, and to delineate firmly: if we cannot attain to the mastery of the great artists—let us, at least, have so much respect for our Art as to prefer it to ourselves: let us not bewilder our successors: let us transmit to them the practice of Poetry, with its boundaries and wholesome regulative laws, under which excellent works may again, perhaps, at some future time, be produced, not yet fallen into oblivion through our neglect, not yet condemned and cancelled by the influence of their eternal enemy, Caprice.

---

17. *Non me . . . hostis*: "Your hot words do not frighten me. . . . The gods frighten me, and Jupiter as my enemy." From Virgil's *Aeneid* 12.894–95.

# Gerald Massey, from
## "Poetry—The Spasmodists" (1858)[1]

Born in poverty, Gerald Massey (1828–1907) was a journalist, ama-
teur Egyptologist, and public speaker known for his lectures on the
arts and Christian socialism; he was also considered a Spasmodic
poet by some. Although the poets whom Victorian critics tended
to label as Spasmodists were considered extremely "modern," their
poetry was often described in terms that today might remind one of
high Romanticism: it was marked by introspection, vivid sensory de-
scriptions, striking imagery, and heightened (if sometimes morbid)
emotions. In this essay, Massey uses the lingering influence of the
Spasmodic school as an opportunity to advance a theory of poetic
creation and poetic value grounded in reality, which recalls George
Eliot's theories of art. In fact, Massey attracted the attention of Eliot,
who drew from his personal story for her novel *Felix Holt*.

There are two worlds in which human existence moves: the world
of thought, and the world of feeling. The world of feeling is more
or less common to all. The highest and the lowest can meet on this
ground, and enter into this bond of human relationship. But it is different
in the world of thought. Many cannot pass from the world of feeling into
that of thought at will, and but few are fitted to translate their feeling into
thought—which is the spiritual apparition of feeling—and thus reproduce
any past experience in such shape as shall give pleasure to the beholder in the
contemplation thereof. This is the work of the poet. He translates from the
world of feeling into that of thought, and thus enables us to realise in thought
what we may have once experienced in feeling. And often, when these re-

1. Gerald Massey, "Poetry—The Spasmodists," *North British Review* (February 1858): 232–33,
235–45, 249–50.

productions are made by the greatest poets in their happiest moments, they seem quite familiar to us, because we have possessed them before in feeling, only we were unable to translate them into thought. When the poet has given us this new rendering of some old experience, it strikes us with the force of a greater reality than did that experience itself, when we were living it. Hence, we believe, has arisen one of the errors respecting the functions of the Imagination. We do not think that the poet adds to the reality, or transcends it in his translation of it, so much as that we ourselves are unaware of all that is contained in the reality, while we are passing through it in feeling. For this reason, while we are in a state of suffering, or enjoyment, we do not speculate upon it in thought; we live it in feeling. Indeed, the more perfect in feeling, the more unconscious are we in thought. But when, by the poet's aid, we come to re-live this feeling in thought, every faculty we turn upon it is now alive with consciousness; and this secondary phase of joy or sorrow often appears more real than the first, because we obtain a conscious interpretation of much that we before experienced unconsciously.

For the time being, then, we shall look upon the poet as a translator of realities which do already exist, and only a creator so far as he shapes an artistic body through which the life is operative; because, by looking upon him in this light we shall be able to see all the more clearly how poetry is coloured by the age in which it is produced, and takes its tints from the various influences that surround it, quickening its life, fostering its strength, or stunting its growth. For not only is the poet a translator of the inner life of man, with its wonder world of thoughts and feelings—its unspeakable love and sorrow, its hopes and aspirations, temptations and lonely wrestlings, darings and doubts, grim passions and gentle affections, its smiles and tears— which, in their changeful lights or gloomy grandeur, play out the great drama of the human heart, but he also translates into his poetry and reflects for us the very spirit of his time. The poetry of every age and epoch comes to us with the likeness of that age or epoch stamped upon it, in features ranging from the heroic type of the noble Elizabethan time, to the sensual cast given by the Merry Monarch and his Circean Restoration.[2] . . .

---

2. *Merry Monarch and his Circean Restoration*: King Charles II (1630–1685) was known as the Merry Monarch. Exiled in 1649, he returned to the throne in 1660, an event known as the "Restoration." "Circean" refers to the mythological enchantress Circe. Massey thus characterizes the period as dangerously seductive.

[Massey goes on to demonstrate his claim by describing poetry from the medieval period to the eighteenth century.]

In briefly noticing how the poet translates historical influences into poetry, we have now arrived at the great rebellion in poetry when Robert Burns[3] strode in among the crowd of the self-enthroned, who sat trying to conjure up the spirit of beauty, by repeating the words of the grand magicians who had passed away, and carried the secret of their enchantment with them, and passed right through them, scattering their fluttering artificialities and sparkling shallownesses on his way back to unsophisticated Nature. With one or two wistful looks at Pope and Shenstone,[4] he turned to the old ballads, with their sinewy strength, smiting tenderness, lilting music, and flashes of feeling. And Cowper,[5] in England, went back all he could to the primal simplicities of Nature, for he had an out-of-doors heart; and when shut indoors from the garden, and fettered there so often by sickness, he would still feel his way back to the woods and fields, and the common human heart, which he touched with so natural a knack that it would be thought a rare feat of genius, had he not done it so easily.

Then came William Wordsworth, who said, Let us go back to Chaucer, sit down beside him and his darling daisy, and learn of him what wealth of meaning there is in the things that lie about our feet; what strength and savour there is in simple speech; and how the poet may rise, Antaeus-like,[6] invincible in strength, so long as he keeps his footing on the common earth. It will do poetry good, said Wordsworth, to take it back, so that it may breathe in new life from the native air of its childhood. Here, then, was a special appeal made to external nature, as a means of getting fresh food for the inner life of man. And a comparatively new influence emanates from this appeal, which mingles largely with all subsequent poetry. Wordsworth becomes the great translator of this influence into his poetry; and after the first flush of the red-rising dawn of the French Revolution, which dazzled his young eyes also, has deepened into blood, he seeks to bring himself and his readers more and more under this influence, and to get further and further away from the sound of the

---

3. Robert Burns (1759–1796), a Scottish poet widely regarded as a precursor of the Romantics.

4. William Shenstone (1714–1763), an English nature poet.

5. William Cowper (1731–1800), an English poet who is also considered to be a pioneering Romantic.

6. *Antaeus-like*: In Greek mythology, Antaeus (son of Poseidon and Gaia) is a strong giant who became as weak as any mortal when his feet no longer touched the ground.

strife, and the smoke of the conflict; because, instead of the Goddess Liberty coming with healing to the nations, he sees a wild Virago[7] dancing round a guillotine, to the sound of the Carmagnole,[8] in wet, red shoes; and he shrinks away, and seeks to dwell apart with a nature that is more beneficent and beautiful, in her grandeur of storm, or blessing of calm. And so, in comparative solitude, he falls back upon those elements which are the very ground-roots of poetry, and attains, in a confused and bewildering time, to that repose in which the bright particles of knowledge are slowly precipitated, and shaped into the larger growth and oneness of accumulated wisdom, instead of their being kept in constant whirl by many disturbing causes, and never becoming anything more than the bright particles of scattered knowledge.

The French Revolution had an incalculable influence in bringing forth the great band of poets that came into being, as it were, through the rents made by the outburst of that Revolution, and produced such a quickening motion of mind, as issued in a very budding and flowering-time of poetry. . . . Tennyson's is the last song that rises up calmly, and rings out clearly with its melodious beauty, in spite of the pressure of our complex time, and the stress of its adverse influences. After him comes that deluge let loose upon us by what has been called the "Spasmodic School."

We fancy there is more meaning and applicability in the name of "Spasmodic," given to so much of the poetry which has been produced of late years, than the first givers of that name saw in it.[9] It is frequently the special characteristic of a nickname, that it shall be too vague and intangible to be seized upon and proved to be false; and so it lives, just because it cannot be caught and put to death. Here, however, the name might be demonstrated as true to the nature. For what constitutes spasm, but weakness trying to be strong, and collapsing in the effort? And what result could be looked for more naturally, than that a good deal of current poetry should be spasmodic, if we carry on into the present time our consideration of the external causes that influence poetry? When the giants of genius shall free themselves from the Etna[10] that now hides them, they may come and make it possible to transmute into poetry those influences which are at present only a hindrance to others, making their own new laws, and breaking old ones, surprising the

---

7. *Virago*: a domineering, manlike woman
8. *Carmagnole*: a popular revolutionary song, dance, and rallying cry
9. William Edmonstoune Aytoun is credited with popularizing the name.
10. *Etna*: a volcano in Sicily

whole world with most magical results; but, till then, poetry, in the hands of
our present writers, is driven into narrower bounds, and left with more lim-
ited means of freeing itself. The greatest poetry always finds its main source
of sustenance in a few common universal elements, which are to it what the
elementary substances are to chemistry. It deals with simple powers. Trust,
for example, we would call one of the simple powers of poetry. Doubt, on
the contrary, we should call a compound, made up of perplexed thought and
uncertain feeling; and, being a compound, it can be divided and destroyed.
Now, many tendencies of the time are at war with the simple powers, and are
in favour of the compounds. The out-flowing tides of feeling are checked and
forced back upon the poet, so that he feels compelled to turn his eyes within
in self-analysis, until, instead of living, he gets bewildered at the mystery of
life, which he cannot solve, and dazzled with the new knowledge, which he
cannot assimilate; instead of telling us what time it is by the face of the clock,
he pores over the problem of the wheels, and for every gain of curious insight
he loses some intuition of more precious value, until at length the conscious
intellect is enthroned in the seat of that unconscious child-like spirit, in which
all that is most human meets with what is most divine, even as the little chil-
dren came near and were taken into the arms of Christ of old. Our spasm-
odists, in a great measure, are dealers in compounds. And not only are they
driven out of the great poet's path by force of many outward circumstances,
and have not sufficient knowledge or grasp of the simple powers by which
poetry is brought home to our business and bosoms, but, in some instances,
they willfully turn from the simple powers to try their experiments with the
compounds, and their only ambition appears to be how to puzzle us with the
subtlety by which they can work for our perplexity and their remote result.
Shelley, in the *Cenci*, says with great truth,

> It is a trick of this same family
> To analyse their own and other minds.
> Such self-anatomy shall teach the will
> Dangerous secrets, for it tempts our powers.[11]

The first condition of being a poet, is to be a man speaking to men. He
who is to image humanity, must at least be able to stand on a common level

---

11. *The Cenci*, 2.2.108–11.

with it, and by his many sympathies enrich his special experience with all that is universal; thus losing the poverty of the individual in the wealth of the species. But it is the evident predilection of our spasmodists toward that "abstruse research" among morbid phenomena, which "tends to steal from his own nature all the natural man," and the habit of their minds to move in the involution[12] of thinking, instead of the evolution of thought. Also, it is their fatal fault to seek for that which is rare and peculiar, and to be afraid of that which is common, and timid of matter-of-fact and mere flesh and blood. If they do not do this intentionally, then so much the worse is it for the class of mind that is so limited and perverse as to take this direction instinctively. Either they seem not to share our ordinary feelings and plain humanities of thought and speech, or they cannot grasp ordinary realities; for the emotion to be sung, or the character to be painted, must have branched off far from the ordinary channel of human affairs, and run into an isolated and particular experience, before it is fitted for their poetic purpose. They refine upon reality till it becomes the faintest shadow, and only attempt to grasp it at the stage in which it cannot be laid hold of.

Now, if a poet possesses his manhood in common with the rest of us, shares our thoughts and has feelings in tune, and has truly a genius for transmuting and translating these into poetic forms, he cannot keep too much on broad human grounds. The charm will be in the common human experience being rendered in his subtler light, and coloured in the prism of his own personality. If he have sufficient genius, it is in universal experience that he will find his greatest strength,—out of it he will draw the universal success; if he have not sufficient genius, then all the seeking in the world, or out of it, for that which is remote and uncommon, will be but of little avail in disguising his weakness. Our spasmodists appear to take for their text, and apply it at all times and in all places, the words of Ecclesiasticus, "A man's mind is *sometimes* wont to tell him more than seven watchmen that sit above in an high tower."[13] They forget that this is only sometimes so, when the darkness of night shuts in the view, for example; and so they will not avail themselves

---

12. *involution*: In biological discourse, a retrograde process of development, the opposite of evolution, degeneration; more generally, it is used to describe being turned in or entangled.

13. *Ecclesiasticus*: Deuterocanonical biblical work, accepted in the Roman Catholic canon, also called the Wisdom of Jesus the Son of Sirach, XXXVII.14

of what the seven watchmen may see when the broad light of day lies on the
land, and reveals the many features of the landscape. Hence their tendency to
look with an introverted vision alone, instead of looking out with wide open
eyes, and deriving advantage from the experience of others, as do the great
objective writers. . . .

The band of young poets who have come before the public during the
last few years, have been called the "Spasmodic School," though there is not
oneness of principle in their efforts sufficient to give consistency to them,
and bind the writers together in any educational brotherhood. Certainly they
include almost every variety of spasm; but there are many spasmodic writ-
ers, in both prose and verse, beside those who have been denominated as
the Spasmodic School. On the other hand, it would be somewhat difficult to
point out any great master as the founder of this school. It appears to us that
Robert Browning is, in a sense, one of the greatest spasmodists, so far as a
wilful delight in remote and involved thinking, abrupt and jerking mental
movements, and "*pernickitieness*"[14] of expression, working, in the higher re-
gions of genius, can constitute a spasmodist. And but for certain spasmodic
peculiarities which seem inherent to Mrs. Browning, "Aurora Leigh" might
have been the greatest poem of our time. In her case, the spasm is manifested
in her sudden transitions from thought to thought and from thing to thing.
Descending to a very low point for illustration, we might also undertake
to show in "Bothwell"[15] some of the meanest possible specimens of *Surrey-
sublime* spasm; all the meaner, because it is the spasm of weakness collaps-
ing, without having to bear any burthen of thought or feeling. Going back
as far as Byron, we shall find the spasmodic element in a large portion of his
poetry. . . .

Following Byron, it appears to us that Lovell Beddoes[16] brings other
spasmodic influences into modern verse of a different kind. Beddoes has

---

14. *pernickitieness*: being overexacting about details; fussiness

15. "Bothwell" (1856) is a dramatic monologue set in the sixteenth century by poet and parodist
William Edmonstoune Aytoun. To characterize this well-received poem as Spasmodic is particularly
(though perhaps pointedly) odd, since Aytoun's parody of the rapturous reviews of the work of the
Spasmodists, as well as his 1854 *Firmilian, or The Student of Badajoz: A Spasmodic Tragedy* (a brilliant
parody of Spasmodic poetry itself) are usually credited with killing serious interest in the productions
of the so-called Spasmodic school.

16. Lovell Beddoes is a doctor and poet associated with the Spasmodic school. He committed
suicide in 1849, distressed about his poetic career.

much in common with the recent revival in poetry, which is somewhat akin to the latter renaissance in painting and architecture, and in which the bacchante[17] is often dearer than the saint. There is, too, more luxuriance of foliage and bloom on their trees than redundancy of fruit. He has the same love of colour, and fondness for all that is striking; he sets upon the banquet table the same rich feast of words, and his expression is mostly at the same pitch of extravagance. He also sprung into full blossom at an early period of youth, and went the way which other spasmodists have gone and are going; his spring blossoms fell in the frosts, and there was no autumn fruitage. His poetry largely possesses a quality which is, perhaps, the most common feature of our spasmodists—it is rich in imagery. This is natural enough for youth, which apprehends life mostly on the sensational side, and is more flowery and fleshly than spiritual. But it is well to note that this imaginal tendency, unless it be the youthful efflorescence of a mind that is quite healthy and full of all manly vigour, is apt to sap the strength from maturer mental qualities, and let it run to waste in a rank luxuriance of undergrowth. . . .

The peculiar nature of Beddoes' mind, which appeared to swarm with morbid instincts, made his end in poetry a melancholy warning. He gradually lost what hold he had upon the warm, rich world of human life, fed with common human affections, and filled with common human sympathies, in pursuit of unnatural mental anatomy, and in search of those mysteries which death renders up in the dissecting-room. For he became an anatomist literally. The poet, no longer satisfied with the beautiful instrument breathing its music, would take it in pieces to see whence the music came, which was a secret death could not reveal. To adapt an image of James Montgomery,[18] he sought to grasp in his own hand the dew-drop, which, when touched, at once loses all its sparkling grace, its shape of beauty, its light from heaven, and is merely a little water, having the one quality of wetness. The gift was taken from him, and died out of him utterly. And little marvel that this should be so: after reducing the ethereal fire to ashes, in search of a mere earthly discovery,—somewhat analogous perhaps to the accidental discovery of glass-making,—it was too much to have expected that the radiant Phoenix

17. *bacchante*: a female follower of Bacchus, god of wine and intoxication, often portrayed in states of violent, erotic frenzy

18. James Montgomery (1771–1854), a British poet.

of poetry would ever soar again from these ashes, when the fire was willfully put out for so paltry a purpose. Beddoes, we say, became an anatomist; and is not this precisely what some of our recent writers in verse have become? They also are probing among the secrets of the skeleton which lies hidden beneath the rosy bloom of flesh, with speculations on bones and membranes, cells and blood-vessels. Oysterlike, they get their pearls from a state of disease. If we were asked to indicate the poem which has been most harmful, and has wrought most evil to the young poetic mind of our time, we should unhesitatingly point to "Festus."[19] Bailey's poem is a vast work, in which egotism is the presiding principle, as it was in building that Babel of old. In going through it, the reader feels as though he were witnessing a series of grand pyrotechnic displays of gorgeous but evanescent brilliance, until his aching eyes are so dazzled, that he feels himself in "a land of darkness."[20] The writer's object throughout appears to be to strike us blind rather than to illumine us, and to leave us breathless rather than breathing. And at last the difficulty of reading the poem becomes bewildering. . . .

"Festus" is not, what it has so often been called, a great poem, because it is altogether wanting in the welding oneness that moulds the great works of imagination. There is no magnet of sufficient purpose passing through its glittering filings of the fancy, and gathering them up into fitting form. And when we use the word "filings" here, we do not do so merely in a figurative sense; for the truth is, that poems of the "Festus" order are principally made up of filings from other men's works—hints and suggestions got while reading the writings of others, sometimes by reading between the lines, often by direct appropriation, however unconscious; thus making the result mainly a parasitic growth, based upon the beginnings of others, instead of an original creation, with the life that shapes into symmetry and oneness energetically running through it, from the lowest ground-root of strength with which it grasps the subject, to the topmost leaf wherewith it breaks into beauty. Here we shall find none of the suspended, poising strength, as of the mountainous repose which marks the climacteric expression of the highest powers in the world of mind, even as they are also the grandest expression of power in our

---

19. "Festus," by Philip James Bailey (1816–1902), was initially published anonymously at Bailey's father's expense in 1839. It went through several editions, getting longer each time.
20. Job 10:21.

physical world; for these can only be attained by the creative mind, that under the dominant idea moves with all its powers at once, each keeping proper place and perfect time, harmoniously to one great end. . . .

"Festus" has also been fatally successful in leading astray, because all phenomena that cannot be explained by known laws open up at once a fresh field to work in; and so long as the phenomena cannot be classified, or the precise amount of their truth ascertained, there is but little fear of the sham and spurious imitation being known from what is true and real. This fact will account for much of the flying-off into space, which characterises recent verse, in order that it may avoid the verdict of an appeal to well-known laws, and not because the writers possess wings at will. If you cannot represent the world of reality, this plan of taking refuge in the impalpable affords a fine chance of fabricating a false world, which may float for a time as a beautiful bubble on the breath of those who puff it. False and futile, however, are all these attempts to create a world apart from that of human life, in which the poet shall be absolved from all known laws, and freed from ordinary conditions, in order that his idiosyncrasies may run riot without let or hindrance. Ordinary human beings cannot enter such a phantom world. Shut up in our house of the senses, with some half-a-dozen windows for outlooks into the infinite, we cannot follow, house and all, on pleasure-excursions into the spirit world, as "Festus" and others would have us, and mingle with its inhabitants on perfectly familiar terms. If Shakespeare, after mirroring so much of our human world so faithfully, had attempted to lead us into the invisible world, we might have followed with a firmer reliance. But he was all too wise, and left that for Milton to do, when God had laid the shadow on his outer eyes, and freed the inner from earthly scales, contenting himself with giving those hints that flash upon us in the high and mystic moods of thought. . . .

We see no reason for going further into detail on the subject of the "Spasmodic School," and we trust that some of our remarks may have gone near enough to the root of the matter, to obviate any necessity for our doing so. On the one hand, we can scarcely undertake to prescribe in the precise language of science for the specialties of the given disease, and the idiosyncrasies of the individual patients in each particular case; and, on the other, we have no wish to give an answer as *ex cathedra*.[21] We urge a return to the lasting and

---

21. *ex cathedra*: Latin; literally "from the chair"; used to denote a teaching authority

true subject-matter of poetry, and a firmer reliance on primal truths; for it is this which has so often given fresh life to both poetry and painting in the past. Crowded as the ground may have been, there is still room for great poets to walk here. Anything that has in it a genuine human interest is sure to win its way to the heart, so irresistible is the touch of real truth. This is the vital and enduring element of the Dutch painters. Their genuine statement of truth is sufficient to keep alive their pictures, though that truth be never so obvious and commonplace. And this is why those books are so successful that treat of the coarser passions. They have in them a real human interest, because they make their appeal to feelings which do exist. We are not here arguing in favour of Dutch pictures or French novels, but for that reality which is the basis of all poetry, and that truth which is the basis of all beauty. As Realists, we do not forget that it is not in the *vulgarity* of common things, nor the mediocrity of average characters, nor the familiarity of familiar affairs, nor the everydayness of everyday lives, that the poetry consists,—not the commonnesses of a common man, but those universal powers and passions which he shares with heroes and martyrs, are the true subjects of poetry. Though we advocate that all beauty must be true, we are not responsible for the converse of the proposition, that assumes all truth therefore beautiful, and that, consequently, "twice two are four" constitutes poetry. Like the consecrated banner of a Cortez, wherein the enthusiastic churchman may see the cross, and the ambitious patriot the crown, but which, to the eyes of the rabble in their train, is merely a waving absolution, this cry for common sense, matter-of-fact, and everyday life, may be followed by some, not for the right in which it originates, but for the wrong to which it may be perverted; but if it be so, they can never arrive at results more lamentable than the crowd who have followed the formulas of "high art" and the "ideal." And if poetry is to get home to us with its better influences, to hearten us in the struggles of life, beguile us of our glooms, take us gently from the dusty high-road, where we have borne the burden in the heat of the day, into the pastures where the grass is green and grateful to the tired feet, the air fragrant, and the shadows are refreshing, and draw us delicately up to loftier heights of being, we must have songs set to the music of the faithful heart,—we must have poetry for men who work, and think, and suffer, and whose hearts would feel faint and their souls grow lean if they fed on such fleeting deliciousness and confectionary trifle as the spasmodists too frequently offer them,—we must have poetry in which natural emotions flow, real passions move, in clash and conflict—in which our higher aims and aspirations are represented, with all that reality of daily life which goes on around us, in its strength and sweetness, its sternness and softness, wearing the smiles of rejoicing, and weeping the bitter tears of pain—weaving the many-coloured woof of Time, and working out the hidden purposes of Him that "sitteth in the heavens."[22]

22. Psalm 2:4.

# Henry James, from
# "Charles Baudelaire" (1876)[1]

This essay is a response to a debate in the pages of the *Nation* about
the relationship between aesthetic and moral value. Henry James
(1843–1916), an American novelist and literary critic, took the con-
troversy (gesturing toward it in the essay's opening paragraph, which
we've omitted) as a launching point for a nuanced meditation on
the question at the heart of Hallam's, Arnold's, and Massey's essays:
What ought to be the proper subject for poetry, and why? James's
critique of Baudelaire's choice of subjects resonates with the early
critical responses to Meredith's "Modern Love" and the "Poems and
Ballads," which were attacked for their focus on sin and misery. See
also Baudelaire's poem "Causerie" in the "Other Poetry" section of
"Contexts," which follow.

[B]audelaire's] celebrity began with the publication of *Les Fleurs du
Mal*,[2] a collection of verses some of which had already appeared in
periodicals. The *Revue des Deux Mondes* had taken the responsibility
of introducing a few of them to the world—or rather, though it held them
at the baptismal font of public opinion, it declined to stand godfather. An
accompanying note in the *Revue* disclaimed all editorial approval of their
morality. This of course procured them a good many readers; and when,
on its appearance, the volume we have mentioned was overhauled by the
police, a still greater number of persons desired to possess it. Yet in spite of
the service rendered him by the censorship, Baudelaire has never become in
any degree popular; the lapse of twenty years has seen but five editions of
*Les Fleurs du Mal*. The foremost feeling of the reader of the present day will
be one of surprise, and even amusement, at Baudelaire's audacities having

---

1. Henry James, "Charles Baudelaire," *Nation* (27 April 1876): 280–81.
2. *Les Fleurs du Mal*: French, "*The Flowers of Evil*"

provoked this degree of scandal. The world has travelled fast since then, and the French censorship must have been, in the year 1857, in a very prudish mood. There is little in *Les Fleurs du Mal* to make the reader of either French or English prose and verse of the present day even open his eyes. We have passed though the fiery furnace and profited by experience. We are like Racine's heroine, who had

Su se faire un front qui ne rougit jamais.[3]

Baudelaire's verses do not strike us as being dictated by a spirit of bravado—though we have heard that, in talk, it was his habit, to an even tiresome degree, to cultivate the quietly outrageous—to pile up monstrosities and blasphemies without winking, and with the air of uttering proper commonplaces.

*Les Fleurs du Mal* is evidently a sincere book—so far as anything for a man of Baudelaire's temper and culture could be sincere. Sincerity seems to us to belong to a range of qualities with which Baudelaire and his friends were but scantily conversant. His great quality was an inordinate cultivation of the sense of the picturesque, and his care was for how things looked, and whether some kind of imaginative amusement was not to be got out of them, much more than for what they meant and whither they led, and what was their use in human life at large. The later editions of *Les Fleurs du Mal* (with some of the interdicted pieces still omitted and others, we believe, restored) contain a long preface by Théophile Gautier,[4] which throws a curious side-light upon what the Spiritualist newspapers would call Baudelaire's "mentality." Of course Baudelaire is not to be held accountable for what Gautier says of him, but we cannot help judging a man in some degree by the company he keeps. To admire Gautier is certainly excellent taste, but to be admired by Gautier we cannot but regard as rather compromising. He gives a magnificently picturesque account of the author of *Les Fleurs du Mal*, in which, indeed, the question of pure veracity is evidently so very subordinate that it seems grossly ill-natured for us to appeal to such a standard. While we are reading him, however, we find ourselves wishing that Baudelaire's analogy with him were either greater or less. Gautier was perfectly sincere, because he dealt only with the picturesque, and pretended to care only for

---

3. *su se faire . . . jamais*: From Racine's *Phaedra: A Tragedy in Five Acts*, 3.3: "put on a face that never blushes."

4. Pierre Jules Théophile Gautier (1811–1872), a French poet, novelist, dramatist, literary and art critic.

appearances. But Baudelaire (who, to our mind, was an altogether inferior genius to Gautier) applied the same process of interpretation to things as regards which it was altogether inadequate; so that one is constantly tempted to suppose he cares more for his process—for making grotesquely-pictorial verse—than for the things themselves. On the whole, as we have said, this inference would be unfair. Baudelaire had a certain groping sense of the moral complexities of life, and if the best that he succeeds in doing is to drag them down into the very turbid element in which he himself plashes and flounders, and there present them to us much besmirched and bespattered, this was not a want of goodwill in him, but rather a dulness and permanent immaturity of vision. For American readers, furthermore, Baudelaire is compromised by his having made himself the apostle of our own Edgar Poe. He translated, very carefully and exactly, all of Poe's prose writings, and, we believe, some of his very valueless verses. With all due respect to the very original genius of the author of the *Tales of Mystery*, it seems to us that to take him with more than a certain degree of seriousness is to lack seriousness one's self. An enthusiasm for Poe is the mark of a decidedly primitive stage of reflection. Baudelaire thought him a profound philosopher, the neglect of whose golden utterances stamped his native land with infamy. Nevertheless, Poe was vastly the greater charlatan of the two, as well as the greater genius.

*Les Fleurs du Mal* was a very happy title for Baudelaire's verses, but it is not altogether a just one. Scattered flowers incontestably do bloom in the quaking swamps of evil, and the poet who does not mind encountering bad odors in his pursuit of sweet ones is quite at liberty to go in search of them. But Baudelaire has, as a general thing, not plucked the flowers—he has plucked the evil-smelling weeds (we take it that he did not use the word flowers in a purely ironical sense), and he has often taken up mere cupfuls of mud and bog-water. He had said to himself that it was a great shame that the realm of evil and unclean things should be fenced off from the domain of poetry; that it was full of subjects, of chances and effects; that it had its light and shade, its logic and its mystery; and that there was the making of some capital verses in it. So he leaped the barrier, and was soon immersed in it up to his neck. Baudelaire's imagination was of a melancholy and sinister kind, and, to a considerable extent, this plunging into darkness and dirt was doubtless very spontaneous and disinterested. But he strikes us on the whole as passionless, and this, in view of the unquestionable pluck and acuteness of his fancy, is a great pity. He knew evil not by experience, not as something within himself, but by contemplation and curiosity, as something outside of himself, by which his own intellectual agility was not in the least discomposed, rather, indeed (as we say his fancy was of a dusky cast), agreeably flattered and stimulated. In the former case, Baudelaire, with his other gifts, might have been a great poet. But, as it is, evil for him begins outside and not inside, and consists primarily of a great deal of lurid landscape and unclean furniture. This is an almost ludicrously puerile view of the matter. Evil is represented as an affair of blood and carrion and physical sickness—there must be stinking corpses and starving prostitutes and empty laudanum bottles in order that the poet shall be effectively inspired.

A good way to embrace Baudelaire at a glance is to say that he was, in his treatment of evil, exactly what Hawthorne was not—Hawthorne,[5] who felt the thing at its source, deep in the human consciousness. Baudelaire's infinitely slighter volume of genius apart, he was a sort of Hawthorne reversed. It is the absence of this metaphysical quality in his treatment of his favorite subjects (Poe was his metaphysician, and his devotion sustained him through a translation of "Eureka!") which exposes him to that class of accusations of which M. Edmond Schérer's[6] talk about his feeding upon *pourriture*[7] is an example; and, in fact, in his pages we never know with what we are dealing. We encounter an inextricable confusion of sad emotions and vile things, and we are at a loss to know whether the subject pretends to appeal to our conscience or—we were going to say—to our olfactories. "*Le Mal?*" we exclaim; "you do yourself too much honor. This is not Evil; it is not the wrong; it is simply the nasty!" Our impatience is of the same order as that which we should feel if a poet, pretending to pluck "the flowers of good," should come and present us, as specimens, a rhapsody on plum-cake and on cologne-water. Independently of the question of his subjects, the charm of Baudelaire's verse is often of a very high order. He belongs to the class of geniuses in whom we ourselves find but a limited pleasure—the laborious, deliberate, economical writers, those who fumble a long time in their pockets before they bring out their hand with a coin in the palm. But the coin, when Baudelaire at last produced it, was often of a high value. He had an extraordinary verbal instinct and an exquisite felicity of epithet. We cannot help wondering, however, at

5. Nathaniel Hawthorne (1804–1864), an American novelist and short story writer.
6. M. Edmond Schérer (1815–1889), a French literary critic, theologian, and politician.
7. *pourriture*: French, "rot" or "decay"

Gautier's extreme admiration for his endowment in this direction; it is the admiration of the writer who flows for the writer who trickles. In one point Baudelaire is extremely remarkable—in his talent for suggesting associations. His epithets seem to have come out of old cupboards and pockets; they have a kind of magical mustiness. Moreover, his natural sense of the superficial picturesqueness of the miserable and the unclean was extremely acute; there may be a difference of opinion as to the advantage of possessing such a sense; but whatever it is worth, Baudelaire had it in a high degree. One of his poems—"To a red-haired Beggar Girl"—is a masterpiece in the way of graceful expression of this high relish of what is shameful:

> Pour moi, poëte chétif,
> Ton jeune corps maladif,
> Plein de taches de rousseur,
> A sa douceur.[8]

Baudelaire repudiated with indignation the charge that he was what is called a realist, and he was doubtless right in doing so. He had too much fancy to adhere strictly to the real; he always embroiders and elaborates and endeavors to impart that touch of strangeness and mystery which is the very *raison d'être*[9] of poetry. Baudelaire was a poet, and for a poet to be a realist is of course nonsense.[10] The idea which Baudelaire imported into his theme was, as a general thing, an intensification of its repulsiveness, but it was at any rate ingenious. When he makes an invocation to "la Débauche aux bras immondes,"[11] one may be sure he means more by it than is evident to the vulgar—he means, that is, an intenser perversity. Occasionally he treats agreeable subjects, and his least sympathetic critics must make a point of admitting that his most successful poem is also his most wholesome and most touching: we allude to "Les Petites Vieilles"—a really masterly production. But if it represents the author's maximum, it is a note which he very rarely struck.

Baudelaire, of course, is a capital text for a discussion of the question as to the importance of the morality—or of the subject-matter in general—of

---

8. *Pour moi . . . douceur*: "For me, puny poet, / Your young sickly body, / Full of freckles / Has its sweetness."

9. *raison d'être*: French, "reason for existing"

10. Cf. Massey's "Poetry—The Spasmodists," which advocates a realist approach to poetry

11. *la Débauche . . . immondes*: French, "debauchery, with filthy arms"

a work of art; for he offers a rare combination of technical zeal and patience and of vicious sentiment. But even if we had space to enter upon such a discussion, we should spare our words, for argument on this point wears to our sense a simply ridiculous aspect. To deny the relevancy of subject-matter and the importance of the moral quality of a work of art strikes us as, in two words, ineffably puerile. We do not know what the great moralists would say about the matter—they would probably treat it very good-humoredly; but that is not the question. There is very little doubt what the great artists would say. These geniuses feel that the whole thinking man is one, and that to count out the moral element in one's appreciation of an artistic total is exactly as sane as it would be (if the total is a poem) to eliminate all the words in three syllables, or to consider only such portions of it as were written by candle-light. The crudity of sentiment of the advocates of "art for art"[12] is often a striking example of the fact that a great deal of what is called culture may fail to dissipate a well-seated provincialism of spirit. They talk of morality as Miss Edgeworth's[13] infantine heroes and heroines talk of "physic"[14]—they allude to its being put in and kept out of a work of art, put in and kept out of one's appreciation of the same, as if it were a colored fluid kept in a big-labelled bottle in some mysterious intellectual closet. It is in reality simply a part of the essential richness of inspiration—it has nothing to do with the artistic process, and it has everything to do with the artistic effect. The more a work of art feels it at its source, the richer it is; the less it feels it, the poorer it is. People of a large taste prefer rich works to poor ones, and they are not inclined to assent to the assumption that the process is the whole work. We are safe in believing that all this is comfortably clear to most of those who have, in any degree, been initiated into art by production. For them the subject is as much a part of their work as their hunger is a part of their dinner. Baudelaire was not so far from being of this way of thinking as some of his admirers would persuade us; yet we may say on the whole that he was the victim of a grotesque illusion. He tried to make fine verses on ignoble subjects, and in our opinion he signally failed. He gives, as a poet, a perpetual impression of

---

12. *"art for art"*: art for art's sake, the English translation of the French *l'Art pour l'Art*, a phrase often attributed to Gautier and associated with the idea—and the movement inspired by the idea—that art need not have a moral or utilitarian function

13. Maria Edgeworth (1767–1849), an Anglo-Irish novelist.

14. *physic*: medicine, medicinal preparation

discomfort and pain. He went in search of corruption, and the ill-conditioned jade proved a thankless muse. The thinking reader, feeling himself, as a critic, all one, as we have said, finds the beauty perverted by the ugliness. What the poet wished, doubtless, was to seem to be always in the poetic attitude; what the reader sees is a gentleman in a painful-looking posture, staring very hard at a mass of things from which we more intelligently avert our heads.

# Gerard Manley Hopkins,
## "Author's Preface" (1883)[1]

The following two selections from Gerard Manley Hopkins's (1844–1889) prose offer a clear picture of the difference between "running rhythm" and "sprung rhythm," and make a strong claim for the positive value of reading poetry aloud. Oddly enough—given the density of his prose—Hopkins, like Wordsworth, believed that poetry ought to correspond to the rhythms of natural speech. Hopkins's poems, by representing the work of poetic inspiration upon the brain though rhythm, unconventional syntax, puns, ellipses, neologisms, repetition, and compound words, allow readers to access what he considered to be the distinctive design that constitutes the dynamic identity of another being. Understanding poetic form is thus paramount to appreciating Hopkins's verse as he intended it. In the "Author's Preface," which follows, Hopkins frames his idiosyncratic practices of scansion, the metrical analysis of verse. In the following letter to friend and fellow poet Robert Bridges, Hopkins discusses the challenges of poetic intelligibility and expresses his intention that Harry Ploughman "be a vivid figure before the mind's eye."

T he poems in this book[2] are written some in Running Rhythm, the common rhythm in English use, some in Sprung Rhythm, and some in a mixture of the two. And those in the common rhythm are some counterpointed, some not.

Common English rhythm, called Running Rhythm above, is measured by feet of either two or three syllables and (putting aside the imperfect feet at the beginning and end of lines and also some unusual measures, in which

---

1. Gerard Manley Hopkins, "Author's Preface," in *Poems of Gerard Manley Hopkins*, ed. Robert Bridges (London: Humphrey Milford, 1918).

2. The preface was written in about 1883 and was part of the manuscript book of Hopkins's poems.

feet seem to be paired together and double or composite feet to arise) never more or less.

Every foot has one principal stress or accent, and this or the syllable it falls on may be called the Stress of the foot and the other part, the one or two unaccented syllables, the Slack. Feet (and the rhythms made out of them) in which the stress comes first are called Falling Feet and Falling Rhythms, feet and rhythm in which the Slack comes first are called Rising Feet and Rhythms, and if the Stress is between two Slacks there will be Rocking Feet and Rhythms. These distinctions are real and true to nature; but for purposes of scanning it is a great convenience to follow the example of music and take the stress always first, as the accent or the chief accent always comes first in a musical bar. If this is done there will be in common English verse only two possible feet—the so-called accentual Trochee and Dactyl, and correspond-ingly only two possible uniform rhythms, the so-called Trochaic and Dac-tylic. But they may be mixed and then what the Greeks called a Logaoedic Rhythm arises. These are the facts and according to these the scanning of ordinary regularly-written English verse is very simple indeed and to bring in other principles is here unnecessary.

But because verse written strictly in these feet and by these principles will become same and tame the poets have brought in licences and depar-tures from rule to give variety, and especially when the natural rhythm is rising, as in the common ten-syllable or five-foot verse, rhymed or blank. These irregularities are chiefly Reversed Feet and Reversed or Counterpoint Rhythm, which two things are two steps or degrees of licence in the same kind. By a reversed foot I mean the putting the stress where, to judge by the rest of the measure, the slack should be and the slack where the stress, and this is done freely at the beginning of a line and, in the course of a line, after a pause; only scarcely ever in the second foot or place and never in the last, unless when the poet designs some extraordinary effect; for these places are characteristic and sensitive and cannot well be touched. But the reversal of the first foot and of some middle foot after a strong pause is a thing so natural that our poets have generally done it, from Chaucer down, without remark and it commonly passes unnoticed and cannot be said to amount to a formal change of rhythm, but rather is that irregularity which all natural growth and motion shows. If however the reversal is repeated in two feet running, espe-cially so as to include the sensitive second foot, it must be due either to great want of ear or else is a calculated effect, the superinducing or *mounting* of a new rhythm upon the old; and since the new or mounted rhythm is actually heard and at the same time the mind naturally supplies the natural or standard foregoing rhythm, for we do not forget what the rhythm is that by rights we should be hearing, two rhythms are in some manner running at once and we have something answerable to counterpoint in music, which is two or more strains of tune going on together, and this is Counterpoint Rhythm. Of this kind of verse Milton is the great master and the choruses of *Samson Agonistes* are written throughout in it—but with the disadvantage that he does not let the reader clearly know what the ground-rhythm is meant to be and so they have struck most readers as merely irregular. And in fact if you counterpoint throughout, since one only of the counter rhythms is actually heard, the other is really destroyed or cannot come to exist and what is written is one rhythm only and probably Sprung Rhythm, of which I now speak.

Sprung Rhythm, as used in this book, is measured by feet of from one to four syllables, regularly, and for particular effects any number of weak or slack syllables may be used. It has one stress, which falls on the only syllable, if there is only one, or, if there are more, then scanning as above, on the first, and so gives rise to four sorts of feet, a monosyllable and the so-called accentual Trochee, Dactyl, and the First Paeon. And there will be four corresponding natural rhythms; but nominally the feet are mixed and any one may follow any other. And hence Sprung Rhythm differs from Running Rhythm in having or being only one nominal rhythm, a mixed or 'logaoedic' one, instead of three, but on the other hand in having twice the flexibility of foot, so that any two stresses may either follow one another running or be divided by one, two, or three slack syllables. But strict Sprung Rhythm cannot be counterpointed. In Sprung Rhythm, as in logaoedic rhythm generally, the feet are assumed to be equally long or strong and their seeming inequality is made up by pause or stressing.

Remark also that it is natural in Sprung Rhythm for the lines to be *rove over*, that is for the scanning of each line immediately to take up that of the one before, so that if the first has one or more syllables at its end the other must have so many the less at its beginning; and in fact the scanning runs on without break from the beginning, say, of a stanza to the end and all the stanza is one long strain, though written in lines asunder.

Two licences are natural to Sprung Rhythm. The one is rests, as in music; but of this an example is scarcely to be found in this book, unless in the *Echos*, second line. The other is *hangers* or *outrides*, that is one, two, or

three slack syllables added to a foot and not counting in the nominal scan-
ning. They are so called because they seem to hang below the line or ride
forward or backward from it in another dimension than the line itself, ac-
cording to a principle needless to explain here. These outriding half feet
or hangers are marked by a loop underneath them, and plenty of them will
be found.

The other marks are easily understood, namely accents, where the reader
might be in doubt which syllable should have the stress; slurs, that is loops
*over* syllables, to tie them together into the time of one; little loops at the end
of a line to show that the rhyme goes on to the first letter of the next line; what
in music are called pauses ⌢, to show that the syllable should be dwelt on; and
twirls ∾, to mark reversed or counterpointed rhythm.

Note on the nature and history of Sprung Rhythm—Sprung Rhythm is
the most natural of things. For (1) it is the rhythm of common speech and of
written prose, when rhythm is perceived in them. (2) It is the rhythm of all
but the most monotonously regular music, so that in the words of choruses
and refrains and in songs written closely to music it arises. (3) It is found
in nursery rhymes, weather saws,[3] and so on; because, however these may
have been once made in running rhythm, the terminations having dropped
off by the change of language, the stresses come together and so the rhythm
is sprung. (4) It arises in common verse when reversed or counterpointed,
for the same reason.

But nevertheless in spite of all this and though Greek and Latin lyric
verse, which is well known, and the old English verse seen in *Pierce Plough-
man*[4] are in sprung rhythm, it has in fact ceased to be used since the Elizabe-
than age, Greene[5] being the last writer who can be said to have recognised
it. For perhaps there was not, down to our days, a single, even short, poem
in English in which sprung rhythm is employed—not for single effects or
in fixed places—but as the governing principle of the scansion. I say this
because the contrary has been asserted: if it is otherwise the poem should be
cited.

---

3. *weather saws*: A saw is a pithy saying; a weather saw would be a saying about the weather.

4. *Pierce Ploughman*: more commonly spelled *Piers Plowman*, by William Langland, considered
one of the greatest works of medieval English literature

5. Robert Greene (1558–1592), Elizabethan playwright, famous for attacking Shakespeare.

Some of the sonnets in this book are in five-foot, some in six-foot or Alexandrine lines.

Nos. 13 and 22 are Curtal-Sonnets, that is they are constructed in proportions resembling those of the sonnet proper, namely $6+4$ instead of $8+6$, with however a halfline tailpiece (so that the equation is rather $12/2 + 9/2 = 21/2 = 10\;\tfrac{1}{2}$).

# Gerard Manley Hopkins, Letter on "Harry Ploughman" (1887)[1]

I want Harry Ploughman to be a vivid figure before the mind's eye; if he is not that the sonnet fails. The difficulties are of syntax no doubt. . . . Dividing a compound word by a clause sandwiched into it was a desperate deed, I feel, and I do not feel that it was an unquestionable success. But which is the line you do not understand? I do myself think, I may say, that it would be an immense advance in notation (so to call it) in writing as the record of speech, to distinguish the subject, verb, object, and in general to express the construction to the eye; as is done already partly in punctuation by everybody, partly in capitals by the Germans, more fully in accentuation by the Hebrews. And I daresay it will come. But it would, I think, not do for me: it seems a confession of unintelligibility. And yet I don't know. At all events there is a difference. My meaning surely *ought* to appear of itself; but in a language like English, and in an age of it like the present, written words are really matter open and indifferent to the receiving of different and alternative verse-forms, some of which the reader cannot possibly be sure are meant unless they are marked for him. Besides metrical marks are for the performer and such marks are proper in every art. Though indeed one might say syntactical marks are for the performer too. But however that reminds me that

1. Gerard Manley Hopkins, 6 November 1887 Letter to Robert Bridges, in *The Letters of Gerard Manley Hopkins to Robert Bridges*, ed. Claude Collier Abbott (London: Oxford University Press, 1970), 265–66. Reprinted by permission of Oxford University Press on behalf of the British Province of the Society of Jesus.

one thing I am now resolved on, it is to prefix short prose *arguments* to some of my pieces. These too will expose me to carping, but I do not mind. Epic and drama and ballad and many, most, things should be at once intelligible; but everything need not and cannot be. Plainly if it is possible to express a subtle and recondite thought on a subtle and recondite subject in a subtle and recondite way and with great felicity and perfection, in the end, something must be sacrificed, with so trying a task, in the process, and this may be the being at once, nay perhaps even the being without explanation at all, intelligible. Neither, in the same light, does it seem to be to me a real objection (though this one I hope not to lay myself open to) that the argument should be even longer than the piece; for the merit of the work may lie for one thing in its terseness. It is like a mate which may be given, one way only, in three moves; otherwise, various ways, in many.

# *Other Poetry*

Demonstrating the wide range of form and content in mid-Victorian poetry, the poems in this section might at first glance seem like an eclectic mix. They were chosen because each exemplifies key elements of Meredith's verse: social commentary, sensory detail and synesthesia, narrativity, and the sonnet form. Reading the *Modern Love* poems in relation to these selections highlights Meredith's use of these poetic devices, revealing the richly diverse nature of his verse.

Any study of Victorian poetry depicting marriage would be incomplete without acknowledging the enormous influence of Coventry Patmore's "The Angel in the House." The poem breathes life into the gender and social expectations articulated in the prose selections in the "Social Commentary" section of this edition. It sets the scene with a compelling vision of marital harmony that would become the *beau ideal* for wifely devotion, though the later parts of this work—far less frequently anthologized—do dramatize a husband's ambivalence.

"Modern Love" takes inspiration from the traditional sonnet form, and by challenging some of the sonnet's formal requirements, turns it into something more modern. John Keats was a master of the form, and a favorite of Meredith, who especially appreciated Keats's pagan imagery. Barrett Browning's *Sonnets from the Portuguese* and Rossetti's "Monna Innominata" offer two examples of the Victorian recuperation of the sonnet sequence. The traditional Petrarchan sequence describes an unrequited, abstracted love—as opposed to a physical or consummated love—and both Barrett Browning and Rossetti's sonnets take that spiritualized version of love as a starting point. Meredith, on the other hand, offers a critique of such disembodied desire by toying with the traditional fourteen-line sonnet and by introducing sensory description, descriptions of physical desire, and complicated, ambivalent emotions.

If Barrett Browning and Rossetti's poems provide examples of more typically Victorian encounters with the amatory sonnet, Baudelaire's and Gerard Manley Hopkins's sonnets present the opposite side of the coin. "Causerie," from Baudelaire's landmark volume *Les Fleurs du Mal* offers an important precedent for "Modern Love," as it imbues the traditional sonnet with synesthesia, detailing sexual desire and repulsion in frank, though beautiful, language. Hopkins's "Harry Ploughman" represents another effort to modernize the sonnet; his subject is a manual laborer—an uncommon subject for a traditional sonnet—and his close attention to vivid description encourages readers to imagine the sensory experience of the poet and his subject. Like Meredith, Hopkins adapts and expands the fourteen-line sonnet form to suit his own purposes.

The exploration of the relationship between physical sensation and emotional experience is also evident in Tennyson's *Maud*. The story of a thwarted lover who descends into madness, it was, like "Modern Love," labeled "Spasmodic" for the introspection and extreme feelings of the poet narrator. *Maud* rejects any single form, instead linking a series of poems with different meters, rhythms, and rhyme schemes, to develop an extended narrative that interweaves elements of tragedy as well as comedy, the sublime and the ridiculous.

# John Keats, from
## "Woman! when I behold thee flippant, vain . . ." (1817) and "On the Sea" (1817)[1]

John Keats (1795–1821) was an English Romantic poet. His associa-
tion with the radical Leigh Hunt made him a target in the Tory press,
which characterized his verse as prurient, overly sensuous, and pre-
tentious. Even Wordsworth called his "Hymn to Pan" a "very pretty
piece of Paganism." It is no wonder, then, that Meredith would re-
gard Keats as a kindred spirit, preferring his work over that of Shel-
ley and Byron. Keats was also a favorite among many in Meredith's
intellectual circle, particularly those belonging to the Pre-Raphaelite
Brotherhood. His mastery of the sonnet form is clear from the two
examples that follow. "Woman! when I behold thee flippant, vain . . ."
comprises three sonnets, the second of which begins "Light feet, dark
violet eyes, and parted hair," and is printed here (the line numbers
refer to the sonnet's position within the series). This sonnet details
the speaker's conflicted desire: despite the woman's obvious pride
and vanity, he is charmed by her beauty and "voice divine." The
husband in "Modern Love" evinces a similar ambivalence toward
his wife. "On the Sea" offers a vision of nature, in the form of the
vast sea, as a curative to those whose senses of sight and sound are
overwhelmed by modern life.

---

1. *The Complete Poetical Works and Letters of John Keats*, ed. Horace E. Scudder (Boston: Hough-
ton, Mifflin, 1899), 3, 37.

## From "Woman! when I behold thee flippant, vain . . ."

Light feet, dark violet eyes, and parted hair;                    15
Soft dimpled hands, white neck, and creamy breast,
Are things on which the dazzled senses rest
Till the fond, fixed eyes, forget they stare.
From such fine pictures, heavens! I cannot dare
To turn my admiration, though unpossess'd
They be of what is worthy,—though not drest
In lovely modesty, and virtues rare.
Yet these I leave as thoughtless as a lark;
These lures I straight forget,—e'en ere[2] I dine,
Or thrice my palate moisten: but when I mark         25
Such charms with mild intelligences shine,
My ear is open like a greedy shark,
To catch the tunings of a voice divine.

---

2. *ere*: before

# On the Sea

It keeps eternal whisperings around
Desolate shores, and with its mighty swell
Gluts twice ten thousand caverns, till the spell
Of Hecate[3] leaves them their old shadowy sound.
Often 'tis in such gentle temper found,
That scarcely will the very smallest shell
Be mov'd for days from where it sometime fell,
When last the winds of Heaven were unbound.
O ye! who have your eyeballs vex'd and tir'd,
Feast them upon the wideness of the Sea;                    10
O ye! whose ears are dinn'd with uproar rude,
Or fed too much with cloying melody,—
Sit ye near some old cavern's mouth, and brood
Until ye start, as if the sea-nymphs quir'd![4]

3. *Hecate*: Greco-Roman goddess associated with borders, doorways, and crossroads
4. *quir'd*: choired, that is, to sing in chorus

# Elizabeth Barrett Browning, from
## *Sonnets from the Portuguese* (1850)[1]

Although her work was deemed unfashionably "Victorian" in the early twentieth century, during her lifetime Elizabeth Barrett Browning was England's most famous and admired woman poet—more famous than her husband, Robert Browning. Their courtship began when Robert Browning, having just read her poetry and never having met her, was nevertheless prompted to express his deep admiration in a letter to her: "I do as I say," he wrote, "love these books with all my heart—and I love you too."[2] Written during the course of their courtship in 1845 and 1846 and first published in 1850 (after they were married), *Sonnets from the Portuguese* was an immediate success. Because they are semiautobiographical, Barrett Browning initially sought to preserve her privacy by suggesting that the sonnets were English translations of Portuguese poems by Luis de Camoëns. In a sequence of forty-four sonnets, Barrett Browning places before her readers a speaker who begins by seeking death, learns she is beloved but cannot accept it, and finally is transformed by love. Although a superficial reading might suggest these are banal love poems (portions of the sequence are often read at weddings), recent critical commentary has explored the ways in which they subvert the traditional courtly-love sonnet.

---

1. Elizabeth Barrett Browning, *Poems* (London: Chapman and Hall, 1862), 188, 193, 201, 229.

2. Robert Browning and Elizabeth Barrett Browning, letter dated 10 January 1845, *The Letters of Robert Browning and Elizabeth Barrett* (London: Harper & Brothers, 1899), 2.

## I.

I thought once how Theocritus had sung
Of the sweet years, the dear and wished-for years,
Who each one in a gracious hand appears
To bear a gift for mortals, old or young:
And, as I mused it in his antique tongue,
I saw, in gradual vision through my tears,
The sweet, sad years, the melancholy years,
Those of my own life, who by turns had flung
A shadow across me. Straightway I was 'ware,
So weeping, how a mystic Shape did move          10
Behind me, and drew me backward by the hair;
And a voice said in mastery, while I strove,—
'Guess now who holds thee?'—'Death,' I said. But, there,
The silver answer rang,—'Not Death, but Love.'

## VI.

Go from me. Yet I feel that I shall stand
Henceforward in thy shadow. Nevermore
Alone upon the threshold of my door
Of individual life, I shall command
The uses of my soul, nor lift my hand
Serenely in the sunshine as before,
Without the sense of that which I forebore—
Thy touch upon the palm. The widest land
Doom takes to part us, leaves thy heart in mine
With pulses that beat double. What I do          10
And what I dream include thee, as the wine
Must taste of its own grapes. And when I sue[3]
God for myself, He hears that name of thine,
And sees within my eyes the tears of two.

3. *sue*: follow

## XIV.

If thou must love me, let it be for nought
Except for love's sake only. Do not say
'I love her for her smile—her look—her way
Of speaking gently,—for a trick of thought
That falls in well with mine, and certes[4] brought
A sense of pleasant ease on such a day'—
For these things in themselves, Belovëd, may
Be changed, or change for thee,—and love, so wrought,
May be unwrought so. Neither love me for
Thine own dear pity's wiping my cheeks dry,—                    10
A creature might forget to weep, who bore
Thy comfort long, and lose thy love thereby!
But love me for love's sake, that evermore
Thou may'st love on, through love's eternity.

## XLII.

'My future will not copy fair my past'—
I wrote that once; and thinking at my side
My ministering life-angel justified
The word by his appealing look upcast
To the white throne of God, I turned at last,
And there, instead, saw thee, not unallied
To angels in thy soul! Then I, long tried
By natural ills, received the comfort fast,
While budding, at thy sight, my pilgrim's staff
Gave out green leaves with morning dews impearled.              10
I seek no copy now of life's first half:
Leave here the pages with long musing curled,
And write me new my future's epigraph,
New angel mine, unhoped for in the world!

---

4. *certes*: certainly

# Coventry Patmore, from
## *The Angel in the House* (1854–62)[1]

Coventry Patmore published his first book of poems, *Poems* (1844), with Edward Moxon, publisher of Tennyson and Robert Browning, when he was only twenty-one. His poetry thematized love, sexuality, medievalism, and intense emotion in the Romantic vein, and he was associated with the Pre-Raphaelite movement, publishing in *The Germ*. Patmore and Meredith were not only connected through the Pre-Raphaelite circle, but also (later in life) through their friendships with the poet and journalist Alice Meynell. *The Angel in the House* was written to be the definitive poem on married love. The first two installments, telling the story of Felix Vaughn's triumph over a rival suitor named Frederick for the hand of Honoria Churchill, were published in 1854 and 1856. The final two installments, offering (for the most part) the now-married Frederick's less-blissful perspective, were published in 1860 and 1862. The poem was not an instant success. Critics lambasted its octosyllabic meter, calling it "humdrum."[2] It became, however, extremely popular toward the end of the century and remained so until well into the twentieth. Included here are "The Chace" and "The Married Lover" from the first two installments, titled "The Angel in the House." We also include two poems from the fourth, lesser-known installment, "The Victories of Love." Published in the same year as *Modern Love*, these epistolary poems, "Frederick to Mrs. Graham" and "From Mrs. Graham," offer the perspective of a husband resigned to life with the woman he married after the disappointment of early rejection by another. Readers will note that both *The Angel in the House* and "Modern Love" use similar tropes and figures for heterosexual courtship and desire.

---

1. Coventry Patmore, *The Angel in the House together with The Victories of Love* (London: Routledge, 1905).

2. Edmund Gosse, *Coventry Patmore* (New York: Scribners, 1905), 68.

# The Chace[3]

She wearies with an ill unknown;
In sleep she sobs and seems to float,
A water-lily, all alone
Within a lonely castle-moat;
And as the full-moon, spectral, lies
Within the crescent's gleaming arms,
The present shows her heedless eyes
A future dim with vague alarms.
She sees, and yet she scarcely sees,
For, life-in-life not yet begun,                    10
Too many are its mysteries
For thought to fix on any one.
She's told that maidens are by youths
Extremely honour'd and desired;
And sighs, 'If those sweet tales be truths,
'What bliss to be so much admired!'
The suitors come; she sees them grieve;
Her coldness fills them with despair;
She'd pity if she could believe;
She's sorry that she cannot care.                   20
But who now meets her on her way?
Comes he as enemy or friend,
Or both? Her bosom seems to say,
He cannot pass, and there an end.
Whom does he love? Does he confer
His heart on worth that answers his?
Or is he come to worship her?
She fears, she hopes, she thinks he is!
Advancing stepless, quick, and still,
As in the grass a serpent glides,                   30
He fascinates her fluttering will,
Then terrifies with dreadful strides.
At first, there's nothing to resist;

---

3. Patmore, *The Angel in the House*, 104–7.

He fights with all the forms of peace;
He comes about her like a mist,
With subtle, swift, unseen increase;
And then, unlook'd for, strikes amain[4]
Some stroke that frightens her to death,
And grows all harmlessness again,
Ere she can cry, or get her breath.                     40
At times she stops, and stands at bay;
But he, in all more strong than she,
Subdues her with his pale dismay,
Or more admired audacity.
She plans some final, fatal blow,
But when she means with frowns to kill
He looks as if he loved her so,
She smiles to him against her will.
How sweetly he implies her praise!
His tender talk, his gentle tone,                        50
The manly worship in his gaze,
They nearly make her heart his own.
With what an air he speaks her name;
His manner always recollects
Her sex, and still the woman's claim
Is taught its scope by his respects.
Her charms, perceived to prosper first
In his beloved advertencies,[5]
When in her glass they are rehearsed,
Prove his most powerful allies.                          60
Ah, whither shall a maiden flee,
When a bold youth so swift pursues,
And siege of tenderest courtesy,
With hope perseverant, still renews!
Why fly so fast? Her flatter'd breast
Thanks him who finds her fair and good;
She loves her fears; veil'd joys arrest

---

4. *amain*: with full force
5. *advertencies*: attentions

The foolish terrors of her blood.
By secret, sweet degrees, her heart,
Vanquish'd, takes warmth from his desire;                    70
She makes it more, with hidden art,
And fuels love's late dreaded fire.
The generous credit he accords
To all the signs of good in her
Redeems itself; his praiseful words
The virtues they impute confer.
Her heart is thrice as rich in bliss,
She's three times gentler than before;
He gains a right to call her his
Now she through him is so much more;                         80
'Tis heaven where'er she turns her head;
'Tis music when she talks; 'tis air
On which, elate, she seems to tread,
The convert of a gladder sphere!
Ah, might he, when by doubts aggrieved,
Behold his tokens next her breast,
At all his words and sighs perceived
Against its blythe upheaval press'd!
But still she flies. Should she be won,
It must not be believed or thought                           90
She yields; she's chased to death, undone,
Surprised, and violently caught.

# The Married Lover[6]

Why, having won her, do I woo?
Because her spirit's vestal[7] grace
Provokes me always to pursue,
But, spirit-like, eludes embrace;
Because her womanhood is such
That, as on court-days subjects kiss
The Queen's hand, yet so near a touch
Affirms no mean familiarness,
Nay, rather marks more fair the height
Which can with safety so neglect                          10
To dread, as lower ladies might,
That grace could meet with disrespect,
Thus she with happy favour feeds
Allegiance from a love so high
That thence no false conceit proceeds
Of difference bridged, or state put by;
Because, although in act and word
As lowly as a wife can be,
Her manners, when they call me lord,
Remind me 'tis by courtesy;                               20
Not with her least consent of will,
Which would my proud affection hurt,
But by the noble style that still
Imputes an unattain'd desert;
Because her gay and lofty brows,
When all is won which hope can ask,
Reflect a light of hopeless snows
That bright in virgin ether bask;
Because, though free of the outer court
I am, this Temple keeps its shrine                        30
Sacred to Heaven; because, in short,
She's not and never can be mine.

---

6. Patmore, *The Angel in the House*, 183.
7. *vestal*: chaste

# Frederick to Mrs. Graham[8]

Honoria, trebly fair and mild
With added loves of lord and child,
Is else unalter'd. Years, which wrong
The rest, touch not her beauty, young
With youth which rather seems her clime,
Than aught that's relative to time.
How beyond hope was heard the prayer
I offer'd in my love's despair!
Could any, whilst there's any woe,
Be wholly blest, then she were so.                    10
She is, and is aware of it,
Her husband's endless benefit;
But, though their daily ways reveal
The depth of private joy they feel,
'Tis not their bearing each to each
That does abroad their secret preach,
But such a lovely good-intent
To all within their government
And friendship as, 'tis well discern'd,
Each of the other must have learn'd;                  20
For no mere dues of neighbourhood
Ever begot so blest a mood.

    And fair, indeed, should be the few
God dowers[9] with nothing else to do,
And liberal of their light, and free
To show themselves, that all may see!
For alms let poor men poorly give
The meat whereby men's bodies live;
But they of wealth are stewards wise
Whose graces are their charities.                     30

✦

---

8. Patmore, *The Angel in the House*, 276–79.
9. *dowers*: endows

The sunny charm about this home
Makes all to shine who thither come.
My own dear Jane has caught its grace,
And, honour'd, honours too the place.
Across the lawn I lately walk'd
Alone, and watch'd where mov'd and talk'd,
Gentle and goddess-like of air,
Honoria and some Stranger fair.
I chose a path unblest by these;
When one of the two Goddesses,                    40
With my Wife's voice, but softer, said,
'Will you not walk with us, dear Fred?'

She moves, indeed, the modest peer
Of all the proudest ladies here.
Unawed she talks with men who stand
Among the leaders of the land,
And women beautiful and wise,
With England's greatness in their eyes.
To high, traditional good-sense,
And knowledge ripe without pretence,             50
And human truth exactly hit
By quiet and conclusive wit,
Listens my little, homely Dove,
Mistakes the points and laughs for love;
And, after, stands and combs her hair,
And calls me much the wittiest there!

With reckless loyalty, dear Wife,
She lays herself about my life!
The joy I might have had of yore
I have not; for 'tis now no more,                60
With me, the lyric time of youth,
And sweet sensation of the truth.
Yet, past my hope or purpose bless'd,
In my chance choice let be confess'd

The tenderer Providence that rules
The fates of children and of fools!

   I kiss'd the kind, warm neck that slept,
And from her side this morning stepp'd,
To bathe my brain from drowsy night
In the sharp air and golden light.                    70
The dew, like frost, was on the pane.
The year begins, though fair, to wane.
There is a fragrance in its breath
Which is not of the flowers, but death;
And green above the ground appear
The lilies of another year.
I wander'd forth, and took my path
Among the bloomless aftermath;
And heard the steadfast robin sing
As if his own warm heart were Spring,          80
And watch'd him feed where, on the yew,
Hung honey'd drops of crimson dew;
And then return'd, by walls of peach,
And pear-trees bending to my reach,
And rose-beds with the roses gone,
To bright-laid breakfast. Mrs. Vaughan
Was there, none with her. I confess
I love her than of yore no less!
But she alone was loved of old;
Now love is twain, nay, manifold;            90
For, somehow, he whose daily life
Adjusts itself to one true wife,
Grows to a nuptial,[10] near degree
With all that's fair and womanly.
Therefore, as more than friends, we met,
Without constraint, without regret;
The wedded yoke that each had donn'd
Seeming a sanction, not a bond.

---

10. *nuptial*: marriage

# From Mrs. Graham[11]

Your love lacks joy, your letter says.
Yes; love requires the focal space
Of recollection or of hope,
E'er it can measure its own scope.
Too soon, too soon comes Death to show
We love more deeply than we know!
The rain, that fell upon the height
Too gently to be call'd delight,
Within the dark vale reappears
As a wild cataract[12] of tears;                          10
And love in life should strive to see
Sometimes what love in death would be!
Easier to love, we so should find,
It is than to be just and kind.

   She's gone: shut close the coffin-lid:
What distance for another did
That death has done for her! The good,
Once gazed upon with heedless mood,
Now fills with tears the famish'd eye,
And turns all else to vanity.                              20
'Tis sad to see, with death between,
The good we have pass'd and have not seen!
How strange appear the words of all!
The looks of those that live appal.
They are the ghosts, and check the breath:
There's no reality but death,
And hunger for some signal given
That we shall have our own in heaven.
But this the God of love lets be
A horrible uncertainty.                                    30

✦

---

11. Patmore, *The Angel in the House*, 280–82.
12. *cataract*: waterfall

How great her smallest virtue seems,
How small her greatest fault! Ill dreams
Were those that foil'd with loftier grace
The homely kindness of her face.
'Twas here she sat and work'd, and there
She comb'd and kiss'd the children's hair;
Or, with one baby at her breast,
Another taught, or hush'd to rest.
Praise does the heart no more refuse
To the chief loveliness of use.                              40
Her humblest good is hence most high
In the heavens of fond memory;
And Love says Amen to the word,
A prudent wife is from the Lord.
Her worst gown's kept, ('tis now the best,
As that in which she oftenest dress'd,)
For memory's sake more precious grown
Than she herself was for her own.
Poor child! foolish it seem'd to fly
To sobs instead of dignity,                                  50
When she was hurt. Now, more than all,
Heart-rending and angelical
That ignorance of what to do,
Bewilder'd still by wrong from you:
For what man ever yet had grace
Ne'er to abuse his power and place?

    No magic of her voice or smile
Suddenly raised a fairy isle,
But fondness for her underwent
An unregarded increment,                                     60
Like that which lifts, through centuries,
The coral-reef within the seas,
Till, lo! the land where was the wave.
Alas! 'tis everywhere her grave.

# Charles Baudelaire,
## "Causerie" (1857)[1]

In addition to being a poet, Charles Baudelaire (1821–1867) was an art critic, essayist, and translator—one credited with popularizing Edgar Allan Poe's work in France. Taking a cue from Poe's gothicism, Baudelaire relished the interstices between the beautiful and the ugly, the sacred and the profane, life and death. Those juxtapositions, along with the parallel synesthesia that pervades his verse, became the touchstone for the Symbolists—poets such as Stéphane Mallarmé, Paul Verlaine, and Arthur Rimbaud, who rejected realism in favor of sensual and sensory description. Though it would come to be regarded as a seminal work of French poetry, Baudelaire's 1857 *Les Fleurs du Mal* (*The Flowers of Evil*) initially inspired derision from most critics, who were appalled by its subject matter. He and his publisher were prosecuted, in fact, for offending the public morality, a charge he did little to discourage. In "Causerie," Baudelaire employs the length, meter, and rhyme scheme of a conventional sonnet while at the same time challenging convention through the torrid subject matter and abrupt interruption in line 11. The speaker's ambivalence—at once bemoaning the misery that women have caused him and desiring the woman at his side—is, like the poem's heterodox approach to form, reminiscent of Meredith's in "Modern Love."

---

1. Charles Baudelaire, *Les Fleurs du Mal* (Paris: Poulet-Malassis et de Brois, 1857), 121. *Causerie* means "chat" or "conversation."

## Causerie

Vous êtes un beau ciel d'automne, clair et rose!
Mais la tristesse en moi monte comme la mer,
Et laisse, en refluant, sur ma lèvre morose
Le souvenir cuisant de son limon amer.

—Ta main se glisse en vain sur mon sein qui se pâme;
Ce qu'elle cherche, amie, est un lieu saccagé
Par la griffe et la dent féroce de la femme.—
Ne cherchez plus mon coeur; des monstres l'ont mangé.

Mon coeur est un palais flétri par la cohue;
On s'y soûle, on s'y tue, on s'y prend aux cheveux                    10
—Un parfum nage autour de votre gorge nue!—

O Beauté, dur fléau des âmes! tu le veux!
Avec tes yeux de feu, brillants comme des fêtes,
Calcine ces lambeaux qu'ont épargnés les bêtes!

# Causerie[2]

You are an autumn sky, suffused with rose . . . .
Yet sadness rises in me like the sea,
And on my sombre lip, when it outflows,
Leaves its salt burning slime for memory.

Over my swooning breast your fingers stray;
In vain, alas! My breast is a void pit
Sacked by the tooth and claw of woman. Nay,
Seek not my heart; the beasts have eaten it!

My heart is as a palace plunderèd
By the wolves, wherein they gorge and rend and kill,            10
A perfume round thy naked throat is shed . . . .

Beauty, strong scourge of souls, O work thy will!
Scorch with thy fiery eyes which shine like feasts
These shreds of flesh rejected by the beasts!

—Sir John Squire

---

2. Sir John Squire, *Poems and Baudelaire Flowers* (London: New Age Press, 1909), 60. Reprinted with permission of the author's estate.

# Alfred, Lord Tennyson,
## from *Maud* (1859)[1]

Alfred, Lord Tennyson became England's Poet Laureate in 1850, on
the heels of the publication of his masterpiece, *In Memoriam*. *Maud*
(which was many, many years in the making) was first published in
1855 (increasingly longer versions appeared in 1856 and 1859). A se-
ries of short lyrics in various meters, *Maud* is divided into three parts;
each of these parts has several subsections (indicated by capitalized
roman numerals), some of which have subsections of their own (in-
dicated by lowercase roman numerals). The poem is said to have
been one of Tennyson's favorites to read aloud. *Maud*'s speaker is an
extremely unhappy young man who desires Maud, the daughter of
the man who drove his father to suicide. When Maud's brother finds
the two lovers in a garden, he strikes the speaker in a fit of rage. The
altercation results in a duel, after which the speaker flees England
for Breton, certain he has killed Maud's brother. He descends into
madness, but finds redemption in fighting against the Russians in the
Crimean War. While the outline of such a story may seem trite, in
Tennyson's hands it nevertheless becomes an opportunity to create
a poetic meditation upon the relationship between the emotions and
physical sensation. The similarities in plot, form, and style between
*Maud* and infamous Spasmodic poems prompted some Victorian
readers to label Tennyson's poem Spasmodic. The line numbers in
the excerpt refer to the poem in its entirety in order to give readers a
sense of the tension between *Maud*'s narrative and lyric impulses.

---

1. Alfred, Lord Tennyson, *Maud, and Other Poems* (London: Edward Moxon, 1859), 1–3, 13–14,
23–24, 102–3.

# From Part I

### I. i.

I hate the dreadful hollow behind the little wood,
Its lips in the field above are dabbled with blood-red heath,
The red-ribb'd ledges drip with a silent horror of blood,
And Echo there, whatever is ask'd her, answers 'Death.'

### I. ii.

For there in the ghastly pit long since a body was found
His who had given me life—O father! O God! was it well?—
Mangled, and flatten'd, and crush'd, and dinted into the ground:
There yet lies the rock that fell with him when he fell.

### I. iii.

Did he fling himself down? who knows, for a vast speculation[2]
    had fail'd,
And ever he mutter'd and madden'd, and ever wann'd with
    despair,                                                    10
And out he walk'd when the wind like a broken worldling wail'd,
And the flying gold of the ruin'd woodlands drove thro' the air.

### I. iv.

I remember the time, for the roots of my hair were stirr'd
By a shuffled step, by a dead weight trail'd, by a whisper'd fright,
And my pulses closed their gates with a shock on my heart as I
    heard
The shrill-edged shriek of a mother divide the shuddering night.

---

2. *speculation*: According to his son, Tennyson described the poem as "a little *Hamlet*, the history of a morbid, poetic soul, under the blighting influence of a recklessly speculative age." Hallam Tennyson, *Alfred Lord Tennyson: A Memoir by his Son* (London: Macmillan, 1897), 396.

III.

Cold and clear-cut face, why come you so cruelly meek,
Breaking a slumber in which all spleenful folly was drown'd,
Pale with the golden beam of an eyelash dead on the cheek,        90
Passionless, pale, cold face, star-sweet on a gloom profound;
Womanlike, taking revenge too deep for a transient wrong
Done but in thought to your beauty, and ever as pale as before
Growing and fading and growing upon me without a sound,
Luminous, gemlike, ghostlike, deathlike, half the night long
Growing and fading and growing, till I could bear it no more,
But arose, and all by myself in my own dark garden ground,
Listening now to the tide in its broad-flung shipwrecking roar,
Now to the scream of a madden'd beach dragg'd down by the
        wave,
Walk'd in a wintry wind by a ghastly glimmer, and found        100
The shining daffodil dead, and Orion[3] low in his grave.

V. i.

A voice by the cedar tree,
In the meadow under the Hall!
She is singing an air that is known to me,
A passionate ballad gallant and gay,
A martial song like a trumpet's call!
Singing alone in the morning of life,
In the happy morning of life and of May,
Singing of men that in battle array,
Ready in heart and ready in hand,        170
March with banner and bugle and fife
To the death, for their native land.

---

3. *Orion*: a constellation resembling a hunter with a sword on his belt

V. ii.

Maud with her exquisite face,
And wild voice pealing up to the sunny sky,
And feet like sunny gems on an English green,
Maud in the light of her youth and her grace,
Singing of Death, and of Honour that cannot die,
Till I well could weep for a time so sordid and mean,
And myself so languid and base.

# From Part II

V. i.[4]

Dead, long dead,
Long dead!                                                   240
And my heart is a handful of dust,
And the wheels go over my head,
And my bones are shaken with pain,
For into a shallow grave they are thrust,
Only a yard beneath the street,
And the hoofs of the horses beat, beat,
The hoofs of the horses beat,
Beat into my scalp and my brain,
With never an end to the stream of passing feet,
Driving, hurrying, marrying, burying,                        250
Clamour and rumble, and ringing and clatter,
And here beneath it is all as bad,
For I thought the dead had peace, but it is not so;
To have no peace in the grave, is that not sad?
But up and down and to and fro,
Ever about me the dead men go;
And then to hear a dead man chatter
Is enough to drive one mad.

---

4. The speaker is now confined to a madhouse, a place that he figures as a shallow grave. He believes that he and the other inhabitants are dead.

# Christina Rossetti, from "Monna Innominata: A Sonnet of Sonnets" (1881)[1]

Christina Rossetti (1830–1894), younger sister to Meredith's friend the Pre-Raphaelite poet and painter Dante Gabriel Rossetti, was a master of poetic form whose witty yet stern poetry often thematized religious belief, love, and death, as well as a conflict between sensory pleasures and their refusal. "Monna Innominata" was first published in 1881, as part of *A Pageant and Other Poems*. Its title is usually translated as "unnamed lady"; its subtitle—"A Sonnet of Sonnets"—refers to the fact that it is a sequence of fourteen 14-line sonnets that (when taken as a whole) function as a meditation on the masculine tradition of courtly-love sonnets—a tradition associated with Dante and Petrarch. In her preface to the poem, Rossetti suggests that their portrayals of their beloveds (Beatrice and Laura, respectively) may not have done these women justice. "Had such a lady spoken for herself," she writes, "the portrait left us might have appeared more tender, if less dignified, than any drawn even by a devoted friend."[2] She goes on to discuss Elizabeth Barrett Browning's *Sonnets from the Portuguese*, suggesting that Barrett Browning's happiness impeded her ability to use poetry to portray the kind of female speaker that Rossetti envisions. Thus, the speaker of "Monna Innominata" tells of her conflicted emotions, focusing not only on her feelings for her earthly lover, but also on how her relationship to him is shaped by her love for God. Perhaps because of her brother William's intimation in his edition of her work and the melancholy tone of the final sonnet, some readers insist upon regarding the sequence as a poetic account of her relationship with Charles Cayley, a suitor Rossetti declined to marry on account of their religious differences.

---

1. Christina Rossetti, "Monna Innominata: A Sonnet of Sonnets," in *A Pageant and Other Poems* (Boston: Roberts Brothers, 1881), 57, 60, 65, 68.
2. Ibid., 54.

## 3.

"O ombre vane, fuor che ne l'aspetto!"—Dante[3]
"Immaginata guida la conduce."—Petrarca[4]

I dream of you to wake: would that I might
    Dream of you and not wake but slumber on;
    Nor find with dreams the dear companion gone,
As Summer ended Summer birds take flight.
In happy dreams I hold you full in sight,
    I blush again who waking look so wan;
    Brighter than sunniest day that ever shone,
In happy dreams your smile makes day of night.
Thus only in a dream we are at one,
    Thus only in a dream we give and take        10
    The faith that maketh rich who take or give;
  If thus to sleep is sweeter than to wake,
    To die were surely sweeter than to live,
Though there be nothing new beneath the sun.[5]

---

3. *"O ombre . . . l'aspetto!"*: "O shades, empty save in semblance!" (*Purgatorio*, 2.79). All epigraph translations for "Monna Innominata" are by William Rossetti. The sources are Dante's *Divine Comedy* and Petrarch's sonnets. The epigraphs underscore Rossetti's reversal of poetic convention, giving voice to the Beatrices and Lauras (adored and idealized objects of Dante's and Petrarch's love, respectively) of so many love poems without silencing the male perspective.

4. *"Immaginata . . . conduce"*: "An imaginary guide conducts her" (277.9).

5. *"Though there be nothing new beneath the sun"*: cf. "The thing that hath been, it is that which shall be; and that which is done is that which shall be done: and there is no new thing under the sun" (Ecclesiastes. 1:9)

## 6.

"Or puoi la quantitate
Comprender de l'amor che a te mi scalda."—Dante[6]
"Non vo'che da tal nodo amor mi scioglia."—Petrarca[7]

Trust me, I have not earned your dear rebuke,
    I love, as you would have me, God the most;
    Would lose not Him, but you, must one be lost,
Nor with Lot's wife cast back a faithless look
Unready to forego what I forsook;
    This say I, having counted up the cost,
    This, though I be the feeblest of God's host,
The sorriest sheep Christ shepherds with His crook.
Yet while I love my God the most, I deem
    That I can never love you overmuch;        10
    I love Him more, so let me love you too;
    Yea, as I apprehend it, love is such
I cannot love you if I love not Him,
    I cannot love Him if I love not you.

---

6. *"Or puoi . . . scalda"*: "Now canst thou comprehend the quantity of the love which glows in me towards thee." (*Purgatorio*, 21.133–34).

7. *"Non vo'che . . . scioglia"*: "I do not choose that Love should release me from such a tie." (59.17).

## II.

"Vien dietro a me e lascia dir le genti."—Dante[8]
"Contando i casi della vita nostra."—Petrarca[9]

Many in aftertimes will say of you
    "He loved her"—while of me what will they say?
    Not that I loved you more than just in play,
For fashion's sake as idle women do.
Even let them prate;[10] who know not what we knew
    Of love and parting in exceeding pain,
    Of parting hopeless here to meet again,
Hopeless on earth, and heaven is out of view.
But by my heart of love laid bare to you,
    My love that you can make not void nor vain,    10
Love that foregoes you but to claim anew
    Beyond this passage of the gate of death,
    I charge you at the Judgment make it plain
    My love of you was life and not a breath.

---

8. *"Vien dietro . . . genti"*: "Come after me, and leave folk to talk." (*Purgatorio*, 5.13).
9. *"Contando . . . nostra"*: "Relating the casualties of our life." (285.12).
10. *prate*: chatter

## 14.

"E la Sua Volontade è nostra pace."—Dante[11]
"Sol con questi pensier, con altre chiome."—Petrarca[12]

Youth gone, and beauty gone if ever there
 Dwelt beauty in so poor a face as this;
 Youth gone and beauty, what remains of bliss?
I will not bind fresh roses in my hair,
To shame a cheek at best but little fair,—
 Leave youth his roses, who can bear a thorn,—
I will not seek for blossoms anywhere,
 Except such common flowers as blow with corn.
Youth gone and beauty gone, what doth remain?
 The longing of a heart pent up forlorn,    10
  A silent heart whose silence loves and longs;
  The silence of a heart which sang its songs
 While youth and beauty made a summer morn,
Silence of love that cannot sing again.

---

11. *"E la Sua . . . pace"*: "And His will is our peace." (*Paradiso*, 3.85)
12. *"Sol con questi . . . chiome"*: "Only with these thoughts, with different locks." (30.32)

# Gerard Manley Hopkins, "Harry Ploughman" (1887)[1]

Hopkins's poetry was first published in 1918, twenty-nine years after his death, by his friend and literary executor, the poet Robert Bridges. His poems are praised for their experimental meter and diction; Hopkins himself was hailed as a pioneer of "Modern" literature—even in the early twentieth century, when his fellow Victorian poets were vociferously derided. Like its companion piece "Tom's Garland," "Harry Ploughman" is a caudate sonnet, that is, a sonnet with a tail consisting of so-called burden lines. The poem asks readers to see God's strength and grace in the body of a common working man and is an excellent example of Hopkins's poetic technique. Joseph Bristow suggests that the image this poem paints may have been inspired by Hamo Thornycroft's *The Sower*, a statue that Hopkins encountered at the Royal Academy exhibition of 1886.[2]

---

1. Gerard Manley Hopkins, "Harry Ploughman," in *Poems of Gerard Manley Hopkins*, ed. Robert Bridges (London: Humphrey Milford, 1918), 65.

2. Joseph Bristow, "'Churlsgrace': Gerard Manley Hopkins and the Working-Class Male Body" *ELH*, 59.3 (Autumn 1992): 705.

# Harry Ploughman

Hard as hurdle arms, with a broth of goldish flue
Breathed round; the rack of ribs; the scooped flank; lank
Rope-over thigh; knee-nave; and barrelled shank—
    Head and foot, shoulder and shank—
By a grey eye's heed steered well, one crew, fall to;
Stand at stress. Each limb's barrowy[3] brawn, his thew[4]
That onewhere curded,[5] onewhere sucked or sank—
    Soared or sank—,
Though as a beechbole[6] firm, finds his, as at a rollcall, rank
And features, in flesh, what deed he each must do—        10
    His sinew-service where do.

He leans to it, Harry bends, look. Back, elbow, and liquid waist
In him, all quail to the wallowing o' the plough: 's cheek crimsons;
    curls
Wag or crossbridle, in a wind lifted, windlaced—
    See his wind-lilylocks-laced;
Churlsgrace,[7] too, child of Amansstrength,[8] how it hangs or hurls
Them—broad in bluff hide his frowning feet lashed! raced
With, along them, cragiron under and cold furls—
    With-a-fountain's shining-shot furls.

---

    3. *barrowy*: Hopkins's neologism; a "barrow" is a mound, so perhaps the word suggests bulging strength.
    4. *thew*: instrument of punishment
    5. *curded*: knotted
    6. *beechbole*: tree trunk
    7. *Churlsgrace*: another neologism, a joining together of *churl* (peasant) and *grace*
    8. *Amansstrength*: compound word; a man's strength

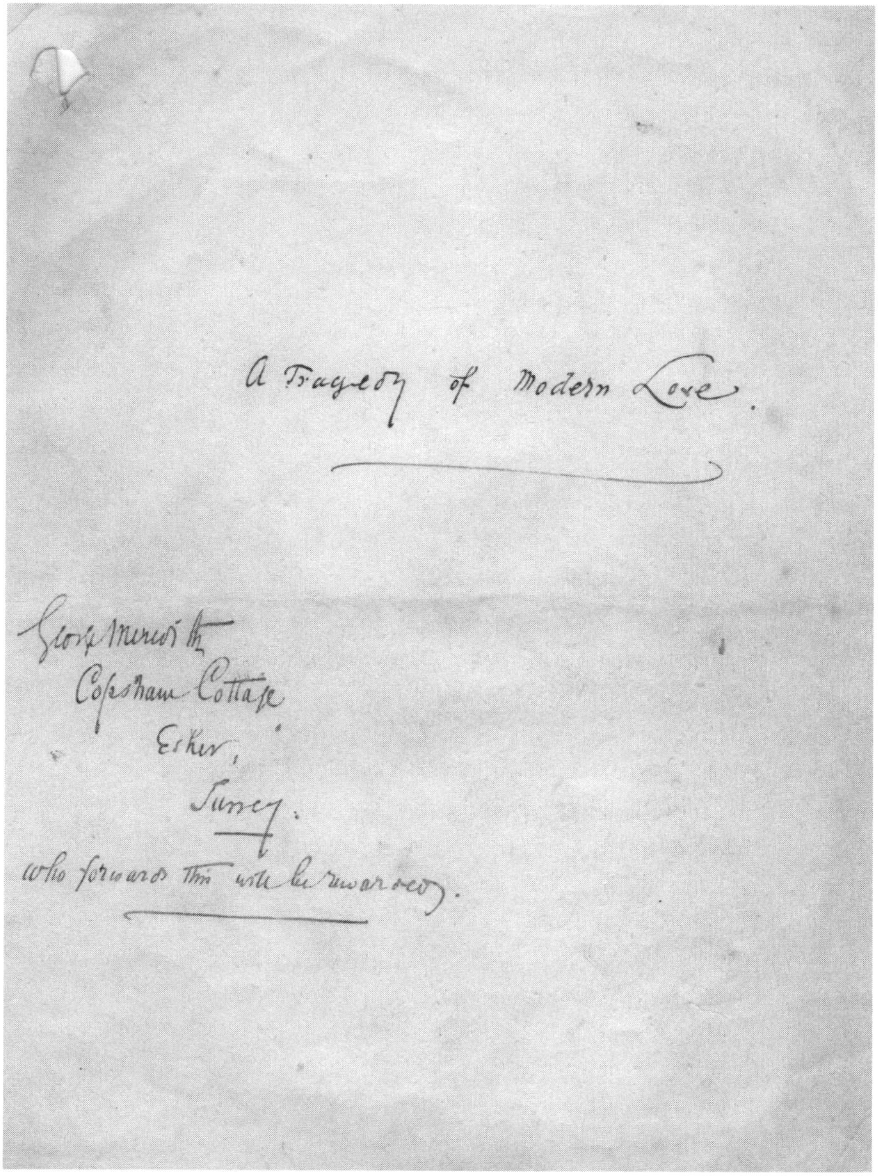

FIGURE 11: Title page from *A Tragedy of Modern Love*, autograph manuscript, signed by George Meredith. Image courtesy of Beinecke Rare Book and Manuscript Library, Yale University, New Haven, CT. MS Vault Shelves, Meredith Notebooks 1–10, 10A. Reproduced with the permission of the Estate of George Meredith.

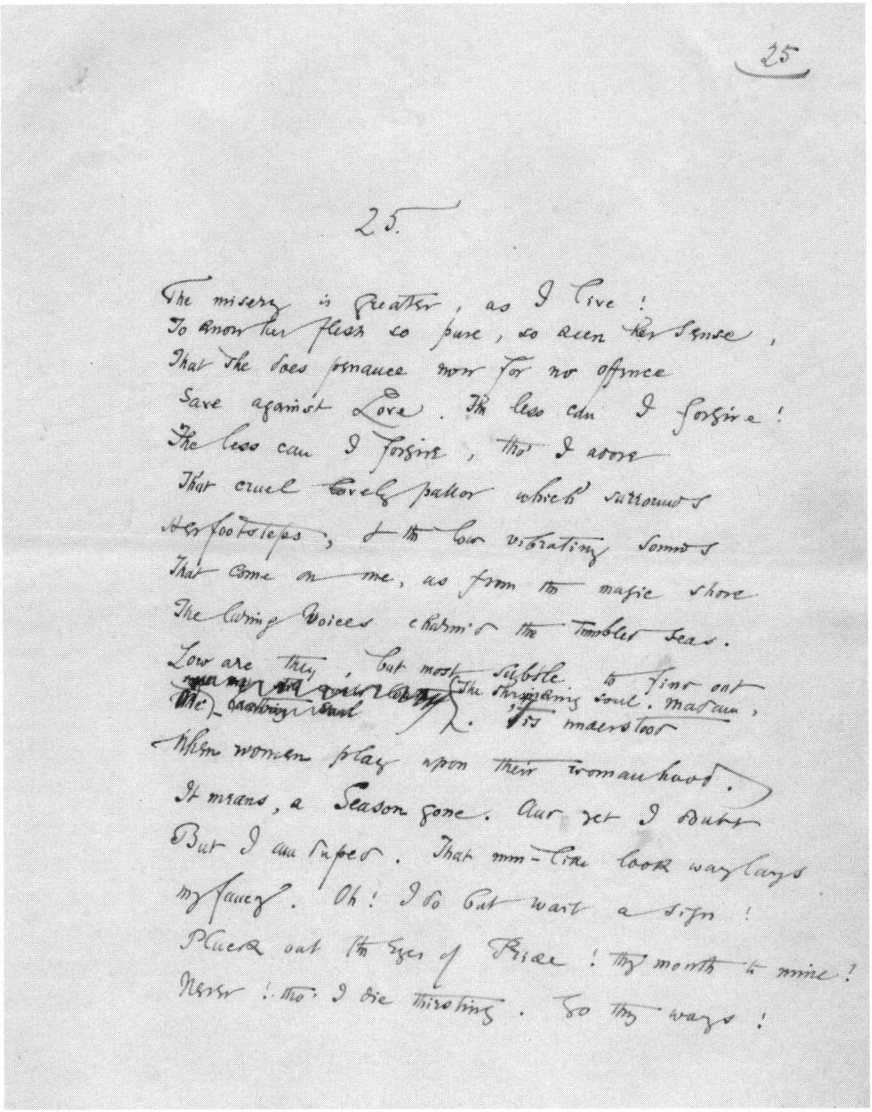
25

25.

The misery is greater, as I live!
To know her flesh so pure, so keen her sense,
That she does penance now for no offence
Save against Love. The less can I forgive!
The less can I forgive, tho' I adore
That cruel lovely pallor which surrounds
Her footsteps, & the low vibrating sounds
That come on me, as from the magic shore
The living voices charm'd the tumbled seas.
Low are they, but most subtle to find out
The shrinking soul. Madam,
'tis understood
When women play upon their womanhood,
It means, a Season gone. And yet I doubt
But I am duped. That nun-like look waylays
My fancy. Oh! I do but wait a sign!
Pluck out the eyes of Pride! thy mouth to mine!
Never! tho' I die thirsting. Go thy ways!

FIGURE 12: Sonnet XXV (Sonnet 24 in the published version) from *A Tragedy of Modern Love*, autograph manuscript signed by George Meredith. Image courtesy of Beinecke Rare Book and Manuscript Library, Yale University, New Haven, CT. MS Vault Shelves, Meredith Notebooks 1–10, 10A. Reproduced with the permission of the Estate of George Meredith.

# Textual Variants

Unlike the 1862 edition, the Edition de Luxe (EdL) does not use double quotation marks to render dialogue—they are omitted altogether, or in case of reported speech, they are exchanged for single quotation marks. Words ending in *'d* in the 1862 edition were rendered as *ed* in the EdL. As these are global changes, we have not recorded each instance here. The running heads and table of contents in EdL are inconsistent; we note the location of the poems in the EdL according to its table of contents.

Meredith frequently used an ampersand instead of *and* in his manuscripts; we have not included those as textual variants. Illegible words in the manuscripts are rendered as [illegible]. Deleted words are rendered with as much fidelity to the manuscript as possible, indicated with a ~~strike through~~. In cases there the manuscript includes two options, one above the other with neither deleted, the words have been separated by a slash (/).

Early draft versions of some of the *Modern Love* poems are included in one notebook held in the Beinecke Rare Book and Manuscript Library (MS Vault Meredith Notebook 1). Meredith worked from both ends of the notebook, and Phyllis Bartlett refers to the front end, which has a bookplate, as Notebook A, and the text beginning from the rear of the notebook as Notebook B. For sake of consistency, we have retained her referents and pagination.

Phyllis Bartlett (PB, 1978) notes Meredith's corrections in a copy of *Modern Love* presented to Swinburne; in 1978, that copy was held in a private collection, but it has since been sold at auction and its location is now unknown. Bartlett's notations from this presentation copy are included in our list of variants below.

Full titles of the abbreviations used below are provided in the "Abbreviations" list at the front of this volume.

GRANDFATHER BRIDGEMAN

Included in EdL XXXI (Poems III), under "Poems from 'Modern Love': 1862"

| | |
|---|---|
| II.3: | EdL reads "scapegrace, offshoot of Methodist" |
| III.2: | EdL line ends without comma |
| III.3: | EdL line ends with comma |
| V.2: | EdL reads "As a warm and dreary"; corrected to "dreamy" in EdL 1911 errata |
| V.4: | EdL line ends with period |
| VII.1: | EdL reads "Yet not from sight had she slipped ere feminine eyes could"; 1862 reads "from sight has she"; as this appears to be a typographical error, editors corrected verb tense for consistency with other stanzas |
| IX.2: | 1862 and EdL read "turned"; GM revised to "tuned" in BEIN MSS 7, BEIN 862.1; as this appears to be a typographical error, the editors revised as per Meredith's corrections |
| IX.4: | EdL reads "but Methodists are mortal" without italics |
| XII.3: | EdL reads "Daddy" |
| XVI.1: | EdL reads "like hedgehogs the Russians rolled" |
| XVII.2: | GM inserted "how" in BEIN MSS 7, BEIN 862.1, BEIN 862.6, and BEIN Purdy; editors include it here |
| XVIII.2: | 1862 omits final single quotation mark at line's end; EdL includes quotation mark; editors revised for consistency |
| XVIII.3: | EdL reads "save it's a serious thing." |
| XXI.6: | 1862 reads "face, our last, time"; EdL excludes comma; editors deleted comma after "last" |
| XXII.3: | 1862 and EdL read "than angel, or"; GM inserted "an" in BEIN 862.1 and BEIN 862.5; editors include it here |
| XXV.1: | EdL line ends with no punctuation |
| XXVI.1: | BEIN 862.2 hand corrected to read "For Mary had swayed" |
| XXVII.6: | 1862 reads "Miss, its clear that"; EdL reads "Miss, it's clear"; editors corrected grammar here as per EdL |
| XXVIII.1: | EdL omits italics for "now" |
| XXVIII.3: | EdL reads "added bluffly: " |
| XXX.6: | EdL reads "this begging-petition" |
| XXXI.2: | EdL reads "share, now, the" |
| XXXII.4: | EdL reads "lids at her 'No.'" |
| XXXIII.5: | EdL reads "with pity's tenderest" |
| XXXIV.3: | EdL reads "Is heaven offended?" |
| XXXIV.6: | EdL line ends with period |
| XXXV.2: | EdL reads "April snowdrifts," |

## THE MEETING

Included in EdL XXXI (Poems III), under "Poems from 'Modern Love': 1862"

| | |
|---|---|
| 1: | OaW omits comma at end of line |
| 2: | EdL reads "With knolls of pine ran white;" |
| 4: | OaW reads "droopt in"; 1862 omits period at end of line; this appears to be a typographical error as it is present in OaW and EdL, so it is included here. |
| 17: | OaW reads "for her babe made prayerful speech" |

## MODERN LOVE

Included in EdL XXIX (Poems I) under the heading "Modern Love"; sonnet sequence preceded by "The Promise in Disturbance."
(fair copy manuscript held in Beinecke)

| | |
|---|---|
| I.3: | ms line ends with comma, as does EdL |
| I.4: | ms identical to 1862 (PB suggests the ms reads "surprize") |
| I.10: | ms reads "pale drug of Silence" with "Silence" capitalized |
| | |
| II.1: | EdL line ends with period |
| II.2: | EdL reads "gates, that let" |
| II.4: | ms reads "Each ~~hid the~~ suck'd a" |
| II.5: | ms reads "But, Oh, the bitter"; EdL reads "But, oh, the" |
| II.6: | ms reads "poison flowers" with no hyphen |
| II.9: | ms reads "and raged deep inward" with no comma after "raged" |
| II.9: | EdL reads "raged deep inward, till" |
| II.11: | EdL reads "murder-spot." |
| II.14: | ms reads "vengefulness + strove" with no comma after "vengefulness" |
| | |
| III.1: | ms reads "what now of the ~~where [illegible] the~~" |
| III.2: | EdL reads "But pass him. If he comes beneath a heel," |
| III.5: | ms reads "only mark" with "only" in lowercase |
| III.6: | EdL reads "striking out from her on him!" |
| III.9: | ms reads "~~her very~~ the thing so fair" |
| III.10: | ms reads "~~[illegible]~~ See that I am" |
| III.16: | ms reads "~~Something~~ The hour has struck, tho' I heard" |
| | |
| IV.1: | EdL reads "other joy of life"; EdL errata corrects to "joys" |
| IV.6: | ms reads "~~[illegible]~~ that went" |
| IV.7: | ms reads "Cold ~~in the whiteness of its own cold Laws,~~ as a mountain in its star-pitch'd tent,"; EdL line ends with comma |

| | |
|---|---|
| IV.12: | ms reads "~~See we our kinship with the quenchless stars!~~ Look we for any kinship with the stars." |
| IV.13: | ms reads "O, wisdom" |
| IV.14: | ms reads "And ~~that~~ the great ~~wealth we squandered for it, worth~~ price we pay for it full worth"; EdL line ends with colon |
| IV.15: | ms reads "We ~~know~~ have it only" |
| | |
| V.6: | EdL line ends with comma |
| V.7: | ms reads "Thro'" |
| V.8: | EdL line ends without punctuation |
| V.13: | ms omits quotation marks around "Come"; EdL reads "In his restraining" |
| V.15: | ms line ends with period |
| | |
| VI.2: | ms reads "~~made droop~~ slanted down" |
| VI.3: | ms reads "confesses Love" with capitalized "Love" |
| VI.4: | ms reads "~~special~~ tender" |
| VI.5: | ms reads "~~can~~ will" |
| VI.7: | ms reads "[illegible] the price of blood drops"; EdL line ends with comma |
| VI.10: | ms reads "but changed its ~~name~~ aim" |
| VI.16: | ms reads "~~We sit~~ They sat, she" |
| | |
| VII.1: | EdL reads "dressing-room" |
| VII.5: | GM corrected printer's erroneous printing of "cur" to "curls" in BEIN MSS 7 and BEIN 862.1; editors have made that change here |
| VII.7: | ms reads "~~And all the~~ The gold-eyed serpent dwelling in [illegible] rich hair" |
| VII.11: | ms reads "in ~~the~~ its den" |
| VII.12: | ms reads "up:—~~is't~~ is it true" |
| VII.12: | EdL reads "is it true we are wed?" |
| VII.15: | ms reads "The former it were not so" with no comma |
| | |
| VIII.3: | EdL reads "Poor twisting worm," |
| VIII.10: | ms reads "~~Ah! sweet the music~~ And they were music till" |
| VIII.11: | ms reads "~~And now~~ Hear, now the" |
| VIII.12: | ms reads "[illegible] Puffs his" |
| | |
| IX.2: | ms reads "so masterfully rude that" with no comma |
| IX.3: | ms reads "to see the ~~tender~~ helpless delicate" |

IX.9:     ms reads "that ~~[illegible] star-like~~ soft starry 'you,' she leaned"

IX.13:    ms reads "and O young"; EdL reads "! and oh"

IX.14:    EdL reads "Of heaven's"

IX.15:    ms line ends with period, not dash

X:       Sonnet 10 as it appears in ms:

          Contest not, we learn much from misery.
          I knew not women till I suffer'd thus:
          ~~All that~~ The things they are, and may be, unto us.
          She gives the key with her inconstancy.
          They must see Love to feel him, & no less
          He dies if his pursuing ~~eyes~~ gaze they miss:
          ~~As~~ Lo, if you break the habit of a kiss,
          And it comes strange, so comes their bashfulness!
          Narrow'd in that hot centre of their life
          Where instincts rule, they bind you to its laws,
          These shifting sandbanks ~~that~~ which the ebb-tide draws!—
          You have a one-month's bride, & then a wife
          Who weens that time deposes her; rebels;
          While you are living upward to the air,
          Those passions that are spawn of low despair,
          She clasps, & gets the comfort that is Hell's.
              ~~for hungry comfort, even Hell's!~~

X.7:    EdL line ends with comma

X.11:    EdL reads "crime is, that the"

XI.1:    EdL reads "meadows, where"

XI.2:    ms reads "Hummeds by us"

XI.4:    ms reads "~~Were~~ Are dropping like a ~~dewy noon,~~ noon-dew, wander we"

XI.5:    ms reads "Or ~~was~~ is it now?"

XI.6:    ms reads "rings shed showers"; EdL reads "running rings pour showers"

XI.7:    ms reads "foot of May ~~was~~ is on"

XI.8:    ms reads "shadows danc'de upon"

XI.9:    ms line ends with question mark

XI.10:    ms reads "Which is the liar? Now, as then, the ~~race~~ grace"

XI.11:    ms reads "~~[illegible]~~ Of heaven seems holding"; EdL reads "heaven seems holding earth"

XI.12:    ms reads "Discerneth she the difference, sad & strange?"

XI.13:          EdL reads "the West."

XI.14:          ms reads "An ~~golden~~ amber cradle ~~hanging~~ near the sun's decline;"

XI.16:          ms and EdL line ends with period, not exclamation point

XII.2:          ms reads "and ~~tha~~te fair life w~~th~~iatch"

XII.6:          ms shows no correction (PB notes correction); EdL reads "Distinction in old times,"

XII.7:          ms reads "Hope:—Earth" with colon instead of comma; EdL reads "earth's"

XII.8:          ms reads "Heaven's high-prompting:—" with dash following colon; EdL reads "heaven's"

XII.12:         ms reads "If ~~that~~ the mad Past"

XII.14:         EdL reads "Past will stay:"

XIII.1:         ms uses single quotation marks, not double quotation marks

XIII.2:         ms uses single open quotation mark before "So"

XIII.3:         ms uses single quotation marks at start and end of line

XIII.5:         EdL line ends with comma

XIII.9:         EdL reads "a seed-bag—there, an"

XIII.10:        ms reads "herself to aught 'twould" with no comma after "aught"

XIII.13:        ms reads "human rose is fair ~~sweet~~"; EdL reads "—but, oh, our human"

XIII.14:        ms reads "Surpassingly!—" with dash following exclamation mark

XIII.14:        ms reads "Lose calmly ~~that~~ Love's great"

XIII.15:        EdL reads "renewed for ever"

XIII.16:        ms reads "hair!—" with dash following exclamation mark; EdL line replaced with "Whirls life within the shower of loosened hair!"

XIV.1:          ms reads "Not such a cure, not such a cure, which brings"

XIV.2:          ms reads "agony to kill!"

XIV.6:          ms reads "Since o~~i~~n that a gold-hair'd lady's eye~~lids~~balls pure,"

XIV.8:          ms reads "loos'd" instead of "loosed"

XIV.9:          EdL reads "Just heaven!"

XIV.11:         ms reads "~~she's~~ she"; EdL line replaced with "Swim somewhat for possessions forfeited?"

XIV.12:         ms reads "you" in lowercase; EdL reads "Madam, you teach"

XIV.13:         EdL line ends with comma

XIV.14:         ms reads "still may love whom ~~tho'~~ they"

XIV.15:         EdL reads "prize not, madam:"

XV.2:           EdL reads "arm toward the" and line ends with semicolon

XV.3:           EdL reads "The face turned"

XV.6:       ms reads "dames. Well, if he did!"; EdL reads "well if he!"

XV.7:       ms reads "upon that ~~open~~ lid"

XV.8:       ms reads "~~That slopes as slopes the bosom~~ "Gentle dove Full-sloping like the ~~bosom~~ breasts beneath. 'Sweet dove!"

XV.9:       ms reads "~~Awake! 'tis I~~ Your sleep is pure. Nay,"

XV.10:      ms reads " "I do not? well!"—"; EdL reads "I do not? good!' Her waking infant-stare"

XV.11:      ms reads "~~Slowly discerns~~ Grows woman to the burden my ~~his~~"

XV.13:      ms reads "thro':—" with dash after colon

XV.16:      ms reads "The words are ~~tone is very wondrous~~ very like: the"


XVI.3:      EdL reads "beheld the red chasm grow"

XVI.11:     ms reads "I never felt it less"

XVI.13:     ms reads "when the fire [illegible] domed blackening"

XVI.15:     ms reads "scale of sobs ~~tears~~ her"


XVII.2:     ms reads "~~Did ever feast run~~ Went the feast ever cheerfuller?"

XVII.5:     ms line ends with colon

XVII.7:     EdL reads "SKELETON, shall"

XVII.9      EdL line ends without punctuation

XVII.10:    ms reads "Enamour'd of ~~each other's acting, feel~~ our acting & our wits,"; EdL line replaced with "Enamoured of an acting nought can tire"

XVII.11:    ms reads "~~An admiration we cannot conceal~~ Admire each other like true hypocrites"; EdL line replaced with "Each other, like true hypocrites, admire;"

XVII.12:    ms reads "~~The~~ Warm-lighted glances, ~~that are~~ Love's ephemerae"; EdL reads "Warm-lighted looks, Love's ephemerioe"

XVII.15:    EdL reads "shows the marriage-knot."

XVII.14–16: ms reads:

~~And we are envied?   Why not? for so complete~~
~~A union few behold & fewer meet.~~
~~Dear Guests,~~
~~[Illegible] for you have seen Love's corpse-light shine.~~
~~[Illegible]~~
~~[Illegible]~~ We waken envy of our happy lot.
Fast, sweet, & golden, shows our marriage-knot.
Dear guests, you now have seen Love's corpse-light shine.

XVII.16     EdL line ends with period


XVIII:      (labeled 19 in ms)

XVIII.1:    ms reads "Here's Jack"

XVIII.4:    ms line ends with colon

XVIII.6:    ms reads "one ~~stream of beer~~ nut-brown stream"

XVIII.10:   ms reads "~~My very first My earliest~~ An early goddess"

XVIII.11:   ms reads "A charm'd ~~[illegible]~~ Amphion-oak, she tripp'd the grass."

XVIII.13:   EdL reads "Heaven keep them happy! Nature they seem near."

XVIII.14    EdL line ends with semicolon

XVIII.15:   ms reads "~~There roars a human bull; here frisks a lamb~~. They have the
            secret of the bull & lamb."

XVIII.16:   ms reads "~~But half of this 'Tis true the whole may find its source in beer.~~
            'Tis true that when we ~~ask~~ seek ~~the~~ its source, 'tis beer!"


XIX:        (labeled 20 in ms)

XIX.3:      ms reads "she who"; 1862 reads "but she who wounds"; GM revised
            "she" to "her" in BEIN MSS 7 and BEIN 862.6; EdL reads "her"; edi-
            tors corrected here per Meredith's corrections

XIX.5:      ms reads "her?—Heaven and Hell!"; EdL reads "heaven and hell"

XIX.6:      ms reads "her cruelly! can I let"

XIX.8:      ms reads "forever" (single word)

XIX.9:      ms reads "one way ~~they~~ Love drifts"

XIX.10:     ms reads "I ~~am [illegible]~~ see not plain:—"

XIX.12:     ms reads "gambler ~~stakes~~ throws his"

XIX.13:     ms reads "If any state be enviable ~~[, illegible]~~ on earth,"

XIX.14:     ms reads "~~Yon village~~ 'Tis yon born"; "[illegible] as days go by,"

XIX. 15:    ms reads "[illegible] Still"; EdL reads "before him, like"

XIX.16:     ms reads "In a ~~strange~~ queer sort of meditative glee ~~mirth~~"


XX:         (labeled 21 in ms)

XX.2:       EdL reads "at vice and, daring"

XX.3:       EdL reads "hope for heaven."

XX.9:       ms has no comma after "coward"

XX.10:      ms reads "With ~~that which comes of~~ what ensues from his"

XX.12:      ms reads "In an old ~~drawer put by~~ desk dusty for"

XX.14:      no deletion in ms (PB notes deletion); EdL reads "That, like some aged
            star, gleam"

XX.15:      EdL reads "If for those times"


XXI:        (labeled 22 in ms)

XXI.1:      ms reads "We ~~[illegible] are sitting on the Summer~~ three are on the
            cedar-shadow'd lawn;"

XXI.4:      ms reads "Struck thro', &"; EdL reads "Struck through, and"

XXI.6:     ms reads "went 'thus':"; 1862 reads "went 'thus:'"; editors corrected punctuation order

XXI.7:     EdL reads "encountering: that we"

XXI.12:    ms reads "~~We laughed [illegible] and pat him, neither~~ And pat him, with light laugh. We have not winced."

XXI.14:    ms reads "happy things in ~~marriage~~ wedlock. When"; EdL line ends with comma

XXI.16:    ms reads "Her [illegible] lost hand"

XXII:      (labeled 23 in ms)

XXII.1:    EdL reads "may the woman"

XXII.4:    EdL reads "of hell in"

XXII.6:    ms line ends with colon

XXII.7:    EdL reads "What sight in view?"

XXII.9:    ms reads "hastily, & tost ~~steals~~"

XXII.10:   ms reads "Irresolute, [illegible] steals shadow-like to"

XXII.13:   ms reads "I ~~must~~ will not ask."

XXII.16:   EdL reads "lower, and a happier"

XXIII:     (labeled 24 in ms)

XXIII.9:   ms reads "Passing, I ~~saw~~ caught the"; EdL reads "coverlet's"

XXIII.11:  EdL reads "tortured me, enchain!"

XXIII.13:  ms reads "The small birds stiffens in the ~~great~~ low starlight."

XXIII.14:  EdL reads "not how, but shuddering"

XXIV:      (labeled 25 in ms)

XXIV.5:    ms reads "tho'"

XXIV.8:    ms has no punctuation at line end

XXIV.9:    ms inserts extra line before printed line 9, omitted from other editions, which reads "The lowing voices charm'd the troubled seas."

XXIV.10:   ms reads "~~The loathing soul The soul that still would loathe~~ The shrinking soul, Madam, 'tis understood"

XXIV.15:   EdL reads "eyes of pride!"

XXIV.16:   ms reads "Never! tho' I die thirsting."

XXV:       (labeled 26 in ms)

XXV.2:     EdL reads "think it quite unnatural."

XXV.3:     ms reads "The actors are, ~~methinks~~ it seems, the"

XXV.5:     ms reads "In England we'll not [illegible] hear of it. Edmond,"

XXV.6:     ms reads "The lover, ~~is most [illegible] penitent~~ her devout chagrin doth share;"

| | |
|---|---|
| XXV.7: | ms reads "are his ~~nourishment~~ penitent fare." |
| XXV.8: | EdL reads "her over-fond:" |
| XXV.11: | ms reads "ere one tear is used." |
| XXV.12: | ms reads "~~Now doth all hang~~ Then hangeth all on one" |
| XXV.14: | ms reads "like a ~~worthy~~ proper wife"; EdL reads "husband, like a" |
| XXV.16: | EdL reads "And life, some think, is" |
| | |
| XXVI: | (labeled 27 in ms) |
| XXVI.6: | ms reads "his ~~[illegible] blood~~ spent pain;" |
| XXVI.8: | EdL reads "ground, with narrow" |
| XXVI.10 | EdL line ends with colon |
| XXVI.16: | ms reads "~~Yea, in a kiss take venom from his tooth!~~ You must bear all the venom of his tooth!" |
| | |
| XXVII: | (labeled 28 in ms) |
| XXVII.2: | EdL reads "my oracle of " |
| XXVII.8: | ms reads "Or fair as ~~twilight Heavens~~ widow'd Heaven,"; EdL reads "Or clear as widowed sky," |
| XXVII.10: | ms reads "And if the devil snare ~~[illegible]~~ me, body and mind" |
| XXVII.12: | ms reads "would ~~[illegible]~~ comfort my" |
| XXVII.13 | EdL reads "world, in which" |
| | |
| XXVIII: | (labeled 29 in ms) |
| XXVIII.4: | ms reads "And with you enter ~~with you~~"; EdL line ends with semicolon |
| XXVIII.5: | "Beauty" capitalized in ms |
| XXVIII.9: | "Beauty" capitalized in ms |
| XXVIII.12: | EdL reads "as a burning sphere;" |
| XXVIII.13: | ms reads "see me, and ~~[illegible]~~ groan" |
| XXVIII.15: | ms reads "I feel the ~~[illegible]~~ promptings of " |
| | |
| XXIX: | (labeled 30 in ms) |
| XXIX.1: | ms reads "For" with word capitalized; "For" capitalized in EdL |
| XXIX.2: | ms reads "about this ~~[illegible]~~ head of gold" |
| XXIX.3: | EdL line ends with semicolon |
| | |
| XXX: | (labeled 31 in ms) |
| XXX.1: | EdL line ends without punctuation |
| XXX.3: | ms reads "~~There~~ Pale lies the ~~heavy~~ distant shadow" |
| XXX.5: | EdL reads "Into which state" |
| XXX.9: | EdL reads "But nature says:" |

| XXX.10: | ms reads "When least they know me" with sign to invert "least" and "they" |
|---|---|
| XXX.11: | ms reads "~~Then~~ Swift doth young Love" |
| XXX.14: | ms reads "but for the day"; EdL ends line with colon |
| XXX.16: | ms reads "this is my ~~love-chant~~ sonnet to your eyes."; EdL reads "my sonnet to" |

| XXXI: | (labeled 32 in ms) |
|---|---|
| XXXI.3: | ms reads "~~She rather likes~~ Some women like a" |
| XXXI.10: | ms reads "these are they" |
| XXXI.11: | ms reads "Who win her homage. Know I what I say?" |
| XXXI.12: | ms reads "Yes, certainly. 'Tis for the world's increase!" |
| XXXI.13: | ms reads "[illegible] Small flattery! Yet has she that rare gift" |
| XXXI.14: | ms reads "To ~~women~~ beauty—" |
| XXXI.15: | EdL line ends with comma |

| XXXII: | (labeled 33 in ms) |
|---|---|
| XXXII.4: | ms reads "Beneath me, while ~~the blue~~ underlids [illegible] uplift," |
| XXXII.8: | ms reads "~~That~~ And has so long" |
| XXXII.10: | EdL reads "my heart or head" |
| XXXII.12: | ms reads "Still ~~fumes~~ frets, tho' Nature" |
| XXXII.13: | ms reads "~~Woman is not her own cure,~~ It means, that woman is not," |
| XXXII.14: | ms reads "~~Its~~Her sex's antidote." |
| XXXII.15: | EdL reads "For serpent's bites?"; ms reads "calm me [illegible] could I clasp" |
| XXXII.16: | ms line ends with period, not exclamation mark |

| XXXIII: | (labeled 34 in ms) |
|---|---|
| XXXIII.1: | ms reads "at the Louvre, ~~I~~ there have I seen" |
| XXXIII.8: | EdL reads "Of heaven might still"; ms reads "thro' the fray." |
| XXXIII.9: | ms reads "the Fiend ~~engage~~ do fight," |
| XXXIII.10: | ms reads "They ~~do not conquer on~~ conquer not upon such" |
| XXXIII.12: | ms reads "~~Let's hope he grows~~ And does he grows half human, ~~from his rage~~ all is right.'" |
| XXXIII.13: | ms reads "This [illegible] to my Lady [illegible] in a distant spot," |
| XXXIII.15: | ms reads "*Gross clay invades it.*' [illegible] If the spy you play," |
| XXXIII.16: | ms reads "My wife, ~~my spy~~ read this! Strange love-talk, is it not? [illegible]"; EdL reads "Strange love talk, is" |

| XXXIV: | (labeled 35 in ms) |
|---|---|
| XXXIV.2: | ms reads "The Deluge, or [illegible] else Fire!"; EdL reads "The Deluge or else" |

XXXIV.3:     ms reads "Our chain thro' silence"; EdL reads "Our chain on silence"
XXXIV.4:     EdL reads "Time leers between, above his twiddling thumbs."
XXXIV.8:     ms reads "~~From earth's hot centre.~~ Niagra is no noisier. ~~Then our eyes~~ By stealth"
XXXIV.9:     ms reads "~~Dart out the~~ Our eyes dart scrutinizing"
XXXIV.15:    EdL reads "With commonplace I"

XXXV:        (labeled 36 in ms)
XXXV.1:      ms reads "~~This~~ It is"
XXXV.13:     ms reads "At Forfeits during snow ~~That night~~ we play'd,"
XXXV.16:     ms reads "Save her? What for? To act this ~~wedded~~ two-scorn'd lie!"

XXXVI:       (labeled 37 in ms; final sonnet in ms)
XXXVI.5:     ms reads "The interview was gracious: [illegible] they anoint"
XXXVI.6:     ms reads "~~Each other subsequently~~ (To me aside) each other"
XXXVI.9:     EdL reads "nose of Nature might"
XXXVI.11:    EdL reads "large-browed steadfastness."
XXXVI.15:    ms reads "~~And open gates at love-time~~ Wide gates, at love-time only."

XXXVII.6     EdL reads "in prae-digestive calm."
XXXVII.11:   EdL reads "the low rosed moon,"
XXXVII.16:   EdL reads "Our tragedy, is"

XXXVIII.6:   EdL reads "whom we can not"
XXXVIII.10:  EdL reads "My soul is arrowy"
XXXVIII.12:  EdL line ends without punctuation

XL.2:        Editors removed italics from "?" in 1862
XL.4:        EdL reads "Commits such folly."
XL.8         EdL line ends with comma
XL.14        EdL line ends with comma

XLI.10       EdL line ends with period

XLII.2:      EdL reads "In woman when"
XLII.5:      EdL line ends without punctuation
XLII.7:      EdL reads "lit a taper"; 1862 reads ""I'm going;""; editors corrected punctuation order

| | |
|---|---|
| XLII.16: | EdL reads "all on an" |
| XLIII.11: | EdL reads "or failing that," |
| XLIV.1: | EdL reads "They say, that" |
| XLIV.13: | EdL reads "sees through" |
| XLIV.14: | EdL line ends with colon |
| XLV.5: | EdL reads "evening heaven round" and line ends without punctuation |
| XLVI.10: | EdL reads "Toward her," |
| XLVII.2: | EdL reads "we heard them noise." |
| XLVII.4: | EdL line ends with colon |
| XLVII.11: | EdL reads "from the West," |
| XLVII.15: | EdL reads "Where I have seen across" |
| XLVIII.1: | EdL line ends with comma |
| XLIX.6: | EdL reads "though shadow-like and" |

## JUGGLING JERRY

Included in EdL XXXI (Poems III), under "Odes: *continued*"

In OaW, the title is "The Last Words of Juggling Jerry" and sections are not numbered.

| | |
|---|---|
| I.8: | OaW reads "Long to have me, and has me now." |
| III.3: | OaW reads "It's easy to think" |
| III.4: | OaW line ends with period |
| IV.3: | OaW reads "Couldn't I juggle the bale off the wicket?" |
| IV.5: | OaW reads "I know 'em" |
| IV.6: | OaW reads "They're old" |
| IV.5: | OaW reads "ale-house. I know 'em" |
| IV.7: | OaW reads "I owe 'em" |
| IX.4: | OaW line ends with period |
| X.6: | OaW reads "Duke might kneel to call you Cook:" |
| X.8: | OaW reads "But old Jerry" |
| XI.7: | OaW reads "makes us to" |
| XII.3: | EdL reads "mortar, brick and putty," |
| XII.8: | OaW reads "But He is" |
| XIII.5: | EdL reads "Crack, went a gun:" |
| XIII.8: | OaW reads "Give me a kiss" |

## THE OLD CHARTIST

Included in EdL XXXI (Poems III), under "Odes: *continued*."

In NB B, p. 69, Meredith writes the title "The Old Chartist" with only two lines of verse below it. We include them here, as they suggest the originally conceived animal was not a water rat but an otter:

> The flower in the prison-vault is pale!
> The otter whistles in the morn

| | |
|---|---|
| I.4: | OaW reads "how to cheat, nor how" |
| III.2: | OaW line ends with period |
| VIII.2: | EdL reads "I could let fly a laugh with all my might." |
| X.1: | EdL line ends with comma |
| XIII.5: | EdL line has three periods instead of four |
| XV.2: | EdL reads "his dress,——" |
| XV.8: | EdL reads "fellow's heaven's neighbor!" |
| XVI.4: | EdL line has no italics |

## THE BEGGAR'S SOLILOQUY

Included in EdL XXXI (Poems III), under "Poems from 'Modern Love': 1862"

| | |
|---|---|
| VI.4: | OaW reads "To myself I'm in tune. I hope" |
| VII.4: | OaW reads "I once was acquainted with his" |
| VII.6: | OaW reads "And, Lord, Sir! didn't" |
| VII.7: | OaW reads "softest of raps," |
| IX.7 | EdL reads "us two, at a" |
| XI.6: | EdL reads "there's here no pride"; corrected in EdL 1911 errata |
| XII.1: | OaW and 1862 read " "all I've got:" "; punctuation order corrected by editors |
| XIII.2 | EdL omits italics |

## THE PATRIOT ENGINEER

Included in EdL XXXIII (Poems IV), under "Poems Written in Youth"; this volume was published after Meredith's death.

| | |
|---|---|
| 24: | EdL reads "Dabbling his" |
| 31: | EdL reads "he seem'd with" |
| 38: | Editors added final quotation mark as per other stanzas and OaW |
| 40: | OaW and EdL read "We breath'd again our" |
| 52: | EdL reads "despots held her" |
| 107: | OaW and EdL read "iron-walled lakes" |
| 114: | OaW and EdL read "High despot of the place" |

## CASSANDRA

Included in EdL XXXI (Poems III), under "Poems from 'Modern Love': 1862"
(ms in Beinecke, Notebook B, p. 10)
NB B contains only two stanzas.

| | |
|---|---|
| I.4: | EdL reads "Speaks Futurity" |
| I.5: | NB B reads "—Death is busy with her grave" |
| I: | NB B includes the following stanza, not printed in 1862, after stanza I: |

        Captive, and a thing of scorn,
        Under that cold alien sky,
        To the death that she must die
        Young/Pale Cassandra walks forlorn:
        —Shrouded is the golden eye.

| | |
|---|---|
| III.1: | EdL reads "Once to many" |
| VII.2: | EdL line ends with period |
| VIII.5: | EdL line ends with period |
| IX.1: | EdL reads "Once to many" |
| XI.1: | EdL reads "See, toward the" |
| XIII.2: | EdL reads "Shadowing heaven" |
| XIV.4: | EdL reads "unsparing Gods," |
| XV.2: | EdL line ends with comma (no dash) |
| XV.3: | EdL reads "She, her soaring" |

## THE YOUNG USURPER

Included in EdL XXXI (Poems III), under "Poems from 'Modern Love': 1862"

## MARGARET'S BRIDAL-EVE

Included in EdL XXXI (Poems III), under "Poems from 'Modern Love': 1862"

| | |
|---|---|
| II.1: | In 1862, each numbered section begins on a new page, with the title "Margaret's Bridal-Eve" |
| II.9: | PB notes variants in GM's copy to Swinburne: "My mother, but when I am kiss'd!" |
| II.11: | PB notes variants in GM's copy to Swinburne: "no mouth then knows what's missed." |
| II.13 | GM revises to "O mother, but when I awake in the dawn!" in BEIN MSS 7 |
| II. 15 | GM revises to "My child, no mouth then knows what's gone" in BEIN MSS 7 |
| III.7: | EdL reads "moonlighted West;" |
| III.9: | EdL reads "the West-cloud breaks" |
| IV.63: | EdL reads "lump on the still dead" |
| IV.65: | EdL reads "and loud the wail," |

MARIAN

Included in EdL XXXI (Poems III), under "Odes: *continued*"
(ms in Berg)
Titled "Song" in Berg

| | |
|---|---|
| I.2: | Berg line ends with colon |
| I.4: | Berg reads "~~her husband's~~ the homely" |
| I.5: | Berg reads "flourish ~~sword~~ staff" |
| I/II: | Berg includes the following stanza between existing stanzas I and II: |

> Such a she who'll match with me
>> Throughout the little island:
> When in green she walks between
>> The barley & rye land?
> Match her for her woman's worth,
>> And its blushing leaven:
> Match her as a thing of Earth,
>> And a Saint of Heaven.

| | |
|---|---|
| II.6: | Berg reads "High/Swift and" |
| II.7: | Berg reads "Mixing with her/its dove" |
| III.1–4: | Berg reads |

> Wild and free, and ~~[illegible]~~ fresh with glee,
>> And tender to/laughing still, her true love:
> Let her veer, but never fear
>> Her old love is her new love.

| | |
|---|---|
| III.6: | Berg reads "Wayward as a maiden:" |

THE HEAD OF BRAN

Included in EdL XXXI (Poems III), under "Poems from 'Modern Love': 1862," and titled "The Head of Bran the Blest."
(manuscript in Beinecke, Notebook B, p. 47)
NB B includes first four stanzas, with variants from 1862 as noted below

| | |
|---|---|
| I.5–8: | NB B reads: |

> He with naked fist
>> Could brain a knight in battle:
> Steel could not resist
>> The weight his ~~blows~~ sword arm would rattle.

| | |
|---|---|
| I.12: | NB B reads "The house he fell'd with slumbers" |
| I.15: | 1862 reads "the head of Bran" |
| I.16: | NB B reads "Shone above/o'er his people." |
| II.22: | EdL reads "That while I die," |

III.8:        EdL reads "in the West!"

IV.8:         EdL reads "Gazing out far foamward."

IV.15:        OaW omits comma at line end

## BY MORNING TWILIGHT

Included in EdL XXXI (Poems III), under "Poems from 'Modern Love': 1862"

1:            EdL reads "Night, like a"

11:           EdL omits second stanza

## AUTUMN EVEN-SONG

Included in EdL XXXI (Poems III), under "Poems from 'Modern Love': 1862"
(manuscript in Berg)

1:            Berg reads "The dark cloud"; EdL reads "streaming grey"

2:            EdL reads "the West;"

6:            Berg reads "~~Wild music shudders up the air.~~"

7–10:         Berg reads:

        The timid breeze pants blue and chill

              Athwart the lake:

        One crow flaps from the western hill;

              And in its wake,

11:           Berg reads "A windy line"

12:           Berg reads "~~In the wind's pauses sing the brooks~~ Lend my [illegible]
              come, the home of the [illegible]." OaW reads "A purple bow the
              shadowless river looks."

13–18:        Berg omits this stanza

22–24:        Berg reads:

            But coming night

        Blacken'd all with its hoard of storm:

        ~~The birds are shelter'd close and warm~~

        Nestle to me, my love, and keep thee warm.

## UNKNOWN FAIR FACES

Included in EdL XXXI (Poems III), under "Poems from 'Modern Love': 1862"

5:            EdL reads "in the Heaven of me"

14:           EdL ends without punctuation

## PHANTASY

Included in EdL XXXI (Poems III), under "Poems from 'Modern Love': 1862"

IV.2:         OaW line ends with colon

VI.1:         EdL spelled "Beguine" as "Benguine"; corrected in EdL 1911 errata to
              "Béguine"

VIII.1:          EdL reads "ballet-beauty, who perked"
VIII.4:          OaW misspelled as "ancles"
IX.1:            EdL reads "twirled, the"
XII.3:           OaW line ends with exclamation mark
XIII.3:          OaW line reads "King Skull, in the black confessionals,"
XXIII.1:         OaW lines ends with semicolon
XXVI.2:          EdL reads "powers that Nature gave"
XXVII.3          EdL line ends with comma
XXXI.4:          OaW omits tilde on Sevilla

## SHEMSELNIHAR

Included in EdL XXXI (Poems III), under "Poems from 'Modern Love': 1862"
(manuscripts in Berg and NB B)
EdL omits stanza numbers
I.1:             EdL reads "O my lover!"
I.3:             EdL reads "How I shuddered—I"
IV.4:            EdL reads "The life that here"
VI.2:            EdL reads "think it my voice!"
VII.3:           EdL reads "of freedom and gorgeousness,"
VII.4:           EdL reads "Bespangle my slavery,"
Berg manuscript transcribed here includes ten stanzas, seven of which appear (in revised
form) in the published poem:

> Let us die, O my lover, in this long kiss:
> > Let us die locked/stretch'd together close close in the night:
> Let me die and be dust when they break our bliss;
> > When they cut thee away from my breast and my sight.
> Let me die and be dust as the pale lilies are,
> For thou are the life blood of Shemselnihar.
>
> O love, O my lover, thy love like a wave
> > Overwhelm'd me, it drown'd me in one deep desire:
> I shudder'd; I knew not that I was a slave
> > Till I look'd on thy face: how the world spun with fire!
> I look'd and remember'd what anguish would mar
> The first and sole passion of Shemselnihar.
>
> And he came, whose I am: O my lover! he came.
> > And his slave still so envied of women was I:
> And I turn'd as a wither'd leaf turns from the flame,
> > And I shrunk into Death in his arms, dark and dry.

Take me close! clasp me now! hide me quite! may no bar
Burn again twixt thy bosom and Shemselnihar.

Yet with thee, like a hot throbbing rose, how I bloom!
    Like a rose by the fountain whose showering we hear,
As we lie, O my lover, in this rich gloom,
    And smell the faint breath of the lemon groves near.
As we lie gazing out on that glowing great star
Which shows thee so darkly to Shemselnihar.

Yet with thee, am I not as a strong climbing vine,
    Firm to bind, free to cherish: deliciously sweet?
Death alone, O my lover! shall e'er disentwine
    The life that reels over thee, neck, waist, and feet.
No! never again shall that jewel'd head jar
With the music thou breathest on Shemselnihar.

Yet with thee, am I not as a fast sailing ship
    That dares the wild tempest—that trusts the strange sea?
Hanging thus over thee, full on thy lip:
    Hoping and trusting/living in nothing but thee:
My over! in thee! and if wreckt shall each spar
Show thee how truthful was Shemselnihar.

Away, far away, where the wandering scents
    Of all flowers are sweetest, white mountains among,
My kindred abide in their green and blue tents:
    Bear me to them, my lover! they lost me so young.
Slip, slip down the stream and mount steed till afar,
None question thy claim upon Shemselnihar.

Away, far away from this radiance that swoons
    Sick in my vision without thee! away
Far, from o my lover the splendor of these hush'd saloons,
    Far! ——How the bulbul slips from the dark/black spray
Scattering to ~~joy~~ bliss his long wail with a bar
Of sweetness like thine over Shemselnihar. . . .

He pants pants with love: only love, only love,
    Only love, O my lover! yearns up in his voice.

The night like a great flower bends from Above,
    Odorous, breathing in sighs that are joys:
Joys even as ours where/tho' the/his keen scimitar
So jealously watches/hovers o'er Shemselnihar.

Would that, less generous, he would oppress,
    Bind me, upbraid me, ~~give~~ brand deep ground for hate,
Than with this tyrannous gorgeousness
    Dress/spangle up my slavery, mock my strange fate:
Would, O my lover! He ~~[illegible]~~ knew to debar
Thy coming, and earn ~~hate~~ curse of Shemselnihar.

NB B, p. 22 includes the following lines:
Let me die, O my lover! in this long kiss
    Of love we can never know:
*Shemselnihar*
Let me die, O my lover! in this long kiss.
    Let us die stretched together close close in the night.
Let us die & be dust when they break ~~my~~ our bliss,
    And cut thee away from my breast & my sight.
Let us die & be dust as the pale flowers are,
For thou art the life-blood of Shemselnihar.

## [A ROAR THRO' THE TALL TWIN ELM-TREES]

Included in EdL XXXI (Poems III), under "Poems from 'Modern Love': 1862"
(manuscript in Beinecke, Notebook B, p. 45)

| | |
|---|---|
| 1: | NB B reads "A roar in the double elm-trees" |
| 2: | NB B reads "The burst of the storm" |
| 3: | NB B reads "The cassia & the willow"; EdL reads "The South-wind seized the willow" |
| 4: | NB B reads "By strenuous gusts were sway'd." |
| 5–8: | NB B reads: |

The ~~anger~~ wasting of the tempest
    Swept chords of shrouded woes
    Awoke me to my woes:
And all night long at my window
    Knock'd the winter rose.

| | |
|---|---|
| 9: | line in NB B ends with period instead of exclamation point |
| 10: | 1862 reads "outcast of must pine"; GM revised "of" to "it" in BEIN MSS 7, BEIN 862.1, BEIN 862.6; 1911 EdL errata reflects revision as well; editors corrected here |

| | |
|---|---|
| 11: | NB B reads "And outcast from thy bosom," |
| 12: | NB B reads "Am I, O lady mine!" |

## [WHEN I WOULD IMAGE HER FEATURES]

Included in EdL XXXI (Poems III), under "Poems from 'Modern Love': 1862"

| | |
|---|---|
| 9: | EdL line ends with comma |
| 10: | EdL reads "domes, and towers" with no comma at line end |

## [I CHAFE AT DARKNESS]

Included in EdL XXXI (Poems III), under "Poems from 'Modern Love': 1862"

| | |
|---|---|
| 1: | EdL line ends with comma |
| 3: | EdL reads "eyes; the" |
| 18: | EdL reads "Waving seem." |

## BY THE ROSANNA

Included in EdL XXXI (Poems III), under "Poems from 'Modern Love': 1862"

| | |
|---|---|
| 20: | EdL ends at line 20 |
| 44: | OaW inserts the following stanzas between line 44 and line 45: |

> And yonder a little boy bellows the Topic:
>> The picture of yesterday clean for a penny:
> Done with a pen so microscopic
>> That we all see ourselves in the face of the many.

> Business, Business, seems the word,
>> In this unvarying On-on-on!
>> The volume coming, the volume gone,
> Shoots, glancing at Beauty, undeterr'd:
> As in the torrent of cabs we both
> Have glanced, borne forward, willing or loth.

| | |
|---|---|
| 113: | OaW reads "Inspiration" with the first letter capitalized |
| 118: | OaW reads "world" with no capitalization |
| 122: | OaW reads "three-fold" |
| 140: | OaW reads "Man" with the first letter capitalized |
| 151: | OaW reads "Come from thy keen Alps down, and, hoarse" |
| 164: | OaW reads "Have I frighted it, frail thing, aghast?" |
| 174: | OaW line ends with dash |

## ODE TO THE SPIRIT OF EARTH IN AUTUMN

Included in EdL XXXI (Poems III), under "Poems from 'Modern Love': 1862"
(manuscript of a fragment appears in Beinecke, Notebook B, p. 49)

| | |
|---|---|
| 6: | EdL line ends with colon |

| | |
|---|---|
| 7: | EdL reads "cherub-mouths" |
| 10: | EdL reads "dumb: then," |
| 15: | EdL reads "thronging figures failed." |
| 21: | EdL reads "glorious South-west." |
| 24: | EdL reads "wings; then sharp the" |
| 30: | EdL reads "some on torn" |
| 53: | EdL reads "the air and rise," |
| 62: | EdL reads "Here stood" |
| 70: | EdL reads "upon their wide roots" |
| 73: | EdL reads "Of mournfulness, not" |
| 74: | EdL reads "For melancholy, but Joy's excess," |
| 91: | 1862 and EdL read "than her who bore"; GM revised "her" to "she" in BEIN MSS 7 and BEIN 862.6; editors corrected here per Meredith's corrections |
| 116: | EdL reads "In the circles" |
| 134: | 1862 reads "Of my life through thro' the"; editors deleted "through" |
| 137: | EdL uses semicolon at end of line; GM revised comma to period in BEIN MSS 7 |
| 141: | EdL reads "Great Mother Nature!" |
| 142: | EdL reads "the season and shun" |
| 170: | EdL line ends with comma |
| 175–219: | EdL omits these lines |
| 226: | EdL reads "when our season" |
| 245: | EdL line ends with colon |

NB B (p. 49) includes a fragment, lines of which were precursors to "Ode to the Spirit of Earth in Autumn." The following transcription of the fragment can be compared to lines 235–53 of the published version:

> Prophetic of the years to be;
> ~~Her dirge swells to a jubilee.~~
> Like the wild western war-chief sinking
> Down to the death he views unblinking,—
> Her dirge ~~becomes~~ swells to a jubilee!
> He for his happy hunting fields
> Forgets the muttered chaunt, and yields
> His ebbing life to exultation:—
> In the proud anticipation
> Shouting the glories of his nation;
> Shouting the grandeur of his race
> ~~Shouting the grandeur of his race;~~
> Shouting his own great deeds of daring:—
> And when at last death ~~sets~~ grasps his face,

And on the grass he lies in peace,
With all his painted terrors staring,-
His tribes know well he leaves ~~he has left~~ the place,
~~And~~ To [paper torn] father's in the chase.

## THE DOE: A FRAGMENT (FROM "WANDERING WILLIE")

Included in EdL XXXI (Poems III), under "Poems from 'Modern Love': 1862"
(manuscript of extended poem in Beinecke, Notebook A; see PB's discussion of the full
poem for composition history)

| | |
|---|---|
| 15: | EdL reads "pointing South," |
| 16: | EdL reads "daintiest, fleetest-footed" |
| 18: | EdL reads "Beyond: her" |
| 25: | EdL reads "As now across" |
| 26: | EdL reads "And now beneath" |
| 37: | EdL reads "Here winding" |
| 39: | EdL reads "water here like" |
| 41: | EdL reads "And—'Let her go;" |
| 43: | EdL reads "sighed: his eyes" |
| 44: | EdL reads "Brimming: ' 'Tis my" |
| 48: | EdL reads "The white gleams" and omits stanza break after line 48 |
| 50: | EdL reads "pillows propped," |
| 53: | EdL reads "A se'nnight—to my" |
| 55: | EdL line ends with colon |
| 63: | EdL reads "fondly: and I" |
| 64: | EdL line ends with colon |
| 65: | EdL reads "nurse nor I" |
| 93: | EdL reads "unheard; the young" |
| 136: | EdL line ends with period |
| 141: | EdL reads "Shut in a" |
| 163: | EdL omits line break between 162 and 163; EdL reads "Colourless, her long" |
| 164: | EdL reads "a tempest tossed" |
| 167: | EdL reads "drooping toward the" |
| 169: | EdL reads "And heaved from sea with" |
| 177: | EdL reads "her wild hair let brush" |
| 181: | EdL reads "sighs they sank;" |
| 191: | EdL line ends with no punctuation |
| 193: | EdL reads "With subtler sweet beneficence" |

# Suggestions for Further Reading

EDITIONS OF MEREDITH'S POETRY

Meredith, George. *The Poems of George Meredith*. 2 vols. Ed. Phyllis Bartlett. New Haven: Yale University Press, 1978.

————. *The Works of George Meredith*. 29 vols. Ed. William Maxse Meredith. London: Constable, 1898–1911.

BIOGRAPHY AND LETTERS

Ellis, S. M. *George Meredith: His Life and Friends in Relation to his Work*. London: Grant Richards, 1919.

Johnson, Diane. *The True History of the First Mrs. Meredith and Other Lesser Lives*. New York: Knopf, 1972.

Meredith, George. *The Letters of George Meredith*. 3 vols. Ed. C. L. Cline. Oxford: Clarendon, 1970.

Sencourt, Robert E. *The Life of George Meredith*. New York: Scribner, 1929.

Stevenson, Lionel. *The Ordeal of George Meredith: A Biography*. New York: Scribner, 1953.

BIBLIOGRAPHY

Collie, Michael. *George Meredith: A Bibliography*. Toronto: University of Toronto Press, 1974.

Esdaile, Arundell. *Bibliography of the Writings in Prose and Verse of George Meredith*. London: W. T. Spencer, 1907.

Forman, Maurice Buxton. *A Bibliography of the Writing in Prose and Verse of George Meredith*. Edinburgh: Bibliographical Society, 1922.

Williams, Ioan. *Meredith: The Critical Heritage*. New York: Barnes and Noble, 1971.

CRITICISM AND SCHOLARSHIP

## Books

Armstrong, Isobel. *Victorian Poetry: Poetry, Poetics and Politics*. London: Routledge, 1993.

Bernstein, Carol L. *Precarious Enchantment: A Reading of Meredith's Poetry*. Washington, DC: Catholic University of America Press, 1979.

Blair, Kirstie. *Victorian Poetry and the Culture of the Heart*. New York: Oxford University Press, 2006.

Fletcher, Ian. *Meredith Now*. London: Routledge & Kegan Paul Books, 1971.

Forman, M. B. *George Meredith: Some Early Appreciations*. London: Chapman & Hall, 1909.

Galland, René. *George Meredith and British Criticism (1851–1902)*. Paris: Les Presses Françaises, 1923.

Kelvin, Norman. *A Troubled Eden: Nature and Society in the Works of George Meredith*. Edinburgh and London: Oliver and Boyd, 1961.

McSweeney, Kerry. *Supreme Attachments: Studies in Victorian Love Poetry*. London: Ashgate, 1998.

Phelan, Joseph. *The Nineteenth-Century Sonnet*. London: Palgrave Macmillan, 2005.

Pinch, Adela. *Thinking about other People in Nineteenth-Century British Writing*. Cambridge, UK: Cambridge University Press, 2010.

Trevelyan, George Macaulay. *The Poetry and Philosophy of George Meredith*. London: T. and A. Constable, 1906.

Van Remoortel, Marianne. *Lives of the Sonnet, 1787–1895: Genre, Gender, and Criticism*. Farnham, UK: Ashgate, 2011.

Wright, Walter F. *Art and Substance in George Meredith: A Study in Narrative*. Lincoln, NE: University of Nebraska Press, 1953.

ARTICLES AND CHAPTERS

## On "Modern Love"

Bogner, Delmar. "The Sexual Side of Meredith's Poetry" *Victorian Poetry* 8, no. 2 (Summer 1970): 107–25.

Bonnecase, Denis. "Meredith's *Modern Love*: Showing/Speaking/Acting Out." *Études Anglaises* 57, no. 1 (2004): 39–52.

Comstock, Cathy. "'Speak, and I see the side-lie of a truth': The Problematics of Truth in Meredith's 'Modern Love.'" *Victorian Poetry* 25, no. 2 (Summer 1987): 129–41.

Cox Wright, Elizabeth. "The Significance of Image Pattern in Meredith's Modern Love." *Victorian Newsletter* 13 (Spring 1958): 1–9.

Crowell, Kenneth. "*Modern Love* and the *Sonetto Caudato*: Comic Intervention through the Satiric Sonnet Form." *Victorian Poetry* 48, no. 4 (Winter 2010): 539–57.

Fletcher, Pauline. "'Trifles light as air' in Meredith's 'Modern Love.'" *Victorian Poetry* 34, no. 1 (Spring 1996): 87–99.

Friedman, Norman. "The Jangled Harp—Symbolic Structure in *Modern Love*." *Modern Language Quarterly* 18, no. 1 (1957): 9–26.

Going, William T. "A Note on 'My Lady' of *Modern Love*." *Modern Language Quarterly* 7, no. 3 (1946): 311–14.

Houston, Natalie. "Affecting Authenticity: *Sonnets from the Portuguese* and *Modern Love*." *Studies in the Literary Imagination* 35, no. 2 (Fall 2002): 99–121.

Kincaid, James. "'The Poem Says': Meredith's *Modern Love*." In *Annoying the Victorians*, 135–48. New York: Routledge, 1994.

Kowalczyk, Richard. "Moral Relativism and the Cult of Love in Meredith's Modern Love." *Research Studies* 37 (1969): 38–53.

Mermin, Dorothy. "Poetry as Fiction: Meredith's Modern Love." *ELH* 43, no. 1 (Spring 1976): 100–19.

Mitchell, Rebecca N. "George Meredith's Poetry and the Critical Imagination." *Literature Compass* 8, no. 3 (March 2011): 142–50.

Pinch, Adela. "Love Thinking." *Victorian Studies* 50, no. 3 (Spring 2008): 379–97.

———. "Transatlantic Modern Love." In *The Traffic in Poems: Nineteenth-Century Poetry and Transatlantic Exchange*. Ed. Meredith L. McGill, 160–84. New Brunswick, NJ: Rutgers University Press, 2008.

Reader, Willie D. "The Autobiographical Author as Fictional Character: Point of View in Meredith's 'Modern Love.'" *Victorian Poetry* 10, no. 2 (Summer 1972): 131–43.

Regan, Stephen. "The Victorian Sonnet, from George Meredith to Gerard Manley Hopkins." *Yearbook of English Studies* 36, no. 2 (2006): 17–34.

Simpson, Arthur. "Meredith's Pessimistic Humanism: A New Reading of 'Modern Love.'" *Modern Philology* 67, no. 4 (May 1970): 341–56.

Tucker, Cynthia. "Meredith's Broken Laurel: 'Modern Love' and the Renaissance Sonnet Tradition." *Victorian Poetry* 10, no. 4 (Winter 1972): 351–65.

Van Remoortel, Marianne. "The Inconstancy of Genre: Meredith's *Modern Love*." In *Lives of the Sonnet, 1787–1895: Genre, Gender and Criticism*, 115–39. Farnham, UK: Ashgate, 2011.

Wilson, Phillip E. "Affective Coherence, a Principle of Abated Action, and Meredith's 'Modern Love.'" *Modern Philology* 72, no. 2 (November 1974): 151–71.

## On Meredith's Oeuvre

Frankel, Nicholas. "Poem, Book, Habitat: The World of George Meredith's Poetry." In *Masking the Text: Essays on Literature and Meditation in the 1890s*. Wycombe, UK: Rivendale Press, 2009.

Hiemstra, Anne. "Reconstructing Milton's Satan: Meredith's 'Lucifer in Starlight.'" *Victorian Poetry* 30, no. 2 (Summer 1992): 123–33.

Hughes, Linda K. "Inventing Poetry and Pictorialism in *Once a Week*: A Magazine of Visual Effects." *Victorian Poetry* 48, no. 1(Spring 2010): 41–72.

Ketcham, Carl H. "Meredith and the Wilis." *Victorian Poetry* 1, no. 4 (November 1963): 241–48.

Morris, John W. "The Germ of Meredith's 'Lucifer in Starlight.'" *Victorian Poetry* 1, no. 1 (January 1963): 76–80.

Simpson, Arthur. "Meredith's Alien Vision: 'In the Woods.'" *Victorian Poetry* 20, no. 2 (Summer 1982): 113–23.

Tompkins, J. M. S. "Meredith's Periander." *The Review of English Studies*, n.s., 11, no. 43 (August 1960): 286–95.

## VICTORIAN POETIC THEORY

Browning, Robert, and W. Tyas Harden. *An Essay On Percy Bysshe Shelley*. London: Reeves and Turner, for the Shelley Society, 1888.

Buchanan, Robert. "The Fleshly School of Poetry." *Contemporary Review* 18 (1871): 334–50.

Hopkins, Gerard Manley. *Further Letters of Gerard Manley Hopkins*. Ed. C. C. Abbott. London: Oxford University Press, 1956.

Patmore, Coventry. "English Metrical Critics." *North British Review* 27 (1857): 127–61.

Prins, Yopi. "Victorian Metres." In *The Cambridge Companion to Victorian Poetry*. Ed. Joseph Bristow, 89–113. London: Cambridge University Press, 2000.

Saintsbury, George. *A History of English Prosody: From the Twelfth Century to the Present Day*. 2nd ed. New York: Russell & Russell, 1961.

# Index of First Lines

# Subject Index